Nordic Health Law in a European Context

– Welfare State Perspectives on Patients' Rights and Biomedicine

ELISABETH RYNNING & METTE HARTLEV (EDS.)

MARTINUS NIJHOFF PUBLISHERS

Liber

Nordic Health Law in a European Context
ISBN 978-91-47-09748-7 (Sweden and Denmark)
ISBN 978-9004-22380-6 (Rest of the world)

Publisher's editor: Carin Laurin
Designed by: Fredrik Elvander
Typeset: Gyllene Snittet

1:1

Printed in Egypt by
Sahara Printing 2012

Distribution:
Sweden and Denmark
Liber AB
S-205 10 Malmö, Sweden
tel +46 40-25 86 00, fax +46 40-97 05 50
http://www.liber.se
Kundtjänst tel +46 8-690 93 30, fax +46 8-690 93 01

All other countries:
Matinus Nijhoff Publishers/ Brill, Leiden
www.brill.nl

Contents

Introduction

1 Nordic Biomedical Law

Biomedical law is a rather recent legal discipline in the Nordic countries, but is expanding strongly. Rapid developments in biomedical science and information technology have contributed to the increased level of attention being given to norms regulating biomedicine, where many important interests are involved. In many Anglo-Saxon jurisdictions, as in continental Europe, biomedical law has long since been accepted as a legal discipline in its own right - sometimes within the combination of "medical law and ethics", or simply as "medical law", "biomedical law", or "health law". In the Nordic countries, however, legal science was more hesitant to establish biomedical law as a special legal discipline; thus, Nordic research into the legal aspects of various activities in biomedicine has primarily been conducted within more traditional fields of law, e.g. public law, criminal law, and private law. Nevertheless, since the 1990s, biomedical law has gradually been establishing itself in the Nordic legal landscape; courses in biomedical law have become part of the legal curriculum at Nordic universities and the first Nordic chair in biomedical law was established at Uppsala University in 2003. Similar positions have also been introduced in Norway, Denmark, and Finland.

Biomedical law is still, however, a comparatively young field of research in the Nordic countries, and has small national research communities. Yet, there is increasing demand for studies concerning the role of law in different types of biomedical activities, as well as analysis of the underlying principles and concepts, in order to foster a more comprehensive understanding of the interaction between the different normative and regulatory systems governing the field of biomedicine. In order to provide a forum for academic discussion, and a stronger basis for Nordic cooperation in this strategically important discipline, the Nordic Network for Research in Biomedical Law was founded at a conference in Uppsala in 2006.[1] The aim of the Nordic Network is to promote both research training and further development of the research methodology particular to biomedical law, and stimulate comparative Nordic research. In 2007, the Network received a NordForsk grant for three years, to finance workshops for research students, Network conferences, and similar activities.[2] This generous funding has contributed significantly to Network activities and created opportunities for looking at biomedical law more systematically from an internal Nordic perspective, and studying how the Nordic countries relate to European and international institutions and regulations in this area of law.

---

1 See website www.nordicnetwork.org. In some definitions, the concepts of health law and biomedical law are perceived to cover somewhat different areas. In this book, however, just as in the Network, these terms are used as synonyms.

2 See website www.nordforsk.no.

The Nordic countries have a considerable shared cultural and historical heritage, and are all strong proponents of the welfare state. They have collaborated closely in their development of legislation during most of the 20th century yet demonstrate a somewhat surprising degree of variation in the field of biomedical law. The divergences and similarities between the Nordic countries have attracted special attention in the activities of the Nordic Network, where conferences and workshops have addressed a variety of issues in areas such as patients' rights (including the protection of weak and vulnerable groups) the organisation of health care systems, challenges to the Nordic welfare models, the regulation of biomedical research, and societal approaches to new technologies. The influence of Europe and EU law has also received attention, as has the general impact made by international human rights law in the field of biomedical law, notably with regard to patients' rights. An additional area of interest concerns the gradual transformation of the Nordic countries from cultural homogeneity to cultural diversity.

This anthology reflects the numerous activities and perspectives explored by the Nordic Network. The contributions have been written, with one exception, by members of the Network, with the authors reflecting the divergence of the Network's membership with regard to gender, age, and nationality. It is a special privilege to present the research findings of some of the many doctoral students who have enthusiastically participated in the Network's activities.

This anthology is divided thematically into three sections where the first deals with foundational and general issues of health law, the second with patients' rights, and the third with issues related to advancements in biomedicine and medical science.

2 Foundational issues

As mentioned in the introduction, biomedical law or health law is a rather recent legal discipline, the development and delimitation of which have been subject to academic reflection and debate. Broadly speaking, biomedical law deals with legal aspects of various biomedical activities and this includes areas such as health care, biomedical research, and forensic medicine, as well as certain aspects of public health and the pharmaceuticals and biotech sectors.

The legal issues addressed also transcend traditional disciplines such as constitutional law, administrative law, private law, criminal law, and public international law. *Human rights law* is often mentioned as an important source of inspiration in the development of health law, and the first two contributions are concerned with the close relationship between human rights and biomedical law.[3] Professor Henriette Roscam Abbing, who is one of the legal pioneers of European health law, explores the historical relationship between these two areas of law and the continuous influ-

3

ence of human rights law in the field of patients' rights. She explains how the focus of international collaboration and regulation has developed from having an interest in protecting Europe against "exotic pestilences", as a primary concern, to a rights-based approach focusing on patients' rights and the necessity to protect the individual – and especially the weak and vulnerable – from exploitation during the encounter with medical science and society. It is stressed that human rights law provides a comprehensive and forward-looking legal background for the further development of biomedical law. Professor Matti Mikkola's contribution is also rooted in human rights law. He addresses the important issue of the right to health, analysing how this right is protected in European human rights law, notably the European Convention on Human Rights and the European Social Charter. Mikkola emphasizes the importance of interplay in this area, between social and economic rights, on the one hand, and political and civil rights, on the other, thus confirming that human rights are indivisible and interrelated.

The right to health is also addressed in Dr Anna-Sara Lind's contribution, but from a constitutional perspective. She examines Nordic constitutional protection of the right to health and shows that, even though perceptions of being a welfare state are taken for granted in all the Nordic countries, the constitutional protection of welfare rights, including the right to health, is rather weak, even though there are differences. Finland and Iceland, which both have fairly new constitutions that have been influenced by public international law, ascribe constitutional protection to the individual's right to health, while this is not the case in the other Nordic countries, which seem reluctant to recognise individual rights within the field of social and economic rights.

The Nordic perspective is also crucial for Professor Mette Hartlev's contribution on the *raison d'être* of Nordic Health Law. After a discussion on the origins, status, and demarcations of health law as a legal discipline, she explores the organisation of the Nordic health care services and the regulation of access to care. Hartlev concludes that, even though – superficially – there are differences between the countries, it is still possible to detect common values within the deep structure of Nordic health law. These common values are closely related to the Nordic welfare societies' aspiration to promote universal and equal access to high-quality health care and to ensure patients fundamental rights.

Interest in Nordic collaboration regarding developments in biotechnology is reflected in the decision taken by the Nordic Council of Ministers to establish a Nordic Committee on Bioethics. Health lawyer and committee member, Sirpa Soini, describes the background and development of the missions and tasks of this committee, which deals with both the ethical and legal aspects, as well as social science perspectives on biotechnology. She discusses whether or not a special Nordic perspective on biotechnology and bioethics is needed, concluding that the Nordic societies seem to have a more permissive attitude towards science and technology than many other societies. This attitude is supported by a general trust in science and society – a trust that can only be maintained through open debate. The Nordic Committee on Bioethics, accordingly, serves the purpose of initiating debate on difficult issues and, thus, the purpose of sustaining Nordic trust in scientific development.

Professor Helle Bødker Madsen addresses a conceptual and fundamental question in her contribution regarding the status of health law as a legal field in Danish law. Although she agrees that health law must be treated as a separate legal discipline, Madsen simultaneously underlines the importance of observing the distinction between public law and private law, not least because the organisational location of health law can be decisive vis-à-vis the rights of patients. From the perspective of legal policy, she thus warns against detaching health law from its legal roots, since this may profoundly undermine the protection that patients are provided by administrative law, not least in a situation where the privatisation of health care services is taking place. This contribution confirms the interdependence of the general, foundational issues and the protection of patients' rights.

3 Patients' rights

Patients' rights is a topic that has attracted special interest within the Nordic biomedical law research environment. This is not surprising as the Nordic countries were among the first to adopt specific patients' rights legislation, thus recognizing the individual patient's rights vis-à-vis the health care services. As the Nordic pioneer, Finland passed a patients' rights Act in 1992 and was quickly followed by Iceland (1997), Denmark (1998), and Norway (1999). Sweden is, thus, the only Nordic country not to have specific legislation on patients' rights. The attention paid to patients' rights fits well with the strong human rights traditions of the Nordic countries, most of which have also signed as well as ratified the Council of Europe Convention on Human Rights and Biomedicine. Patients' rights encompass a cluster of rights that include the right to be a patient, the right to self-determination, the right to obtain information, the right to privacy and confidentiality, and the right to complain and receive compensation in cases of error and malpractice.

Professor Asbjørn Kjønstad explores the development of patients' rights in Norway and lists a number of factors that have been influential for the shift from a doctor and duty perspective on patient relationships with health care services to a rights-based approach. Among other factors, he emphasizes the importance of the networked society where different actors – grass roots organizations, the health administration, the media, legal complaint mechanisms, and legal science – through complex interactions have paved the way for the creation of patients' rights. In contrast to the other Nordic countries, Sweden does not have a patients' rights Act; it is also the only Nordic country which has so far refrained from ratifying the Council of Europe Convention on Human Rights and Biomedicine. The reasons and implications regarding the Swedish legislative strategy constitute the topic of Professor Elisabeth Rynning's contribution. She outlines four legal tools and strategies for promoting patients' rights, using this as a basis for a critical analysis of the Swedish legislative attitude to patients' rights. It is shown that, even though there have been important developments in certain areas, the lack of a comprehensive and coherent Swedish legal strategy has implications; especially for weak and vulnerable patients whose rights have remained inadequately protected.

Respect for patient autonomy and the right to self-determination are two of the core legal principles in biomedical law. However, there are situations where it may be justified to restrict the patient's right to self-determination, in the interests of public health or public security or in deference to the interests and rights of others. The patient's own best interests may also, in some cases, justify restrictions to the right to self-determination. Professor Aslak Syse discusses justification of the use of coercion in Norwegian health law, from a human rights perspective. As in many other countries, the use of coercion may be legitimate in psychiatric care and with regard to communicable diseases, with the Norwegian legislation in these areas being in line with general human rights standards. However, Syse draws the reader's attention to the new UN Convention on the Rights of Persons with Disabilities, which institutes a paradigm shift in attitudes to those with disabilities. This new approach may demand extensive alterations to Nordic legislation in the psychiatric field. Syse also outlines new provisions in Norwegian legislation justifying the delivery of care to incapacitated adults who oppose such care. Norway is the first Nordic country to introduce such legislation with the purpose of ensuring that incapacitated patients receive essential care in order to prevent the serious deterioration of and harm to their health.

Professor Karl Harald Søvig's contribution also deals with the use of coercion. He explores a new topic in Nordic biomedical law, which is the detention of pregnant women in order to protect the foetus. It is well known that the consumption of alcohol and other substances during pregnancy may be harmful to the foetus, with health injuries to children that are caused by their mothers constituting a health problem in most Western societies. However, the use of detention and coercion on pregnant women gives rise to difficult ethical and legal considerations, including the legal status of the foetus. Norway is the only Nordic country with specific legislation justifying the detention of pregnant substance addicts for the purposes of protecting the foetus. Søvig discusses the use of coercion in such cases from a human rights perspective and concludes that detention may be in line with human rights standards, but that human rights, on the other hand, do not obligate national authorities to intervene with a view to protecting the foetus. In his conclusion, Søvig emphasizes that Norwegian experiences show that the possibility of detaining pregnant substance abusers may have an impact on the individual case, but that it certainly does not solve the public health problem of children being exposed to intoxicating substances during pregnancy.

During the past 30-40 years, the Nordic countries have shifted from cultural homogeneity to increased cultural diversity. This development raises complex issues regarding cultural accommodation, issues which also affect health care services. The following three contributions all deal with this issue. Professor Oddny Mjöll Arnardottir explores the normative foundations of a general claim for cultural accommodation, as well as the limits to such accommodation, seen from the perspective of human rights. She shows that the claim for attention to cultural appropriateness, together with the principle of equal treatment and non-discrimination, can be seen as the two normative pillars of cultural accommodation. However, she also stresses the importance of keeping an eye on human rights when accommodating cultural traditions, using guidelines issued by the Icelandic health care authorities as an example demonstrating the necessity to carefully balance human rights when dealing with this sensitive issue.

Female genital mutilation is an example of a cultural tradition that has given rise to widespread concern. Professor Henriette Sinding Aasen examines the legal response to this practice and, based on an analysis of human rights law, she establishes that female genital mutilation clearly involves a violation of the individual's human rights, which is also considered a criminal offence in all the Nordic countries. Hence, this is without doubt an example where no cultural accommodation is expedient. However, Aasen also draws attention to a challenging dilemma facing authorities in their efforts to prevent female genital mutilation, because the measures used – e.g. non-voluntary medical check-ups – may involve procedures which could also be problematic from a human rights perspective, and thus hard to justify. While female genital mutilation is a comparatively new issue in the Nordic societies, male circumcision has been practiced there for many years within certain communities. In contrast to female genital mutilation, the acceptability of male circumcision has only been legally challenged recently, despite being debated in some countries. This may be due to a respect for religious freedom, but it may also be seen as an example of cultural accommodation. Professor Raimo Lahti addresses this issue in his comprehensive analysis of the Finnish response to this practice. He pays special attention to the ruling by the Finnish Supreme Court, in a criminal case, that the Court did not find it illegal for a mother to have her Muslim son aged 4½ circumcised for religious reasons. Lahti makes a thorough and critical assessment of the ruling, both from a criminal law perspective and a human rights perspective, concluding that legislation would be appropriate as regards ensuring that sufficient notice is paid to the different human rights aspects involved in this complex question.

Patients' rights are not only important with regard to the patient's – legal – relationship with health care services, since assessments and decisions made by health care services may also affect the patient's right to other entitlements, e.g. social benefits. This topic is addressed by Professor Lotta Vahlne Westerhäll in her contribution regarding the challenges facing migrant workers when applying for social benefits due to sickness and incapacity for work. Divergent conceptions of "sickness" and "incapacity for work", within both the Nordic countries and the EU, may cause significant problems for migrant workers in a rehabilitative situation. This is not only a question of lack of legal uniformity, but also one of professional agreement regarding evidence of specific medical procedures and mutual perceptions of e.g. the concept of sickness. Vahlne Westerhäll points to the necessity to find a solution, which may not necessarily be a uniform perception of such concepts, but could be a recognition of other states' ways of assessing the content of such concepts in a legal setting.

4 Biomedical science

As previously mentioned, the Nordic people are generally very positively inclined towards research, showing considerable trust in researchers and the improvements new technology can bring to society. Even so, it is clear that rapid developments in biomedical science – sometimes combined with new information technology – can also give rise to questions about risks to fundamental human rights and human dignity. This is pointed out in the preamble to the Biomedicine Convention, where it is also affirmed that progress in biology and medicine should be used for the benefit of both present and future generations. In some areas, the Nordic countries have been quite quick to recognise the need for new legislation safeguarding important interests concerned by developments in biomedicine. Most of the contributions in this section discuss such regulatory initiatives. In the first article, however, Dr Laura Walin addresses a more overarching topic, in her analysis of the key concept of "human dignity". Understanding of this concept has become increasingly complicated, with developments in biomedicine that include, for example, new uses of human organs, tissue and genes, as well as increasingly strong commercial interests. Walin explores the changing use and interpretation of human dignity as a legal concept, from the traditional approach where the human dignity argument was primarily used to protect the individual autonomy and self-determination of born human beings, to more recent use of the concept to restrict certain human activities, e.g. in embryo research. She concludes that human dignity is a changing concept that works as a universal argument only if it is left undefined; once invoked in order to restrict individual rights or to impose new obligations on individuals, the concept has to be defined for a specific society in a given timeframe.

The fact that values and interpretations may vary from society to society is also a key issue in Dr Sigmund Simonsen's article on the challenges facing European integration, featuring examples from regulations in the field of biomedical research. Simonsen discusses whether or not European integration and regulatory harmony are legally feasible and even a mandatory consideration in the interpretation of legal instruments in this field, focusing primarily on the issue of acceptable risks in research, as described in the Council of Europe Biomedicine convention, the EU Clinical Trials Directive, and Norwegian law. Despite the challenges pertaining to, for instance, the differences in wording, as well as in the actual standards, he argues that legal insecurity and conflicts of law must be overcome. Even though the legal framework is not harmonised, harmonising interpretation can be applied; Simonsen thus considers European integration in biomedical research law to be feasible in practice, as well as legally possible, even a legal requirement.

With new potential uses of human biological material, one important question has been what kind of protection should be offered in the interests of the donors of such material, the researchers, industry etc. Legislation governing so-called biobanks was adopted in Iceland in 2000, with several other Nordic countries following suit within the next few years. Professor Marit Halvorsen, in her contribution, questions why Norwegian policymakers have been so quick to discard the property law approach to this field, without any serious consideration or analysis of the traditional property law concepts that might offer some fruitful insights. She points to the fact that some types of human biological material can indeed be bought and sold, but she also stresses that legal constrictions on an owner's right to commercialize biological material would not be an anomaly. Looking to the legal categories used in Roman law, Halvorsen discusses whether or not the concept of *res extra commercium* – things exempted from the commercial sphere – could be a suitable analogy, but finds arguments against this solution. She maintains, however, that there are good reasons to start by considering the individual as the owner of materials stemming from his/her body and that a coherent doctrine for human material could be built on traditional Norwegian property law. Dr Salla Silvola starts by discussing the biobank concept, and goes on to compare the biobank regulation in Finland with the other Nordic countries. Interesting variations are found even in the structure and nature of the different regulatory instruments. Finland, so far, has no comprehensive biobanks Act, but a government Bill, presented in 2010, is still pending. Silvola looks at the different provisions regulating the preconditions for setting up a biobank, consent issues (including withdrawal and proxy consent), information to the public, and financial aspects and benefit sharing. She argues that the national level of regulation can be assumed to reflect the trust placed in the research community, and discusses the example of presumed consent, which is used in the different Nordic countries to varying degrees. However, Silvola concludes, the significant differences between the Nordic biobank regulations demonstrate that none of the efforts made by various international bodies to harmonise standards in this field have so far been efficient enough to result in common standards, even in the small and culturally-homogenous Nordic region.

One of the recent possibilities for using human biological material concerns genetic analysis, whereby unforeseeable quantities of sensitive personal information can be gained, not only about the present and future health of the person from whom the biological sample is taken, including his/her identity, but also about genetic relatives. Questions about who is really concerned by the information about a hereditary disease, and other family-related health problems, are thus seen in a new light. Although warnings against so-called genetic exceptionalism have been abundant, many countries have felt a need to adopt special regulations on the procurement and use of genetic information. Assistant Professor Line Bune Juhl brings together traditional patients' rights and biomedical science as she explores the Danish legal situation regarding the conflicts that may arise in relation to genetic diagnosis. While some of the other Nordic countries have chosen to adopt special rules relating to genetic privacy, this field is almost entirely governed by more general legislation in Denmark. Using the case example of patient George and his family, Juhl identifies a number of potential conflicts relating to the right to know, the right not to know, and the right to confidentiality. She goes on to discuss possible ways of solving the conflicts, concluding that the outcome of the necessary weighing up and balancing will be influenced by whether or not a duty of solidarity is supported by the competent policymaker, a question that should be more clearly addressed in Danish law.

Questions about life and death are inherent to the field of biomedical law, although domestic legislation may vary substantially from country to country. In a way, the final contribution to this anthology can be said to address both these issues, bringing them together with perceptions of human dignity and the use of human biological material as well. In her article Death before Life, Assistant Professor Janne Rothmar Herrmann analyses the status of deceased foetuses in Danish law, exploring both the traditional legal classification of the foetus and the approach that takes in more recent legislation on abortion and the use of foetal tissue. She demonstrates that the dead foetus can be placed in a number of legal categories, defined as a dead child, as tissue identical to the woman who has carried the foetus, as tissue which is separate to her, or sometimes as biological waste. Herrmann concludes that, while the use of different legal categories, based on a number of governing parameters, may be accepted in relation to dead foetuses, there seems to be a stronger reluctance towards applying the same dynamic and flexible legal status to the developing embryo and foetus *in vivo*.

5 Nordic health law in a European context

As mentioned at the outset, this anthology aims to provide some Nordic perspectives on the young and evolving field of biomedical law by reflecting on issues that have been explored within the activities of the NordForsk-funded Nordic Network for Research in Biomedical Law. In the evolution of this fairly new legal discipline, it has been very clear that the Nordic region forms a part of Europe that has been strongly influenced by both hard and soft law initiatives from the European Union and the Council of Europe. Naturally, the legal issues relating to the field of biomedicine are shared by many countries and discussions about possible solutions should thus not stop at geographical boundaries.

At the same time, however, Nordic identity, culture, and collaboration clearly remain an important factor in the legal development of our particular region. Just as in other countries, the need for integration and harmonisation must be balanced against domestic – sometimes pan-Nordic – values and traditions. Our readers will have to decide for themselves whether or not there is sufficient reason to speak of Nordic Biomedical Law or Nordic Health Law as a special legal approach to the field of biomedicine.

Elisabeth Rynning & Mette Hartlev (Eds.)

Part 1

Foundational Issues

Health and Human Rights in the European Context

By Professor dr. Henriette D.C. Roscam Abbing[1]

1 Introduction

Historically, in Europe, the primary focus of international health law was on the health consequences of increased international mobility and traffic. Contrary to what might be expected, concerted action between governments in the field of health cannot be traced back to humanitarian considerations for the health of individuals. It was rather the growing concern to remove hindrances to trade and export, while at the same time protecting Europe against "exotic pestilences", that formed the basis of the first international health legislation in the early years of the 20th Century. Since then, cross border mobility of patients and cross frontier co-operation in the provision of health services and medical research have substantially increased. At the same time, the individual human rights of patients and their possibilities of equal access to affordable, safe and good quality health care services as a social right have become the subject of shared principles; the first time was in 1994, with a Declaration on the Promotion of Patients' Rights in Europe.[2] The observance of patients' rights is an important instrument for enabling patients in their relationship with medical professionals to cope with dependence and vulnerability due to their state of health. This is of particular importance, because in Europe, health systems have become increasingly complex and bureaucratic, health has become a lucrative market and healthcare and research are increasingly becoming commercialised. The call, made in December of 2010, to improve the doctor-patient relationship by better informing and more involving patients in decisions about their medical care is a sign of the time[3]; as is the statement made in 2009 by the European Committee of Social

---

1 Professor Henriette Roscam Abbing's expertise lies in international health law. In her quality as a legal counselor to the Minister of Health she participated directly in the preparation of the Council of Europe's Biomedicine Convention. Since her retirement, she continues with scientific research, is one of the editors of the European Journal of Health Law, vice-chair of the European Association of health law and active as a health law counselor (asylum seekers and irregular migrants).

2 World Health Organisation, Regional Office for Europe.

3 *The Salzburg Statement on Shared Decision Making*, December 2010, Salzburg Global Seminar. <www.SalzburgGlobal.org/go/477>

Rights (Council of Europe)[4] that "the economic crisis should not have as a consequence the reduction of the protection of the rights recognized by the Charter".[5] The preservation of human dignity is a core issue in relation to advances in science and their application to medicine and biology.

In this contribution, I will first provide a brief sketch of the importance of human rights to the health of the individual and the implications that medical developments have for human rights. This is followed by some remarks on the limits of personal freedom in relation to health (paragraph 4), with paragraph 6 dealing with the diversity of norms and values in relation to health(care). In paragraph 6, the human rights challenges posed by expected developments in the field of genetics are briefly discussed. In my final remarks, patients' responsibilities are addressed.

2 The importance of human rights for health

Human dignity, freedom, equality and solidarity are basic values that underpin individual and social human rights. These values are codified in human rights instruments as far as is necessary for the regulation of societal issues. Human rights instruments constitute the legal framework to test human action against. Free choice and self-determination are fundamental constituents of life. "The very essence of the Convention is respect for human dignity and human freedom and the notions of self-determination and personal autonomy are important principles underlying its guarantees."[6]

Where individual human rights are primarily an expression of human freedom, social rights are an expression of solidarity. States have a positive obligation to protect and promote the health of the individual, and of the public at large, as far as available resources allow.[7]

What is reasonable in terms of volume and range of services available, as well as the degree of sophistication of the technology and specialisation, will depend on political, social and economic factors. To avoid discrimination in access to healthcare, health policies should take into account differences in health needs. Genetic, cultural, ethnic, and socio-economic differences are the most significant causes of differences in the health patterns of the population. To avoid physical harm to patients, health care delivery must take place in a safe environment and in accordance with professional skills. In matters of health, there is no watertight division between individual and social rights. "Human dignity is the fundamental value and indeed the core of positive European human rights law, whether un-

4 The Committee entrusted with the monitoring of the European Social Charter (ESC,1961, revised in 1996).

5 European Committee of Social Rights, *Activity report 2009*, 25 June 2010, p. 17. <www.coe.int>

6 *Jehova's Witnesses of Moscow v. Russia*, 10 June 2010, ECHR, no. 302/02 (First section), 17 *European Journal of Health Law* (2010), pp. 507-513.

7 Social security systems (partially) guarantee the financial accessibility of health services.

der the European Social Charter or under the European Convention on Human Rights ... and health care is a prerequisite for the preservation of human dignity."[8]

States must protect their citizens against threats to their lives emanating from serious environmental, and similar, health risks. The responsibility of the State applies particularly to persons who are deprived of their liberty (prisoners, or persons compulsorily confined to a hospital). Prisoners must receive adequate treatment that will preserve their health and well-being. A lack of medical assistance for serious health problems not suffered prior to detention, may amount to a violation of the prohibition of torture, or to degrading treatment or punishment (Article 3, ECHR).[9] It may be the case that the practical demands of imprisonment (limited resources) influence the scope of the duty to provide detainees with care, so that the principle of the equivalence of prison health care with that of the outside world is not complied with. However, the prisoner's dignity, together with the prohibition of discrimination when it comes to access to health care, limits deviations from the standard of care.

Respect for private life (Article 8, ECHR) plays a part in relation to health and health care in many aspects. Private life is a broad concept. It encompasses, *inter alia,* aspects of an individual's physical and social identity and mental health, it plays a role after death,[10] in relation to bio-banks,[11]and information failures.[12] It incorporates the right to respect the decision to become, and not to become, a parent, including becoming a genetic parent.[13] Legislation dissuading health professionals from assisting in home births is an interference with the exercising of the right to respect the private life of the prospective mother. "The notion of a freedom implies some measure of choice as to its exercise"... "Therefore the right to become a parent includes the right of choosing circumstances of becoming a parent."[14] Without appropriate safeguards against the disclosure of medical information, those in need of medical assistance may lose confidence in the medical profession, and in the health services in general; they may be deterred from seeking medical assistance and this may be to the detriment of their health.[15] The right of the patient to hold control over his (her) personal information has become vulnerable for violation because of the application of information and communication technology in health care and

8 *Digest of the case law of the European Committee of Social rights,* 1 September 2008, Council of Europe, p. 81. <.www.coe.int>

9 *Pakhomov v. Russia,* 30 September 2010, no. 4491/08 (First section), 18 *European Journal of Health Law* (2011), pp. 83-79.

10 *Odievre v. France,* 13 February 2003, no. 42326/98; *Bioethics and the case law of the Court, Report of the Research Division of the European Court of Human Rights, working document* (2009), pp. 50-51.

11 *Van der Velden v. the Netherlands,* 7 December 2006, no. 29514/05, supra note 10, pp. 47-48.

12 *Codarcea v. Romania,* 2 June 2009, no 31675/04, 16 *European Journal of Health Law* (2009), pp. 370-372.

13 The prohibition of discrimination, Article 14 ECHR, is relevant also. *S.H. and others v. Austria,* 1 April 2010, no. 57813/00 (First section), 17 *European Journal of Health Law* (2010), pp 307-313. Paras 58-60 provide an overview of the notion of "private life" (article 8) as seen by the Court.

14 *Ternovsky v. Hungary,* 14 December 2010, no. 67545/09 (second Section), 18 *European Journal of Health Law,* (2011), pp. 221-237.

15 *Z against Finland,* 25 February 1997, no. 9/1996/627/811, 4 *European Journal of Health Law* (1997), pp. 303-308.

the inherent possibilities to use medical data and bodily material stored in data- and bio-banks for non-medical purposes.

The acts and omissions of the authorities in the field of health care policy may also, in certain circumstances, engage their responsibilities under the obligation to protect the right to life (Article 2), e.g. by taking measures to prevent prisoners committing suicide and by compelling hospitals to take appropriate measures to protect patients' lives. Also, it is not excluded, per se, that a positive obligation might arise in order to eradicate or prevent the spread of a particular disease or infection. However, in matters of health care policy, in particular with regard to general preventative measures, the domestic authorities are best placed to assess priorities, use of resources, and social needs.[16] Under the European Social Charter (Articles 11 and 23), states are required to prevent risks to health by offering proven effective screening programmes. Other obligations under the Charter include measures to limit waiting times, to have humane conditions in psychiatric institutions and care facilities for the elderly, and to prevent discrimination on the basis of age. The system of health care must be accessible to the entire population. To that end states should take as their main criterion for judging the success of health system reforms effective access to health care for all, without discrimination, as a basic human right. This is particularly important given the high price tag attached to new scientific and technological developments, while resources are limited and legislative reforms of health systems that favour competition invoke undesired side-effects.

3 Medical developments and human rights

Developments in (medical) science and technology raise fundamental questions about the interpretation and application of human rights, and about their underlying basis. The interpretation of human rights cannot be dissociated from scientific and technological innovation and changes in society. The consequences of developments in medical science and technology for the interpretation of human rights are reflected in the jurisprudence of the European Court of Human Rights. In doing so, the Court makes a dynamic interpretation, in the light of "present days conditions" or "present days circumstances". In the Court's view, the ECHR is not designed to guarantee rights that are theoretical, but rights that are practical and effective. Human rights instruments are "living instruments"; the codification of fundamental values in human rights instruments does not take away the philosophical and moral concept of the norm - the norm, so to speak, "floats" in the sphere of those concepts and remains a stimulant for innovative jurisprudence and fresh regulation. In its jurisprudence related to developments in medicine, the Court draws on the Council of Europe Convention on Human Rights and Biomedicine (Oviedo Convention, 1997). This Convention was drawn up out of concern for the ambivalent nature and dark

16 *Shelly v. the United Kingdom*, 4 January 2008, no. 23800/06, supra note 10, p. 43.

side of many of the advances in science and their application to medicine and biology. For this purpose, the primacy of the human being over the sole interest of society or science is explicitly laid down (Article 2). The human being has to be shielded from any threat resulting from the improper use of scientific developments. This Kantian requirement of the non-instrumentalisation (non-commodification) of individuals is particularly addressed in the articles dealing with medical scientific research that involves human beings and the prohibition of financial gain from the human body and its parts. The prohibition of the creation of human embryos for research purposes (Article 18.2) expresses the concern for preserving the dignity and identity of the human being. Yet, this prohibition raises the question of whether or not it is justified in the event such research were to be the sole method of finding ways of preventing and curing very serious illnesses.[17]

Like the Oviedo Convention, the content of the Charter of Fundamental Rights of the European Union[18] is an update of human rights in the light of changes in society and scientific and technological developments. In Article 3 (the right to integrity of the person), it follows closely the Oviedo Convention (informed consent according to the procedures laid down by law; the prohibition of eugenic practices, in particular those aimed at the selection of persons; the prohibition of making the human body and its parts, per se, a source of financial gain; the prohibition of the reproductive cloning of human beings).[19] The European Court, when dealing with a plea brought by the Netherlands, that the patentability of isolated parts of the human body, as provided by the European Directive on the legal protection of biotechnological inventions, reduces living human material to a means to an end and undermines dignity, observed that having respect for the right to human dignity and integrity constitutes a fundamental right and that it is up to the Court to ensure that it is complied with. According to the Court, the right to human integrity encompasses, in the context of medicine and biology, the free informed consent of the donor and the recipient.[20]

To ensure compliance with the Charter, the Commission will submit new proposals for European Union regulations to a "human rights proof test".[21] It is without question that the implementation of current EU law should also pass the human rights proof test. Particularly where this implementation touches upon the core of human rights, regulatory diversity is not indicated. This concerns, for instance, the

17 EU Network of Independent Experts on Fundamental Rights, *Commentary of the Charter of Fundamental Rights of the European Union*, (June 2006) p. 28. <ec.europa.eu/justice_home/cfr_cdf/index_en.htm>

18 2000, legally binding since the coming into force of the Treaty of Lisbon, 2009.

19 The Charter is primarily aimed to the institutions of the European Union. It applies to member states when implementing EU law. The EU will adhere to the ECHR. The Charter's dispositions will only take precedence when they provide more ample protection.

20 C-377/98 *Netherlands v Parliament & Council*, 8 *European Journal of Health Law* (2001), pp. 373-374.

21 European Commission, *Strategy for the effective implementation of the Charter of Fundamental Rights by the Eruopean Union*, COM(2010) 573 final, p. 5.

prohibition of financial gain from the human body and its parts,[22], [23] an important principle to be observed, especially given the ongoing commodification and commercialisation in this domain. Umbilical Cord Blood Banking (private or profit-making enterprises), whereby parents pay for services without any realistic use in the foreseeable future, may also be considered to fall under this prohibition.[24] For national rules implementing the Clinical Trial Directive[25] to be compatible with the Charter,[26] the legal (human rights) conditions for involving incapacitated persons in research on human beings, as laid down in the Oviedo Convention and the Additional Protocol on Human Rights and Biomedicine concerning biomedical research,[27]are to be observed.

4 Health and personal freedom

"The ability to conduct one's life in a manner of one's own choosing includes the opportunity to pursue activities perceived to be of a physically harmful or dangerous nature for the individual concerned. In the sphere of medical assistance, even where the refusal to accept a particular treatment might lead to a fatal outcome, the imposition of medical treatment without the consent of a mentally-competent adult patient would interfere with his/her right to physical integrity and impinge on the rights protected under Article 8 of the Convention. The freedom to accept or refuse medical treatment, or to select an alternative form of treatment, is vital to the principle of self-determination and personal autonomy." The Court emphasised that "absent any indication of the need to protect third parties, for example, mandatory vaccination during an epidemic, the State must abstain from interfering with the individual freedom of choice in the sphere of healthcare for such interference can only lessen and not enhance the value of life."[28]

Self-determination is not unlimited. In relation to one's right to care for health, personal choices are limited to what is affordable and available and because one can only expect the health professional to act in accordance with the relevant professional standards (Oviedo Convention, Article 4). Limits may be inherent to one's mental capacities, to the rights and freedoms of others, or may be imposed by reasons of public health (e.g. contagious diseases). The isolation of a person to prevent the

22 Stipulated in Article 3.2 Charter and Article 21 Oviedo Convention.

23 Directive on human cells and tissues, 2004/23/EC; Blood Directive, 2002/98/EC.

24 For a potentially different viewpoint, see Takis Vidallis, A matter of health? Private umbilical cord blood banking, 18 *European Journal of Health Law* (2011), p. 125.

25 2001/20/EC.

26 Article 3: physical integrtiy and Article 24.2: the best interest of the child as a primary consideration in all actions relating to children whether taken by public authorities or private institutions.

27 Steering Committiee on Bioethics (Council of Europe), *Guide for Research Ethics Committee Members*, 7 February 2011, CDBI/INF(2011)2.

28 *Jehova's Witnesses of Moscow v. Russia*, supra note 6.

spreading of a contagious disease[29] is justified only on condition that the disease is a real danger to public health and safety, that the measure is a last resort, and that the disease cannot be prevented effectively with less severe measures. Restrictions must be based on societal and medical reasons, not only focusing on the protection of public safety, but also on the protection of the individual (the principle of proportionality and the prohibition of arbitrariness).[30] A person who has a mental disorder of a serious nature may be subjected, without his/her consent, to an intervention aimed at treating his/her mental disorder. The reasons justifying such treatment are the prevention of serious harm to the person concerned and the protection of others.[31] In case of compulsory treatment, the therapeutic necessity in accordance with well established principles of medicine, is a necessary condition.[32]

Restrictions to one's personal freedom are radical because of the fundamental nature of self-determination, they require strong arguments; touchstones for their legitimacy are the principles of necessity, proportionality, and subsidiarity. Grounds for restrictions must be prescribed by law. Every restriction must respect the essence of the rights and freedoms concerned.[33] When resources are limited, it is tempting to fall back on compulsory measures in situations where these are not supposed to be applied, striking vulnerable persons, like psychiatric and psycho-geriatric patients and the mentally handicapped. In relation to health, decisions concerning dependent persons must be taken from their perspective only. The duty of the professional care-giver is not compatible with the excessive (undue) application, or with too little, of restrictive measures; restrictive measures should only be applied as a last resort. Failing to care for dependent people is a potential attack on human dignity and can amount to torture, or to inhuman and degrading treatment (Article 3, ECHR). Regular evaluation of the practice of measures forced on patients in institutions and in ambulatory care is vital. To avoid relatives of vulnerable persons influencing arbitrary decisions being made by health professionals "for the person's own good", another conceivable attack on the individual's personal freedom, the appointment of a representative and the drawing up of advanced directives should become standard practice.

29 Article 5.1 of ECHR.

30 *Enhorn v. Sweden*, 25 January 2005, no. 56529/00, 12 *European Journal of Health Law* (2005), pp. 169-173.

31 Articles 7 and 26, respectively, Oviedo Convention.

32 *Bogumil vs Portugal*, 7 October 2008, no. 35228/03, supra note 10, pp. 25-27.

33 Article 52, Charter.

5 Diversity of norms and values

5.1 Sensitive issues

European consensus on shared values concerning the application of biology and medicine does not prevent views differing on their exact scope and content. There are different religious and philosophical views on where exactly the protection of human dignity starts. Depending on the area to be protected, some use a higher threshold than others.

The European Commission (EC) respects differences of views in sensitive matters in the area of medicine, where fundamental values are at stake. For instance, research projects that include the use of embryonic stem cells are excluded from financial support by the Commission. The Advanced Therapy Medicinal Products Regulation[34] respects member states' legislations prohibiting or restricting the sale, supply, or use of medicinal products containing, consisting of, or derived from any specific type of human cells (e.g. embryonic stem cells).

The European Court of Human Rights allows the states a wide margin of appreciation in matters of morals, where there is no uniform European conception in the legal and social orders of the States Parties to the ECHR. The state is, in principle, best placed to provide an opinion on the exact content of the requirements of morals, particularly in an area which touches upon matters of belief concerning the nature of human life, against the backdrop of fast moving medical and scientific developments. The margin of appreciation extends, in principle, both to the state's decision to intervene in such an area and, once having intervened, to the rules it lays down in order to achieve a balance between competing public and private interests. This legal framework must be shaped in a coherent manner which allows the different legitimate interests involved to be adequately taken into account and in accordance with the obligations deriving from the Convention.

Medically-assisted procreation is an example of a field where a broad margin of appreciation remains. The use of in vitro fertilisation techniques (IVF), in particular, gives rise to sensitive moral and ethical issues in an area where there are no shared views among the member states. There is no obligation on a state to enact legislation allowing for artificial procreation in general. But once a positive decision has been taken, concerns based on moral considerations, or on social acceptability, are not in themselves considered sufficient reasons for a complete ban on a specific technique of artificial procreation, unless it is the only means of effectively preventing serious repercussions.[35] For instance, the prohibition of ova and sperm donation for IVF is not proportional when there are regulatory possibilities of safeguarding against the risks associated with the technique (health risks, the exploitation of women by remunerating them for ova donations, and the abuse of techniques for gender selec-

34 Regulation 1394/2007, Preamble no. 7.

35 Right to protection of private life and the prohibition of discrimination, Articles 8 and 14, ECHR.

tion). Possible safeguards include restricting the method to specialised doctors, who are bound by the ethical rules of their profession, and the prohibition of remunerations for ova and sperm donation.[36] If not proportional, the regulation is discriminatory.[37]

5.2 *Beginning of life*

In relation to abortion, some states protect human life from the moment of conception, while in other states, protection starts from the moment of viability of the foetus. According to jurisprudence under the ECHR thus far, the full protection of life starts at birth, and there is at least some protection of life before birth, depending on the interpretation of other rights (protection of the life and health of the pregnant woman). In the absence of European consensus on the scientific and legal definition of the beginning of life, the margin of appreciation of how the state protects the unborn child necessarily translates into a margin of appreciation as to how it balances conflicting rights. Legislation regulating the interruption of pregnancy touches upon the sphere of private life, since whenever a woman is pregnant, her private life becomes closely connected with the developing foetus. Therefore, in the case of a collision between two fundamental rights, representing two different human dignity positions (e.g. that of an embryo and that of the pregnant woman wanting an abortion), a careful balance must be struck. "In a concrete case, however, this may result in one of the positions having to fully stand back."[38] A restriction of a human right, as a result of such a balance must be compatible with the Convention. For example, in the case A.B. and C. v. Ireland,[39] the Court concluded that the Irish prohibition of abortion – in giving precedence to the pregnant woman over the interests of the (future) life of the unborn child only in a life-threatening situation for the woman – had struck a fair balance between a woman's right to respect for her private life and the rights of the unborn child. For the broader situation regarding the health and well-being of the woman (touching upon Article 8, ECHR), information about seeking abortion abroad was available, as were both guarantees under the law and professional medical guidelines regarding the availability of the necessary medical treatment pre- and post-abortion. However, the state failed in its positive obligations to secure effective respect for the private life, as neither the medical consultation nor the litigation options constituted effective and accessible procedures that would allow the establishment of the right to a lawful abortion in Ireland. Women were risk-

36 *S. H. and others v. Austria*, 1 April 2010, no. 57813/00 (First section), 17 *European Journal of Health Law* (2010), pp. 307-313.

37 A difference in treatment must have an objective and reasonable justification, which means that it does not pursue "a legitimate aim", or that there is no objective or reasonable justification between the means employed and the aim sought to be realised.

38 *Commentary of the Charter of Fundamental Rights of the European Union*, June 2006, supra note 17, p. 29.

39 *A.B. and C. v. Ireland*, 16 December 2010, Application no. 25579/05, 18 *European Journal of Health Law* (2011), pp. 224-231 (2nd Chamber).

ing conviction and doctors were risking both conviction and disciplinary action. This leaves the question about the role formal medical professional guidelines could have played in determining whether or not an abortion would have been lawful (see Article 4, Oviedo Convention).

The criminalisation of abortion can have a serious impact on women's access to safe healthcare services in a life-threatening situation (so-called therapeutic abortion). In the event that abortion is decriminalised, the legal framework must be structured in such a manner that there are real possibilities to obtain it.[40] Post-factum reviews of decisions to deny access to abortion services are inadequate. Whether or not, and if so under what conditions, the interest of the future child can justify the compulsory confinement of a woman who refuses treatment of the foetus at the stage of viability, another issue where views differ, has not yet been subjected to scrutiny under the ECHR.

5.3 *End of life*

The right to determine how and in what manner one's life should end is another aspect of the right to respect for private life where European consensus is lacking. In the Pretty case, the Court concluded that "no right to die whether at the hands of a third person or with the assistance of a public authority can be derived from article 2 of the Convention".[41] Where the strict domestic criminal prohibition of euthanasia and assisted suicide is in accordance with the ECHR, this does not imply that such a criminal prohibition is required by the positive state obligation to protect the right to life. The decriminalisation of euthanasia and assisted suicide requires from states a careful balancing of the positive obligation to respect and protect the right to life, and to respect the right of a person to die with dignity. When decriminalised, ample restrictions by the state are still deemed compatible with the Convention. For instance, in case states have an obligation to adopt measures facilitating suicide in a humane manner, the objective of a prescription necessary for the lawful procurement of the medicaments, namely the prevention of abuse and of over-hasty decisions, can justify a refusal by a medical doctor to prescribe the medicaments. In that case however, the person concerned should have another possibility of gaining lawful access to the medicaments.[42]

40 *Tysiac v. Poland*, 20 March 2007, appl. No.5410/03 (4th section), supra note 10, p. 4.

41 *Commentary of the Charter of fundamental Rights of the European Union*, supra note 17, p. 34; *Pretty v. United Kingdom*, 29 april 2002, appl no. 2346/02, 9 *European Journal of Health Law* (2002), pp. 263-279.

42 *Haas v. Switzerland*, appl. no. 31322/07, 20 January 2011(Section I), *European Court of Human rights/Information Note no. 137*, January 2011, p. 16. <echr.coe.int>

5.4 Conscientious objections

Health professionals and patients can express their religious views in relation to healthcare by raising conscientious objections. This is part of the right to freedom of thought, conscience and religion[43] Conscientious objections by health professionals are notably raised in relation to medical services that interfere directly with human life (abortion, artificial procreation techniques, contraception, euthanasia and assisted suicide). Conscientious objection cancels these professionals' duty of care, except in emergency situations, under the condition of the timely referral of the patient to another qualified health care practitioner. Conscientious objection should not in any way deprive a person of the possibility of having access to the legally-recognised medical service in question. A doctor who, for reasons of conscience, withholds important information on the status of the foetus from a pregnant woman, and fails to refer in a timely way to another gynaecologist, is acting negligently. Such behaviour deprives the woman of the possibility of making a decision as regards whether or not to interrupt the pregnancy.[44] Yet, in spite of the case law under the ECHR, conscientious objections continue to stand in the way of a woman's right to obtain lawful medical care in relation to reproductive health. Disappointingly, an attempt failed in 2010 to draft comprehensive European guidelines regulating the invocation of conscientious objections by health professionals working in reproductive health.[45] In a case against French pharmacists who refused to deliver medically-prescribed contraceptives, the European Court of Human Rights considered that "as long as the sale of contraceptives is legal and occurs on medical prescription nowhere other than in a pharmacy, the applicants cannot give precedence to their religious beliefs and impose them on others as justification for their refusal to sell such products, since they can manifest their beliefs in many ways outside the professional sphere".[46]As seen in the previous paragraph, a similar argument can be made in relation to medically-prescribed drugs in the context of legally-permitted euthanasia and suicide. Also, effective remedies should be available to challenge any refusal by a medical service which is subject to conscientious objection. Otherwise, there is a risk of patients being deprived of access to services that are, in principle, available to all within a state, or of being treated in a discriminatory manner. Not only the accessibility of health care, but a variety of other reasons can also justify restrictions to health personnel's right to freedom of religion. They include the safety of patients (e.g. hygienic clothing guidelines for health personnel) and the proper functioning of a

43 Article 9, ECHR. In Article 10.2 of the Charter, the right to conscientious objection is explicitely recognised.

44 EU Network of Independent Experts on Fundamental Rights, opinion no. 4-200, *The right to Conscientious objection and the conclusion by EU Member States of concordats with the Holy See*, 14 December 2005, p. 13. CFR-CDF.Opinion 4-2005.doc.

45 The text of a Parliamentary Assembly Resolution on the right to conscientious objection in lawful medical care was severely diluted (Resolution 1763 92010, 7 October 2010). <assembly@coe.int/ASP>

46 *Pichon and Sajous v. France*, no. 498853/99, 2 October 2001. As the Court did not consider the applicants' convictions for refusing to sell medicaments to be an interference with the exercising of the rights guranteed under Article 9, the application was declared manifestedly ill-founded. Supra note 44, p. 23.

health service (e.g. when a choice made by a patient, of a healthcare provider of a specific gender for religious reasons, is inversely proportional to the acuteness of the situation).

For patients, religious beliefs may be a reason to refuse (certain) medical interventions (principle of self-determination). Even when the refusal relates to a potentially life-saving medical intervention, the personal autonomy right in the sphere of physical integrity and religious beliefs takes precedence over states' duty to protect the life and health of their citizens.[47] For instance, the refusal to award custody to the mother of a child for reasons of protecting the health of that child, because the mother is a member of the Jehovah's Witnesses religious community, is in itself a legitimate aim. But when the distinction is essentially based on a difference of religion, it falls short of proportionality between the means employed and the aim pursued, and is therefore unacceptable.[48] However, protecting the health and rights of children is a legitimate reason for state interference when parents make decisions regarding their children that are based on religion rather than on the interests of the child.[49] Furthermore, parents should not, in principle, ask for religion-based medical interventions for their children if the intervention is not medically indicated. Female genital mutilation is considered a form of child abuse. For male circumcision, the situation is different; particularly when both parents give their consent, when the child's viewpoints are taken into account, and when the intervention is performed by a qualified person. In all circumstances, the doctor must convince him-/herself that the act is in conformity with the child's best interests.

6 Human rights challenges of medical developments

Advances in science and medicine have considerably broadened patients' options for prevention and treatment. Medical perspectives (substantiated or not) in the preventative sphere incite an almost unlimited individual claim right to health-related information. But the developments of medicine and technology also have a dark side. Medical technology developments are fast, both with regard to breadth and depth. They bring a paradigm change from illness to health, they intrude more into the private sphere, and they have the potency of manipulating the individual (cognitive enhancement). Developments in science and medicine, especially in the field of genetics, promote, at first sight, individual freedom of choice; however, greater choice also implies more difficult decisions. Personal decisions will increasingly come under the influence of public opinion and society. In how far will the social climate still leave room for the individual to choose not to know, or to take decisions on the basis of personal health related information according to one owns

---

47 *Jehovah's Witnesses of Moscow v. Russia*, supra note 6.

48 *Hoffmann v Austria*, 23 June 1993, no. 12875/87, supra note 10, pp. 18-20.

49 UN Convention on the Rights of the Child, Article 3; Oviedo Convention, Article 6; EU Charter of Fundamental Rights, Article 24.

views? Gene testing during pregnancy may be offered without constraint, in order either to continue with, or to end the pregnancy; however, that is often more theory than practice. Developments in genetics raise serious questions about the interpretation of human rights, and about responsibilities and legal duties. Genetic information entails lifelong consequences; it plays a part before life starts and can be relevant after death. It is not dependent on symptoms or complaints; it always involves more than one person. Genetic information can be used to people's disadvantage as it provides the opportunity to select them vis-à-vis jobs and insurance. The mere availability of genetic screening and testing puts the right not to know under pressure. Direct-to-consumer genetic testing for health-related purposes is currently on the market for monogenic and severe genetic disorders. Many of these tests make misleading claims, without adequate pre-test information, counselling or psychological support; good quality is not guaranteed and the medical relevance is doubtful. The predictive genetic testing of asymptomatic minors that is available on the market, if applied with parental consent, is an infringement of these minors' privacy; it deprives them of their autonomy to know or not to know. Traditional health services are being unnecessarily burdened as a result of poor quality direct-to-consumer genetic tests. In particular, the analysis of a person's entire genetic code (full genome sequencing, FGS and full genome analysis, FGA) will have serious implications for human rights, once it becomes a medically-accepted service and becomes more cost effective than other methods. When there is no medical answer to a health problem revealed by such analysis, the information will be stored for future use, just in case. Almost any biological sample can provide the genetic material necessary for these techniques. FGA may, under certain circumstances, be the only possibility of reaching a diagnosis of an illness for which the genetic background is as yet unknown. But, in general, the information will be more confrontational than is the case with (predictive) findings for specific diseases. It may reveal abnormalities regarding which there are, as yet, no medical answers, or which will never pose a health problem. Knowledge of the susceptibility to a severe, as yet untreatable, disease will cause serious mental harm; it may undermine a person's life perspective. The information may also have serious societal implications (private insurance, employment, stigmatisation). It raises questions about informed consent, the right not to know, and limits to the professional duty to inform the person concerned. Individuals are, in principle, entitled to health information about themselves, including genetic information However, the medical utility of such information should be clear. If there is no proven clinical utility, the mere right to know must be balanced against the positive duty of the state to protect the individual against the potential harm of the intervention necessary to obtain the required information (protection of the person's right to private life). It is just a matter of time before FGS and FGA flood the market. Rules have been formulated governing the appropriate use of genetic technology and information.[50] However, more is needed to counter the negative implications of genetic technology that is of poor quality. Genetic tests and screening which are potentially harmful to the health of the individual, and an unnecessary burden on health care, must be barred from the market. The European Commission and the states have a positive duty, which is based on the human rights they are committed to, to develop policies and regulations in such a way that tests and screening are only admitted to the market once there is evidence of clinical utility and efficiency (similar to the market authorisation system for high-risk medicaments).

7 Final remarks

The focus of this essay was on human rights in relation to health. This does not imply that people do not have responsibilities and duties, for their own health, for the health of others and for the unborn child, to co-operate in their own treatment, to avoid medical consumerism and not to unnecessarily burden health care. Under Article 11 of the ESC, states have a duty to undertake activities that encourage individual responsibility. The European Court of Human Rights assigns a major role to a person's own behaviour. For instance, in relation to the legal right to an abortion in Ireland, the applicant, who complained about the lack of abortion services in that country in connection with a lethal foetal abnormality, in not having sought legal advice regarding her eligibility for an abortion, did not comply with the requirement to exhaust domestic remedies.[51]

50 *Additional Protocol to the Oviedo Convention on Human Rights and Biomedicine, concerning Genetic Testing for Health Purposes*, Council of Europe, Strasbourg (2008); *OECD Guidelines for Quality Assurance in Genetic Testing*, Organisation for Economic Co-operation and Development (2007); European Society of Human Genetics, "Statement of the ESHG on direct-to-consumer genetic testing for health-related purposes", 18 *European Journal of Human genetics (2010)*, pp. 1-3.

51 *D. v Ireland*, 27 June 2006, no. 26499/02, inadmissable, supra note 10, p. 2.

Right to Health as a Human Right in Europe[1]

By Professor Matti Mikkola, University of Helsinki[2]

This article is dedicated to the discussion on health as a human right on the basis of the two key European legal instruments; the Convention on Human Rights and the Social Charter and on the case law of their supervisory bodies, in addition to which the strengthening of their material scope will be discussed.

1 General

The basic functions of health care include promoting health and treating illness. Both functions are pertinent to the whole population; every individual person and his or her well-being. Without a population-wide perspective, health care fails to perform its task; without striving to maintain the health of and to treat the illnesses of every individual, health care fails to produce results that are better than mediocre.

1.1 Concept of health

When founded, the World Health Organization (WHO) defined health as "a state of complete physical, mental and social well-being and not merely the absence of disease or infirmity" (1947). Health was thus defined as being dependent on both personal and social factors. The terms *physical* and *mental* referred to personal qualities, whereas *social well-being* emphasised the interpersonal and communal nature of health.

Four decades later (1989), the WHO raised, or at least changed, this standard by defining health as having *good means of achieving a balance of physical, psychological and social adaptation and moral character.* The revised definition was better suited to guiding the development of the health care systems of welfare states.

The maintenance of health covers the protection of health, the promotion of health, and the prevention of disease. The *care of ill-health* includes research, diagnosis, treatment, and medication, in addition to rehabilitation.

---

1 The text is largely based on the author's latest book: *Social Human Rights of Europe*. Legisactio 2010.

2 Matti Mikkola is Professor of Labour Law at the University of Helsinki. Previous member of the Charte-Rel Committee of the Council of Europe, revising the Social Charter in 1992–94; member of the European Committee of Social Rights in 1995–2006, chairman in 1999–2000; legal adviser of the Finnish Ministry of Social Affairs and Health of Finland in 1981–94 and consultant of World Bank and the EU in Estonia, Bulgaria, Ukraine and Russian Federation in 1993–2011.

Fig. 1: Functionality focus

ACTIVITY AREAS	MEASURES
MAINTENANCE OF HEALTH	
1. Protection	quality of food, air and drinking water, safety in traffic, health and safety at work, safe housing, social inclusion, consciousness of conditions of good health, product safety, chemical safety, protection from radiation, as well as safeguards against forces of nature and pollution
2. Promotion	health education, healthy lifestyle, self-care and preventive rehabilitation
3. Prevention	vaccination, screening, as well as measures against ill-treatment, accidents and spread of epidemic diseases
CARE OF ILL-HEALTH	
1. Examination	family doctors, medical centres, polyclinics and hospitals
2. Diagnoses	family doctors, medical centres, policlinics and hospitals
3. Treatment and medication	surgery, internal and psychiatric care of disorders and diseases
4. Rehabilitation	medical, social and occupational

The *subject* of the maintenance of health and care of ill-health is the *population* on the whole. However, since the negative consequences of malpractice, prolonged illness, or medical neglect are always experienced by *individuals*, the right to health should also be understood as a subjective right. From the viewpoint of an individual, the focus is on protection from health threats, adequate medical treatment when needed, and the right to a remedy when one's rights have been violated.

The maintenance of health and the treatment of disease are the primary medical issues facing citizens. Legislation does not cover actual treatment decisions; who to treat and how. Those decisions are the responsibility of treatment providers, of doctors in particular. Control over decisions and a good quality of care are mainly left to their professionalism and their *code of ethics and professional conduct.*

Legal measures are important when defining the scope and quality of care, as well as the jurisdiction over resources; however, in the treatment of disease, the role of legislation has been secondary. That role still prevails.

1.2 Resources

No desired activity is possible without adequate care measures. The single most important resource of health care is staff who are well-educated, motivated, competent, and who exist in sufficient numbers. Different countries have similar curricula, degrees, and required professional qualifications. Moreover, the WHO and the Council of Europe have created a joint policy and ethical standards for treatment practices. Common European standards have improved health care in many areas. At the same time, the convergence of labour markets has resulted in greater mobility in the workforce, which has left some areas short of staff, and thus in danger of not being able to provide adequate health care.

The bulk of health care expenditure is made up of salaries and wages. That proportion of overall health care expenditure increases as salaries and wages increase generally. Moreover, the more demanding a treatment, the more staff are required. – Due to these factors, the growth in health care resources needs to be paired with *continued rationalisation measures,* if health care expenditure is to be brought under control.

Current tendencies in the reorganisation of hospital care are; 1) from hospital beds to less expensive beds and non-residential care at local health centres, 2) from care services to the maintenance of health, and 3) from less-resourced rehabilitation to systematic rehabilitation, preventative rehabilitation, and self-care.

Fig. 2: Rationalisation of resources

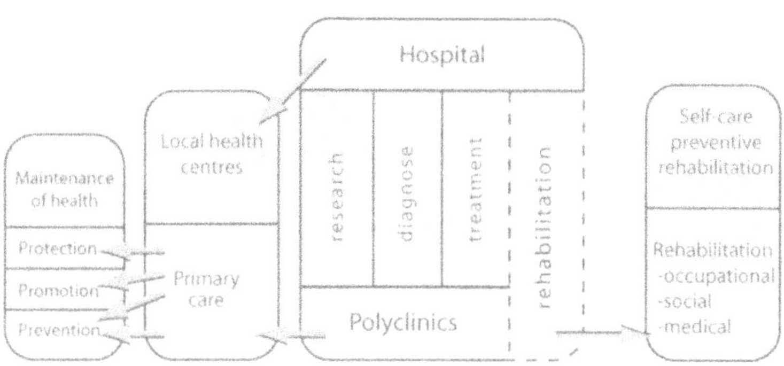

In recent years, public health care crises have been staved off by setting *priorities* for different health care services and for different individuals who are entitled to health care, something which has led to fundamental ethical discussions. The exercise has also led to the transfer of power over treatment decisions from doctors to hospitals' financial administrations, in turn increasing the need to strengthen patients' rights.

From a lifecycle perspective, the most expensive care is provided during the "fourth life", i.e. during the final years of elderly persons' lives. The higher the proportion of dependent elderly citizens, and the greater the need for health care, the more pressure there will be to increase expenditure.

However, there are also other factors affecting expenditure. For many years, the Organisation for Economic Co-operation and Development (OECD) has stressed that countries should prioritise resources for their economically active populations (and not their passive ones). In many countries, that is what has been done.

1.3 Legal approach

Legal regulation has especially focused on matters of health protection, on health education, and on the prevention of disease. Regarding care services, regulation has traditionally centred primarily on the health care system, its resources, and its waiting lists. Actual treatment decisions have been left to health care staff, which has led to an emphasis being placed on their professionalism, code of ethics, and professional conduct.

The use of modern technology in medical research and treatment has traditionally been regulated by professional ethical standards. This has been the case with treatment priorities, too. The law has provided more regulations on the framework conditions of health care systems and resources, organisation of the care, staff and management, finance, as well as interventions, in order to guarantee the health and safety of citizens and workers.

The importance of a legal approach increases when law becomes more of a measure for protecting the good practises and the equal treatment of patients, i.e. when: a) the availability or accessibility of health care services or measures taken to protect and promote health and to prevent disease is not adequate; b) measures taken include possible restrictions to civil rights; c) the responsibility for providing care is unclear; d) patients are treated unequally; e) the effectiveness and cost of treatment are not reasonable; f) the patient's right to self-determination or remedies has been violated. – Although the legal perspective is *secondary* to health care activities, it serves a purpose in the whole.

Fig. 3: Regulation of health care

Legislation governing *patients' rights* enables the regulation of the patient's status during the course of his/her care, consultation with the patient, and treatment options. Laws may also be used to provide access to services, to control the adequacy of their quality and their cost, and to ensure remedies for patients. However, legal regulation alone is seldom a sufficient solution when it comes to ensuring the rights of patients.

2 Protection of health in the ECHR

2.1 Key provisions

The European Convention on Human Rights (the ECHR) regulates, in addition to civil rights, many social rights. Its hard core is formed of Articles 2, 3, and 4, which concern the protection of life and human dignity and protecting anyone against abuse. Non-discrimination is provided under Article 14 and Protocol 12.

Among other things, Article 2 aims to offer protection against threats to life and health. The European Court of Human Rights has treated dangerous emissions from industrial and power production as such a threat and has focused, in particular, on the insufficient information given to local residents about such a threat.

The issue was initially raised in a 1998 case brought against the UK government, although no human rights violation was eventually found.[3] A turning point was the case of *Öneryildiz v. Turkey* (2005),[4] where the Court ruled that a licence, or other *compulsory system of supervision* to prevent risk, is necessary when it comes to dangerous activities and that there is a *positive obligation to inform* of the existence of risks. *Chantal Gallant,* in a 2006 report to the Steering Committee for Human

3 *L.C.B. v. United Kingdom,* judgement of 9 June 1998.

4 *Öneryildiz v. Turkey,* Grand Chamber judgement of 30 November 2004.

Rights,[5] concluded that public authorities have a particular obligation to supervise construction in environmentally-damaged areas, inform local residents of the risks, and regulate it by law.

Recently, the Court decided, in the case of *Bacila v. Romania,* that everyone has the right to an unpolluted environment under the protection of family life and the home.[6]

In the application of Article 2, the ECtHR has also ruled that states must have an adequate system of health care services, which must be available to everyone in the case of a life-threatening loss of health. However, providing sufficient evidence of a possible violation could be difficult.[7]

A form of insecurity, which is not life-threatening, may still constitute a violation of a person's human rights under Article 3 of the Convention. That insecurity may be related to a shorter life-expectancy, serious pain, suffering, hunger, homelessness, a lost or compromised ability to function, constricting a person's ability to live his/her life in human dignity.

2.2 Non-discrimination

Each of the aforementioned rights may be addressed in situations where the treatment of individual persons or families is not equal to that given to others. This is provided under Article 14 of the Convention. The provision is general and prohibits all discrimination in relation to the rights provided by the Convention.

Protocol No. 12 came into force in April 2005. It *prohibits discrimination on any grounds* (also outside the Convention) in relation to the rights in force within the contracting states. It also entails the provisions of the Convention and the Social Charter becoming even more overlapping.

3 Protection of health under the ESC

3.1 Provisions

The European Social Charter (the ESC) includes three types of provisions: one group of norm sentences has the intention of maintaining health, the aim of another group is to guarantee access to services, while the third group calls for additional positive action in order to protect employees and the most vulnerable in society.

5 *Gallant, C.:* CDDH(2006)006, p. 7.

6 *Bacila v. Romania,* judgement 30 March 2010.

7 See *Cyprus v. Turkey,* Grand Chamber judgement of 10 May 2001; *Nitecki v. Poland,* judgement of 21 March 2002 and *Pentiacova v. Moldova,* decision of 4 January 2005.

*Right to health under the ESC**

Maintenance of health

- protection, Art. 11 § 1,
- promotion, Art. 11 § 2,
- prevention, Art. 11 § 3,
- protection at work, Art. 3,
- special protection of young workers, Arts. 7 § 2 and 7 § 9
- during maternity, Art. 8 § 1.

Access to care services

- within a reasonable waiting time
- financing for insured persons, Art. 12 § 1,
- financing for those without sufficient means, Art. 13,

Positive action

- occupational health care, Art. 3 § 4,
- for children, Art. 17 § 1a,
- for the elderly, Art. 23 § 2b
- rehabilitation, including the disabled, Art. 1 § 4
- services for the socially-excluded, Art. 30

3.2 Maintenance of health

3.2.1 Protection of health (Art. 11 § 1)

Up until the last decade, the European Committee of Social Rights (the ECSR), the controlling body of the Charter, paid very little attention to health care services. Its main focus was the protection and promotion of health, as well as the prevention of ill-health. During recent years, the Committee has focused on refining the indicators of health maintenance, as well as on setting requirements for certain services as conditions of an adequate health care system. The key indicators for the assessment of adequacy are the substantive and personnel coverage of the system and, as the hard core, the infant mortality and that of the mothers giving child birth.

The Committee has also had an impact on the interpretation of Article 11 § 1 of the Charter in two ways. It has been used as a reference point for determining the minimum standards of environmental health, and for evaluating the adequacy of a

* Articles 23 and 30 of the revised European Social Charter only. In addition, Articles 3 and 17 of the Revised Charter contain additions not found in the Charter of 1961.

state's health care system. The ECSR has adopted the view that health protection requires functioning health care services.

"The right to protection of health guaranteed in Article 11 of the Charter complements Articles 2 and 3 of the European Convention on Human Rights - as interpreted by the European Court of Human Rights - by imposing a range of positive obligations designed to secure its effective exercise."[8] The Committee has emphasised that the rights relating to health that are embodied in the two treaties are inextricably linked, since "human dignity is the fundamental value and indeed the core of positive European human rights law – whether under the European Social Charter or under the European Convention on Human Rights - and health care is a prerequisite for the preservation of human dignity"[9].

The ECSR has required that the prevention of *environmental health risks* be regulated by means of sufficiently developed and specific legislation, which is supported by a state budget reasonable with regard to this aim.[10] Assessment has so far concentrated on air quality, radiation risks to those living near radioactive facilities, risks relating to asbestos, and food safety.[11]

The Committee also considers preventative and protective measures that are related to water and noise pollution, as well as the enforcement of public health standards in housing.[12] In each case, the Committee considers both the relevant legislation and the measures for implementing it[13]. – Although pollution can be caused by a community or by a single enterprise, the main responsibility rests with the state.[14]

3.2.2 Promotion of health (Art. 11 § 2)

The promotion of health is achieved by means of enlightenment, health education, awareness-raising campaigns, advice for groups at risk, and by means of medical examinations and mass screenings. The last-mentioned may also be part of a set of measures falling under Article 11 § 3.

The intention of the second paragraph of Article 11 is to emphasise the role of institutions and the importance of individual responsibility in maintaining health. To promote this, health education, advisory services, and general enlightenment in the mass media should be used. Measures must be adopted to prevent risks arising from damaging living habits, e.g. alcohol consumption, smoking, and drug abuse, and to invoke a sense of personal responsibility for both environmental degradation and unhealthy dietary and living habits.

8 Statement of Interpretation of Article 11, general introduction to Conclusions XVII-2 and Conclusions 2005, para. 5.

9 *International Federation of Human Rights Leagues (FIDH) v. France*, Complaint No. 14/2003, Decision on the merits of 3 November 2004, § 31.

10 Addendum to Conclusions XV-2, Slovakia, pp. 201-205.

11 Digest 8/2006, pp. 71-72.

12 In the case of states that have not accepted Article 31 (right to housing), Conclusions XVII-2, Portugal, pp. 685-689.

13 In connection with noise pollution, see Conclusions XVII-2, Portugal, p. 687.

14 *Marangopoulos Foundation for Human Rights (MFHR) v. Greece*, Collective Complaint no. 30/2005 (on website of ECSR).

Here, the ECSR has increased its requirements for states to promote the health of their populations, following WHO instructions.[15]

States are also required to adopt measures for *youth health education* in particular, including sexual and reproductive education. Health education must be provided throughout primary school and it must be *integrated into school curricula.*[16]

The Committee feels that, after family, school is the most appropriate setting for health education because the general purpose of education is to impart the knowledge and skills necessary for life. It refers, in particular, to Committee of Ministers Recommendation No R(88)7 on school health education and the role and training of teachers. Health education must cover, as a minimum, such topics as smoking and alcohol abuse, sexual and reproductive education, in particular with regard to sexually-transmitted diseases and AIDS, road safety, and healthy eating habits. The precise extent of these activities may vary with the nature of the public health problems in the countries concerned[17].

In the same context, the ECSR has adopted decisions about *advisory clinics for mothers and children* and about screening. Moreover, requirements have been issued for school health care to be available and health checks to be carried out throughout school. *Mass screenings* must be arranged also, if they can help to prevent premature deaths caused by diseases with a high risk of fatality. – On this point, paragraph 2 overlaps the next paragraph, paragraph 3, of Article 11.

3.2.3 Preventative measures (Art. 11 § 3)

Screenings, examinations, and vaccinations

Standards in the prevention of ill-health have been the main focus of the ECSR during recent decades, requiring that:

1) There must be free and regular screening for pregnant women and children throughout the country[18].
2) Free medical checks must be carried out throughout school. In assessing compliance, the Committee takes into account the frequency of school medical examinations, their objectives, the proportion of pupils concerned, and the level of staffing[19].
3) There should be screening, preferably systematic, for all the diseases that constitute the principal causes of death[20]. The Committee has ruled that "where it has proved to be an effective means of prevention, screening must be used to the full"[21].

15 Digest 12/2008, p. 84.

16 Digest 12/2006, p. 93.

17 Conclusions XV-2, Belgium, p. 99.

18 Conclusions 2005, Moldova, p. 452.

19 Conclusions XV-2, France, p. 210.

20 Conclusions 2005, Moldova, p. 452.

21 Conclusions XV-2, Belgium, p. 99.

4) States must operate widely-accessible immunisation programmes. They must maintain high coverage rates, not only to reduce the incidence of diseases, but also to neutralise the reservoir of the virus and thus achieve the goals set by the WHO to eradicate several infectious diseases[22].
5) Countries must demonstrate their ability to cope with infectious diseases, e.g. arrangements for reporting and notifying diseases, special treatment for AIDS patients, and emergency measures in the case of epidemics[23].
6) Vaccination programmes are the more usual preventative measures. States must demonstrate that targeted vaccination programmes cover the whole of the target population, not only in order to prevent disease, but to eradicate particular strains of virus, as with the WHO programmes. States must demonstrate their ability to control contagious disease and potential epidemics, and to communicate urgent treatment information effectively.

If a state lacks the preparedness to protect all its citizens with vaccinations, it must have an official and transparent priority listing in place. Also, in cases where a vaccination is intended only for at-risk groups, official rules must be prepared in advance that will establish who belongs to those groups and who the primary recipients of the vaccinations will be. As already stated above, for general emergency situations, the priorities for protection should be guaranteed by law.

The Committee puts particular emphasis on anti-smoking measures when considering compliance with Article 11, since smoking is a major cause of avoidable death in the developed countries (in Europe, 30 % of deaths from cancer are attributable to smoking) and associated with a wide range of diseases (cardiac and circulatory diseases, cancers, pulmonary diseases, etc.).

To be effective, any prevention policy must restrict the supply of tobacco through controls on production, distribution, advertising and pricing[24]. In particular, the sale of tobacco to young persons must be banned[25], as must smoking in public places, including transportation, and advertising on posters and in the press[26]. The Committee assesses the effectiveness of such policies on the basis of statistics on tobacco consumption[27].

This approach also applies *mutatis mutandis* to anti-alcoholism and drug addiction measures[28].

Based on the revised Social Charter, the ECSR has investigated the possibility of setting standards for the five most frequent categories of *accidents:* i.e. 1) traffic ac-

22 Conclusions XV-2, Belgium, p. 103.

23 Conclusions XVII-2, Latvia, p. 504.

24 Conclusions XVII-2, Malta, pp. 560-561.

25 Conclusions XVII-2, Portugal, p. 499.

26 Conclusions XV-2, Greece, pp. 252-253.

27 Conclusions XVII-2, Malta, pp. 560-561.

28 Ibid.

cidents, 2) domestic accidents, 3) injuries suffered doing leisure time activities, including injuries caused by animals, 4) accidents at work or at school, or 5) accidents caused by dangerous chemicals or products, e.g. unhealthy or dangerous toys. Work accidents are covered by a separate provision in Article 3, which will be dealt with later. Article 17 regulates, among other things, the environment of children and its risks. However, the ECSR has decided to include the evaluation of children's accidents in the context of Article 11 § 3, and to monitor risk factors and injuries separately.

The discussion regarding influencing citizens' attitudes with the aim of preventing accidents also belongs to the context of Article 11 § 2. The evaluation of the health care system as a whole may justify the treatment of fatal accidents under Article 11 § 1 too. As preventative measures, the ECSR usually evaluates the environmental risks under paragraph 11 § 3. The general comment on this point is as follows:[29]

Under the Charter, overcoming pollution is an objective that can only be achieved gradually. Nevertheless, a contracting state must strive to attain this objective within a reasonable time, by showing measurable progress and making best possible use of the resources at their disposal.[30] The measures taken by states are assessed with reference to their national legislation and regulations and undertakings entered into with regard to the European Union and the United Nations[31] and in terms of how the relevant law is applied in practice.

3.3 *Access to care*

3.3.1 Adequate health care system

Recently, ECSR case law has extended to requiring that states should have effective health care systems. Based on Article E in relation to Article 11 § 1, the requirement is that[32]; 1) the whole population is covered by the services, regardless of place of residence, ethnic or social group, or other such factor. In addition, it is also required that 2) health care be financed collectively[33], 3) insurance or service fees must not become an excessively heavy cost that may lead to exclusion from services[34], 4) there are adequate staff and facilities, and services are available within reasonable waiting times. In fact, the Committee is requesting that states submit full information about their resources and their organisation of health care.

The Committee feels that there must be adequate staffing and facilities. In the

29 Digest 12/2008, p. 85.

30 *Marangopoulos Foundation for Human Rights (MFHR) v. Greece*, Complaint no.° 30/2005, decision on the merits of 6 December 2006, §§ 203 and 205.

31 Conclusions XV-2, Italy, Article 11 § 3, p. 332.

32 Digest 12/2008, p. 83.

33 Statement of Interpretation of Article 11, Conclusions I, pp. 59-60; Conclusions XV-2, Addendum, Cyprus, pp. 26-28.

34 Conclusions XVII-2, Portugal, p. 681.

case of hospitals, the Committee refers to the objective laid down by the WHO, for the developing countries, of 3 beds per thousand of population[35]. The Committee also feels that a very low density of hospital beds, combined with waiting lists, could be an obstacle to access to health care for the largest possible number of people[36]. Conditions during a stay in hospital, including psychiatric hospitals, must be satisfactory and compatible with human dignity[37].

Arrangements for access to care must not lead to unnecessary delays in the provision of that care. The management of health care waiting lists and times is considered in the light of Committee of Ministers Recommendation (99) 21 on the criteria for such management. Access to treatment must be based on transparent criteria, agreed at the national level, taking into account the risk of deterioration in either clinical conditions or quality of life[38].

3.3.2 *From ethical to legal norms*

The member states of the Council of Europe have agreed on several conventions regulating ethical standards and rules of medical research and treatment. The founding principles are;

a) that in medical research and treatment, risks disproportionate to the potential benefits should be avoided;
b) that children and young people, in particular, should be protected from disproportionate risk;
c) that human genetic engineering, organ and tissue removal, or the disposal of human body parts for financial gain, and human cloning are all to be prohibited by law.

3.3.3 *Accessibility and affordability*

The health care system must be accessible to everyone.[39] Restrictions on the application of Article 11 may not be interpreted in such a way as to impede disadvantaged groups from exercising their right to health. This interpretation is the logical consequence of the non-discrimination provision in Article E of the Revised Charter, in conjunction with the substantive rights of the Charter. The ECSR pointed out that this approach calls for a strict interpretation of the way the personal scope of the Charter is applied in conjunction with Article 11 on the right to the protection of health, particularly with its first paragraph on access to health care[40]. In this respect,

35 Conclusions XV-2, Addendum, Turkey, p. 257.

36 Conclusions XV-2, Denmark, p. 128.

37 Conclusions XVII-2 and 2005, aforementioned statement of interpretation; Conclusions 2005, Romania, pp. 600-601.

38 Conclusions XV-2, United Kingdom, p. 599.

39 Digest 12/2008, p. 82.

40 Conclusions XVII-2 and 2005, aforementioned statement of interpretation of Article 11.

it referred to its interpretation of the Charter's personal scope in which it noted that "the Parties to the Charter (in its 1961 and revised 1996 versions) have guaranteed to foreigners not covered by the Charter rights identical to or inseparable from those of the Charter by ratifying human rights treaties – in particular the European Convention on Human Rights – or by adopting domestic rules whether constitutional, legislative or otherwise without distinguishing between persons referred to explicitly in the Appendix and other non-nationals. In so doing, the Parties have undertaken these obligations."[41]

The Committee considered the conditions governing access to care in the light of Parliamentary Assembly Recommendation 1626 (2003) on "the reform of health care systems in Europe: reconciling equity, quality and efficiency", which invites member states to take as their main criterion for judging the success of health system reforms effective access to health care for all, without discrimination, as a basic human right[42].

There may be separate *waiting times* for contact with the care provider, access to an examination, and the start of treatment. In the case of the first-mentioned, the waiting time may be a few days, while in the second it may be weeks, and in the third it may be a few months, at maximum. So far, the Committee has not confirmed its stance, except that the waiting time for treatment should not be unreasonable.

Poland received a negative conclusion because of its unreasonably long waiting times for specialised medical services and because of the lack of appropriate waiting lists. [43]

Likewise, there has been no clear formulation of a stance in respect of the maximum level of *client fees*, or how to compensate for non-payment in cases where an individual's own resources are insufficient. To ensure the adequacy of health care systems, it would also be important to assess how social and ethnic minorities' rights, as health care recipients, are being fulfilled.

Another issue meriting discussion is positive guarantees, for the most vulnerable population groups, that ensure their access to the protection of health and the care of ill-health. - The ethical code that protects them might do as regards ensuring their interests during normal times, but in unusual situations, caused by epidemics, environmental catastrophes, or a nuclear hazard, their position and the priority of children, pregnant women, and the parents of small children should be guaranteed by law.

3.4 *Positive action*

Other provisions of the Charter pertaining to the maintenance of health, and the care of ill-health, are as follows:

41 General introduction to Conclusions XVII-1 and 2004, p. 10.

42 Conclusions XVII-2 and 2005, aforementioned statement of interpretation of Article 11.

43 Conclusion XVI-2, vol.2, Poland, p. 642.

- Social security, including the *financing of health services* is provided by Article 12 § 1, which states with insurance-based financing use to regulate sickness benefits, both in cash and in kind — from the patient's point of view, such a system regulates both access to health care and the quality of treatment;
- The right to *safe and healthy working conditions* in general, which have been augmented in the Revised Charter with the right to *occupational health care* (Art. 3);
- Employers are required to provide special protection to children and young persons, and to provide them (the under 18s) with a *medical examination* upon starting in a job and at regular intervals thereafter (Art. 7 § 9);
- The protection of *maternity* and *motherhood* and the right to associated benefits is provided by Article 8;
- *Rehabilitation services* for all employees are provided by Article 1 § 4, and rehabilitation for disabled persons by Article 15;
- Appropriate public services for *children*, including maternity clinics and school health care, are provided by Article 17 § 1; the Article also covers the rights of children in public custody to obtain appropriate health care, as well as the right of young people using intoxicants or drugs to obtain appropriate care, which is also regulated by Article 7 § 10. – Due to this incoherence, the ECSR has opted to supervise the adequacy of, and access to, children's and young people's health care services in the context of Article 11 § 1;
- The right of *the elderly* to obtain adequate services, including health care, is provided by Article 23; and
- Finally, Articles 13 § 1, 13 § 4, and 30 are aimed at ensuring that citizens and *legal residents with inadequate resources* have the right to emergency medical care (or to income assistance vouchers valid for health care expenses), and to any health care service deemed necessary to prevent their own or their family's social exclusion.

These provisions may provide grounds for requiring *positive action* from states to guarantee inclusion in the maintenance of health, as well as access to caring for ill-health, for the most vulnerable population groups. In cases where small children, the chronically ill, or the very old are in danger of dying from bird flu, pig flu, or some other epidemic, these should be *prioritised as regards preventative measures* (vaccination) and the necessary treatment.

The requirement for positive action might also lead to different care strategies, different patient treatments, or additional care for the most vulnerable groups of patients.

For the active population, the Revised Charter sets a requirement to develop a system of occupational health care (Art. 3) progressively, so that such a system would cover all, or at least a great number of, employees within a reasonable timeframe. It is the states' responsibility to organise this, by means of public or private services, or in public-private partnership.

4 Scope of persons

The measures for maintaining health should cover the whole population. In principle, the requirements of Articles 2 and 3 of the Convention and Articles 3 and 11 of the Charter have a *universal nature*, except as provisions of the care of ill-health. The restriction regarding the scope of persons under the Appendix to the Charter must not be understood in terms of removing anyone's most fundamental right to dignity, and neither in terms of limiting the self-determination, privacy, or respect vis-à-vis family life from that of the Convention without justified reason (8 § 2). As already discussed above, under section 3.3 (Access to care), restrictions to personal coverage in the Charter should be interpreted on this point strictly.

As regards access to health services under Articles 11 § 1, 12 § 1 and 13 § 1 of the Charter, the situation is different. The scope of persons is limited to those who are *legally resident or permanently working* in the relevant country. Visitors, who are nationals of any of the states parties, are also covered (Art. 13 § 4). – Here, the notion of reciprocity still lives on in the background, but it is not applicable in practice.

According to ECSR case law, access to health care services for third country citizens and irregular migrants could be limited to life-threatening situations.[44] Children, however, who have a limited capacity to influence decisions regarding their migration, should always be treated adequately, even in case of the illegal migration of the family (Art. 17).[45]

5 Strengthening of legal protection

5.1 In relation to Oviedo Convention

In the first Chapter of the BMC, there are also requirements concerning the sufficiency of health care services, the quality of health care, and non-discrimination. However, it must be noted immediately that the Convention does not put quantifiable requirements on the states, or requirements that would concern geographical coverage. Equal treatment is required, but only within the framework of existing resources. The Convention is neutral in relation to the scale of service provision.

44 *FIDH v. France*, Collective Complaint 14/2003, Decision of 5 September 2003.

45 Ibid.

The Convention is mainly made up of provisions concerning relations between health care staff and patients, standards for mutual understanding, and the prevention of abuse of the human body, which are provided under Chapters 2-8 and focus on:

1. Consent
2. Private life and right to information
3. Human genome
4. Scientific research
5. Organ and tissue removal from living donors for transplantation purposes
6. Prohibition of financial gain and disposal of human body parts
7. Infringements of the provisions of the Convention

The Oviedo Convention's greatest significance, in principle, is that earlier norms, which were held to be ethical ones, were changed by the treaty into norms of professional ethics and legal norms.

5.2 *Proposed Article 32 on health care services*[46]

The European Health Committee (CDSP) of the Council of Europe has proposed a new Article 32 on health care services to be added to the revised Social Charter. The following section is an examination of the draft article's content as regards the general motivation, the text of the article, specifications listed in the Appendix, and the explanatory report.[47]

The proposed article would regulate in more detail: 1) the provision of comprehensive and adequate health care services, 2) the participation of persons, 3) ethical standards, 4) equal treatment and non-discrimination, 5) access to emergency treatment, 6) patients' rights, and 7) adequate remedies.

5.3 *Challenges*

In the evolution of health care, there are certain bad options where:

1) resources flow to expensive special treatments while the development of primary care stops,
2) health becomes perceived as a commodity purchased in the marketplace and

46 All the explanatory texts under this section were quoted from a proposal made by the consultant to the European Health Committee.

47 The author, acting on a request made by the European Health Committee, made a proposal for new additional provisions to the Social Charter in March 2002. The proposal concerned Article 32 on the right to health care services. The *ad hoc* Reviewing Committee appointed by the Health Committee a) added paragraph 2 to the proposal concerning participation and b) replaced "legal remedies" with the word "remedies" (para. 7). In other respects, the proposal was accepted and the Health Committee submitted it for review by the Government Committee.

3) the population is divided into a) those who have immediate access to health services and who receive care while in good health, and b) those who must wait in line or who are not treated, even when in ill-health.

The progress to date in US health care should serve as a warning sign of expensive and bad choices, as well as the difficulties of returning to a systematic health care system.

Investments in the maintenance of health, immediate access to primary health care services, and investments in the health of the population as a whole all improve, in particular, the possibility of providing adequate care to those who cannot afford high patient fees or private health services. The pursuit of systemic and universal health care ultimately benefits everyone. The improvement of the health of the underprivileged will also bring improved health and well-being to those who are better off.

References

Literature

Dutertre, G. (2003), *Key Case Law Extracts*, European Court of Human Rights, Strasbourg: Council of Europe.

Gallant, C., *CDDH(2006)022: Recent developments in the field of social rights*, background paper for the Steering Committee for Human Rights (CDDH) of 17 October 2006.

Gallant, C., *CDDH(2008)006: Summary of the second background paper on recent developments in the field of social rights*, prepared by the Reporter on Social Rights for the CDDH of 19 March 2008.

Mikkola, M. (2010), *Social Human Rights of Europe*. Legisactio.

Treaties and official publications

The ESC, the Charter, European Social Charter (1961), Revised (1996).

The ECHR, the Convention, European Convention for the Protection of Human Rights and Fundamental Freedoms (1950).

Digest of the Case Law of the ECSR. March 2005, December 2006, September 2007, February 2008 and September 2008.

Case law of the European Court of Human Rights

Bacila v. Romania, judgement of 30 March 2010.

Cyprus v. Turkey, Grand Chamber judgement of 10 May 2001.

L.C.B. v. United Kingdom, judgement of 9 June 1998.

Nitecki v. Poland, judgement of 21 march 2002.
Pentiacova v. Moldova, decision of 4 January 2005.
Öneryildiz v. Turkey, Grand Chamber judgement of 30 November 2004.

Case law of the European Committee of Human Rights

Autisme Europe v. France, Collective Complaint 13/2002, Decision of 4 November 2003.
International Federation of Human Rights Leagues (FIDH) v. France, Collective Complaint No. 14/2003, Decision of 3 November 2004.
Marangopoulos Foundation for Human Rights (MFHR) v. Greece, Collective Complaint No. 30/2005, Decision of 6 December 2006.
Addendum to Conclusions XV-2, Slovakia, pp. 201-205.
Conclusions XVII-2, Portugal, pp. 685-689.
Conclusions XVII-2 and 2005, aforementioned statement of interpretation of Article 11.
Conclusions XV-2, Addendum, Cyprus, pp. 26-28.
Conclusions XVII-2, Portugal, p. 681.
Conclusions XV-2, United Kingdom, p. 599.
Conclusions XV-2, Addendum, Turkey, p. 257.
Conclusions XV-2, Denmark, p. 128.
Conclusions XVII-2 and 2005, aforementioned statement of interpretation; Conclusions 2005, Romania, pp. 600-601.
Conclusion XVI-2, vol.2, Poland, p. 642.
Conclusions XV-2, Belgium, p. 99.
Conclusions 2005, Moldova, p. 452.
Conclusions XV-2, France, p. 210.
Conclusions XV-2, Belgium, p. 103.
Conclusions XVII-2, Latvia, p. 504.
Conclusions XVII-2, Malta, pp. 560-561.
Conclusions XVII-2, Portugal, p. 499.
Conclusions XV-2, Greece, pp. 252-253.
Conclusions XV-2, Italy, Article 11 § 3, p. 332.
Statement of Interpretation of Article 11, Conclusions I, pp. 59-60.
Statement of Interpretation of Article 11, general introduction to Conclusions XVII-2 and Conclusions 2005, para. 5.
General introduction to Conclusions XVII-1 and 2004, p. 10.

The *raison d'être* of Nordic Health Law

By Professor Mette Hartlev, University of Copenhagen[1]

1 Introduction[2]

This aim of this contribution is to investigate the *raison d'être* of Nordic health law. The expression *raison d'être* normally means 'reason for existence'. Accordingly, looking for the *raison d'être* of Nordic health law means searching for the reason for its existence.

It would be pointless to investigate the *raison d'être* of Nordic health law without simultaneously assuming that it is possible to perceive 'health law' as a distinct field of law with special characteristics separating it from other legal domains. This assumption is not indisputable, and will thus be considered more thoroughly in Section 2. However, before we embark on any further analyses, it is important to note that the concept of 'health law' is, without doubt, a living reality among Nordic legal scholars. Since the end of the 1970s, numerous legal publications – including a number of doctoral dissertations – have dealt with various issues in health law. Moreover, special courses in health law have been included in law studies programmes at Nordic universities since the beginning of the 1990s.[3] Finally, there is also an increasing number of chairs in health law at Nordic universities.[4] Consequently, health law is indeed a visible phenomenon in Nordic academic life; however, it is essential to con-

---

1 Mette Hartlev, PhD, LL.D, is professor of health law at the Faculty of law, University of Copenhagen. Her major research interests include health law, patients' rights, biolaw and bioethics, and science and technology studies. She is a member of the editorial board of European Journal of Health and has participated in a number of EU-funded research projects.

2 This contribution is based on a keynote speech held at a conference entitled Nordic Health Law: Trends and Challenges, held in Copenhagen on 10-12 April 2010. The author would like to thank Professor Oddný Mjöll Arnardottir, Professor Elisabeth Rynning, Professor Raimo Lahti, PhD student Sandra Liede, and Professor Henriette Sinding Aasen who all provided valuable information about their national health systems in preparation for the speech. However, the author takes full responsibility for the content of the article.

3 Courses in health law were introduced in Denmark (*sundhedsret/health law*) in 1992 (initially at the University of Aarhus and the following year at the University of Copenhagen), in Sweden (*medicinsk rätt/medical law*) in 1993, in Finland (*medical law and bio-law*) in 1997, and in Iceland in 2004. In Norway, at the University of Oslo, central issues in health law have been part of the course in social welfare law (*socialrett/social security law*) since the mid-1970s, later being separated into an independent subject (*helserett/health law*).

4 Uppsala University established a chair in health law, located in the law faculty, in 2003, the Universities of Copenhagen and Aarhus have established chairs in both health law (2006 in Copenhagen) and administrative law, with a special focus on health law (Aarhus 2010). Helsinki University announced a chair (Associate Professorship) in health law in 2011.

sider more carefully what we mean when we talk about health law and whether or not there are any mutual traits in national health law that could justify the hypothesis that there is a *raison d'être* for Nordic health law.

This leads to another assumption, i.e. that it is possible to demarcate something which could be characterised as 'Nordic' health law. This requires the existence of some relatively stable commonalities between health regulation and the approach to health law in the Nordic countries.[5] Whether or not this is the case will be explored further in Section 4. A few observations and reflections are appropriate, however, at this point. It is well known that the Nordic countries share the same cultural roots, and that there is a longstanding tradition of collaboration and mutual inspiration between them in the field of legislation.[6] Although the aim of such collaboration is more modest nowadays than previously, cross-border inspiration is still influential, and references to the legal state of affairs in the other Nordic countries are common – almost mandatory – in white papers and in other preparatory legislative work. However, at the same time, there are also variations among the Nordic countries with regard to the prioritisation of values and how such values should be reflected in regulatory frameworks. Looking at the activities of the Nordic Network for Research in Biomedical Law, as well as other Nordic activities in the field of health law, it is clear that there are both similarities and differences in how the various Nordic countries address legal issues related to health care services.[7] This anthology is also an illustrative example of the divergences as well as the commonalities of Nordic health law. Taking this blurred picture into account, one could ask whether or not it is justified to assume the existence of Nordic health law. In this respect, it is important to weigh the detected differences against the commonalities. It will be argued that, despite certain differences, it may still be possible to detect some common underlying values on a very fundamental level – in the deep structure of law[8] – which constitute the rationale or the reasoning behind a specifically Nordic approach to health law. Accordingly, the focus of this contribution will be the commonalities across the Nordic countries in their approaches to the legal regulation of health care services and the role of health law.

5 For similar reflections regarding European health law, see S. Gevers Health Law in Europe: From the Present to the Future, 15 *European Journal of Health Law* (2008), pp. 261-272.

6 Elisabeth Rynning, Oddný Mjöll Arnardottir, Mette Hartlev, Henriette Sinding Aasen and Sirpa Soini, Recent Developments in Nordic Health Law, 17 *European Journal of Health Law* (2010), pp. 279-294.

7 See, for instance, Nordic Committee on Bioethics, Assisted Reproduction in the Nordic Countries: A Comparative Study of Policies and Regulation 2006: 505 *TemaNord* (Nordic Council of Ministers, Copenhagen, 2006), E. Rynning, Legal Challenges and Strategies in the Regulation of Research Biobanking, in J.H. Solbakk et al. (eds), *The Ethics of Research Biobanking* (Springer, New York, 2009), pp. 277-313 (especially pp. 295-301), L. Wallin, Ambiguity of the Embryo Protection in the Human rights and, Biomedicine Convention: Experiences from the Nordic Countries, 14 *European Journal of Health Law*, (2007), pp. 131-148, and Mette Hartlev, Legislation and Regulation in the Nordic Countries: Is there a Nordic dimension?, in I. Jóndsdottir (ed.), *PGD and Embryo Selection: Report from an International Conference on Preimplantation Genetic Diagnosis and Embryo Selection*, 2005: 291 *TemaNord* (Nordic Council of Ministers, Copenhagen, 2005), pp. 111-122.

8 K. Tuori, *Critical legal positivism* (Aldershot 2002).

2 Health law as a legal discipline

How, then, can we understand and conceptualize health law as a legal discipline? First, it is necessary to consider whether or not we are treating health law as a collection of *legal sources* (statutes and case law), or as the *legal activities* that study this collection of legal sources, whether from an academic or a more practical perspective.[9] Irrespective of how we look at this question, we must also consider and determine which issues and areas to include in health law. Consequently, are we only looking at the rights of the patient vis-à-vis the health care services, or are issues such as the regulation of pharmaceuticals, food security, and environmental health also part of health law? And finally, it must be considered whether health law could be understood as a legal discipline in its own right, or whether it should more rightly be understood as a variety of legal disciplines dealing with the same object, or as a special branch of more established legal disciplines such as human rights law, criminal law, administrative law, or contract law.

These issues were discussed very thoroughly by Sjef Gevers in his keynote speech at the foundational conference of the European Association of Health Law in 2008, in which he concluded that health law is both a *body of law* and the *activities* concerned with this body. However, he also stressed the importance of detecting and framing the *identity* of health law with regard to both the body of law it studies and the way it deals with the object.[10] According to Gevers, it would be too broad to see health law as all laws relating to health care and health protection. Health law should rather be delimited more narrowly to the rules and regulations addressing the *organization, financing,* and *delivery of care,* which are the concerns specifically attributed to the health care services. In contrast, food security, environmental safety, and other issues, which may also affect the protection of health, should instead be dealt with in other legal disciplines. Gevers further stresses that health law is not restricted to the laws directed specifically at dealing with health care (e.g. patients' rights Acts); it also includes other laws such as criminal law, administrative law, and tort, which are applicable to the organisation and delivery of care. A similar approach seems to be in operation among Nordic health lawyers. Consequently, Asbjørn Kjønstad lists five areas of concern for health law: organisations and the financing of health-care services, special diseases and intervention (e.g. compulsory care, organ donation, medical research), pharmaceutical regulation, health-care professionals' rights and duties, and finally patients' rights.[11]

9 Gevers, supra note 5.

10 Ibid.

11 A. Kjønstad and A. Syse, *Velferdsrett I [Welfare law]* (Gyldendal Akademisk, Oslo 2008) pp. 38 ff. See also M. Hartlev, Respekt og beskyttelse i sundhedsretten [Respect and protection in health law], in C. Henrichsen, S. Rønsholdt and P. Blume (eds.), *Forvaltningsretlige perspektiver [Perspectives on administrative law]* (Jurist- og Økonomforbundets Forlag, Copenhagen 2006) pp. 495-522. Kjønstad systematises the area a little differently in his article Twelve main principles in Norwegian health law, 33:3 *Retfærd* (2010), pp. 60-78, but the scope of health law seems to be the same.

Even with this restriction, health law is still a rather complex legal field that deals with a variety of topics across the legal landscape, e.g. issues relating to criminal law, administrative law, contract law, tort, human rights law, EU law, and family law. This complexity raises the question of the *status of health law*. Is it to be considered a legal discipline in its own right, or should it rather be understood as a variety of legal disciplines dealing with the same object, or as a sub-discipline of better established legal disciplines? In the European and international literature, the dominant understanding seems to be that health law is a legal category deserving its own place within the legal academy.[12] For this reason, Derek Morgan claims that 'Whether medical law is a legal category in itself is beside the point' and Ian Kennedy stresses that health law is more than the sum of its parts.[13] Gevers also perceives health law to be a separate, complex legal discipline based on a broad normative foundation.[14] International academic support for the status of health law as an independent legal category is also shown in the fact that there are several international academic journals within the field of health law and medical law, as well as a number of international health law organisations.

Until recently, however, the ontological question regarding the status of health law has not attracted any particular theoretical attention from Nordic scholars. Rather, it seems that health law has established itself gradually as a separate legal discipline, with research activities, special courses, textbooks, and chairs, without any special consideration being paid to the conceptual nature of its existence.[15] However, there have been some discussions about the *legal origins* of health law, and recently also about the *status of health law* as a legal discipline.

The question of the *origin* of health law has been addressed in a number of publications, most of them rooted in the public law–private law dichotomy.[16] What can be deduced from this discussion is that health law is influenced by both legal fields and that public and private law can jointly be seen as the parents of this new legal discipline. However, there are also other positions. Hence, it has been argued that

12 H.J.J. Leenen, Rights of Patients in Europe, 1 *European Journal of Health Law* (1994), pp. 5-13, and H. Roscam Abbing, Founding a European Association of Health Law, 13 *European Journal of Health Law* (2006), pp. 203-207.

13 D. Morgan, *Issues in Medical Law and Ethics* (Routledge Cavendish, 2001), p. 5, and I. Kennedy, *Treat me Right: Essays in Medical Law and Ethics* (Oxford 1988), pp. 1 ff.

14 Gevers, supra note 5.

15 Some of the first academic publications to use the concept of 'health law' were published in Norway and Sweden; A. Kjønstad, *Helserett, helsevern og pasientrettigheter, rett og rettferdighet ved fordeling av helsetjenester, taushetsplikt og bruk av edb i helsesektoren, krav om samtykke fra forsøksperson/pasient ved medisinsk forskning [Health law, health protection and patients' rights, law and justice in distribution of health care services, confidentiality and use of IT in the health care sector, consent obligation in biomedical research]* (Tano, Oslo, 1987) and L. Westerhäll, *Medical Law: An Introduction* (Nordstedts Juridik, Stockholm, 1994). See also L. Fallberg, Patients Rights in the Nordic Countries, 7 *European Journal of Health Law* (2000), pp. 123-144. For teaching activities, see supra note 3.

16 A. Kjønstad, Pasienters rettigheter: kontraktsrett eller forvaltningsrett? [Patients' rights: Contract law or administrative law], in *Lov og Frihet: Festskrift til Johs. Andenæs [Law and Liberty: Miscellany in honour of Johs. Andenæs]* (Universitetsforlaget, Oslo, 1982), pp. 587 ff.; E. Rynning, *Samtycke til medicinsk vård och behandling: En rättsvetenskaplig studie [Consent to medical care and treatment]* (Iustus, Uppsala, 1994), pp. 64 ff.; M. Hartlev, *Fortrolighed i sundhedsretten: Et patientretligt perspektiv [Confidentiality in health law; A patient's rights perspective]* (Thomson, Copenhagen 2005), pp. 123-141; and H.B. Madsen, *Privatisering og patientrettigheder [Privatisation and patients' rights]* (Jurist- og Økonomforbundets Forlag, Copenhagen, 2010), pp. 97-107. H. Bødker Madsen, Health Law as a legal discipline, in this volume.

health law primarily belongs to administrative law and must be understood as a sub-discipline of it (thus depicting health law as the child of a single mother).[17] The importance of administrative law in the health care sector is, without doubt, very high, and administrative law is definitely also part of health law; however, according to other Nordic scholars, it alone does not encapsulate the complex nature of health law. These scholars emphasize instead the importance of, for example, criminal law and human rights law in this field of law.[18] Consequently, health law may turn out not be the child of a liaison between the two major legal categories, but a hybrid of many legal disciplines.[19]

As may be clear, there are many different perceptions of the origins of health law and its relation to other legal disciplines. However, it seems that the predominant position is that, despite its multifaceted origins, health law must be considered a legal discipline in its own right, a legal discipline which is not only based on other legal disciplines and principles but has developed its own legal principles and methodologies.[20] Consequently, instead of perceiving health law as a rebellious teenager claiming independence from his/her parents, I would argue that the teenager has left the parents and formed a family of his/her own with mixed legal roots. As part of this process, health law has developed its own legal principles very much inspired by human rights law; principles which transcend the normal frontiers between traditional legal disciplines such as private and public law.

3 Searching for a *raison d'être*

3.1 Normative patterns

How, then, can we identify the reasoning behind Nordic health law? The methodology used in this contribution, in order to identify its commonalities and hence its *raison d'être*, is inspired by the Swedish legal sociologist Anna Christensen, who developed a theory of law as normative patterns in a normative field.[21] The general idea behind this theory is that it is possible to discover normative patterns in a very complex set of legal norms, and that these patterns reflect the foundational values of society and of social practices. The patterns can be detected through a study of specific fields of law – in this case, selected fields of health legislation in the Nordic countries – with the purpose of identifying and describing the normative content of legal norms.

17 H.B. Madsen, ibid.

18 H.S. Aasen, *Patiensens rett til selvbestemmelse ved medisinsk behandling [Patient's right to self-determination in medical care]* (Bergen, 2000), pp. 221 ff.; Hartlev, supra notes 11, 16.

19 Hartlev, supra note 11.

20 A. Kjønstad, Twelve main principles in Norwegian health law, 33:3 *Retfærd* (2010), pp. 60-78; Hartlev, supra note 11.

21 A. Christensen, Skydd för etableret position: ett normativt grundmönster [Protection of established position: A general normative pattern], *Tidsskrift for Retsvitenskap* (1996), pp. 519 ff.

In approaching this task, it may be useful to have a general idea of the overall social structure and normative framework of the Nordic societies. In this respect, there are two characteristics that could serve as a point of departure. First, all the Nordic countries are considered to be *welfare societies*, and the development of health law is closely related to the development of the welfare state. Secondly, the Nordic countries are known to be strong proponents of *human rights* and, as the development of health law is closely connected to that of human rights law, it is justified to assume that this characteristic also influences the foundational values of health law in the Nordic societies. In this section, we will explore these characteristics a little further, while the normative patterns will be traced in the subsequent sections. In looking for the normative patterns, it has been necessary to restrict the analyses to selected areas of health law. The main focus will therefore be on the organisation and delivery of health care, including individual rights to health care.

3.2 The Nordic welfare state model

According to social scientists, it is possible to identify different welfare state models, among which there is a special Nordic model.[22] Compared to other welfare state models, the Nordic model is characterised by *universalism*, which means that entitlements to social benefits are based on residence instead of specific need, employment relationship, or other conditions. Furthermore, the Nordic model favours *extensive public participation* in various areas of economic and social life to promote *equality of the highest standard*, whereas other models are satisfied with covering basic needs.

Magnussen et al. argue that, in addition to a separate Nordic welfare model, one may also identify a 'Nordic model of health care' characterised by a number of common features. Nordic health care services are, for example, primarily funded by taxes. This is also true of a number of other welfare societies; however, most of the Nordic countries have a decentralised governance structure whereby elected local governments are authorised to raise local taxes. In addition, there is also widespread public ownership or control of the delivery of health care services. Furthermore, these health care services focus on achieving geographical and social equity. Finally, there is a large amount of public participation. According to the authors, this can be summarised in two basic values: *equity* and *participation*.[23] While the authors argue in favour of the existence of a Nordic (welfare state) model of health care services, they also acknowledge that recent developments in health care reforms in the Nordic countries suggest that the Nordic health care systems are in the process of

22 G. Esping-Andersen, *The Three Worlds of Welfare Capitalism* (Polity Press, Cambridge, 1990) and J. Magnussen, K. Vrangbæk, R.B. Saltman and P.E. Martinussen, Introduction: the Nordic model of health care, in J. Magnussen, K. Vrangbæk and R.B. Saltman, *Nordic Health Care Systems: Recent Reforms and Current Policy Challenges* (European Observatory on Health Systems and Policies Series, Open University Press, Berkshire, 2009), pp. 3-20.

23 Magnussen,Vrangbæk, Saltman and Martinussen ibid.

'losing the unique characteristics that would justify referring to a Nordic model'.[24] We should be aware of this tendency when looking for normative patterns in Nordic health legislation.

The welfare state also has certain characteristics, from a legal perspective. Often, the legal regulation of the welfare state is discussed in comparison with the legal tradition of its predecessor, the *Rechtsstaat*. While the *Rechtsstaat* is characterised by a strong emphasis on the rule of law, transparency, and political and civil rights, the welfare state leaves more room for flexibility and administrative discretion in the application of rules and regulations. This serves the purpose of accommodating individual needs with regard to social and economic rights. However, welfare state regulation has gradually assumed the shape of traditional *Rechtsstat* regulation in providing more substantial as well as procedural rights with regard to welfare services. This development matches the other main characteristic of the Nordic societies well, i.e. their strong support for human rights thinking.

3.3 *The human rights tradition*

Modern human rights and health law developed simultaneously as a reaction to the atrocities experienced by the world community during World War II, some of which could be related to the doctor–patient relationship. Human rights and health law also share the same basic legal principles, e.g. respect for dignity, integrity, and autonomy, with both legal disciplines emphasizing the importance of recognizing the freedom of the individual while simultaneously acknowledging the vulnerability and dignity of all human beings.[25]

The Nordic countries have a longstanding and strong tradition of protecting human rights. Consequently, it is not surprising that they were among the first to adopt specific patients' rights legislation, and in doing so recognizing the individual patient's rights in relation to health care services. Finland was the first country to pass a patients' rights Act in 1993, soon followed by Iceland (1997), Denmark (1998), and Norway (2000). Sweden does not have a specific law governing patients' rights; however, patients are assured the same fundamental rights under other laws.[26] Most of the Nordic countries have also ratified and signed the Council of Europe Convention on Human Rights and Biomedicine, as well as a number of the additional protocols, thus showing their commitment to human rights in this field.[27]

24 Magnussen,Vrangbæk, Saltman and Martinussen ibid., p. 18.

25 J. Dute, The Leading Principles of the Convention on Human Rights and Biomedicine', in J.K.M. Gevers, E.H. Hondius and J.H. Hubben (eds.), *Health Law, Human Rights and the Biomedicine Convention: Essays in Honour of Henriette Roscam Abbing* (Leiden: Koninklijke Brill NV, 2005), pp. 3-12; and Mette Hartlev, Diversity and Harmonisation: Trends and Challenges in European Health Law, *European Journal of Health Law* 17 (2010), pp. 37-50; H. Roscam Abbing, Health and human rights in a Europan Context and M. Mikkola, Right to health as human right in Europe in this volume.

26 Fallberg, supra note 15; Rynning, Arnardottir, Hartlev, Aasen and Soini, supra note 6.

27 Rynning, Arnardottir, Hartlev, Aasen and Soini, supra note 6.

However, respect for patients' individual rights must be weighed against the rights of others, as well as important public interests. As the focus on having collective responsibility for social services is very prevalent in the welfare state, there may be a special need to weigh individual rights against collective interests in this context. Consequently, it might be expected that there is a stronger emphasis on collective interests in the Nordic welfare societies than in other societies. Whether or not this is the case will be investigated further in Section 5.

4 The organization and delivery of health care services

4.1 Universal coverage

The purpose of this section is to investigate the delivery and organization of health services in the Nordic countries, including an examination of the extent to which the public are involved in the delivery of health care and the role played by private providers. The financing of health services – including patient charges – will also be addressed. This may provide an impression of the values underpinning Nordic health legislation.

As a point of departure, it is important to stress that all Nordic countries have a *universal health care system* in which access to health care services is primarily based on residence and not on any other, additional criteria such as economic need or circumstances of employment.[28] Even though there are examples of additional schemes, such as private or employer-paid health insurance, these only have a marginal significance compared to the universal coverage offered by public, national systems.

If we look more closely at the *organization* of the Nordic health care systems, it is important to distinguish between care provided by hospitals (in-patient care) and care provided by general practitioners, specialist doctors, dentists and other health-care providers outside the hospital system (out-patient care).

4.2 The hospital sector – in-patient care

Starting with the *hospital sector*, it can be observed that all the Nordic countries have *publicly* run hospital services. A few private hospitals exist, but the number of beds available at private hospitals is rather modest, and their importance is marginal com-

28 See Sweden: § 4 of the Health and Medical Service Act (1987:763), Denmark: § 7 of the Health Care Act (Consolidating Act no. 913 of 13 July 2010), Norway: § 2-1 of the Municipal Health Services Act (Act no. 66 of 19 November 1982), and § 2-1 of the Patients' Rights Act (Act no. 63 of 2 July 1999), Iceland Article 10 of the Health Insurance Act (Act no. 112/2008), while in Finland, access to health care is a constitutional right for all, section 19 of the Finnish Constitution (731/1999) and the right to health care is also stipulated in section 3 of the Status and Rights of Patients Act (785/1992).

pared with public hospitals.[29] However, this may be an area where changes could occur. Consequently, in Denmark, the private hospitals have gained importance during recent years due to the introduction of extended waiting-time rules, entailing that the public purse pays for treatment at private hospitals if waiting times are too long (currently more than one month).[30] In certain situations, Norwegian patients are also entitled to access to private hospitals if the regions are unable to provide timely care.[31] In Sweden, private hospitals also appear to have gained importance and, as in other countries, this growth seems to have profited from contracts with public health care providers. Thus, most of the treatment at private hospitals is paid for from the public purse.[32]

As hospital services are operated by the public sector, it is not surprising that *funding* is primarily based on public money (taxation or mandatory national health insurance systems) Thus, in countries where private hospitals are used more systematically to reduce waiting lists (especially in Denmark), funding is still primarily public. However, private health insurance also pays for care at private hospitals, especially for selected treatments, typically elective surgery. In Finland and Iceland, there are some out-of-pocket payments for in-patient wards, whereas this is not the case in the other Nordic countries.[33] However, there are examples of user charges with regard to special kinds of treatments, e.g. artificial reproduction and sterilization.

Despite the existence of some private providers and private contributions (patient charges or private insurance), it seems justified to conclude that both organizationally and financially, the hospital sector is still primarily a public matter in the Nordic countries. This supports the picture of the Nordic countries as welfare societies with a strong commitment towards promoting equality. It should be added, however, that, in recent years, there has been a trend in several Nordic countries whereby private providers are increasingly being integrated into the provision of

29 In Norway, the number of somatic beds at private hospitals was 284 in 2004. In comparison, there were 13,000 beds available at public hospitals, J.R. Johnsen, *Health Care System in Transition: Norway* (WHO Regional Office for Europe on behalf of the European Observatory on Health Systems and Policies, Copenhagen, 2006), p. 21. The same picture may be observed in Denmark, where the number of private hospitals and clinics has grown from 43 (in 2001) to 221 (in 2009); see Ministry of Health, Sundhedsvæsenet i nationalt perspektiv [The health care services in a national perspective], 2010. Retrieved 25 May 2011, http://www.sum.dk/~/media/Filer%20-%20Publikationer_i_pdf/2010/Tal%20og%20analyser/Det%20danske%20 sundhedsvaesen%20i%20nationalt%20perspektiv/Sundhedsvæsenet%20i%20nationalt%20perspektiv%20juni2010.ashx Sweden only has a few private hospitals, A.H. Glenngård, F. Hjalte, M. Svensson, A. Anell and V. Bankauskaite *Health Systems in Transition: Sweden.* (WHO Regional Office for Europe on behalf of the European Observatory on Health Systems and Policies, Copenhagen, 2005), pp. 1 and 25. In Finland, there are a number of private hospitals, but they are rather small, L. Vuorenkoski, P. Mladovsky and E. Mossialos *Finland: Health system review. Health Systems in Transition.* (WHO Regional Office for Europe on behalf of the European Observatory on Health Systems and Policies, Copenhagen, 2008), pp. 111-112.

30 § 87 of the Health Care Act (Consolidating Act no. 913 of 13 July 2010).

31 § 2-1 of the Patients' Rights Act (Act no. 63 of 2 July 1999), Johnsen, supra note 29, p. 54.

32 Glenngård, Hjalte, Svensson, Anell, Bankauskaite, supra note 29.

33 For Finland, see Vuorenkoski, Mladovsky and Mossialos supra note 29, pp. 63 ff. and for Iceland, see Article 29 of the Iceland Health Insurance Act (Act 112/2008). In Finland, patient charges are subject to an annual cost ceiling.

hospital care.[34] Likewise, in some countries, private health insurance has also gained ground. Consequently, as stressed by Magnussen et al., this may be an area where Nordic health care systems are gradually losing the special characteristics of the Nordic health care model.[35]

4.3 Out-patient care

If we turn our attention to out-patient care, the picture becomes more diverse, both organizationally and financially. *General practitioners* – GPs – are normally of great importance to the health care system, serving as so-called 'gate-keepers' between the patient and more specialized health care services.[36] This is also true in the Nordic countries. However, the way GPs are organised differs greatly. In some countries, they are mainly public sector employees. This is the case in Iceland and Finland, and has also been the point of departure in the Swedish system. The Finnish system seems to be the most complex in the Nordic countries, with three different interacting systems: municipal health care, providing basic care for all citizens; a national health insurance system (NHI), subsidising pharmaceuticals and health care visits in private facilities; and occupational health (which may also include access to a private GP). However, from the organisational perspective, the three systems are publicly rooted, and as such the system could be characterized as public.[37]

Compared to the other Nordic countries, Denmark stands out, with a system of 100 % self-employed physicians – a system which has its historic roots in the privately-financed health care insurance system in operation until the late 1970s. However, it seems that both Norway and Sweden have taken inspiration from the Danish system, and that – on the Nordic level – there is a general trend away from primarily publicly-employed GPs towards a system that favours self-employed GPs. Hence, in certain Swedish counties, there are significant numbers of self-employed physicians; it is estimated that 27 % of visits to physicians in 2002 were to private GPs.[38] This may since have increased, due to new legislation on free choice.[39] Norway changed its GP system significantly in 2001. Previously, patients were allocated to a local health centre equipped with a group of publicly-employed doctors and other health-care professionals. The municipalities are still free to choose whether they will provide

34 There are also examples of private providers offering health care services which are not covered by the general public scheme, e.g. cosmetic treatments – Bemærk: Det er særlige former for behandling/treatments – og ikke leverandøren/providers som er undtaget fra den offentlige finansiering. As a special case, there have been plans in Iceland to create two private hospitals for health tourism.

35 Magnussen,Vrangbæk, Saltman and Martinussen ibid., p. 18.

36 In Sweden, however, in certain situations, patients may have direct access to specialist care of their own choice; see Glenngård, Hjalte, Svensson, Anell, Bankauskaite, supra note 29, p. 28.

37 For further details, see Vuorenkoski, Mladovsky and Mossialos, supra note 29, p. 104.

38 Glenngård, Hjalte, Svensson, Anell, Bankauskaite, supra note 29, pp. 23, 25, 33-35, 50 ff.

39 Act 2008:962 governing free choice and Act 2009:140. See also Rynning, Arnardottir, Hartlev, Aasen and Soini, supra note 6, p. 292.

health care services using public health care facilities or by contracting them out to private actors; however, the reform initiated a personal doctor system which, in turn, also had an impact on the organisation of GP services, whereby a significant number of GPs have been transformed from public employees into self-employed contractors.[40] In Finland, the system of personal doctors also exists in half of all municipalities, although these doctors are still public employees.[41] However, private providers are also increasingly common in Finland, e.g. with regard to emergency services at primary health care centres.[42] Finally, it should be mentioned that some changes have also occurred in Iceland. Primary care – including GPs – is provided by local (public) health centres. However, the state can contract out the health centres, and tenders have been invited since 2003.[43]

Despite the differences in organizational structure, the financing of the health care services provided by GPs is primarily a public matter in all countries. In countries where some or all GPs are self-employed, the public health service has negotiated general contracts or agreements regarding GP services, ensuring that patient care is paid for by the public. However, some patient contributions are not uncommon in the Nordic countries. Apart from Denmark, all the other countries require out-of-pocket payments for services provided by GPs. Charges vary between the countries, and normally, specific groups of patients (e.g. children) and those with special diseases (e.g. HIV) are exempt from payment, or subject to a lower cost ceiling, in order to ensure that patients, especially the weak and vulnerable, are not excluded from the necessary care.[44]

If patients need more specialized care, they may be referred to a *specialist*. The provision of specialist care by doctors is organized in more or less the same way as the GP system in all the Nordic countries. This means that there is a mixture of publicly-employed and self-employed specialists. In Iceland, however, specialist care is provided by self-employed doctors, in contrast to the GP system, whereby care is provided by publicly-employed physicians.[45] Financing generally also follows the same rules as regards the GPs. Consequently, in countries where there are patient contributions, this also applies to health care provided by specialists.

If we go one step further, and look at other health care actors in out-patient care, e.g. dentists, physiotherapists, chiropractors, and psychologists, it can be observed that the public provision of care has less importance. However, the picture

40 J.R. Johnsen, supra note 29, pp. 131 ff.

41 Vuorenkoski, Mladovsky and Mossialos, supra note 29, p. 108.

42 U. Häkkinen and P. M. Jonsson, Harnessing diversity of provision, in J. Magnussen, K. Vrangbæk and R.B. Saltman, *Nordic Health Care Systems: Recent Reforms and Current Policy Challenges* (European Observatory on Health Systems and Policies Series, Open University Press, Berkshire, 2009), pp. 198-213.

43 M. Halldorsson, *Health care systems in transition: Iceland* (WHO Regional Office for Europe on behalf of the European Observatory on Health Systems and Policies, Copenhagen, 2003), p. 19.

44 In addition, patients must also pay for services not covered by the publicly-financed health care schemes, e.g. travel vaccinations, cosmetic surgery etc.

45 Halldorsson, supra note 43, pp. 19-20.

is still very diverse. In general, *dental care* seems to be offered by self-employed providers more often than is the case with GPs and specialist care. However, Finland has a large proportion of publicly-employed dentists. In the other countries, dentists are primarily self-employed. However, in all countries, there are schemes whereby dental care is available publicly to specific groups such as children and the elderly. If we include physiotherapists, chiropractors, and psychologists in our analysis, it appears that these groups are predominantly self-employed in most countries. However, there may be special arrangements for particular groups of patients and, in countries with local health centres (Finland and Iceland), both physiotherapists and psychologists may be available at these centers. Most of the Nordic countries have a system of charges for out-patient care, and this also applies to dental care and treatment offered by other health care providers, e.g. physiotherapists, chiropractors and psychologists. Denmark is the only Nordic country not to have out-of-pocket payment for treatment by a physician (both GPs and specialists); however, with regard to other health care services, Danish patients also have a system of patient contributions.

Looking generally at out-patient care in the Nordic countries, it is clear that there is great variation in its *organization*. However, when it comes to financing, public funding is the primary source, irrespective of whether care is provided directly by public health care providers (e.g. municipal health care centers) or by self-employed health care providers under contract. In contrast to in-patient care, some patient contributions are normal; however, in general, out-of-pocket payments are rather modest vis-à-vis the treatment provided by GPs and specialist doctors. When it comes to dental care, and treatment provided by other health care providers, contributions are higher. This leaves the impression that the level of patient contribution is determined by what is considered to be an urgent need, and that patient charges should not be an impediment to equal access to the necessary patient care. Accordingly, patient contributions regarding core services seem mainly to be used to promote economically-responsible patient behaviour and thus to sustain a system of universal welfare coverage.

4.4 Equal access

All in all, it can be concluded that, with regard to the *organization* of Nordic health care systems, it seems to be the case that the public has a dominant role. This is most evident with regard to hospital care, but public involvement is still very prominent in relation to GPs and specialist doctors. However, with regard to both hospital care and out-patient care, there seems to be a trend towards the greater integration of private providers. In the hospital sector, private hospitals and clinics are slowly but surely becoming integrated, while in out-patient care, GPs are now mostly self-employed. To a greater extent, other forms of out-patient care (dentists, physiotherapists, chiropractors, and psychologists) have been an arena for private providers, albeit with a public safety net for weak and vulnerable patients.

Turning to the *financing* of the health care system, it can be observed that public involvement is very dominant when we look at the funding of core health services (hospitals, GPs, specialists). In other areas, there is significantly less public funding, and it seems that the degree of public funding depends on perceptions of how necessary services are. Consequently, irrespective of the shift in the organisation of health care towards the increasing integration of private providers, financing is still considered to be a public responsibility in order to ensure that all citizens have equal access to core health care services.

5 Human rights perspectives

5.1 Health law, human rights, and the welfare state

As previously mentioned, there is a very manifest link between human rights and health law and, with their historic tradition of supporting human rights, it is no surprise that the Nordic countries were among the first to adopt patients' rights legislation. All the Nordic countries have signed the Council of Europe Convention on Human Rights and Biomedicine as well as a number of its additional protocols, and most of them have also ratified the convention. Accordingly, the Nordic countries are strong promoters of both the welfare state and human rights thinking.

However, there is an immanent tension between the ideology of the welfare state and human rights thinking.[46] Human rights are characterized by an emphasis on human liberty and respect for and protection of the individual. It is, however, also accepted that individual rights in certain situations may be overruled by the vital interests of other persons or by the collective interests of societies. The welfare state is also concerned with the individual; however, in contrast to human rights thinking, the ideology of the welfare state is more receptive to accepting interventions in the rights of the individual in order to promote the collective interest in fair distribution. Accordingly, human rights will be inclined to pull in the direction of individual rights, whereas the ideology of the welfare state, conversely, tends to pull towards collective interests.

The Nordic countries are not frequent guests of the European Court of Human Rights in Strasbourg; however, there are a few cases where the issue of balancing patients' rights with the interests of society has come before the Court. Most of these cases concern respect for patients' private lives and confidentiality.[47] M.S. v. Sweden is of particular interest, because it illustrates the tension between the ideology of the welfare state and human rights thinking.

46 See H.S. Aasen, R. Halvorsen and A.B. da Silva (eds.), *Human Rights, Dignity and Autonomy in Health Care and Social Services* (Intersentia, Antwerp 2009).

47 *M.S. v. Sweden*, 27 August 1997, ECHR no. 20837/92, *I v. Finland*, 17 July 2008, ECHR no. 20511/03 and *Z v Finland*, 25 February 1997, ECHR no. 22009/93. Another important case is Enhorn v. Sweden, 25 January 2005, ECHR no. 56529/00, which concerns the deprivation of liberty.

> The case concerns a woman who had applied for compensation from the Social Insurance Office (SIO) due to a back injury she had suffered at work. The SIO had demanded, and had been provided with, information about her medical condition from the hospital clinic where she had been treated for her back condition, and for other health problems. Her application was turned down as the SIO had found that her back condition was caused by a chronic disorder and not by the work-related injury. The woman claimed there was a violation of her right to a private life under Article 8 of the ECHR because the clinic had provided more extensive information about her medical condition to the SIO than was justified by her application. The disclosed medical data included, for instance, information about an abortion she had requested due to severe back pain. She also claimed that she should have been consulted prior to her medical data being disclosed to the SIO.

The Swedish government presented an interesting argument (paragraph 35), claiming that the woman, through having initiated the compensation proceedings, had waived her right to privacy under Article 8. Consequently, it seems that the government takes the position that citizens have to sacrifice their human rights if they want to have access to welfare benefits from the state. The Court was not convinced by this argument and found that Article 8 was applicable and that there had been a violation of the woman's right to a private life. The government's argument, however, demonstrates how human rights thinking can be considered alien in a welfare state context.

The Court's arguments, as regards reaching the conclusion that the intervention was justified under Article 8.2, are also interesting. The Court observes (paragraph 38) that; 'The communication of the data was potentially decisive for the allocation of public funds to deserving claimants', further noting that; 'It could thus be regarded as having pursued the aim of protecting the economic well-being of the country.' Consequently, the collective (economic) interest of a welfare state is acknowledged as a legitimate aim. In the Court's final assessment of necessity and proportionality under Article 8.2, it is worth noting that it does not specifically address the woman's argument of not having been consulted prior to disclosure.[48] Instead, the Court observes that the SIO had a legitimate need to access information in order to determine whether or not the claim was well-founded (paragraph 42). While it is certainly true that the SIO must have sufficient information to make a proper decision, it is debatable whether or not it was actually *necessary* to disclose information *without consulting the woman in advance.* Hence, it could be argued that the legitimate need of the SIO could just as easily have been met by asking for her prior consent. If she did not agree to the disclosure of all the relevant medical data, the SIO would have been able to refuse her application based on the lack of objective data. In conclusion, it is worth remarking that the European Court of Human Rights seems to be rather receptive to arguments put forward by governments based on the ideology of the welfare state.

48 This question is addressed in more detail by the ECtHR in its assessment of a possible violation of Article 6 of the ECHR.

The case law of the European Court of Human Rights does not, of course, provide a comprehensive picture of how individual rights and collective interests are balanced in Nordic health care services. A number of the other contributions made to this book offer important insights into the status of human rights in areas such as compulsory care, multiculturalism, children's rights, and the protection of patients participating in biomedical research. In what follows, I will take a closer look at the protection of patients' rights with regard to access to care. The patient's right to health – including the right of access to care – is stipulated in a number of human rights instruments. The right to health is considered to be a social human right, and it is well known that the legal status of social and economic rights vis-à-vis political and civic rights has been debated.[49] However, nowadays, the dominant position among human rights scholars is that these rights are indivisible and interdependent.[50] Still, it is necessary to consider the scope and limits of a right to health and to analyze how this is recognized in a Nordic welfare state context.

5.2 Access to care

The question of access to care as a component of the right to health can be approach from a variety of angles. Consequently, issues such as *which* kind of care (including the *quality* of care), *waiting* times, and the patient's *right to choose his/her provider* are all important when assessing the patient's right to care.

As a point of departure, it is important to note that, for patients, access to care is never totally unlimited. Even countries with a private health care system will have professionally-determined limits on care. Hence, doctors and other health care providers are under a professional duty to provide due care, and may be punished if they embark on treatment that is irresponsible or dangerous to the patient. Consequently, a patient never has the right to treatment that is not in line with due care.

In a publicly-funded health care system, there will normally be further limits to the patient's right of access to care in order to ensure administrative and economic efficiency. There may, for example, be waiting times, restrictions regarding choice of provider, and restrictions regarding the quantity and quality of care. In a privately-funded health care system, patients with sufficient economic resources will not face the same obstacles.

In all the Nordic countries, patients have a right to *emergency care*, which must be easily available in hospital emergency wards or from GPs. In other situations – i.e. *planned treatment* – access to care is dependent on a number of factors. First of all, a medical assessment is required and the patient's medical condition must justify further activities on the part of health care services. If the doctor does not find a

49 For an introduction to the human right to health, see B. Toebes, Right to Health, in A. Eide, K. Krause and A. Rosas (eds.), *Economic, Social and Cultural Rights. A Textbook*, 2. rev. ed. (Martinus Nijhoff Publishers, Dordrecht 2001), pp. 169-190.

50 I.E. Koch, The Justiciability of Indivisible Rights, *Nordic Journal of International Law* 72 (2003), pp. 3-39.

medical reason for further examination or treatment, in some Nordic countries, the patient has a right to a *second opinion*. This is the case in Norway and Iceland, but certain conditions and limitations may apply, e.g. a prescription from the GP, and only one second opinion for each condition.[51] In Denmark and Sweden, access to a second opinion is restricted to patients with severe or life-threatening conditions.[52]

A separate question concerns the *quality* of care. In general, the patients' rights legislation in most of the Nordic countries stipulates that patients should be provided with care of a certain standard, but the wording differs. In Denmark, the goal is to provide treatment of a *high quality*, while in Finland and Sweden, the aim is to deliver *good quality* health care.[53] The Icelandic legislation stipulates that patients are entitled to "... the *best health service available* at each time", and furthermore as regards services "... appropriate to his/her condition and prognosis at each time and the *best knowledge available*".[54] The wording of the Icelandic legislation suggests that the standard is *relative*, as it is dependent on the treatment options actually available within the allocated resources. In Norway, patients are entitled to the *necessary* health care, which seems to be 'less ambitious' than in the other countries. It is also stipulated in the Norwegian legislation that, even though patients are entitled to the necessary health care, the cost of that care must be proportionate to the expected benefit to the patient.[55] Despite the different wordings, there seems to be a clear ambition to ensure that patients have access to care that is of a good, and in some instances even high, standard. The aim is more modest in Iceland and Norway than it is in the other countries, but this may be because these countries take such legal provisions more seriously and consider them to be legally binding, and not mainly an expression of a political aspiration.

Waiting times are an issue in all the Nordic countries. Patients may have to wait to get an appointment with a health care professional in order to be examined and diagnosed; after their examinations, they may face waiting times for further analysis and treatment. To ensure transparency, there are rules regarding the right to obtain information about waiting times in all the Nordic countries; in some of the Nordic countries, such information might also be instrumental in satisfying other patients' rights (see below).[56]

---

51 Iceland: Article 20 of the Patients' Rights Act (Act no. 94/1997), Norway: § 3-2 of the Patients' Rights Act (Act no. 63 of 2 July 1999).

52 Denmark: § 29.3 of the Health Act (Consolidated Act no. 913 of 13 July 2010) and section 29 of administrative order no. 62 of 20 January 2010 on the right to hospital treatment, Sweden: § 3a of the Health and Medical Service Act (Act no. 1982:763).

53 Denmark: § 2 of the Health Act (Consolidated Act no. 913 of 13 July 2010), Finland: section 3 of the Status and Rights of Patients Act (Act no. 785/1992) and Sweden: § 2 of the Health and Medical Service Act (Act no. 1982:763).

54 Iceland: Article 3 of the Patients' Rights Act (Act no. 94/1997).

55 § 2-1 of the Patients' Rights Act (Act no. 63 of 2 July 1999).

56 Denmark: § 90 of the Health Act (Consolidated Act no. 913 of 13 July 2010), Finland: sections 4 and 4a of the Status and Rights of Patients Act (Act no. 785/1992), Iceland: Article 18 of the Patients' Rights Act (Act no. 94/1997), Norway: § 2-1 and § 2-2 of the Patients' Rights Act (Act no. 63 of 2 July 1999), and Sweden: § 2b of the Health and Medical Service Act (Act no. 1982:763).

From an economic perspective, waiting times are a necessary evil, but if they are too long, they may be a violation of the patient's right to health. Denmark, Norway, and Sweden have legislated on rules regarding *maximum waiting times*.[57] In Denmark, patients are entitled to have access to hospital care within a specific period of time (Denmark – currently one month), while in Norway, the specific waiting time should be assessed for each patient. In Sweden, the system is more elaborate and covers all sorts of specialist treatment.[58] Furthermore, there are more specific waiting time rules in Denmark for patients suffering from life-threatening diseases. If the local hospital cannot ensure timely care, patients will be entitled to seek care at other hospitals in the country, or even cross-border care.

While the rules regarding maximum waiting times give patients a rather strong right to access care, there are also other means of empowering the patient's right to health care. Rights which give patients a *free choice* of provider could make it possible for them to seek care at hospitals or from health care professionals with shorter waiting times than other providers, while at the same time also offering patients an opportunity to choose a provider of their own convenience. Free choice seems to be an issue that is attracting increasing attention in Nordic health law. In most of the Nordic countries, patients are free to choose their own GPs; in Sweden, patients have free access to specialists and do not need a referral from their GP, while in Norway, Sweden, and Denmark, patients can freely choose a hospital.[59] Iceland seems to have the most liberal free-choice systems, which allow patients 'notwithstanding the division of the country into health regions (...) to attend the healthcare centre or healthcare facility most accessible to them at any time'.[60]

Looking at the different issues related to access to care, the overall impression is that Nordic patients have rather elaborate individual rights, and that the Nordic countries, consequently, strive to protect and fulfill the individual's social and economic human rights in this area. There are some differences between the countries, especially with regard to the regulation of waiting time, second opinions, and freely choosing a provider, but there seems to be a trend against more legal uniformity in these issues. Consequently, on the whole, it would seem that the Nordic countries have succeeded in finding a way of balancing patients' individual rights to health with the interests of the welfare state in ensuring economic and administrative efficiency, as well as the fair distribution of resources.

---

57 Denmark: § 87 of the Health Act (Consolidated Act no. 913 of 13 July 2010) and Norway: § 2-1 and § 2-2 of the Patients' Rights Act (Act no. 63 of 2 July 1999), and Sweden: § 3g of the Health and Medical Service Act (Act no. 1982:763).

58 A so-called '1-7-90-90' rule applies, entailing that the patient is entitled to come into contact with a doctor on the first day, get to see the one within 7 days, have access to a specialist within a further 90 days, and finally have access to specialist treatment within another 90 days.

59 Denmark: §§ 86-87h of the Health Act (Consolidated Act no. 913 of 13 July 2010), Norway: § 2-4 of the Patients' Rights Act (Act no. 63 of 2 July 1999) and Sweden: Act on Systems for Free Choice (Act no. 2008/962).

60 Denmark: §§ 86-87h of the Health Act (Consolidated Act no. 913 of 13 July 2010), Iceland: Article 20 the Patients' Rights Act (Act no. 94/1997) and Article 5.2 of the Health Services Act (Act no. 40/2007), Norway: § 2-4 of the Patients' Rights Act (Act no. 63 of 2 July 1999).

6 Concluding remarks

More specific analyses are certainly needed in order to provide a comprehensive and thorough picture of the *raison d'être* of Nordic health law. However, despite the limited character of this contribution, it seems justified to conclude that there are commonalities in Nordic health law that support the hypothesis that there is a common Nordic rationale. On the surface, there are, indeed, differences between the Nordic countries, but the normative patterns show that, in the deep structure of Nordic health law, we find some common values closely linked to the aspiration of the Nordic welfare societies to promote universal and equal access to health care that is of a high standard. We also find values supporting the fundamental rights of individuals, even in areas of social and economic rights, which are often less recognized and less protected in national laws. Hence, rules regarding maximum waiting times, free choice, and second opinions are all important when it comes to supporting the individual's ability to access timely and good quality care.

There are, however, other trends in Nordic health legislation that point towards a possible shift in rationale. The increasing number of private health-care providers is not, in itself, so important, as long as the public financing of health care services remains intact. However, it could be a sign of a shifting rationale if private health insurance becomes more and more common and if patient contributions escalate. The Nordic health care model is being challenged by an ageing population, as well as by the development of new and expensive treatments and pharmaceuticals.[61] The impact of the European Union on cross-border care also presents a challenge to health care systems based on public funding and benefit-in-kind health services.[62] Whether or not it will still be possible to provide equal access to care of the highest standard in the future remains to be seen.

61 Magnussen, Vrangbæk, Saltman and Martinussen, supra note 22.

62 See, for instance, C. Jaqueson and U. Neergaard, Liberaliseringen af det danske hospitalsbehandlingsvæsen i et EU-retligt lys [EU-law perspectives on the liberalisation of the Danish hospital services], in R. Madell, T. Bekkedal and U. Neergaard (eds.), *Den Nordiska Välfärden och marknaden. Nordiska erfarenheter av tjänster av allmänt intresse i en EU-rättslig kontext [The Nordic welfare and the market. Nordic experiences with services of general interest in an EU-law context]* (Iustus Forlag, Uppsala 2011), pp. 133-166 and M. Hartlev, supra note 25.

The Right to Health from a Constitutional Perspective – the Example of the Nordic Countries

By Dr. Anna-Sara Lind, Uppsala University[1]

1 Point of departure: the paradigm of the welfare state

It is well known, that the Nordic countries are deeply rooted in the welfare state. The realisation of social rights as part of the welfare state is, in practice, considered fundamental in these countries.[2] However fundamental, this is shown to varying extent in the constitutions of the five Nordic countries.[3] In this short article, I will make some reflections on the constitutional status of the right to health, taking the wording of the Nordic constitutions as the point of departure for my reflections.[4]

The realisation of social rights is, thus, one aspect of the welfare state; a common feature of the five countries is the fact that statutory legislation and regional and local self-government are the means chosen in order to materialise social rights. Traditionally, constitutionally-granted individual rights have not been part of the Nordic tradition.[5] Thus, the connection between social rights and political will is intimate.[6]

1 Anna-Sara Lind, LL.D., Senior Lecturer of Public Law at the Faculty of Law, Uppsala University. She defended her thesis *Sociala rättigheter i förändring [Social Rights undergoing Changes]* in constitutional law in November 2009. Lind's research interests focus on fundamental rights in national constitutional and administrative law as well as in a European constitutional context. Lind is on the editorial board of *Nordisk socialrättslig tidskrift*.

2 Asbjørn Kjønstad, *Trygderettighetenes grunnlovsvern [The Constitutional Protection of Security Rights]*, Ad Notam Gyldendal, 1994, p. 14.

3 The Nordic Network of Research in Biomedical Law has existed for five years and several interesting seminars have been conducted by the researchers of the Network. Many of the encounters are comparative in nature; see Elisabeth Rynning, Oddny Mjöll Arnardottír, Mette Hartlev, Henriette Sinding Aasen, and Sirpa Soini, "Recent Developments in Nordic Health Law". *European Journal of Health Law*, 17, 2010, pp. 279–294, especially at pp. 281–282.

4 I do not suggest that this article is a profound comparative study. That has to be done in another context. Such a study would also include the legislation materialising constitutional rules and more of the case law from the courts etc. interpreting and applying the law.

5 Martin Scheinin, "Protection of Economic, Social and Cultural Rights in Finland – A Rights-Based Variant of the Welfare State?", in: Martin Scheinin (ed.) *The Welfare State and Constitutionalism in the Nordic Countries – Nordic Perspectives*, Nord 2001:5, pp. 245–285, at p. 245.

6 Which is always the case, maybe even more so in constitutional law. Cf. Jaakko Husa, *Nordic Reflections on Constitutional Law*, Peter Lang, 2002, pp. 20–22.

This becomes even clearer when we take a closer look at the right to health. The realisation of this right demands a lot from a country's financial and logistical resources. With scientific progress, an ageing population, and financial pressures and restrictions, the right to health is becoming more crucial than ever before. At the same time, realising the right to health is fundamental to living a decent life with human dignity and being able to, as well as capable of, taking one's place in society as a citizen.[7]

This essay is structured as follows. First, the "presence" of the right to health (care) in the five constitutions is discussed, from the literal wording of the fundamental texts. Similarities and differences are outlined. Next, some of the challenges that the right to health care imposes on society, and is itself exposed to, will be discussed from a perspective of constitutional law.

2 A different or similar Nordic standpoint?

2.1 Introduction

Of course, a most relevant question to consider is whether or not a constitutional discussion concerning if there is a right to health at all would be of interest. The constitution serves several aims. One is to set the limits and state the tools for the elected representatives as regards how to perform their duties while serving the people and using the power they have been given. Another is to guarantee the fundamental aims that should prevail over a longer period of time in a country, in order to guarantee foreseeable legislation and stability. In this part, the constitutional protection of the right to health in the Nordic countries will be analysed on the basis of the wording of the five constitutions. As we shall see, the presence of a right to health in the Nordic constitutions differs from country to country. That is also the case, in general, regarding the welfare state in these constitutions; it is not clearly expressed or visible in all the Nordic Constitutions.

2.2 Earlier constitutions – "older" rights? The cases of Denmark and Norway

The oldest constitution in force in the Nordic countries is that of Norway, from 1814. In this constitution, there is no explicit provision regarding the right to health care, with the position of social rights being weak in general. However, the right to property is stated in Article 105:

> If the welfare of the State requires that any person shall surrender his movable or immovable property for the public use, he shall receive full compensation from the Treasury.

7 Cf. T.H. Marshall, *Class, Citizenship and Social Development*, Doubleday and Company, Inc, 1964, pp. 28–29.

The first paragraph of Article 110 mirrors the importance of work to those without property: "It is the responsibility of the authorities of the State to create conditions enabling every person capable of work to earn a living by his work."[8] These two articles, together with Article 97 which generally prohibits retroactivity, have been the basis for recent cases concerning social protection.[9]

A specific or general right to health is not included; however, in the newer Article 110b, the right to environment includes some health aspects since it states that "every person has a right to an environment that is conducive to health and to a natural environment whose productivity and diversity are maintained". In addition, since 1999 the Human Rights Act implements the European Convention for the Protection of Human Rights and Fundamental Freedoms and the two United Nations' Conventions from 1966 on Civil and Political Rights and Economic, Social and Cultural Rights.[10] Accordingly, these conventions take precedence over national rules that conflict with them. The right to health that follow from these conventions has thus, from a constitutional perspective, been strengthened.[11]

In the Danish constitution, from 1849 (with amendments in 1953), Articles 71–80 contain fundamental and human rights. The right to health is not expressed in the wording of this constitution;[12] however, as the right to property is expressed in Article 73, social rights have been considered to be covered (to some extent) by it, in paragraph 1: "The right of property shall be inviolable. No person shall be ordered to surrender his property except where required in the public interest. It shall be done only as provided by statute and against full compensation." However, as is the case in the Norwegian constitution, those who cannot support themselves are entitled to some protection under the constitution. Article 75 paragraph 2 states that these persons are entitled to public assistance if they meet the conditions stipulated by law.[13] When comparing the constitutions of Norway and Denmark, we can see some similarities. The explicit general values referring to the welfare state are not included. Social protection has not been constitutionally protected, nor has the individual right to health. In both countries, the European Convention has left constitutional traces (or brought about a constitutional revolution?). The European Convention became part of Danish law in 1992 and, in Norway, the constitution nowadays states that it is the responsibility of the authorities of the state to respect and ensure human rights (Article 110c). We will return to this question in Part 3.

---

8 Ole-Erik Øie, "Rettsvernet for grunnpensjonen" [Legal protection for basic pension], in: Asbjørn Kjønstad (ed.), *Trygderettighetenes grunnlovsvern [The Constitutional Protection of Security Rights]*, pp. 171.

9 Asbjørn Kjønstad, *Trygderettighetenes grunnlovsvern [The Constitutional Protection of Security Rights]*, Ad Notam Gyldendal, 1994, pp. 31–52, 60 and 73. See also Ole-Erik Øie, *Rettsvernet for grunnpensjonen [Legal protection for basic pension]*, pp. 166–169.

10 Act of 21 May 1999.

11 See also the Act of 2 July 1999 no. 63, the Patients' Rights Act. For more information about recent legislation in the field of health care in Norway, see Rynning et.al., op. cit., pp. 289–291.

12 The right to health care is instead regulated in the Health Care Act [Sundhedsloven] no. 913 of 13 July 2010.

13 This paragraph is self-standing and not dependent on other paragraphs or rights, such as the right to property (Article 73). See Henrik Zahle, *Menneske rettigheder [Human Rights]*, Christian Ejlers' Forlag, 1989, pp. 221–222.

2.3 *The affirmation of the welfare state in the constitutions? The cases of Iceland and Sweden*

The constitution of Iceland dates from 1944, but has been amended since.[14] Even though it is quite "young" as a constitution, it is not that modern in its style,[15] which could be explained by Iceland's long traditions and close links to the legal cultures and legislations of Denmark and, to some extent, Norway.[16] But this might change. Iceland, at the time writing, is experiencing a dynamic constitutional period due to a constitutional process that started in the wake of the financial crisis of last year. The current Article 76, introduced into the constitution in 1995, of the present constitution, states: "The law shall guarantee for everyone the necessary assistance in case of sickness, invalidity, infirmity by reason of old age, unemployment and similar circumstances." The result of the process is not foreseeable as yet,[17] but it has been indicated that welfare rights are strengthened in the proposal for a new constitution presented at the end of July 2011.[18] Accordingly, the right to health services is recognised in Article 23 and social rights in Article 22. These rights are to be legally guaranteed, e.g. defined in law.[19] Unfortunately, at the time writing, no explanations to the proposal are available.

Combined with the prohibition of discrimination, in Article 65, case law from the Supreme Court indicates that the constitutionally-protected social rights in Article 76 are strengthened and can be justiciable.[20] The case shows several interesting features. One of these is that the Supreme Court seeks to interpret the constitutional provisions in the light of Iceland's international obligations. The Court bases its arguments on the European Social Charter and the International Convention on Economic, Social and Cultural Rights as well as ILO Convention no. 102 Concerning Minimum Standards of Social Security. The Articles in the two conventions mentioned initially concern both the right to health and the prohibition of discrimination. This was done despite Iceland being a dualist country, in addition to the other Nordic countries, and despite the fact that none of the conventions have been incor-

---

14 See Kristín Benediktsdottír, "On the States' Obligation to Provide the Elderly a Decent Standard of Living. The Example of Iceland". *Cuadernos Constitucionales de la Cátedra Fadrique Furió Ceriol* no 64/65, pp. 5–17, at p. 12.

15 See also Kirsten Ketscher, "Contrasting legal concepts of active citizenship. Europe and the Nordic countries", in: Bjørd Hvinden & Håkan Johansson, *Citizenship in the Nordic Welfare States*, Routledge, 2007, pp. 142–143, and Kirsten Ketscher, *Socialret*, Förlaget Thomson, 2nd ed., 2004.

16 Compare with Paavo Kastari, "Constitutional experience in the Nordic countries". *Israel Law Review*, No. 4, 1970, pp. 513–526, at p. 523.

17 For information in English, on the constitutional reforms taking place in Iceland, see http://stjornlagarad.is/english.

18 The proposal for a new constitution was presented on 27 July 2011. No official translation of the proposal has yet been made.

19 See Rynning et.al., op.cit., p. 287 for a description of the laws regulating health care in Iceland.

20 See the case no. 125/2000 from the Supreme Court of Iceland (*Tryggingastofnun ríkisins v. Öryrkjabandalag Íslands; The Organisation of Disabled in Iceland v. the Icelandic State*).

porated into national law.[21] The European Convention on Human Rights was implemented into Icelandic national law in the middle of the 1990s.[22] The case shows that social rights as minimum rights are constitutionally protected and the outcome of the case was that a provision in the Social Security Act, which reduced social security payments to disabled persons, was deemed unlawful.

The Swedish Instrument of Government (IoG) does not contain an individual, justiciable right to health either which is explained to some extent by the development of constitutionally-granted rights in Sweden. The present IoG came into force in 1975. It was the result of a lengthy transformation of the constitutional structures of Sweden that had started with the affirmation, in practice, of parliamentarianism at the beginning of the 1920s. Through different reforms in the 1950s and 1960s, Sweden's parliament [Riksdag] was granted the position of the supreme power in Sweden and this development was concluded by the new IoG. The new constitutional law that was intended to lay down the most important features of how the public power should be organised and foremost set up the frame for the work of the elected politicians.

During the 20th century, the constitution did not, accordingly, play a crucial role. From the 1920s and on, most political differences were handled through dialogue and political compromise, and not by applying or referring to the constitution. An important observation to make, in this context, is that the Social Democratic Party, in fact, had been forming majority governments for decades and thus had great opportunity to steer societal evolution. The affirmation of the welfare state, according to the government, was to be handled efficiently by the different political actors using legislative measures. The result of this is that the question of constitutionally-granted rights was not given a high priority, with the party in power expressing, on several occasions, concerns about including (and an unwillingness to do so) individual rights in the constitution. They feared that such rights could threaten the strong expansion of the welfare state and give too much power to the courts. Even more difficult to accept were constitutional *social* rights considered to be.[23] No political party was striving for social rights that would be subject to judicial control, nor guaranteeing a certain minimum level or core of rights. The result is, thus, that we have social rights formulated as goals or aims in the constitution, Chapter 1 Article 2 paragraph 2, and that this article only is being subject of political control not capable of being tried by the courts:

21 The fact that the cited articles were expressly mentioned in the explanatory note to an amendment to the Constitution in 1995 could have played a crucial role. For a short introducion on the Icelandic legal environment, see Oddny Mjöll Arnardottír, Davíd Thór Björgvinsson, and Vidar Már Matthíasson, "The Icelandic Health Sector Data Base". *European Journal of Health Law*, vol. 6, 1999, pp. 307–362, at pp. 308–309. See also Davíd Thór Björgvinsson, *Constitution and Government*, 1996.

22 Law no. 68/1994.

23 Anna-Sara Lind, *Sociala rättigheter i förändring [Social Rights undergoing Changes]*, Uppsala universitet, 2009, pp. 69–76.

> The personal, economic and cultural welfare of the private person shall be fundamental aims of public activity. In particular, it shall be incumbent upon the public institutions to secure employment, housing and education, and to promote social care and social security and good conditions for health.[24]

Accordingly, social rights are materialised through statutory law which in turn, to a large extent, hands a certain margin of appreciation over to the national agencies and the decision-makers at the local and regional levels. Regarding the right to health, this is the case with the Health and Medical Services Act (1982:763), the HMSA, a framework-oriented law. Its first article defines health and medical care while its second defines the obligation to provide good health care on equal terms to the entire population. Thus, the right to health is not an individual, subjective right; although the obligations of the state, the counties, and the municipalities are laid down in the HMSA.

2.4 A stronger constitutional right to health? – The case of Finland

The constitution of Finland has the most extensive article on social rights, in comparison with the other Nordic countries. Its Article 19 reads:

> Those who cannot obtain the means necessary for a life of dignity have the right to receive indispensable subsistence and care.
>
> Everyone shall be guaranteed by an Act the right to basic subsistence in the event of unemployment, illness, and disability and during old age as well as at the birth of a child or the loss of a provider.
>
> The public authorities shall guarantee for everyone, as provided in more detail by an Act, adequate social, health and medical services and promote the health of the population.
>
> Moreover, the public authorities shall support families and others responsible for providing for children so that they have the ability to ensure the wellbeing and personal development of the children.
>
> The public authorities shall promote the right of everyone to housing and the opportunity to arrange their own housing.

24 Author's translation. The IoG changed on January 1st 2011 and, as yet, there is no official translation. Until January 1st 2011, the wording was: "The personal, economic and cultural welfare of the private person shall be fundamental aims of public activity. In particular, it shall be incumbent upon the public institutions to secure the right to health, employment, housing and education, and to promote social care and social security." Health was introduced into IoG Chapter 1 Article 2 in 2002, see Government Bill 2001/02:72, pp. 23–25.

Aspects of the right to health are expressly stated in some of its paragraphs, but a closer reading of the *travaux préparatoires* and the decisions of the Constitutional Law Committee shows that the right to health is relevant when interpreting all of the paragraphs. The Article is supposed to correspond to the international social rights obligations that Finland has vis-à-vis the International Convention on Economic, Social and Cultural Rights, as well as the European Social Charter and the Additional Protocol to the European Social Charter.[25]

To start with, the institutional aspects of social security are formulated in Article 19 paragraph 3. The authorities are accordingly obliged to safeguard access to social services, health and medical care, and also to promote public health.[26] Statutory legislation is thus a very important tool in realising this Article of the constitution, since the wording of the paragraph does not explain how these services are to be organised.[27] Private social and health care services are allowed under the constitution but they have to respect and comply with the conditions stated laid down in Article 124 as regards how public tasks are to be performed by other bodies than public authorities.[28] The importance of the public sector supplying enough services so that all individuals can be full members of society is stressed in the *travaux préparatoires*.[29] It is thus important that services are of such quality that this goal is realised and that everyone has a real chance of becoming a full member.[30]

The third paragraph does not define how health and medical care services should be organised, but focuses on the fact that access to sufficient services must be guaranteed by the means of legislation. Access to and the way the services are organised are also dependent on other articles in the constitution; i.e. equality, the non discrimination rule, privacy and safety, the right to life, etc. Of course, human rights pursuant to Finland's international agreements should also be respected.[31]

The exact content of the rights expressed in paragraph 3 is not easily read from the literal wording of the paragraph. According to the Constitutional Law Committee of the Parliament [Grundlagsutskottet], the content of the right is decided by how the freedoms and rights are construed in combination with ordinary legislation.[32] The

25 See Government Bill 309/1993.

26 Constitutional Law Committee, hereafter CLC [Grundlagsutskottet, GrUU] 37/2000, p. 2; CLC 10/2009, p. 2.

27 CLC 20/2004, p. 2.

28 Article 124: "A public administrative task may be delegated to others than public authorities only by an Act or by virtue of an Act, if this is necessary for the appropriate performance of the task and if basic rights and liberties, legal remedies and other requirements of good governance are not endangered. However, a task involving significant exercise of public powers can only be delegated to public authorities." See also the Health and Medical Services Act (2010/1326), the Private Health and Medical Care Act (152/1990), the Social Care Act (710/1982), the Public Health Act (66/1972), and the Specialised Sickness Care Act (1062/1989).

29 Government Bill 309/1993, p. 75, according to Markuu Suksi, *Finlands statsrätt [Constitutional Law of Finland]*, Institutet för mänskliga rättigheter vid Åbo akademi, 2002, p. 200 n. 103.

30 CLC 20/2004, p. 2, with reference to Government Bill 309/1993; see also CLC 10/2009, p. 3.

31 Government Bill 309/1993 Motivering II/III rd. Detaljmotivering rörande 15 a § [Explanation II/III rd. Detailed explanation concerning Article 15 a]. See also CLC 20/2004, p. 2; CLC 37/2000, p. 2; CLC 10/2009, p. 2.

32 See CLC 20/2004, p. 2.

Committee has adhered to the opinion expressed in the preparatory works, i.e. that it is absolutely important that remunerations paid by the state to the municipalities be raised so that the municipalities may have a real possibility of meeting their obligations in the field of health and medical care.[33] Promoting public health includes both preventative social and health care measures as part of health care activities, in addition to a more general aspiration that society should evolve in such a way that advances public health.[34]

An individual and subjective right to social assistance is expressed in Article 19 paragraph 1 and is applicable when the social guarantees of Article 19 paragraphs 2–4 are not enough for the needs of the individual to be met or when the applicant cannot get help from other persons such as family members. The first paragraph includes services aimed at guaranteeing a life in dignity, including the right to emergency health care.[35] The constitution of Finland contains, accordingly, an individual and justiciable right to health care that has been defined by the Constitutional Law Committee. The individual right in the first paragraph entails that patients must have the possibility of accessing and obtaining health care at all hours and during weekends and holidays, in order to get emergency health care.[36] Furthermore, a life in dignity is to be defined on the basis of a cultural and historical context.[37] This is closely related to the right to life, as stated in Article 7 of the constitution.[38]

The right to the security of basic livelihood, paragraph 2, is aimed at certain situations where the individual encounters specific social risks, such as illness.[39] The right that ensues from this paragraph is thus broader than the minimum right guaranteed in the first paragraph.[40] It was not intended that the right to indispensable subsistence could be considered enough. Both the situation of the individual and the whole system of social security and care are to be considered when deciding whether or not the second paragraph is applicable.[41] The income level and the services that are to be provided according to the first paragraph – indispensable subsistence and care – are accordingly the ones that safeguard the preconditions needed to lead a life in dignity. Examples include the right to food and housing to the extent necessary to retain

33 Government Bill 309/1993, p. 28; CLC Report (GrUB) 25/1994, p. 3; CLC 37/2000, p. 2; CLC 20/2004, p. 3 (that also adds that the effects of reforms must be followed closely). On local self-governance for the municipalities, see Article 121 of the constitution.

34 CLC 37/2005, p. 2, where the Constitutional Law Committee refers to the right to environment in Article 20 GL.

35 CLC 20/2004, p. 2, with reference to Government Bill 309/1993; CLC 10/2009, p. 3.

36 CLC 20/2004, p. 3. See also Government Bill 309/1993, pp. 73–74 and CLC 20/2004, p. 2.

37 As described by Jan-Erik Helenelund, "Den subjektiva rätten till boende i grundrättighetssystemet" [The subjective right to housing in the system of fundamental rights], *JFT* 2/2005, p. 149, with references to Tuori.

38 Government Bill 309/1993 (Explanation II/III rd. Detailed explanation concerning Article 15 a).

39 Paula Ilveskivi, "Fundamental Social Rights in the Finnish Constitution, with Special Reference to Their Enforcement by the Administration", in: Martin Scheinin (ed.), *The Welfare State and Constitutionalism in the Nordic Countries – Nordic Perspectives*, pp. 219–244, at pp. 224–225.

40 CLC 48/2006, p. 2.

41 CLC 33/2004, p. 2; CLC 48/2006, p. 2.

one's health and "life spirit".[42] According to the preparatory works for Article 19 paragraph 1, even aspects of the right to housing are included insofar as the core of the right is concerned. This core cannot be limited and is aimed at guaranteeing health and life. The decisions of the Council also show that material standards have been defined concerning the content of the legislation. Accordingly, the subjective right to housing must meet health care demands and respect the protection of the home and private life.[43] As part of the first paragraph, the right is individual and justiciable. The Article ensures that everyone has a right to social security, even foreign citizens. In line with this, the Constitutional Law Committee has stated that it is absolutely important that legislative Bills respect the rules enshrined in EU law, the European Social Charter, and the United Nation's Convention on the Rights of the Child.[44]

Since the first paragraph lays down an individual and justiciable right, the Constitutional Law Committee has defined the right as having an absolute core which the legislator cannot limit by enacting statutory legislation. The "core" is made up of the fundamental aspects of, and preconditions for, a dignified life.[45] The indispensible subsistence is not to be questioned by the authorities or withdrawn due to, for example, a lack of cooperation on the part of the individual in need. The same is to be said of the indispensible care, for example the right to health care.[46]

3 Challenges facing the Nordic countries – the need for considering the right to health care in a constitutional context

As we have seen, the constitutions of the Nordic countries show similarities on as regards how the notion of the welfare state is expressed at the constitutional level. A common feature is the decentralised state, whereby a lot of latitude is given to the regional and local levels. But there are also significant differences, due to constitutional traditions and choices. These differences are of importance when the realisation of social rights is at stake and, of course, when we study the protection of the right to health. A common feature of the constitutions is that, although the protection of the right to health is expressly stated in some constitutions, this protection is rather weak, giving quite a lot of latitude to the legislator and the decision-maker in individual cases. Finland is the exception to this general "rule", with individual social rights (e.g. the right to health) included in its constitution.

All the Nordic countries are under the influence of other legal orders than the national ones, with their international obligations within the United Nations and the

42 Government Bill 309/1993 (Explanation II/III rd. Detailed explanation concerning Article 15 a). Compare with Article 13.1 of the European Social Charter.

43 The Social Care Act (710/1982) and the Subsistence Act (1412/1997) realise the individual right in Article 19 paragraph 1.

44 CLC 22/2004, p. 3, and CLC 48/2006, p. 4.

45 Compare with Article 7 of the constitution.

46 It should be added that the exclusion of asylum seekers from the application of Article 19 paragraph 1 was to be regulated via statutory legislation, and not by regulation.

Council of Europe increasing. Interestingly enough, the importance of these obligations, as regards the effect of the national legal orders, differs between the Nordic countries. All five countries are dualistic and have all incorporated the European Convention on Human Rights. The difference detected in this paper is that the more recent constitutional reforms of Iceland and Finland have paved the way for the application of international conventions in the national legal order, even though the conventions have not been incorporated. The exception is Sweden; nowhere is it suggested in the *travaux préparatoires* for the last reform[47] that international agreements should be applicable without incorporation and neither is it expressed that these agreements should guide the courts in deciding whether or not a provision, in an individual case, should be considered unconstitutional.

According to recent developments in public international law, the right to health is clearly defined and stressed as one of the core rights regarding what is to be considered an existence that is in line with "human dignity".[48] This has greatly inspired the Finnish constitutional reform, and the 1995 reform in Iceland to some extent. This is not alien to the Nordic view of the welfare state, as expressed in national legislation strongly committed to equal access to health care. The notion of the welfare state is taken for granted, but is not clearly expressed or defined in most of the Nordic constitutions. Maybe that is part of how we choose to consider our national constitutions; maybe the time has come to ask ourselves if the welfare state should be mirrored in these constitutions in terms of expressing a fundamental value commonly held by the Nordic peoples.

The right to health is, perhaps, the social right being put to the test and challenged the most today. In times of financial crisis, the realisation of this right is threatened, something which in turn might lead to a negative impact on the most vulnerable in society, e.g. those who lack resources or the voice to get what they need. Another challenge is the more and more intensive cooperation within the European Union, which effects resource allocation, planning, and the realisation of the right to health. The rules governing financial constraint, free movement, state aid etc. all narrow the scope of the national legislator in steering the evolution of the welfare state. A constitutionally-protected right to health would, accordingly, strengthen the right of the individual (and people in general) since it would put demands and restrictions on the legislator. It would also be a signal, nationally, about the important value of the right to health.[49] Internationally, in particular with regard to the European Union, it could be the clear communication of a fundamental and nationally important value.

47 Swedish Government Reports 2008:125; Government Bill 2009/10:80.

48 See Lind, op. cit., Chapter 3 with references.

49 Eleanor D. Kinney and Brian Alexander Clark, "Provisions for Health and Health Care in the Constitutions of the Countries of the World". *Cornell International Law Journal*, Vol. 37, 2004, pp. 285–355 at p. 304.

Health Law as a Legal Discipline

By Professor Helle Bødker Madsen, Aarhus University[1]

1 Introduction

1.1 The subject of the article

The purpose of this article is to discuss the positioning of health law as a legal discipline. This topic has previously been discussed in my dissertation *Privatisering og patientrettigheder*, to which reference is made in what follows.[2] In my dissertation, I am critical of Mette Hartlev's ideas about the position of health law expressed in *Respekt og beskyttelse i sundhedsretten* and *Fortrolighed i sundhedsretten – et patientretligt perspektiv*.[3]

In what follows, there is a discussion about whether one can characterise health law as 'an area of law with an independent existence' as Mette Hartlev does, or whether health law should instead be described as a special area of law, in line with other specialist disciplines, something which is rooted in the general principles of law, public law (administrative law), or private law (contract law) (see Section 2 below).[4] There is also some discussion about whether it is relevant to maintain the traditional distinction between public law and private law in a health law context (see Section 3), and whether the legal status of the parties is relevant to which set of rules will apply in a given situation (Section 4). Finally, in Section 5, there is some discussion about the significance of general administrative law in connection with

1 Helle Bødker Madsen is professor, dr.jur. at the Department of Law, Aarhus University. Her research field is health law and administrative law, and she also lectures in these subjects. Her doctoral degree was obtained on the basis of the dissertation *Privatisering og patientrettigheder [Privatization and Patients' Rights]* (2010).

She has published the books *Patientbehandling og forvaltningsret [Patient Treatment and Administrative Law]* (2000) and *Sundhedsret [Health Law]* (2nd ed. 2010).

2 H. Bødker Madsen, *Privatisering og patientrettigheder* (Jurist- og Økonomforbundets Forlag, Copenhagen, 2010). This article also contains an extract from my contribution to an anthology on Nordic welfare; see T. Madell et al. (eds.), *Den nordiska välfärden och marknaden* (Iustus Förlag, Uppsala, 2011), pp. 369-390.

3 M. Hartlev, 'Respekt og beskyttelse i sundhedsretten', in C. Henrichsen et al. (eds.), *Forvaltningsretlige perspektiver* (Jurist- og Økonomforbundets Forlag, Copenhagen, 2006); and M. Hartlev, *Fortrolighed i sundhedsretten – et patientretligt perspektiv* (Thomson, Copenhagen, 2005). The subject has also been dealt with in Norwegian law, see Asbjørn Kjønstad, 'Pasienters rettigheter – kontraktsrett eller forvaltningsrett?', in A. Bratholm et al. (eds.), *Lov og frihet. Festskrift til Johs. Andenæs* (Universitetsforlaget, Oslo, 1982).

4 Hartlev, 'Respekt og beskyttelse i sundhedsretten', supra note 3, p. 496.

the treatment of patients, including whether or not it is relevant to patients' rights whether, in a given case, administrative law or contract law will apply in connection with treatment. Section 6 contains concluding remarks.

1.2 'Patients' rights'

The terms 'patient', 'treatment', and 'rights' play key roles when discussing the issues raised in the introduction. Thus, it is necessary to start by determining what is meant by these terms in the present context.

The term 'patient' is not expressly defined in the Health Act. However, Part III of the Act, on the rights of patients, which has been carried forward from the now repealed Patients' Rights Act, is based on the assumption that a patient is a user of health services, whether he/she is healthy or ill.[5] According to Section 13[6] of the Health Act, Part III of the Act applies to patients of the health system, and elsewhere where professional health services are provided, who receive or have received treatment from health personnel.[7] Thus, persons who are or who have been treated are covered by the rules. However, in what follows, a wider concept of 'patient' is used. The term also covers those who are waiting to receive treatment, e.g. those on a waiting list to receive a preliminary examination at a hospital.

The term 'treatment' can also have either a narrow or a broad definition. Within the meaning of the Health Act, it covers examination, diagnosis, the treatment of illness, maternity help, rehabilitation, nursing care, and prevention and health promotion in relation to individual patients (see Section 5). This is supplemented by Section 13 which, as stated, stipulates that Part III, regarding patients' rights, will apply to patients who receive or have received treatment from health personnel, whether within the health services or somewhere else where professional health services are provided.[8] One can thus say that, in a narrow sense, treatment concerns professional health services, including decisions made about patient treatment by health professionals.[9] In the present context, the term also covers decisions taken before treatment is initiated. Thus, the term includes decisions taken regarding the right to receive treatment, including the prioritisation of patients on waiting lists, and decisions relating to a stay in the place of treatment, e.g. the right to use a mobile telephone, listen to the radio, and receive bedside visits. This also covers patient care, e.g. telephone services, the behaviour of staff etc. Rather than talking about treatment in

5 Pregnant women and those in receipt of district health services are thus also patients under the Health Act; see *Folketingstidende* 1997-98, 2nd series, Annex A, p. 521.

6 Consolidated Law No 913 of 13 July 2010.

7 Under the Health Act, 'health personnel' are those who are authorised, under special legislation, to undertake professional health tasks, and those who act on their behalf; see Section 6.

8 Part III contains the general rules on patient participation in decision-making, the right to decide in special cases, the right of determination with regard to biological material, the right of access to medical records, the duty of confidentiality and vis-à-vis the passing on of health information, and the right to use interpreters.

9 On the concept of 'professional health services', which is dynamic, see Bødker Madsen, supra note 2, p. 294 ff.

a wider sense, one could talk of associated activities and decisions taken in connection with them.

As for the concept of rights what follows focuses on the rules that give patients a legal status. What is of interest is patients' legal entitlements. Methodologically, the assessment of patients' legal entitlements is based on a traditional interpretation of the relevant legal rules. In the first instance, these are the rules that are specific to health services. Next, this concerns rules that operate in conjunction with these, e.g. the general rules of contract and administrative law. Rules that are derived from contracts or collective agreements between the authorities responsible for providing health services and the private actors in the health sector, e.g. privately-owned hospitals and private sector practitioners, can also constitute legal rules. This will depend on the protective intention of the rules in question. The decisive thing is whether or not, as is generally understood, a rule must be regarded as intended to protect the interests of patients (third parties). Examples of rules derived from contracts or collective agreements, which can presumably be relied on by insured patients, include rules in the national agreement on general medical assistance regarding the obligation of doctors to be available, and the rule in the general agreement regarding the expanded freedom of choice of hospital, which binds privately-owned hospitals to refuse to examine/treat a patient who is referred under the agreement purely on the grounds of a lack of resources or on professional grounds, and to give written information to the patient about the reason for the refusal.[10]

The concept of patients' rights can be understood both broadly and narrowly. In a narrow sense, the concept covers the legal rights of patients who either are or who have been treated. These rights concern the rules that are specific to the health sector. Examples of these include the rights of patients, under the Health Act, to obtain information about their state of health, the possibilities of treatment, the risk of complications etc. (see Section 16), the right of access to medical records and confidentiality (Sections 37 and 40), and the rights of patients, under the Practice of Medicine Act, to obtain treatment which, in each individual case, does not fall below the current generally applicable professional standards for the sector (see Section 17).[11]

In a broad sense, patients' rights also include rights derived from general legal rules supplementing the rules that are specific to the health sector (see Section 2 below). These include, for example, the Personal Data Protection Act, the Public Administration Act, the Freedom of Information Act, administrative law principles, contract law, and EU law. Here, the term is used in its broader sense.

10 Bødker Madsen, supra note 2, p. 377 ff.

11 Consolidated Law No 1350 of 17 December 2008.

2 Health-specific rules and their interaction with general legal rules

Health-specific rules are those that are specifically aimed at the health sector and its activities, including treatment in a narrow sense. These include the general rules of the Health Act, the Practice of Medicine Act, the Claims and Compensation Act, and the special rules of the Mental Health Act and the Assisted Reproduction Act. In a number of cases, these rules cover both public and private health service providers. For example, the rules of the Practice of Medicine Act, as well as the confidentiality obligations of the Health Act, apply to health professionals in both the private and public sectors.[12]

However, health-specific rules do not exist in a vacuum and they do not provide exhaustive answers to the issues raised in connection with the decisions taken about, and in connection with, patient treatment. For example, the rules only govern patients' rights of access to their health records, but not access to the hospital's internal rules about referrals, procedure, and documentation when there are complaints, about the prioritising of patients on waiting lists, the obligation of private hospitals to accept a patient for treatment, payment for treatment at a private hospital, and about a patient's obligation to pay a charge if he/she misses an appointment. Nor do the health-specific rules govern whether or not advice has to be given about making complaints and the right to be advised about the reason for a decision. In order to provide answers to these questions, it is necessary to draw on the general legal rules in this area, both public and private law rules, e.g. under general administrative and contract law. Exactly which of these general rules is relevant in a given situation will depend on how the health service providers in question are organised (see Section 4 below).

Thus, the health-specific rules are supplemented by generally applicable rules, whether under public or private law. This can also be expressed thus: the health-specific rules have their roots in general legal rules. For this reason, I do not agree with Mette Hartlev when she characterises health law as 'an area of law with an independent existence', understood as an autonomous area of the law.[13]

On the other hand, this does not mean that I deny the significance of health law as an independent legal discipline. Health law has its own special rules and characteristics, e.g. the fundamental principle of a patient's right to self-determination, which justify and necessitate health law being treated as a separate legal discipline. If a patient is treated in the public health sector, it will be possible to draw parallels with

12 Bødker Madsen, supra note 2, p. 109 ff. However, it is also possible to provide examples of health-specific rules that are only binding on the authorities responsible for the health services, regional or local authorities, e.g. the obligation to provide a patient, who is referred for hospital treatment, with specific information by a given deadline (Section 90 of the Health Act), and the obligation to provide patient counselling services (Section 51 of the Health Act).

13 Hartlev, 'Respekt og beskyttelse i sundhedsretten', supra note 3, p. 496. In the same place, Hartlev goes further and states that health law is not a special branch of administrative law, but rather a form of hybrid, located in both public and private law, as well as under the influence of EU and human rights law. In doing so, Hartlev seems to acknowledge that these general rules are relevant.

special disciplines such as social welfare law, tax law, and environmental law; in other words, special administrative law. If a patient is treated in the private health sector, it will be possible to draw parallels with tenancy law and consumer law; in other words, special property law.

Thus, I believe that health law is an independent legal discipline and, in common with other special disciplines, it is based on general legal rules.

3 The distinction between public and private law

A distinction is traditionally made between public and private law. However, Mette Hartlev does not believe that the distinction between public and private law per se helps to clarify what she calls the 'normative space' that surrounds an area of law. Instead, in relation to health law, Mette Hartlev believes that, in order to clarify this, one must start out from the position of the rights of individual patients and then analyse the public and private law aspects of these rights.[14]

As part of her argument as to why one should start out from the traditional distinction between public and private law, Mette Hartlev states that freedom of contract is restricted by mandatory rules and, in relation to the general practice sector, by the provisions of the collective agreement (e.g. the rules obligating doctors to be available). On the public law aspect of patients' rights, Mette Hartlev states that several contract law elements are involved, and she refers to the example of freedom of choice of hospital, and to the fact that treatment is dependent on the patient's informed consent.[15]

I do not agree that the fact that mandatory rules govern a particular area of the law means that contract law is deprived of all significance. Contract law still applies within the framework of the mandatory rules, including health-specific rules and general legal rules, such as those prohibiting discrimination on the grounds of race and ethnicity etc. An example situation in the private health sector, based on contract law, is whether or not a patient is to be accepted for treatment; i.e. an agreement can be entered into regarding acceptance for treatment. Also, questions of payment and the timing of treatment are, in principle, subjects for agreement; i.e. agreements can be entered into as regards scheduling and payment. Besides, the question of the patient's right of access to documentation other than his/her medical records is based on an agreement; thus, procedural agreements can be entered into. To a limited extent, depending on the circumstances, there is also scope for agreements about treatment in a narrow sense, i.e. treatment agreements. Thus, it is possible to agree on more specialised examination, e.g. MRI scanning and examination by specialists, additional post-surgery check-ups, or more preventive health examinations, than is the norm.[16]

14 Hartlev, *Fortrolighed i sundhedsretten*, supra note 3, p. 124 ff.

15 Ibid., supra note 3, p. 126 ff. and p. 131.

16 Bødker Madsen, supra note 2, p. 302 ff.

As for the public law rules, it can be said that these are mandatory in the same way as the rules governing professional health service provision. Legal regulation, binding effect, and foreseeability (legal certainty) are characteristic of public law. Comprehensive legal regulation means that there is only very limited scope for freedom of contract.[17] Freedom of choice of hospital does not depend on contract law, as asserted by Mette Hartlev. This patient's right, provided by means of legislation, is based on health-specific mandatory rules contained in the Health Act; thus, freedom of choice of hospital cannot be offered as an example of a contractual element of public law. The same can be said of the requirement for informed consent, which is similarly based on mandatory rules contained in the Health Act (Sections 15-16).

Thus, I do not believe there are grounds for departing from the traditional distinction between public and private law. On the contrary, without any basis in the general legal rules and their characteristics, there is a risk of overlooking the interaction between the health-specific provisions and the generally-applicable rules, and the differing results arrived at under private and public law from the perspective of patients' rights.[18]

With regard to the fundamental difference between private and public law, broadly speaking, it can be said that private law is characterised by having little legislative regulation. Freedom of contract prevails, and it is the agreement that constitutes the 'law' for the parties. It is different with public law, which is characterised by having comprehensive legal regulation, aimed at protecting the legal rights of citizens. This is discussed in more depth in Section 5.

4 Legal status of the parties

As a starting point, the legal status of the parties is relevant to which rules will apply to the relations between them. For example, the rules contained in the Health Act regarding informed consent will apply if one of the parties is a health professional and the other is a patient, while administrative law will apply if one of the parties is an administrative authority. However, Mette Hartlev has criticised this doctrine regarding the status of the parties, i.e. the doctrine that the status of the parties is relevant to which rules of general law (private or public law) govern individual cases.[19] Mette Hartlev also denies, in principle, the significance to fundamental patients' rights of the organisational form of a service provider.[20]

I disagree with these views. Private law does, in fact, apply to relations between two individuals.[21] If a patient's treatment takes place in the private sector, it will prin-

17 Ibid., p. 289 ff.

18 Ibid., pp. 293-294.

19 Rather, Mette Hartlev concentrates on the public and private law aspects; see Bødker Madsen, supra note 2, p. 132 ff.

20 Hartlev, *Fortrolighed i sundhedsretten*, supra note 3, p. 142.

21 Bødker Madsen, supra note 2, p. 279 ff.

cipally be private law, general contract law, that will supplement the health-specific rules. As established in my dissertation, this also applies in cases where treatment in the private health sector takes place subject to an agreement between the authorities responsible for the health services, i.e. regional or local authorities, and where the treatment is publicly financed, either in whole or in part.[22] Furthermore, legislation, including health-specific rules, does not address the issue of the application of administrative law when health authorities delegate health service provision to private actors.[23] This means that one must fall back on the general starting point where, in defining the concept of 'the public administration', and thus the scope of administrative law, there is an emphasis on the formal and organisational rather than on the functional. If an entity is organised under private law, then private law is applicable even if it actually carries out administrative functions. Conversely, administrative law will apply if a body is organised under public law.

The relationship between an administrative authority and a private individual is, in fact, regulated by administrative law.[24] Where treatment is provided by a public body, for example by publicly-employed hospital doctors, it is public law, including general administrative law, which supplements the health-specific rules. Under Section 3(1) of the Health Act, the responsibilities of public authorities rest with regional and local authorities; in other words, this is a public welfare task so the general principles of administrative law will play a key role in connection with patient treatment.[25] According to Section 2(1) of the Public Administration Act, this Act applies to cases where decisions are, or will be, taken by an administrative authority.[26] This is traditionally aimed at determining what is, or should be, the law in a given case. As in recent years patient treatment has increasingly become a legal question, administrative law has become increasingly important in this area.[27] To this extent, in contrast to what Mette Hartlev argues, one can characterise health law as special administrative law.[28]

In conclusion, it must be maintained that, in a situation involving a private health service provider, e.g. a private general practitioner, and a patient, the health-specific rules, including those governing health professionals, are supplemented by general contract law; while in a situation involving a public health service provider, e.g. a hospital doctor, and a patient, it is general administrative law, along with other man-

---

22 Ibid., p. 117 ff. There is general authorisation to cooperate with private health service providers in the provision of health services in Section 3(2) of the Health Act. This provision is supplemented by special provisions which obligate health authorities to cooperate with private actors in carrying out the tasks of hospitals and general practice; see Section 75(3) and (4), Section 87(5), and Section 87(c) and (g) of the Health Act.

23 Bødker Madsen, supra note 2, p. 43 ff.

24 See, for instance, J. Garde et al., *Forvaltningsret, sagsbehandling*, 6th ed. (Jurist- og Økonomforbundets Forlag, Copenhagen, 2007), p. 1.

25 Bødker Madsen, supra note 2, p. 97 ff.

26 Consolidated Law No 1365 of 7 December 2007.

27 Bødker Madsen, supra note 2, p. 217 ff.

28 Hartlev, 'Respekt og beskyttelse i sundhedsretten', supra note 3, p. 495.

datory public law rules such as EU law, that will supplement the health-specific rules. In my dissertation, I have argued that, with regard to the fundamental principles of administrative law (or the fundamental principles of quasi-administrative law), e.g. the requirement for impartiality, there is a sufficient basis for departing from the traditional starting point of the definition of 'the public administration' in relation to general practitioners who are party to a collective agreement with public authorities regarding the free treatment of patients insured in Group 1. This group of doctors occupy such a powerful position, both in fact and in law, that, in my view, there is both a basis and a need for applying the fundamental principles of administrative law.[29] This view of the law is maintained in the present context.

5 Health-specific rules and contract or administrative law

5.1 Field of application

The rules governing professional health service provision, and a number of other health-specific rules that apply to treatment, e.g. regarding self-determination, access to documentation, and the duty of confidentiality, cover both publicly-employed and private-practising health professionals.[30] To this extent, it makes no difference to a patient whether treatment is provided in the public or the private sector.

It is different with regard to the generally-applicable rules which supplement the health-specific rules. As I have shown in my dissertation, from the patient's point of view, it can be relevant whether contract or administrative law supplements the health-specific rules in a given case. Thus, it is also relevant to the legal position of a patient whether treatment is provided by authorities responsible for health services, i.e. regional or local authorities, or by private health service providers under an agreement between these authorities. This is discussed in more detail in what follows.

5.2 Contract and administrative law

In Section 3 above, I have given an account of the differences between public and private law. In respect of private law, I stated that there is little legal regulation. Freedom of contract thus prevails, with the contract being the 'law' between the parties. In contrast, public law is characterised by having comprehensive legal regulation, binding effect, and foreseeability (legal certainty). The following looks at how this difference is manifested in concrete situations.

By way of introduction, it can be said that the two areas of the law differ with regard to openness (publicity). In contrast to administrative law, contract law has no

29 Bødker Madsen, supra note 2, p. 168 ff.

30 Ibid., p. 109 ff.

general principle of openness. This means, for example, that a patient who is treated in the private health sector does not have the right to see the internal guidelines applying to the treatment of patients in the place where the treatment is provided, as is the case where the health service providers are subject to public law (see the Freedom of Information Act, Section 8(4)).[31] This can involve, for example, rules about referrals, professional instructions, and procedural rules etc. The lack of openness means that contract law lacks a core patient right, which is found in administrative law.

The general procedural requirements of administrative law do not apply to contract law. This means, for example, that a patient who is treated in the private health sector does not generally have the right to obtain advice, the automatic right to be heard, or the right to be advised of the reasons for decisions and on making complaints (see the Public Administration Act, Sections 7, 19, 22, and 25).[32] For example, a patient who is denied access to a private hospital has no general entitlement to receive written justification of this. Nor does contract law contain any special rules about legal capacity. This means that a private GP can make a referral for treatment even if there is, or there is a risk of a lack of, impartiality because of a family connection, friendship etc. Neither sympathy nor antipathy prevents a private practitioner from taking important decisions about a patient.

All in all, it can be said that, compared with administrative law, contract law lacks rules for securing the legal position of patients.

If we next look at the requirements of administrative law as regards the content of an offer of treatment (i.e. questions about what treatment options must be offered with regard to their nature, time, place, extent and quality, and to which persons or groups of persons existing treatment options must be offered, including the priority according to which patients must be offered treatment), it can be said that, under administrative law, there is an obligation to ensure that such decisions are based on proper considerations. Proper considerations are, first and foremost, the seriousness of the illness, the urgency, the possibilities of treatment and cure, the risk of complications etc., as well as certain associated considerations. This means that public health service providers have an obligation to accept a patient for treatment if there is a need for treatment in that specific case. In other words, in the public sector a patient has a vaguely defined right to treatment.

Under contract law, a private health service provider is free to enter into an agreement to accept a patient for treatment, and free not to. Both private specialist doctors and private hospitals are thus free to decide whether or not a patient will be accepted for treatment. In principle, there is no obligation to enter into a contract. The terms upon which a patient is accepted for treatment are also based on an agreement. Thus, there is no general requirement for impartiality. This means that a private health ser-

31 Law No 572 of 15 December 1985, with amendments.

32 Consolidated Law No 1365 of 7 December 2007.

vice provider can refuse to accept a patient for treatment even if the patient needs treatment; in other words, the patient has no legal right to treatment. For example, a private doctor can refuse to treat a person with whom he is on bad terms. A private hospital or clinic can adopt rules which entail that only certain groups of persons can receive treatment, e.g. because they are covered by a special health insurance scheme, because they are elite sportsmen/women etc., or because they can decide that such people will go to the head of the queue. A private specialist doctor will be able to provide treatment earlier, or offer a highly-specialised examination, e.g. using MRI scanning, just because the patient is covered by special health insurance or because the patient is a powerful politician or a relation.[33] A doctor can refuse to see a 'lifestyle' patient (smokers, obese persons etc.) or acute or criminal patients, and can put a patient at the front of the queue who is willing to pay more, or a friend or a relation. A private clinic will also be able to provide certain groups of patients, e.g. celebrities, with especially favourable conditions during their stay at the clinic. As stated, this also applies in cases where private health service providers provide treatment under an agreement with a public body, and where the fees are paid by that public body.

Compared with administrative law, contract law lacks rules protecting the legal position of the patient. Thus, administrative law contains rules which are not found in contract law and which are aimed at protecting the legal position of the patient.[34]

5.3 *Health-specific rules and administrative law*

If, to start with, one compares the mandatory, health-specific rules, including those applicable to professional health services, with general administrative law, it can be seen that, in principle, the general administrative law procedures only apply where decisions are, or will be, made (see the Public Administration Act, Section 2(1)).[35] Thus, it is not decisive whether a particular instance concerns an actual treatment situation. The provisions of the Public Administration Act can also be relied on by patients who are awaiting treatment. The same applies to the provisions of the Freedom of Information Act.

On the other hand, the health-specific procedural rules only apply where there is, or has been, a treatment situation (see the Health Act, Section 13). Thus it is not decisive whether decisions are by nature "decisions" within the meaning of the Public Administration Act, or decisions that fall outside its scope. But the health-specific procedural rules do not apply to patients who are awaiting treatment.

---

33 In the press, there has recently been a number of examples of persons covered by special health insurance getting appointments with a specialist within a couple of days, while patients who are covered by ordinary health insurance often have to wait for months. There have also been descriptions of how ordinary GPs have referred patients covered by special health insurance for advanced examinations, even when there was no proper medical justification for doing so. This is unacceptable; see section 5.4 below.

34 Bødker Madsen, supra note 2, pp. 323-327.

35 On the concept of decision-making in relation to the treatment of patients in the public health services sector, see Bødker Madsen, supra note 2, p. 217 ff.

Under the health-specific rules, persons who have been treated can demand access to their medical records (see the Health Act, Section 37). On the other hand, the Health Act does not provide the right of access to other documentation, e.g. internal rules about referrals to the place of treatment, or documents in connection with complaints. With regard to openness, general administrative law gives legal rights to patients that are not contained in the health-specific rules.

In certain cases, under the health-specific rules, there is a requirement for the doctor providing the treatment to be impartial. This applies to the issuing of death certificates etc. (see Executive Order No. 320 of 27 March 2007), to transplants (see the Health Act, Section 54(2)), and to involuntary hospital admissions (see the Mental Health Act, Section 7(2), second and third sentences). On the other hand, there is no general requirement, as under administrative law, that health personnel must possess a legal capacity. Thus, a doctor can treat a close relation.

A patient who is undergoing treatment must be informed of the treatment options and the risk of complications and side-effects; he/she must also give his/her consent before treatment is initiated (see the Health Act, Sections 15 and 16). These are patients' rights in a narrow sense, and they cannot be claimed by patients who are on a waiting list. It is different under the rules of the Public Administration Act regarding the right of a party to be heard, rules which also cover people who are awaiting treatment. Thus, on this point too, the rules of the Public Administration Act have an independent significance for the legal rights of patients.

It is the responsibility of health professionals, at their own initiative, to make patients aware of injuries that may confer on them the right to compensation from the Patient Insurance Association (see the Claims and Compensation Act, Section 23).[36] On the other hand, the health-specific rules do not contain a general requirement for health professionals to advise patients on their rights, e.g. the freedom to choose a hospital. Thus, the duty to advise in Section 7(21) of the Public Administration Act has an independent significance for the legal rights of patients.

Under the health-specific rules, there is no general obligation to justify a refusal, e.g. regarding access to medical records or treatment. Such an obligation arises under the Public Administration Act, Section 22, which thus has an independent significance for the legal rights of patients. Nor is there a general duty, under the health-specific rules, to advise about complaints.[37] Finally, under the health-specific rules, there is no general right to an examination other than in the context of treatment.

All in all, compared with administrative law, the health-specific procedural rules lack provisions protecting patients' legal rights.

36 Consolidated Law No 24 of 21 January 2009.

37 Under the rules that have applied hitherto, a doctor could refuse to give a woman or a couple fertility treatment if that doctor's assessment was that one or other of the persons in question was not a suitable parent. The doctor was then required to inform the woman or the couple about their right to appeal to the Appeal Tribunal; see Executive Order No 119 of 7 February 2007, Section 6(2). These rules were repealed by Executive Order No 74 of 28 January 2011, pursuant to which the State Administration decides in such cases.

If one compares the substantive rules regarding the terms and content of an offer of treatment, it follows from the general rules governing professional health services as regards the duty to provide proper professional treatment, once a treatment situation has been established, that there are considerations which must be taken into account in each case. Here, reference should be made to Case No. 0127410 of the Patients' Board of Complaints, where it was stated that, in assessing whether or not a patient can undergo a complex course of treatment, including an organ transplant, it is necessary to include an assessment of the patient's ability to cooperate. However, there is no general requirement for impartiality, as under administrative law. Subject to the restrictions governing doctors' general duty to provide assistance (the duty to give the first necessary medical assistance), the provisions of the Racial Discrimination Act, and the principle of the equal treatment of men and women, private health service providers are free to decide whether or not they will accept a patient for treatment, and if so, on which terms. This means that private health service providers are free to select their patients, including the use of selection criteria which would be improper under administrative law, e.g. insurance status, friendship, family relationship etc., and thus free to exclude patients whom the health professional does not want to treat, perhaps on the grounds of political considerations, social status, lifestyle, personal antipathy etc. In other words, there is no legal right to be accepted for treatment, even where there is a need for it.

According to the rules governing professional health services, in a treatment situation, a health professional must make an overall assessment of the health of the patient (see Case No. 0127410 of the Patients' Board of Complaints). In this case, the Board has stated that the lack of language ability did not in itself justify the refusal of an organ transplant. An overall health assessment should have been made, including an assessment of whether or not the patient would be able to understand and follow the requirements for the treatment. Discretionary assessments cannot be made subject to a rule in a treatment situation. However, as stated, private health service providers are free to decide whether or not, and on which terms, they will accept a patient for treatment. They can establish rules that lead to certain groups of persons being excluded from treatment, or that only certain groups of persons are accepted for treatment, e.g. persons who are covered by some particular health insurance scheme. On this point too, general administrative law has an independent significance for the legal rights of patients.

Administrative law also has an independent significance in relation to the principle of proportionality. This generally applies to public bodies, both when making decisions and when carrying out their administrative tasks. Under the health-specific rules, the principle only applies in a treatment situation. This means, for example, that a patient who has been admitted to a private hospital can be subject to restrictions, e.g. on visiting times and the right to watch television and listen to the radio, which go further than required for their purposes.

While public health service providers are subject to an 'administrative best practice' norm, on the basis of the Ombudsman's expanded basis for assessment, there is no general 'administrative best practice' norm for the private health care sector. The ethical norms for the medical professions do not help to establish best practice standards for medical services. Thus, the 'administrative best practice' norm has an independent significance for undertakings that are associated with the treatment of patients.[38]

5.4 Patients lose rights when treated by private rather than public health service providers

All in all, it can be concluded that administrative law has an independent significance for the legal rights of patients. Compared with administrative law, health-specific rules and contract law lack rules that ensure the legal rights of patients in a number of important areas. This means that the legal rights of patients are weakened when their treatment is administered by private health service providers, private practitioners, private hospitals, private clinics and so on, under agreements with the authorities responsible for health services rather than when treatment is administered by these authorities themselves. This also means that Mette Hartlev's argument, i.e. that the starting point for a legal assessment within health law is the patient while within administrative law it is the system, can and must be rejected.[39] The main purposes of the general rules of administrative law, such as under the Public Administration Act, the Freedom of Information Act, and the unwritten fundamental principles of impartiality and proportionality, are indeed to protect the interests of individual citizens against the powers of the public administration.[40]

The difference between the legal positions of patients in the private and public health sectors is particularly marked when they are not actually undergoing treatment, i.e. when waiting for it.

Procedurally, patients in the private sector have no legal right of access to documentation, including internal regulations such as rules for referrals, and there are no special procedural requirements. For example, patients do not have the general right of impartiality on the part of health personnel when these decide on the conditions of treatment. Also, patients do not have the general right to obtain advice about making complaints, or to be advised of the reasons for decisions.

Substantively, patients who are treated in the private sector do not have the legal right to be accepted for treatment, nor that decisions taken in this regard should be based on considerations that are impartial. A privately practising health professional

38 Bødker Madsen, supra note 2, pp. 369-370.

39 Hartlev, 'Respekt og beskyttelse i sundhedsretten', supra note 3, p. 518.

40 Bødker Madsen, supra note 2, p. 99 ff.

can reject a patient in individual cases, or give them a lower priority, or establish conditions whereby certain groups of patients are rejected on grounds that would be improper under administrative law.

As stated, this also applies as a clear main rule where treatment is provided by private health service providers under agreements with the authorities responsible for the health services, and at their expense.

The conclusion is, thus, that it is relevant to patients' rights, broadly understood, including their legal certainty, whether or not treatment is being provided by private health service providers, under outsourcing agreements with the authorities responsible for health services, or by these authorities themselves.

This means that, from the perspective of patients' legal rights, the privatisation of the health service gives rise to legal concerns, in principle.

5.5 Considerations of legal policy

On the basis of the conclusion of the dissertation, according to which the legal rights of patients' are weakened because administrative law does not follow them into the private sector, I recommend that consideration be given to legislating on the application of administrative law, including whether it should apply in whole or in part wherever the private health sector provides treatment under an agreement with the authorities responsible for health services.[41] It is argued that a legislative approach would be preferable to deciding the question in individual outsourcing agreements. Rules addressing citizens ought to be made public. Moreover, it is recommended that the rules should be laid down in authorising laws, i.e. in the Health Act, and not in a general framework act, so as to take care of the special considerations and needs in conjunction with the treatment of patients.

The right to receive treatment for an illness is highly important to individual citizens. One could say that health services lie at the heart of welfare. For this reason, it is important that legal rights are not weakened when such core tasks are delegated to private health service providers.

On this basis, the general administrative law principles of impartiality, equal treatment, and proportionality should unquestionably apply when private practitioners, private hospitals, private clinics and so on carry out tasks under agreements with the authorities responsible for health services (and at their expense).

I also believe that there is a need to develop best practice standards in line with those that exist for public bodies (administrative best practice), e.g. in connection with telephone services in general practice.

The rules of the Freedom of Information Act, regarding access to documentation and the obligation to keep records, should also be applicable. Patients who are treated in private practice and private hospitals, as part of their freedom to choose a

41 Ibid., p. 463 ff.

hospital, also need to have some insight into documentation other than their medical records, e.g. rules about referrals and professional instructions.

In principle, the Public Administration Act should apply when health service tasks are carried out by private health service providers under outsourcing agreements with public bodies. This should unconditionally apply to the rules about legal capacity, access to documentation, and advice, including advice about complaints. As for the rules governing the automatic right of parties to be heard and to be advised of the reasons for decisions, the situation is not so clear. On the one hand, they are core guarantees of legal rights, suggesting that these rules should apply; but on the other, providing an automatic right for parties to be heard and advised of the reasons for decisions demands relatively large resources, because the rules, the main considerations, and the facts relating to patient treatment involve professional medical criteria. In many situations, it would be necessary to have technical language translated into layman's language if a patient is to have the possibility of protecting his/her interests. This requires administration, and thus resources would be displaced from the core activity of clinical work in order to administer that, and this is an argument against the application of the rules.[42] The legislative authority must weigh these two conflicting considerations against each other. It is also possible to choose a middle road, whereby legislation could provide for the Public Administration Act only applying to patient treatment decisions that are particularly critical, e.g. the refusal of treatment or only admitting for treatment after a long waiting period.[43]

6 Concluding remarks

As shown above, there are fundamental differences between the approach of Mette Hartlev and my approach to health law.

In summary, while I consider health law to be a special legal discipline based on the general rules of public and private law, Mette Hartlev considers health law to be 'an area of law with an independent existence'. While I believe the distinction between public and private law to be relevant, and worthy, therefore, of being maintained within the context of patients' rights, Mette Hartlev does not believe that this distinction contributes to clarity in this area. And, while I believe that the organisational placing of health service providers is decisive for the rights of patients, including their legal rights, Mette Hartlev does not believe, in principle, that this is relevant to the fundamental rights of patients.

Even though these two theoretical views differ significantly, this does not necessarily entail significant differences when addressing specific problems of health law. It can thus be argued that this debate is only of academic interest. However, I do

42 In the Norwegian Patients' Rights Act, Law No 1999-07-02-63, it is expressly stipulated that the Public Administration Act does not apply to decisions about necessary medical treatment, the right to an examination and a second opinion, choice of hospital, individual treatment plans, and medical transport; Section 2-7.

43 Bødker Madsen, supra note 2, p. 465 ff.

not believe this to be the case. In my view, considering and presenting health law as something entirely special, as divorced from the known existing legal rules and principles and thus different in essence to other special disciplines, makes health law unnecessarily problematic. In this, there is a risk of overlooking the supplementary general legal rules, the fundamental differences between public and private law and the different results that arise under private and public law rules, including the aspects of legal certainty that are a special feature of administrative law. This puts barriers in the way of exhaustively answering questions of health law. Thus, the different approaches to health law are not merely of theoretical interest, but of practical relevance as well. It is highly important that the theory of health law includes an awareness that public law gives patients significant legal guarantees which are present neither in private law nor in the health-specific rules, and that patients lose their key rights when contract law, rather than general administrative law, supplements the health-specific rules, for example with the privatisation of the health service.

The Nordic Committee on Bioethics

By Sirpa Soini, University of Helsinki[1]

1 Introduction

The Nordic Committee on Bioethics (subsequently referred to as the Bioethics Committee)[2], as we know it today, was established in 1996. Its roots, however, are in the Nordic Collaboration Programme for Biotechnology 1988-92 when an independent Nordic Committee for Ethics related to Biotechnology (*Nordisk utvalg for etikk innen bioteknologi*) was created.

The birth of such a committee was a characteristic of the time at the beginning of 1990s. Both the national and world communities were confronted with rapidly emerging new biotechnological inventions and applications, e.g. gene patenting, cloning, a variety of novel *in vitro* fertilisation techniques and applications, genetically-modified organisms, and the human genome project, just to name a few. These developments raised fears in the public and the research community as regards how to ensure the appropriate use of novel techniques and assess their potential threat to humanity.

In order to respond to new needs to monitor and discuss bioethical issues, the Council of Europe set up an *ad hoc* Committee of experts on Bioethics (CAHBI) in 1985, which later became the Steering Committee on Bioethics (CDBI) in 1992. UNESCO, for its part, established the International Bioethics Committee (IBC) in 1993. Both the CDBI and the IBC are also highly influential today and contribute towards policy-making. Sweden and Denmark were among the first countries in Europe to found national ethical councils; Sweden founded the National Council on Medical Ethics (*SMER - Statens Medicinsk-Etiska Råd*) in 1985 and Denmark founded the Danish Council of Ethics (*Det etiske råd*) in 1987, just few years after France had established its National Consultative Ethics Committee (*CCNE - Comité Consultatif National d'Ethique*) in 1983.

---

1 Sirpa Soini is a lawyer specialised on health law. She works at the Finnish National Institute for Health and Welfare (THL), and as a part-time teacher in the Faculty of Law at the University of Helsinki. Soini is a member of the board of the Nordic Committee on Bioethics.

2 www.ncbio.org.

The need for Nordic collaboration in the field of biotechnology was expressed at a meeting of Nordic Prime Ministers and Collaboration Ministers held in November 1986. Subsequently, the Nordic Council of Ministers appointed a programme committee to work on a collaboration plan on 14 May 1987. National priorities were worked out. The programme committee made a proposal for a concrete Nordic Biotechnology programme.[3] The Nordic Council of Ministers approved the idea and initiated a Nordic collaboration programme for the period 1988-92, and gave it an annual budget.[4] In addition, the Nordic Council of Ministers had appointed *ad hoc* committees in 1988 and 1990 to address patenting issues in biotechnology.

2 Mandate of the Nordic Committee on Bioethics

2.1 Organisation

The Nordic Council of Ministers initiates the Bioethics Committee. Its activities and budget are included in the annual action plan of the Nordic Council of Ministers.[5] The mandate of the Bioethics Committee has, since being established in 1996, continued in three-year periods; 1996-1998, 1999-2001, 2002-2004, 2005-2007, 2008-2010. The current and sixth mandate started on 1 January 2011.

The Nordic Council of Ministers was formed in 1971 as a collaboration organisation between the Nordic governments. Nordic cooperation started in 1952 when Denmark, Iceland, Norway, and Sweden established the Nordic Council; Finland joined in 1955. In 1962, the Nordic countries formalised their co-operation by drafting the Treaty of Co-operation between Denmark, Finland, Iceland, Norway and Sweden (the Helsinki Treaty). The Faroe Islands, Greenland, and Åland are also represented in the Nordic organisations.

The Bioethics Committee has two members from each Nordic country.[6] The Nordic Council of Ministers appoints the committee members for three-year periods on the basis of nominations made by the respective national governments. In addition, the Faroe Islands holds observer status on the Bioethics Committee. Members can be appointed for a maximum of two consecutive terms of office. The Bioethics Committee's aim is a multidisciplinary discourse, thus its members represent, for instance, philosophy, medicine, sociology, biology, theology, and law. The Bioethics Committee selects its chair from its members and the chairmanship rotates annually between the Nordic countries. The Bioethics Committee also appoints a secretariat.[7] The committee members are not paid for their work; however, their travel expenses are reimbursed.

---

3 *Nordisk Programkomité for Bioteknologi* 1987.

4 *Nordisk Programkomité for Bioteknologi* 1991, p. 14.

5 *Nordiska ministerrådet* 2011, pp. 95-96.

6 The author of this text is the other Finnish committee member, currently serving her second term of office.

7 Since 2008, the secretary has been Lotta Knutsson Bråkenhielm, a Swedish PhD student of theology.

2.2 History

As mentioned above, the Nordic Collaboration Programme for Biotechnology was established for the period 1988-92 at the initiative of the Nordic ministers in 1986. The programme was arranged into three sub-programmes under the responsibility of the Nordic Programme Committee for Biotechnology (*NBP – Nordisk programkomité for bioteknologi*), the Nordic Fund for Technology and Industrial Development (*NI – Nordic industrifond*), and the Nordic Senior Executives Committee for Agricultural and Forestry Questions (*NEJS – Nordisk embetsmannskomité for jord- og skogbruksspørsmål*). The NBP had the overall, and coordinating, responsibility.

At the time, the programme prioritised the following areas[8]:

- Gene technology
- Protein Engineering
- Plant Cell biotechnology
- Biotechnology applied to domestic animals
- Aquaculture
- Food biotechnology
- Bioprosessing and enzyme technology
- Environmental biotechnology

Human Genomics (HUGO) and genetically-modified organisms (GMOs) would soon be considered deserving of special attention, too.[9]

The proposal for a collaboration programme emphasised the significance of a joint Nordic evaluation of the ethical norms that would form the basis for biotechnological research and application. It suggested the creation of a separate organisation to promote an inter-Nordic debate on ethics and biotechnology.[10] Consequently, the Nordic Committee for Ethics Related to Biotechnology was founded (*Nordisk utvalg for etikk innen bioteknologi*). It was to function as a central and integral part of the collaboration between the three sub-programmes. The committee was financed by the NBP and they collaborated closely. It was a predecessor of today's Bioethics Committee.

The Nordic Committee for Ethics Related to Biotechnology had its first meeting in May 1989. Its first representatives were; Karen Højte Jensen and Else Marie Sejer Larsen from Denmark; Paula Kokkonen and Matti Sarvas from Finland; Jorunn Erla Eyfjörd and Arnor Hannibalsson from Iceland; Gudbrand Bakken and Jul-

8 Supra note 4, p. 7.

9 Supra note 4, p. 9.

10 Supra note 4, p. 48.

ie Skjæraasen from Norway; and Göran Herméren and Lars Rask from Sweden. Johs Kjosbakken was its first secretary.

The committee concretised its mandate as follows:

1) To collect and draft background material for fruitful discussions on ethical issues in the Nordic countries.
2) To examine possible joint Nordic reference points for the ethical assessment of biotechnological research and applications.
3) To contribute to ethical risk-assessments relating to biotechnology.
4) To advise the NPB within the sphere of the Nordic Biotechnology Programme.[11]

2.3 Development of the mission and the tasks of the Bioethics Committee

Finally, the Bioethics Committee was established in 1996, for a three-year period, to replace the previous Nordic Committee. Unfortunately, given the timeframe, the documentation relating to its establishment could not be located and accessed for this overview. The minutes, annual reports, and other documents (mandates and their drafts, seminar material, and correspondence) of the Committee, since 2000, are being stored in the Finnish National Archives. During the early years, the secretariat moved from country to country, and it is not known whether documents have been archived or not. This will be a subject for further research. Still, documents in the Finnish archives show that the continuation of the mandate and the development of the tasks have been at the initiative of the Bioethics Committee.

In 1998, the Bioethics Committee drafted a paper *Nordisk bioetikk inn i det 21. århundrede. Förslag till mandat 3.2.1998*[12] (Nordic bioethics in front of 21st century. A proposal for a mandate 3.2.1998) for the Nordic Council of Minister to propose continuation of its activities for the next term. In the paper, the Bioethics Committee discussed the importance of continuing its work, describing its mission, tasks, and working methods. As its mission, it set the fostering of Nordic co-operation and information exchange regarding the ethical aspects of biotechnological R&D and application between researchers, MPs, and moulders of public opinion.[13] The current mandate and mission of the Bioethics Committee are still based on this paper.

The paper designated the following tasks for the Bioethics Committee:

- identifying ethical problems arising from genetic and other biotechnology research; the development and modification of microorganisms, plants, animals and humans.
- promoting Nordic collaboration between researchers, moulders of public

11 Supra note 4, p. 49.

12 Helland and Erland 1998.

13 Ibid.

opinion, and parliamentarians on bioethical issues by means of cooperating with national research institutions, authorities, and ethics committees, and, by the same token, creating opportunities for the exchange of information.

- contributing to a joint Nordic debate on bioethical questions by disseminating material that can be used in constructive discussions about bioethics issues.
- monitoring biotechnological developments, both in the Nordic region and internationally.
- keeping abreast of the Nordic and international debate on ethical questions arising from biotechnology R&D and application.
- following legislative developments within the sphere of biotechnology in the Nordic countries.

Working methods were proposed as follows:

- The Committee would have regular internal meetings.
- The Committee would be able to assign of experts vis-à-vis its activities.
- The Committee would arrange working groups, hearings, conferences, symposia, and public lectures to support the exchange of information between researchers, MPs, and moulders of public opinion concerning contemporary bioethical issues.
- The Committee would publish reports and other background papers in order to start up a Nordic debate on bioethical issues.

Further, it was proposed that the Bioethics Committee would consist of two members from each Nordic country and represent broad knowledge in the area of biotechnology and bioethics. The chairmanship would circulate.

3 Activities

3.1 General

The Bioethics Committee holds regular internal meetings, arranges conferences and workshops, publishes books, follows national and international debates and developments, and collaborates with national ethics committees.

Human biomedicine has been a prevailing theme in the activities of the Bioethics Committee, even though the initial mandate was not limited to the directly human application of biotechnology. However, there have also been conferences or workshops on the following themes; 'Bioprophecy', 'Bioethics of the Sea', in 2004,

'Bioethics of the Sea II', in 2008, and 'Bioethics and Bioenergy', in 2009. In 2010, the Bioethics Committee showed that it was following the latest bioethical trends by arranging a conference on Public Health Ethics, thus responding to demands to broaden the bioethical discourse.

3.2 *Mapping the legislation*

The Nordic countries have adopted different regulatory approaches to sensitive biotechnological issues, e.g. in assisted reproduction and stem cell research. Bioethics was the main theme for the Nordic Council's 52nd session in 2000. As one outcome of the meeting, the Nordic Council recommended charting the legislation and regulations pertaining to biotechnology in the Nordic countries. The Bioethics Committee started up the process in 2001 as regards assisted reproduction and preimplantation genetic diagnostics, genetic testing and gene therapy, biobanks and embryo research, stem cell research, cloning, during the second stage adding preimplantation genetic diagnosis, abortion, prenatal diagnosis, clinical research on humans, and animal experimentation. The first report was published in 2003, with a second, broader overview coming in 2006.[14]

The Bioethics Committee also assigned a researcher to conduct a study on assisted reproduction in the Nordic countries[15]. The aim of the study was to look into the various backgrounds and processes that have led to different legal situations with regard to assisted reproduction in the Nordic countries. There have been some motions even to harmonise the legislation, but these have not succeeded.[16] Dr. Riitta Burrell from Finland, who was assigned to conduct the study, examined the social, cultural, and political processes behind perceptions and the regulation of assisted reproduction in the Nordic countries. The report was presented at a seminar entitled Nordic Biolaw – Focus on Assisted Reproduction, in 2005.

In 2007, the Bioethics Committee reported to NordForsk on stem cell research in the Nordic countries. It demonstrated the national moral approaches to embryo research within the Nordic bloc. In addition, legislation and regulations relating to stem cell research in the Nordic countries were systematically examined.[17]

3.3 *Teaching bioethics as a specific theme*

Since the early days of the Bioethics Committee, it has held the teaching of bioethics as one of its prioritised activities. It arranged a conference entitled Teaching Bioethics, in 2001, in order to obtain an overview of what was being done in the field

14 Nordic Committee on Bioethics 2006a.

15 Nordic Committee on Bioethics 2006b.

16 Ibid., pp. 73-74.

17 Lötjönen et al. 2007.

of bioethics education within the Nordic bloc. This conference indicated gaps in bioethics education; additionally, quality and quantity seemed to vary between the countries. Based on the findings and results of the conference in 2001, the Bioethics Committee arranged a workshop in 2003. Presentations and summaries of both occasions were compiled into publications.[18]

In 2008, the Bioethics Committee moved its work forward by arranging a third thematic meeting concerning bioethics teaching, this time entitled Teaching Material in Bioethics. The purpose of the workshop was to identify excellent educational resources in bioethics which were already available in one or more of the Nordic languages, Finnish included; resources that could be translated and modified in order to make them available in all the languages used in the Nordic countries. The Bioethics Committee decided to establish a working group that would give it specific advice on how to continue the work of developing teaching materials. The working group advocated the importance of teaching bioethics at schools because "[e]thical discussions are an important part of young people's training to become involved citizens in our democratic societies. Working with bioethics is a means of training in critical and creative thinking that can improve the active participation that is an important part of democratic citizenship."[19] The development of teaching materials for primary school pupils and teachers is included in the Bioethics Committee's Action Plan 2011.[20]

Furthermore, an idea raised at the pan-Nordic meeting of the national ethics committees in 2011 would influence politicians in such a way that bioethics would be included in the undergraduate schools' curriculum, as already is in Norway.

3.4 Collaboration with national ethics committees, councils, and boards

One of the tasks of the Bioethics Committee is to correspond with the national ethics committees in order to promote joint Nordic collaboration. The ways of doing this are manifold: members of the Bioethics Committee collaborate in their respective national contexts, representatives of the national ethics committees participate in conferences and workshops organised by the Bioethics Committee, sharing material they have developed with each other. Many of the members of the Bioethics Committee are also members of some national committees, so information and news circulate on a regular basis. Sometimes, they arrange joint conferences, e.g. Chimera Research - ethical and legal aspects, arranged with the Danish Ethical Council in Copenhagen in 2008, and Prenatal Diagnosis - Individuals and Society, arranged with the Norwegian Biotechnology Advisory Board at Holmenkollen in 2010.

18 Nordic Committee on Bioethics 2002; Erland and von Troil 2004.

19 Nordic Committee on Bioethics 2008.

20 Supra note 5.

The Bioethics Committee has invited national committees to attend meetings in order to enhance collaboration, to discuss contemporary issues, and to identify national anxieties. In 1999, the Bioethics Committee arranged a workshop with national ethics committees in Copenhagen to discuss their activities, prioritisations, and working methods. This workshop resulted in a publication giving an overview of the bioethics committees of the Nordic countries.[21] A similar meeting was arranged in Copenhagen in March 2011. The national committees introduced their work and listed some ethical questions arising in the context of biobanks, and various types of registers, genetic tests, including whole genome sequencing, prioritisation in healthcare, clinical trials, euthanasia, emergency research, and the role of children in research.

In 2003, the Bioethics Committee organised the seminar Biomedical Research Ethics, in order to discuss ethical challenges in contemporary research, with the national RECs from both the Nordic and Baltic regions.

However, joint meetings face a challenge in the fact that none of the national ethics committees are alike. They have different tasks, focuses, and obligations. For instance, the role of the National Ethical Advisory Committees, Councils, or Boards is very different to that of the (Medical) Research Ethics Committees (RECs) which are usually statutory public agencies tasked with previewing research protocols within the framework of specific legal regulation[22]. Instead, the mission of the advisory councils is to discuss, reflect, and raise awareness of the bioethical issues in society, and to give their opinions, for instance[23]. Even though the RECs also need to appraise the ethical aspects of a given protocol, the process is formal compared to the free discourse of the National Ethics Committees. The different needs were once again evident at a meeting convened by the Nordic Committee on Bioethics in Copenhagen on 21 March 2011 because it was difficult to identify issues that would be beneficial to both RECs and Councils having an advisory role.

Given the mission of the Nordic Committee on Bioethics, its activities are more in parallel with national ethical advisory boards such as the National Advisory Board on Social Welfare and Health Care Ethics (*ETENE)*, in Finland, the National Council on Medical Ethics (*SMER)*, in Sweden, the Danish Council of Ethics (*Det Etiske Råd)*, and the Norwegian Biotechnology Advisory Board (*Bioteknologinemnda)*. In Norway, the Biotechnological Advisory Board has both an advisory and a statutorily authoritative role. Iceland is currently lacking a national ethical council with a general advisory mission similar to that of the other Nordic countries. The Danish Council of Ethics and the Norwegian Biotechnology Advisory Board both seem to have gained wide societal recognition and their contribution has truly influenced and stimulated public debate. In Finland, it is the opposite, *ETENE's* impact as an initiator of public debate has remained relatively vague. The reason, however, is not only

21 Erland and Helland 1999.

22 Launis 2008, pp. 47-52.

23 Kappel 2008, pp. 27-29.

its modest way of addressing the issues, the Finnish public simply seems to be rather uninterested in bioethical issues.

4 The future

Is the Nordic Committee on Bioethics needed in the Nordic debate? Is Nordic bioethics different to that of central Europe? In my opinion, the answer is yes to both questions. Our societies are based on a welfare model and trust in the state. Biomedical regulation is relatively permissive and the Nordic people are very much *pro science*. The Eurobarometer survey carried out in 2010 further indicated the positive public perceptions that exist of science in the Nordic countries, even though attitudes to bioethical issues vary to some degree between the Nordic countries.[24] Given our cultural, social, political, and intellectual atmosphere, our approach to bioethical issues is different to that of many other societies. We have excellent research and we rapidly adopt novel techniques, but we also need to discuss them openly.

Our key challenge lies in maintaining Nordic trust. The stakeholders are many; from laymen to the scientific community, funders, politicians, interest groups, industry, and government. It is very important in the biotechnological arena to openly address the ethical and scientific issues. But how will the information be disseminated, and by whom? Who can be relied on? These questions were on the agenda at two conferences arranged by the Nordic Committee on Bioethics; Business and Bioethics, in 2006, and Bioethics or Biopolitics?, in 2007. The first conference was aimed at identifying roles and potential conflicts of interest between scientists, the biotechnological industry, and policy-makers. The latter analysed the decision-making patterns and the interrelationship between bioethics, politics, and other players in the field, e.g. the media and expert organisations. Presentations given at the two conferences resulted in a publication called Bioethics, Politics and Business, in 2008[25].

The Nordic Committee on Bioethics exists in order to respond to this challenge. It should keep up its work of addressing bioethical issues and collaborating with national ethics committees in order to stimulate public debate. It could also take a more active role in drawing the attention of the Nordic Council of Ministers when it thinks an issue needs more political handling, or even intervention. In fact, the Nordic Council and the Bioethics Committee once jointly arranged a seminar to discuss Nordic Biopolitics with parliamentarians in 2005.[26] This kind of discussion should be on the agenda in the future, too.

The feedback from the Nordic Council of Ministers regarding the activities of the Bioethics Committee has been positive. In 2011, this work will be evaluated and we are excited about what the conclusions will be.

24 Gaskell et al. 2010.

25 Lötjönen and von Troil 2008.

26 Klingenberg 2005.

References

J. Elster and H. von Troil (eds.), *How to best teach bioethics?* Report from a workshop in 2003 (Nordic Council of Ministers, Copenhagen, 2004).

S. Erdal and D.E. Helland (eds.), *Nordiske komiteer innen Bioetikk [Nordic Committees on Bioethics]*. (Nordic Council of Ministers, Copenhagen, 1999).

G. Gaskell et al, *Europeans and biotechnology in 2010. Winds of change?* A report to the European Commission's Directorate-General for Research. Eurobarometer 73.1 (European Commission, 2010).

D.E. Helland and S.Erdal, *Nordisk bioetikk inn i det 21. århundrede. Forslag til videreføring av aktiviteten til Nordisk Ministerråds Komité for Bioetikk for perioden 1999-2001. Forslag til Mandat [The Nordic bioethics in front of the 21st century. A proposal for a mandate 1999-2001]*, (A paper from 3 February 1998, in the Archives of the Nordic Committee on Bioethics, Finnish National Archives, Helsinki).

K. Kappel, National Ethics Advisory Boards: Do they have a Legitimate Role in Liberal Democracy?, in S. Lötjönen and H. von Troil (eds.), *Bioethics, Politics and Business* (Nordic Council of Ministers, Copenhagen, 2008), pp. 27-29.

S. Klingenberg, *Mot en nordisk biopolitik?* Rapport fra seminar om bioteknologi og bioetikk [*Towards a Nordic biopolitics?* A report from a seminar on biotechnology and bioethics] (Nordic Council, Copenhagen, 2005).

V. Launis, Research Ethics Committees: Their Role, Opinion Formation and Justification, in S. Lötjönen and H. von Troil (eds.), *Bioethics, Politics and Business* (Nordic Council of Ministers, Copenhagen, 2008), pp. 47-54.

S. Lötjönen, L.Walin and I. Jónsdóttir, Legislation on stem cell research in the Nordic countries, in *Stem Cell Research in the Nordic Countries – Science, Ethics, Public Debate and Law,* NordForsk Policy Briefs 2007-2 (NordForsk, Oslo, 2007).

Nordic Committee on Bioethics, *A Nordic Initiative in Bioethical Educational Resources.* Report from a working group on educational resources in bioethics (2008). <http://ncbio.org/nordisk/arkiv/teach-bioethics-lysebu.pdf>, visited on 30 March 2011.

Nordic Committee on Bioethics, *Legislation on Biotechnology in the Nordic Countries* (Nordic Council of Ministers, Copenhagen, 2006a).

Nordic Committee on Bioethics, *Assisted Reproduction in the Nordic Countries.* A comparative study of policies and regulation (Nordic Council of Ministers, Copenhagen, 2006b).

Nordic Committee on Bioethics, *Teaching bioethics.* Report from a seminar (Nordic Council of Ministers, Copenhagen, 2002).

Nordisk Programkomité for Bioteknologi av Nordisk Ministerråd [The Nordic Council of Ministers' Nordic Programme Committee for Biotechnology], *Bioteknologisk samarbeidsprogram 1988-92 – midtveisrapport [Programme for biotechnological collaboration 1988-92 – mid-term report]* (Nordic Council of Ministers, Copenhagen, 1991).

Nordisk Programkomité for Bioteknologi av Nordisk Ministerråd [The Nordic Council of Ministers' Nordic Programme Committee for Biotechnology], *Nordisk Bioteknologi – förslag till samarbetsprogram [Nordic biotechnology – proposal for a collaboration programme]* (Nordic Council of Ministers, Copenhagen, 1987).

Nordiska ministerrådet [Nordic Council of Ministers], *Planer och budget 2011 [Plans and budget 2011]* (Nordic Council of Ministers, Copenhagen, 2011).

Part 2

Patients' Rights

The Development of Patients' Rights in Norway

By Professor dr. juris Asbjørn Kjønstad, University of Oslo[1]

1 Introduction[2]

In this article I will present the history of the development of patients' rights in Norway. Although the emphasis is on development, I will also discuss the concept of rights and the reasons for establishing the new rules in this respect, see point 2.

According to the Norwegian Constitution, parliament [Stortinget] is the legislative body empowered to establish patients' rights, see point 3. However, the courts also have a legislative function, and have contributed toward establishing and clarifying a large number of patients' rights, see point 4. Other important institutions that have contributed towards establishing and maintaining patients' rights are administrative bodies, patients' associations, the media, and other institutions: in other words, the networked society, see point 5.

Legal research is also a driving force in the establishment of new legal rules. Researchers collect and compare material, and review it in relation to fundamental legal principles and social development. New concepts, theories, and views that appear in the legal literature have become important premises for committees of inquiry, ministries, legislators, lawyers, courts, patients' associations, the media, and other institutions. I will discuss the contributions made by legal research to the growth of patients' rights under point 6.

A summary is presented under point 7.

---

1 Asbjørn Kjønstad has been professor of Law at the University of Oslo since 1978. He is the author of a large number of articles and books on health law, social security law, tort law and constitutional law. He has been Head of the Department of Private Law, Dean of the Faculty of Law and a member of the Board of the University of Oslo. He is currently the leader of the Law Division of the Norwegian Academy of Science and Letters, and Chair of the Board of the Centre for Advanced Studies at this Academy.

2 For a more detailed review, see Kjønstad 2007, pp. 69-140.

2 The development of the concept of 'right'

2.1 *The treatment model and the legal model*

Over the course of the 20th century, Norwegian society invested enormous resources in the development of public health services. However, as a general rule, citizens were not given individual legal rights in relation to public health bodies. The formation and distribution of health services was delegated to head surgeons and other health workers, who were generally able to make decisions based on professional and ethical judgments. The health services have largely been built up on the basis of a treatment model.

The philosophy behind health law differs from the philosophy behind social security law: ever since the first social security statutes were passed more than 100 years ago, the Norwegian national insurance system has been based upon a legal model. A comprehensive network of statutes and regulations dictates the conditions for entitlement to social security benefits and prescribes rules determining how benefit sums should be calculated.[3] The premiums which national insurance has collected, and the sums which the state has contributed to social security, have been distributed to those with an individual right to social security benefits. National insurance pensions and other benefits are only to a limited extent paid out on a discretionary basis.

Approximately half of all national insurance funds are paid to persons suffering from sickness, injury, or disability, in the form of sickness benefit, disability pension, and industrial injury compensation. These are important patients' rights which have been established and gradually extended from the first social security statute of 1894. These rights have, however, systematically not been treated as health law, but as social security law.

During the last 30-40 years, the health service has been subjected to increased political governance and legal control. The main responsibility for the execution of health policies is delegated to state health authorities and to municipal health services. Moreover, patients have been given legal rights. A comprehensive network of statutes and regulations has set up the conditions for being entitled to health services.

Rules bestowing patients' rights have reduced the discretionary powers that health workers, health administrators, and politicians have exercised. These are no longer free to allocate resources between different kinds of services, or to determine patient priority. Legislation conferring the right to treatment on patients requires increased resources and may necessitate growth in public budgets.

---

3 The system of rules gradually became so complicated that safeguards for citizens were weakened. In 1990, a public commission presented the report NOU 1990:20 *Forenklet folketrygdlov [A Simplified National Insurance Act]*, which was the basis for the new Act of 28-02-1997 relating to Social Security.

2.2 *Reasons for the development of patients' rights*

During the 1980s, 'patients' rights' developed into a central concept within Norwegian legal research, the public debate, health administration, and the administration of justice. The concept of patients' rights held particularly positive connotations, and was accorded great significance in health politics. Although patients held certain rights prior to the 1980s, it was only then that the development of rights and legal safeguards for patients really began to gain momentum.

Some general reasons for the development of patients' rights and the growing interest in them during the 1970s and 1980s were as follows:

- Norway had become materially wealthier than during previous decades, hence there was an economic basis for the establishment of certain patients' rights.
- In public bodies as well as institutions, both resources and authority were being extended to a steadily growing number of healthcare workers, with a great deal of power and knowledge regarding patients. In order to maintain the balance of power, it was important to improve the rights of patients, and enact legal safeguards.
- This trend had begun in other sectors of public administration with the post-war debate on the rule of law, which led to the enactment of the Ombudsman Act of 1962, the Public Administration Act of 1967, and the Public Documents Act of 1970.[4]
- Throughout the 1970s, protecting the rights and interests of individuals was a recurring issue in Norway, as evidenced by, for example, the Personal Data Registers Act of 1978.[5]
- After WWII, international human rights conventions – which also bestow individual rights – had become increasingly important. The right to health services was classified as a human right.[6]
- Patients' rights became a central ideology in Anglo-American health law; for example, through the requirement for informed consent prior to medical examinations and treatment, the protection of participants in medical research projects, and the development of tort law.[7]
- Developments abroad, including the enactment of consumer protection legislation, product liability, and increased interest in patients' rights, were important factors influencing the development of patients' rights in Norway.

---

4 The Act 22-06-1962, No. 8 relating to the Parliamentary Ombudsman for Public Administration; the Act of 10-02-1967, relating to Procedure in cases concerning the Public Administration (Public Administration Act); and the Act of 19-06-1970, No. 69 relating to Public Access to Documents in the Public Administration (Freedom of Information Act).

5 The Act of 09-06-1978, No. 48 relating to Personal Data Filing Systems, etc.

6 Rehof and Trier 1990, Chapter 24.

7 See Mason and Smith 1987.

- Throughout the post-WWII period, there were demands to increase the influence of workers, culminating in a constitutional amendment in 1980.[8] At the same time, citizens were given increased powers to influence the administrative decisions which affected them. It was natural, therefore, that patients, too, should be given greater powers to exert an influence within the health service.
- A one-thousand-year-old paternalistic medical tradition with roots in the Hippocratic Oath was gradually replaced by a doctor/patient relationship giving greater weight to equality between the two parties.[9]
- Furthermore, the creation of new legal rules and principles had a cumulative effect. Once certain patients' rights had been introduced, it appeared to be easier to gain support for new ones.

The development of patients' rights during the 1970s and 1980s culminated in the passing of the Patients' Rights Act of 1999.[10] This Act partly codified existing law, partly further developed existing law, and partly established a number of new legal principles. It contains a comprehensive program of rights for patients.

2.3 *An overview of patients' rights*

Patients' rights can be divided into three main groups:
1. The right to become a patient: for example, the right to immediate medical treatment when urgently needed, and the right to obtain the necessary primary and specialized medical assistance from municipal and state health services.
2. The rights which patients hold once they have attained the status of patient: for example, the right to confidentiality and the right to refuse treatment.
3. Formal rights consisting of procedural rules to ensure the patient receives the rights mentioned in points (1) and (2) above: for example, the right to appeal against health authority decisions and the right to a second opinion.

Two important patients' rights fall within groups (2) and (3), namely the right to obtain information and the right of access to one's own medical records. These rights enable patients to exert an influence in their relationships with health workers and the health service and also to promote legal safeguards; for example, when demanding treatment or claiming compensation.

8 Article 110 (2) of the Norwegian Constitution; see Doc. No. 13 (1975-76); Innst. S. No. 207 (1979-80); and Stortingets forhandlinger [Proceedings of the Parliament] 05-05-1980.

9 Syse 1992, pp. 9-37.

10 Act of 02-07-1999, No. 63 relating to Patients' Rights.

3 Legislation

3.1 Introduction

The first Norwegian statute governing medical practitioners was the 1927 Act relating to the Rights and Duties of Medical Practitioners. There were two major characteristics of this Act: first, the legal relationships between society, medical practitioners, and patients were described entirely from the perspective of the medical profession; and second, the Act imposed a number of duties upon medical practitioners which could confer corresponding rights for patients. A new Medical Practitioners Act was passed in 1980. This Act imposed further duties upon medical practitioners, some of which conferred corresponding rights for patients.[11]

3.2 The right to become a patient

Provisions relating to the right to obtain assistance from a midwife and the right to obtain immediate assistance from a doctor have existed since 1898 and 1927, respectively. Rights to obtain emergency assistance from hospitals, maternity homes, and mental institutions were introduced in the 1970s.[12]

The Sickness Insurance Act of 1909 and the Medical Service Act of 1912 laid the foundations for the rights of the working classes to obtain assistance from doctors and hospitals.

In 1982, the right to obtain the "necessary health assistance" from the primary health service was introduced via the Municipal Health Services Act.[13] In 1983, certain priority groups were given the right to obtain the "necessary dental treatment".[14]

In 1999, the right to obtain the necessary health assistance from hospitals and other specialist health services was introduced via the Patients' Rights Act.[15]

3.3 Rights as a patient

General rules relating to the compulsory treatment of the mentally ill and potential spreaders of contagious diseases were enacted via the Mental Diseases Act of 1848 and the Public Health Act of 1860. In this and subsequent legislation,[16] conditions governing the use of force have been framed in discretionary terms, which has necessitated guarantees of the rule of law. These conditions have given rise to conflict

11 Act of 13-06-1980, No. 42 relating to Medical Practitioners.

12 Act of 19-06-1969, No. 57 relating to Hospitals, section 6 included an "emergency help provision" and a similar provision was introduced into the Act of 12-06-1981, No. 73 relating to Mental Health.

13 Act of 19-11-1982, No. 66 relating to Municipal Health Services, section 2-1.

14 Act of 03-06-1983, No. 54 relating to Dental Health Services.

15 Act of 02-07-1999, No. 63 relating to Patients' Rights, section 2-1. The main principles in Norwegian health law currently in force are described by Kjønstad 2011.

16 Act of 05-08-1994, No. 55 relating to the Control of Communicable Diseases.

between the protection of society, on the one hand, and the protection of personal freedom and the right to self-determination, on the other.

As early as 1848, the Mental Sickness Act introduced a system of commissioners to control conditions in mental hospitals. In 1969, special provisions were introduced, which provided for the judicial review of administrative decisions relating to the deprivation of liberty and other coercive infringements under the Mental Health Care Act.[17]

The duty of confidentiality has existed for thousands of years as a moral norm. It was introduced into Norwegian legislation in the Penal Code of 1902, and later on into the various statutes relating to the health professions.

The Medical Practitioners Act of 1980 granted patients the statutory right to obtain information regarding their state of health and treatment, the right of access to their medical records, and the right to participation during treatment. These three rights apply equally to relationships between patients and other health sector workers.

In 1999, the patient's right to self-determination was introduced.[18] Before that time, the right to informed consent only applied in special cases, e.g. abortion and sterilization.[19]

The Medical Practitioners Act of 1980 also granted patients the statutory right to "reasonable care with regard to treatment", which was previously only a principle in tort law. In tort law, however, principles of reasonableness and guilt are losing ground to principles of tort based on objective (strict) liability.[20] In 1999, the right to obtain "sound professional medical practice and considerate care" was introduced into the Health Personnel Act, section 4. This applies to all health workers.[21]

3.4 *Procedural rules*

The Public Administration Act of 1967 contains by far the most important procedural rules relating to public administration. However, as a main principle, the guarantees of the rule of law contained in this Act do not apply to decisions made by health personnel. But, if a patient lodges a complaint with the Board of Health Supervision in the Norwegian counties, the Public Administration Act will apply.

The establishment of procedural rules in health law is in itself important for improving the position of the patient vis-à-vis the various health service bodies. There is consensus among health law researchers in Norway that the procedural

17 Act of 19-06-1969, No. 52 relating to the Act of 13-08-1915, No. 6 relating to Procedure in Civil Cases, Chapter 33.

18 The Patients' Rights Act, Chapters 3 and 4.

19 Act of 13-06-1975, No. 50 relating to the Termination of Pregnancy; and the Act of 03-06-1977, No. 57 relating to Sterilization.

20 Act of 15-06-2001, No. 53 relating to Patient Injury Compensation. The main principles of Norwegian health law currently in force are described by Jørstad 2011.

21 The main principles of Norwegian health law currently in force are described by Braut 2011.

position of patients ought to be improved, and that there is no reason why these should have a weaker legal position than the recipients of other public benefits and services.

3.5 *Preventative healthcare*

The Public Health Act of 1860 emphasized preventative healthcare, in line with prevailing beliefs regarding the role of social medicine in the fight against disease. With the growth of modern medicine, the preventative aspect was given less importance, while greater attention was paid to the development of different forms of treatment.

In recent years, prevention has once again attracted a certain amount of attention, which is reflected in the Municipal Health Services Act of 1982. However, it is only in the Tobacco Act of 1973[22], the Communicable Diseases Act of 1994[23], and the Dental Health Services Act of 1983[24] that preventative measures are particularly prominent.

On the whole, preventative healthcare has played a limited role in Norwegian health legislation.[25] It has been considered more important to extend the right to reasonable care, as regards treating those who are already ill, than to prevent people from becoming ill. It has also been underlined that, if priority were to be given to preventative health measures, this would necessarily imply taking from the sick in order to give to the healthy.[26]

4 Judicial law

4.1 *Introduction*

The main task of the courts is to settle conflicts on the basis of current legislation and the general principles of law. But the courts also contribute towards clarifying and specifying the content of rules; in Norway, they sometimes create new laws. This has particularly been the case in the area of tort law, but also in other areas.

4.2 *Tort law*

A question of interest amongst lawyers is that of liability in tort relating to doctors and hospitals. This is also the sector of health law that concerns most judicial prac-

22 Act of 09-03-1973, No. 14 relating to the prevention of the harmful effects of tobacco.

23 Act of 05-08-1994, No. 55 relating to the control of communicable diseases.

24 Act of 03-06-1983, No. 54 relating to dental health services.

25 The Ministry of Health and Social Affairs has published a report, NOU 1991:10 *Flere gode leveår for alle. Forebyggingsstrategier [Many good years for all. Preventative strategies]*.

26 Former Director of Health, Torbjørn Mork 1992, pp. 4-7.

tice. In many cases, the Norwegian Supreme Court has exercised caution in imposing liability in tort upon doctors and health institutions.[27] The duty of care of health workers has traditionally been less strict than in other areas.[28]

However, over the last 30 years, the doctor's duty of care has become more rigorous. This has primarily taken place through cases which have imposed increased requirements upon doctors to document the details of treatment by completing medical records.[29] It is possible that the stricter requirements placed upon doctors by the courts are in some way connected to the general improvement in patients' rights which has taken place through legislation, particularly during the 1980s, see point 3 above.

4.3 Important precedents

The Supreme Court has played a major role in the development of patients' rights in Norway:

First, and of particular importance, is the Medical Records Case from 1977, which gave patients the right to access their own medical records.[30]

Second, following a judgment from 1981, it has become easier for patients to discharge themselves from mental hospitals. The Supreme Court has argued that the true benefit to the patient that services provided by health institutions represent must be given importance.[31]

Third, in a decision from 1984, the Supreme Court held that the guarantees of the rule of law which apply to patients under the mental health service apply equally to prisoners serving sentences at a mental diseases hospital.[32]

Fourth, a decision from 1987 imposed strict liability in tort where a person was unlawfully refused permission to leave a mental diseases hospital.[33]

Fifth, in a decision from 1990, the Supreme Court held that a severely handicapped woman had the legal right to be nursed at home by her municipality.[34]

Finally, in the Pill Case from 1992, the Supreme Court held that the duty of care of the manufacturers of pharmaceutical products was one of strict liability.[35] Following the coming into force of the Product Liability Act of 1988, there was no doubt whatsoever that the duty of care of manufacturers of pharmaceutical products is one

27 Norwegian Supreme Court cases are published consecutively in *Norsk Retstidende* (Supreme Court Reporter), and cited with the abbreviation Rt., followed by the year and page reference.

28 Regarding cases where the duty of care has been particularly low, see Rt. 1919 p. 1; Rt. 1935 p. 1090; Rt. 1963 p. 161; Rt. 1978 p. 482; and Rt. 1981 p. 728. See also Brunsvig 1983, p. 243.

29 Rt. 1988 p. 244; and Rt. 1989 p. 674.

30 Rt. 1977 p. 1035.

31 Rt. 1981 p. 770.

32 Rt. 1984 p. 1175.

33 Rt. 1987 p. 1495.

34 Rt. 1990 p. 874.

35 Rt. 1992 p. 64.

of strict liability, cf. section 3-3. What is interesting about the Pill Case is that the facts arose before the Product Liability Act came into force.

4.4 Lawyers and medical experts

The activity of the courts in judge-made law is largely dependent upon the work of attorneys and other lawyers. They are the ones who bring cases to court, and who appeal against decisions if there is any possibility of achieving a different result in the Appeal Courts or in the Supreme Court. More importantly, it is lawyers who research the relevant sources of law to argue their cases in court.

In patient cases, expert opinion also plays a vital role. If there is consensus among the experts, the courts will almost never diverge from that expert opinion. Certain trends can be traced during recent years: experts disagree on certain issues more often than previously, and certain experts are more positively disposed towards patients than previously. Both of these factors give the courts increased leeway in creating new laws.

5 The networked society, with contributions coming from a variety of institutions and individuals

5.1 Introduction

In a democratic society, many institutions and individuals contribute towards the creation of new legal rules and principles. Practices employed in the relationship between the patient and the health worker arises from a combination of knowledge of health, medical ethics, and law. Amendments to any one of these three factors will therefore necessarily affect the relationship between the patient and the health worker.

The issue of amending these principles will often arise at the grassroots level: in the health service, at health conferences, in healthcare workers' organizations, in patients' societies, in the media, in the health authority administration, in city, town, and county councils, and in many other places. Points of view voiced in one forum will often be reiterated in others such that society itself can be seen as a network in which new thoughts and ideas are developed and disseminated.[36]

However, this does not necessarily mean that there is harmony and good communication between the various institutions and individuals. The main point is that many entities contribute towards development, and that this is not directed by the kind of hierarchy which is often prevalent in legal theory. Patients' rights have been created in a networked society.

36 Sand 1992.

5.2 The state health administration

The highest political leadership of the state health administration, and administration in general, affects patients' rights in several ways:
1. The Ministry of Health and Care Services and the government appoint law commissions and present Bills to parliament.
2. The government issues parliamentary reports, which form the basis of parliamentary debate, in which the highest political body in the country lays down guidelines for health policy. One important example is parliament's handling of the principles of determining priority between the various health services and among patients.[37]
3. The government and the Ministry of Health and Care Services issue regulations which are binding, and which can be just as important as new statutory provisions.
4. The government and the Ministry of Health and Care Services establish schemes which have a bearing on the position of the patients, but do not require statutory authority: for example, the establishment in 1985 of ethics committees to consider and control medical research projects, and the introduction in 1988 of a patient compensation scheme based on strict liability.
5. The Ministry of Health and Care Services and the Norwegian Directorate of Health practice and interpret statutes and regulations, particularly through directives. These directives contain important guidelines for the application of law within the health service. Because the law is usually applied by civil servants who are not lawyers, the health service quite often looks upon these regulations as legally binding.

5.3 Media debate and conflicts of interest

Institutions and persons outside the formal state administration have also been significant in establishing patients' rights. A number of scandals in the Norwegian health service, and the media coverage these have received, have played a major role.

Since the mid-1980s, the Norwegian Consumer Council[38] and the Norwegian Patients' Association have been working to improve patients' rights. Their efforts have resulted in a perspective and a way of thinking that is more developed than previously.

Legal protection and legal safeguards for patients have been improved within a network of interacting – although sometimes opposing – institutions and persons. The fact that many of these have cooperated, and then mostly in the same direction, has had a cumulative effect on patients' rights.

37 Parliamentary Report No. 41 (1987-88) Helsepolitikken mot år 2000. Nasjonal Helseplan [Health Policies towards the year 2000. A National Health Plan].

38 These initiatives resulted, among other things, in two publications by the Norwegian Consumer Council: *Pasientrettigheter [Patients' Rights]*, Oslo 1983; and *Pasientrettigheter – hva nå? [Patients' Rights – What Now?]*, Oslo 1985.

5.4 *Complaint procedures and ombudsman schemes*

One important aspect of the rule of law is that a person, who is dissatisfied with a decision, will have the opportunity to have that decision reviewed by an independent body. A few decades ago, patients had no right to complain; however, there have been changes in this area and certain rules regarding complaints have been introduced:

A person who is refused access to his or her medical records, or who is refused the "necessary health assistance" or the "necessary dental treatment", has the right to complain.[39] When a complaint is lodged, the Board of Health Supervision and the Boards of Health Supervision of the Norwegian counties are obliged to carry out certain investigations.[40] In recent years, there has been a dramatic increase in the number of such complaints.

Through the powers conferred upon it by the Personal Data Filing Systems Act, the Norwegian Data Inspectorate has played quite an important role in securing patients' privacy and in protecting information that is subject to the duty of confidentiality. The Data Inspectorate has given its support to demands made by patients for the correction of medical records wherein information has been incorrect or incomplete. The Data Inspectorate has thus functioned as an ombudsman in issues relating to privacy protection.

Some 20 complaints have been dealt with annually by the Parliamentary Ombudsman for Public Administration. These complaints have represented less than 2 % of all cases reviewed by the Ombudsman.[41] Taking into consideration the importance of the health service within the public administration as a whole, it must be admitted that the Ombudsman plays a minor role in securing legal safeguards for patients from a quantitative point of view.

Since the mid-1980s, all county authorities have established patient ombudsman schemes. The introduction of these schemes is an indication that hospitals wanted to protect the rights of patients and to channel dissatisfaction to the ombudsmen instead of to the media and others. The patient ombudsman at the National Hospital of Norway [Rikshospitalet], concluded that the ombudsman schemes have made a valuable contribution to legal safeguards in the health sector. He also states: "The experience of the ombudsmen can become an important part of quality control".[42]

The patient ombudsman represents an important new development in Norwegian health law. The rules of office are now described in the Patients' Rights Act, Chapter 8. In 2009, the title was changed to Patient and Social Service Ombudsman, and complaints can be accepted from patients of primary or/and specialist health services, as well as from clients of social services.

39 See the Patients' Rights Act, Chapter 7; the Municipal Health Services Act, Section 2-3; and the Dental Health Services Act, Section 2-3.

40 Act of 30-03-1984, No. 15 relating to the public supervision of health services.

41 Os 1985, p. 115.

42 Molven 1991, pp. 195-220.

6 Legal research

6.1 Introduction to health law research

The task of legal research is to take up legal issues of major theoretical and practical interest, to collect and to systematize relevant sources of law, to analyze these and other considerations which ought to be given weight, and to draw conclusions on the basis of these sources and analyses.

In an article published in 1981, the author of this article drew attention to the fact that the position of the patients had been stronger, both *de jure* and *de facto*, some decades earlier. At that time, a clear, bipartite contractual relationship existed between the individual doctor and the individual patient, to which the contractual guarantees of the rule of law applied.[43]

Throughout the 20th century, more and more health workers were gradually being employed by hospitals and other parts of the public health service, and the bipartite relationship was replaced by a tripartite relationship. Within this triangular relationship, there was only a weak direct legal relationship between the individual patient and the individual health worker. The relationship between health workers and hospitals, and other employers, is governed by labor law. On the other hand, the relationship between the individual patient and the hospital/health center is governed by administrative law. However, the administrative guarantees of the rule of law, which are generally so important in the relationship between the individual and the public administration, only had a limited application. There was, in other words, a vacuum, as far as the rule of law was concerned, where neither private nor public law provided the patient with sufficient safeguards.[44]

After WWII, researchers of public and international law, and the sociology of law at the University of Oslo, attached great importance to legal safeguards for the individual, as well as to the legal position of weaker groups in society. This provided an important backdrop for health law research in Norway, which began in the 1970s.

6.2 The breakthrough of the patient's perspective

During the 1980s, there was considerable growth in health law research in Norway, with patients' rights and legal safeguards being given a stronger profile. Previously, the only legal literature in existence was a handful of articles and a few textbook pages covering the liability of the doctor in tort law and criminal law, and the duty of confidentiality.

The concept of patients' rights was adopted into the Norwegian legal literature in around 1980. A doctor's perspective was replaced by a patient's perspective – a perspective 'from below.'

43 Kjønstad 1981, p. 142.

44 Kjønstad 1982, p. 587.

Furthermore, attention was not only given to the legal position of patients vis-à-vis doctors, but also vis-à-vis other professions within the healthcare sector, and, above all, vis-à-vis the public health service itself. The areas of interest were no longer limited to tort law, criminal law, and the duty of confidentiality, but were extended to cover issues such as the requirement for informed consent, the right to become a patient, complaints, ombudsmen, the procedures of the Public Administration Act, and legal issues governing birth, death, AIDS, and mental disability.

6.3 Legal right to healthcare versus competition over limited resources

In analyzing health law, legal theory distinguishes between cases where citizens have a clear right to healthcare services and cases where they must compete over limited healthcare resources:

1. In some cases, people who have diseases have a legal right to care. In these cases public authorities cannot refuse to help due to a lack of resources; they must ensure that sufficient resources are provided to fulfill their legal obligation. Legal rights on the part of citizens and legal obligations on the part of the public authorities, as a rule, only exist as a result of legislation, or of regulations that have a legal basis. If those meeting the requirements of the legislation or regulations do not receive the healthcare to which they are entitled, they may sue the public authorities in order to force them to perform their duty.
2. In many cases, people who have diseases do not have a legal right to obtain healthcare, but they do have a right to compete for limited resources. In these cases, no legislation or regulations exist that specify the conditions for allotting a benefit to a person. The opportunity for an individual to receive healthcare depends on need, what is available, how many other people are interested in receiving the same care, their needs, other distinguishing characteristics of the people interested in the care, and other decisive factors.

6.4 An important part of Norwegian jurisprudence

There are now a number of competent health law researchers in Norway who have published some 200 articles and other works.[45] This research represents one of the most expansive areas of law within modern Norwegian jurisprudence. Health law – with patients' rights as one of its core subjects – is an important, independent, and established legal discipline.

45 For a summary of the most important works systematized by theme, see Kjønstad 2007, pp. 131-140.

7 Summary

The 1980s can be described as the golden age of patients' rights. In 1999, the legislators crowned past developments by passing the Patients' Rights Act, and this act has become very important. Although, to a large extent, the Patients' Rights Act only codified previous law, it was crucial that this was properly documented, and that vague principles were defined in the legislation.

This article has outlined when and how the growth of various patients' rights has occurred. Here in this summary, I will provide a systematic overview of twelve main principles in Norwegian health law currently in force:[46]

The first three principles are related to treatment: the patient's right to access treatment, the patient's right to obtain sound professional medical help and considerate care, and state supervision and control of health personnel and health services.

The second three principles are related to lines of communication in the health sector: the patient's right to protection against the spread of confidential information, the patient's right to verbal information, and the patient's right of access his/her own medical records.

The third three principles are particularly applicable post-treatment: the patient's right to lodge a complaint, the patient's right to compensation when treatment has resulted in injury, and the patient's protection under criminal law.

The fourth three principles are related to the right to autonomy: the patient's autonomy, the professional autonomy of healthcare workers, and Parliament's [Stortinget's] budgetary freedom and municipal autonomy. The autonomy of Parliament and the municipalities, and the autonomy of healthcare personnel, does not constitute patients' rights, but rather the most important limitation on patients' rights.

References

Braut, Geir Sverre (2011), "The requirement to practice in accordance with sound professional standards". In O. Molven and J. Ferkis (Ed.), *Healthcare, Welfare and Law*, Oslo, p. 139-149.

Brunsvig, Jørgen (1983), "Culpanormen for leger" [Doctors' Duty of Care and Tort Law], *Jussens Venner* (Students law journal), 1983, p. 243.

Jørstad, Rolf Gunnar (2011), "Patient injury – the right to claim compensation". In O. Molven and J. Ferkis, *Healthcare, Welfare and Law*, Oslo, p. 176-185.

Kjønstad, Asbjørn (1981), "Pasienters rättigheter" [Patients' Rights]. In *Förhandlingarna vid Det tjugonionde juristmøtet [Proceedings from the 29th Nordic Meeting of Lawyers]*, Part 1, Stockholm, p. 142.

Kjønstad, Asbjørn (1982), "Pasienters rettigheter – Kontraktsrett eller forvaltningsrett" [Patients' Rights – Contract Law or Public Administration Law]. In *Lov og*

46 See Kjønstad 2007 pp. 41-53; and Kjønstad 2010.

Frihet, Festskrift til Johs. Andenæs [Law and Freedom, in honour of Johs. Andenæs], Oslo, p. 587.

Kjønstad, Asbjørn (2007), "Pasientrettighetenes framvekst" [The Development of Patients' Rights]. In A. Kjønstad, *Helserett [Health Law]*, Oslo, pp. 69-140.

Kjønstad, Asbjørn (2010), "Twelve main principles in Norwegian health law". In *Retfærd* (Nordic Journal of Law) 2010, pp. 60-78.

Kjønstad, Asbjørn (2011), "The right to primary healthcare" and "The right to specialized healthcare". In O. Molven and J. Ferkis (Ed.), *Healthcare, Welfare and Law*, Oslo, pp. 58-92.

Mason, J.K. and Smith, R.A. McCall (1987), *Butterworth's Medico-Legal Encyclopaedia*, London, Boston.

Molven, Olav (1991), "Pasientombudsordningen – et bidrag til rettssikkerhet og kvalitet i helsevesenet?" [The Patient Ombudsman Scheme – A Contribution to Legal Safeguards and Quality in the Health Service?], *Lov og Rett* (Norwegian Law Journal) 1991, pp. 195-220.

Mork, Torbjørn (1992), "Trenger vi en verdidebatt i helsetjenesten?" [Do we need a debate on values in the health service?], *Helsetjenesten Medisinsk Teknikk [Health Service Mediocal Technology]* 1992, pp. 4-9.

Os, Audvar (1985), "Erfaringer med Pasientklager" [Experiences with Patients' Complaints]. In *Pasientrettigheter – hva nå? [Patients' Rights – What Now?]*, Oslo, p. 115.

Rehof, Lars A. and Trier, Trygve (1990), *Menneskerett [Human Rights]*, Copenhagen, Oslo.

Sand, Inger Johanne (1992), "En skisse til tre rettslige statsmodeller: Rettsstaten, forvaltningsstaten, nettverkstaten" [A Draft of Three Models of State: Legal State, Administrative State and Network State]. In *Festskrift til Gunnar de Capua [In honour of Gunnar de Capua]*, Oslo, pp. 54-63.

Syse, Aslak (1992), "Historiske streiflys på lege/pasientforholdet – medisinsk-etisk og rettslig" [A Historical Glimpse of the Relationship between Doctor and Patient – Medico-ethical and legal]. In A. Kjønstad and A. Syse (Ed.), *Helseprioriteringer og pasientrettigheter [Priorities of Health and Patients' Rights]*, Oslo, pp. 9-37.

Still no Patients' Act in Sweden – Reasons and Implications

By Professor Elisabeth Rynning, Uppsala University[1]

1 A Nordic point of departure

For several decades, there has been a clear ambition in all the Nordic countries to strengthen the legal position of the patient.[2] This aim can, of course, be pursued by means of different legal tools and strategies; however, there are two points in this trend where Sweden quite markedly deviates from the other members of the Nordic family. Sweden is thus the only Nordic country not to have introduced a special Patients' Rights Act, and neither has it ratified the Council of Europe Convention on Human Rights and Biomedicine (1997) yet. As will be shown below, this should not be misinterpreted as a Swedish lack of interest in the status of the patient; however, it does undeniably tell us something about the focus of Swedish health care policy and the legal strategies that have been favoured.

Having started as early on as the 1970s, the Nordic legal discussion on patients' rights grew stronger during the 1980s. The rights of patients thus constituted one of the topics at the 1981 Nordic Law Convention,[3] and before long, several of the Nordic countries had started to prepare special legislation in this field. The first statutory law governing the status and rights of the patient was adopted in Finland in 1992; however, Denmark, Iceland, and Norway all followed suit before the turn of the cen-

---

1 Elisabeth Rynning, LL.D. Professor of Medical Law at Uppsala University (www.jur.uu.se). Research interests include patients' rights, privacy and the use of new technology in health care and research. Has participated in a number of European research projects and since 2006 coordinates the Nordic Network for Research in Biomedical Law. Former legal expert of the Swedish National Council on Medical Ethics (1997-2008) and a number of law commissions in the areas of health care and research.

This chapter is partly based on the more comprehensive Swedish essay Patientens rättsliga ställning – två steg fram och ett tillbaka? [The Legal Status of the Patient – Two Steps Forward and One Backwards?], in *Festskrift till Lotta Vahlne Westerhäll* (Santérus Förlag, Stockholm, 2011), pp. 307-335.

2 See, for instance, E. Rynning, O. M. Arnardottir, M. Hartlev, H. S. Aasen, and S. Soini, Recent Developments in Nordic Health Law, 17 *European Journal of Health Law* (2010), pp. 279-294.

3 See J. Lett, Patienters rettigheder [Patients Rights], in *Förhandlingarna vid det tjugonionde nordiska juristmötet i Stockholm 19-21 augusti 1981 [Proceedings from the 29th Nordic Law Convention, Stockholm 19-21 August 1981]*, Part 1 pp. 137-1667, and Part 2 pp. 73-92, http//:jura.ku.dk/njm/29/lett-jesper/ visited 2011-07-06.

tury.[4] As mentioned above, however, this was not the case in Sweden, despite the fact that there had been calls for patient-focused legislation as far back as the introduction of the Health and Medical Services Act (1982:763).[5] Since then, the issue has been raised recurrently over the years. However, even in 2011, there is still no comprehensive Swedish legislation on the status and rights of the patient. Many patient-related issues have instead been addressed in various provisions dealing with the obligations of health care providers and health care staff, while others are only regulated via more general rules governing, for instance, legal necessity or the rights and duties of custody holders. Why Sweden has no special legislation on the status and rights of the patient, and what the implications of this may be, are questions that will be discussed in this essay.

The Nordic trend in the field of patients' rights has, of course, been strongly influenced and inspired by the parallel European debate and the introduction of documents such as the numerous Council of Europe recommendations dealing with health care issues, the WHO 1994 Declaration on the Rights of Patients in Europe, and, not least, the European Convention on Human Rights and Biomedicine, with its additional protocols. In these documents, the meaning of fundamental human rights and freedoms is specified and contextualised with regard to the particular fields of health care and biomedical research.[6]

When the Biomedicine Convention was opened for signatures in April 1997, all the Nordic countries immediately signed. Denmark then ratified the Convention in 1999, followed by Iceland in 2004, Norway in 2006, and, most recently, Finland in 2009. Meanwhile, Sweden has still not been able to meet some of the European minimum standards laid down for the protection of human rights and human dignity in health care and biomedical research. It will be argued that there is indeed a connection between Sweden's lack of patient-focused legislation and its difficulties meeting the standards of the Biomedicine Convention.

2 Patients' rights?

The concept of patients' rights can be defined in different ways, encompassing somewhat varied aspects. As described by Mette Hartlev, the traditional Nordic health care model has been based on a strong emphasis on *collective* interests and responsibility, although *individual* rights have clearly been given increasing consideration

4 Finland's Lag om patientens ställning och rättigheter [Act on the Status and Rights of the Patient] 785/1992, followed by Iceland's Rights of Patients Act, no. 74/1997; Denmark's Lov om patienters retsstilling [Act on the Status of Patients] no. 482 of 01/07/1998 and Norway's Lov om pasientrettigheter (pasientrettighetsloven) [Act on Patients' Rights] 1999-07-02 no. 63. The Norwegian Act only came into force in 2001. The Danish law was subsequently incorporated into the comprehensive Health Care Act, [Sundhedsloven] (no. 95 of 07/02/2008; later no. 913 of 13/07/2010), where the provisions governing the status of the patient can be found in Chapters 4-11.

5 See government Bill 1981/82:97 Hälso- och sjukvårdslag m.m. [Health and Medical Services Act etc.], p. 49.

6 For further aspects of European health law, see also H.R. Abbing and M. Mikkola, pp??. in this book.

over the past few decades.[7] Even so, the Nordic regulatory approach to patients' rights is still primarily the public law approach, whereby patients, in principle, have no avenue of direct action against the health care provider. This means that many of the rights referred to in this context are not justiciable individual rights, but rather social rights that allow individual patients equitable access to the limited resources of the publicly-funded health care sector. Even though some patients' rights may be judicially enforceable by appeal to a court, or other administrative body, dissatisfied patients are more often reduced to making use of various complaint procedures involving disciplinary sanctions or criticism directed at the professionals or health care providers concerned. Criminal proceedings are rare and economic compensation for healthcare-related injuries is normally provided by the special patient insurance schemes,[8] rather than by way of ordinary torts litigation.

To call something a "right" in statutory law, when this right cannot be legally enforced, could, of course, give rise to misunderstandings. If patients expect such statutory rights to be justiciable, they may end up feeling disappointed or even deceived. It is therefore understandable that the Finnish statute was named the *Status* and Rights of Patients Act, and that the Danish legislator completely avoided the term "rights" when the *Legal Status* of Patients Act was introduced. Iceland and Norway seem to have been less concerned about this terminological issue, both have Patients' Rights Acts.

Whether so-called patients' rights are justiciable or not, they are often divided into three main categories:[9]

1. Rights related to access to health care (sometimes described as the right to become a patient)
2. Rights related to the content of the health care services provided as well as certain other aspects of the relationship between the patient and health care providers/staff (i.e. the right to obtain information, access to medical records, quality of care, respect for autonomy, privacy etc.)
3. Procedural or formal rights, aimed at providing guarantees for the fulfilment of rights under the two first categories, or compensation/judicial sanctions when infringements of such rights occur.

7 M. Hartlev, *Raison d'être* of Nordic Health Law, in this volume.

8 This kind of insurance system has constituted a common feature in Nordic health law, since the mid-1970s. See, for instance, B. von Eyben, Alternative Compensation Systems, 41 *Scandinavian Studies in Law* (2009), pp. 193-232, www.scandinavianlaw.se, visited on 2011-07-06; or C. Hodges, Nordic compensation schemes for drug injuries, 29(2) *Journal of Consumer Policy* June (2006), pp. 143-175.

9 See, for instance, A. Kjønstad, The development of patients' rights in Norway, in this volume. See also L. Westerhäll, Rätten att bli patient – patienträttigheter [The Right to Become a Patient – Patients' Rights], in *Om våra rättigheter IV [On Our Rights, part IV]*, (Rättsfonden, Stockholm, 1990), pp. 133-163, and *Patienträttigheter [Patients' Rights]*, (Nerenius & Santerus Förlag, Stockholm, 1994), and the WHO Declaration on the Rights of Patients in Europe, 1994.

The development of patients' rights has had the aim of strengthening the position of the patient in various ways. As a group, patients are undeniably in a vulnerable position, in that they are dependent on the services of the health care sector for their well-being or even their survival. It goes without saying that patients expect health care staff to be well educated and to perform their work in accordance with high professional standards. In the old paternalistic tradition of the medical profession, however, patients had a very limited influence on their own health care. This policy ceased to be acceptable a long time ago.

The individual needs of the patient should thus be made clearly visible, just as patients themselves must be allowed a more influential and central role in the health care setting. The provision of adequate information and respect for patient autonomy constitute necessary prerequisites for the empowerment of patients.

Some patients are more vulnerable than others, however, and cannot realistically adopt the role of an active and autonomous health care consumer. In this category, we find incapacitated adults and minors who have an insufficient decision-making capacity, as well as other groups of less resourceful citizens. This means that patients' rights cannot only be about autonomy and choice, but also about human dignity, protection, and care. Furthermore, even the most autonomous patients may be highly vulnerable with regard to the sensitive personal information that must be processed for health-related purposes. Adequate protection of informational privacy is thus not only a fundamental human right, but also vital for maintaining public trust in health care.

3 Legal tools and strategies for advancing patients' rights

A number of different legal tools and strategies can be used to strengthen the position of the patient. One alternative could be to apply a truly rights-focused strategy, whereby patients are provided with more *justiciable, individual rights,* maybe even an enforceable right to health care, with the possibility to appeal. Although far from the primary strategy in the Nordic countries, this method has been used to varying degrees. The main counterargument would seem to concern the difficulties involved in forming a suitable body for appeal, whereby health care decisions can be reviewed in a competent and sufficiently timely way.[10] There may also be financial objections to justiciable rights which are likely to put additional strain on health care budgets. The objections mentioned would primarily be relevant to rights in the first category above, i.e. rights related to access to health care, but also to decisions concerning choosing between different treatment methods. Other positive rights, e.g. the right to obtain information and to access medical records, would seem easier to make legally enforceable. With regard to negative rights, e.g. respect for private life and liberty, the need for adequate judicial protection is already commonly agreed upon.

10 See section 4.1 below.

Infringements of, for instance, the right to bodily autonomy, through coercive treatment or the deprivation of liberty, certainly require access to effective legal remedies.[11]

Where it is not considered feasible or desirable to introduce new justiciable health care rights, *comprehensive legislation on the status of patients* can still be of great value, both as a matter of principle and to facilitate access to the relevant provisions. Patient-focused legislation can be introduced in a separate Act (as in Finland, Iceland, and Norway), or in special chapters that form part of a more general health care Act (as in Denmark after 2008).[12] Objections normally raised concern the disadvantages of duplicating rules already laid down in legislation on the duties of health care providers and personnel.

If the competent policy-makers do not wish to introduce special patient legislation, a third strategy could be to *clarify the obligations of health care providers and staff* and formulate their duties in more patient-focused rules. New supplementary obligations can be introduced with the specific aim of strengthening the position of the patient. Although considerable improvements can also be achieved using this strategy, the lack of a comprehensive patient-centric approach is associated with a clear risk of fragmentisation, whereby an overview of the relevant provisions becomes more difficult and important issues may be overlooked.

The fourth and final legal tool to be mentioned here is *access to legal remedies.*[13] When patients are provided with a right of appeal, this, of course, turns the right in question into a justiciable right of the kind discussed above. In other cases, legal remedies will involve a *post factum* review of the alleged infringement, allowing the patient redress by way of financial compensation and the imposition of disciplinary sanctions or similar measures. The right will still have been violated, but the patient will be offered some kind of satisfaction.

In the sections below, the use of these four strategies in Swedish health care policy will be investigated.

4 Strategies applied to Swedish health care policy

4.1 Few enforceable individual rights

Swedish law provides patients with very few enforceable positive rights. Those normally mentioned include the right to abortion and the right to sterilisation, since a decision refusing the patient such an intervention can be overruled by the National Board of Health and Welfare.[14] The patient's right to access his/her own medical records is also a right that can be legally enforced, by appeal to the competent Ad-

11 Cf. Article 13 of the European Convention on the Protection of Human Rights and Fundamental Freedoms (1950).

12 Supra note 4.

13 Cf. Articles 23-25 of the Biomedicine Convention.

14 See Section 4 of the Abortion Act (1974:595) and Section 2 of the Sterilisation Act (1975:580).

ministrative Court of Appeal.[15] When it comes to the protection of negative rights, e.g. the right to refuse treatment, the Compulsory Psychiatric Care Act (1991:1128) provides for certain judicial review by the Administrative Court system,[16] as does the Protection Against Communicable Diseases Act (2004:168).

From the preparatory works of the Health and Medical Services Act, it is clear that the possibility of rights-based regulation was not considered a realistic alternative, at least not in the form of an enforceable right of access to health care.[17] It is interesting to note, by way of comparison, that individual positive rights were introduced in the area of social welfare at this very time.[18] The fact that enforceable rights could be a powerful tool for strengthening the position of the individual in health care too, has not been denied in the continuing debate, but it has not been considered possible to overcome the problems related to such a system.[19] The problems referred to primarily concern the difficulties involved in establishing a satisfactory review system, as well as conflicts with the principle of autonomous local governance which is applicable to public health care providers.

4.2 Comprehensive patient-focused legislation

When justiciable rights were once again rejected as a possible tool for addressing problems of prioritisation, during the debate of the early 1990s, there was no real discussion about the other aspects of special patient legislation.[20] Some years later, the 1997 official report *The Patient is Right* underlined the fact that patient legislation need not necessarily be rights-based, and it was agreed that more patient-focused regulation would have considerable advantages with regard to overview and accessibility of the relevant provisions, for patients as well as health care staff.[21] The marginalised position of the patient in the existing duty-based legislation was also considered problematic. However, as pointed out in the report, some important issues had not, as yet, been made subject to any special regulation at all, e.g. the status of minors in health care, decision-making on behalf of incapacitated adult patients,

15 As regards publicly-run health care, this right was established as early on as 1951, by the Administrative Supreme Court (Yearbook of the Administrative Supreme Court 1951 ref. 29). An equivalent right for patients in the private sector was first introduced in the Monitoring of Health Care Staff Act (1980:11) and is now regulated by Chapter 8 Section 2 of the Patient Data Act.

16 For a comprehensive analysis of compulsory psychiatric care in Sweden, from a rule of law perspective, see E. Gustafsson, *Psykiatrisk tvångsvård och rättssäkerhet [Compulsory Psychiatric Care and the Rule of Law]*, (Studentlitteratur, Lund, 2010).

17 See, for instance, government Bill 1981/82:97 Hälso- och sjukvårdslag m.m [Health and Medical Services Act etc.], p. 54.

18 See, for instance, L. Vahlne Westerhäll, *Den starka statens fall? [The Fall of the Strong State?]*, Norstedts Juridik, Stockholm, 2002), pp.14–17.

19 See government Bill 1997/98:189 Patientens ställning [The Status of the Patient], p. xx, and the official report Patienten har rätt [The Patient is Right], (Swedish Government Official Report 1997:154), p. 118.

20 See Vårdens svåra val [The Difficult Choices in Health Care], (Swedish Government Official Reports 1993:93 and 1995:5), in particular the latter, pp. 185 ff.

21 This view was held by both the government and the Parliamentary Committee on Health and Welfare, see government Bill 1997/98:189 Patientens ställning [The Status of the Patient], pp. 14-17, and the committee report 1998/99:SoU03 Stärkt patientinflytande m.m. (Increased Patient Influence). See also Swedish Government Official Report 1997:154, pp. 123 ff.

and health care interventions in emergency situations. In 1998, the government thus declared its intention to arrange a patient-focused review of Swedish health care legislation.[22] Unfortunately, no such review was initiated.

The issue was raised once again during the early years of the new millennium and, in 2007, another official report recommended the introduction of a comprehensive Patients' Act.[23] Although many provisions could be transferred or copied from already-existing legislation, there were still, however, areas where additional rules needed to be developed, e.g. concerning the status of minors in health care.

The government then decided to appoint a commission of inquiry with the specific task of proposing how the status and influence of patients could be improved.[24] The reports subsequently presented by the commission, in 2008 and 2009, primarily focused, however, on issues related to individual access to health care and, although a comprehensive Patients Act was also considered recommendable, no draft of any such legislation was ever presented.[25]

The incumbent Swedish government has since come to the repeat conclusion that a special Patients' Act is needed; in March 2011, another commission was appointed with the explicit task of drafting such an Act.[26] This time, too, access issues are being given quite a lot of attention in the terms of reference and, although the commission is required to survey the status of minors in health care, other important issues, e.g. emergency care, advance directives, and decision-making on behalf of incapacitated patients, are not being mentioned.

In conclusion: Despite clear consensus regarding the need for more comprehensive patient-focused legislation in Sweden, no such legislation has actually been prepared during the thirteen years that have elapsed since official agreement was first reached on this point.

Instead, the legal strategy most favoured in Sweden's evolution of patients' "rights" has doubtless been to clarify, develop, and supplement the duties of health care providers and their staff, in order for them to better meet the needs of the individual patient.

22 Government Bill, supra note 22.

23 Swedish Government Official Report 2007:10, Hållbar samhällsorganisation med utvecklingskraft [Endurable Organisation of Society, with Developmental Power], pp. 141 ff. and p. 151.

24 See terms of reference (Dir 2007:90) Patientens rätt i vården [The Rights of the Patient in Health Care].

25 Swedish Government Official Reports 2008:127, pp. 184 ff., and 2009:84 Regler för etablering av vårdgivare [Rules for Establishment of Health Care Providers], p. 109.

26 See terms of reference (Dir 2011:25) Stärkt ställning för patienten genom en ny patientlagstiftning [Improved Status of the Patient by Way of a New Patients' Act].

4.3 *Clarified and extended duties for health care providers and staff*

4.3.1 *Equal access to health care*

Accessibility has been one of the difficult areas of Swedish health care, with at times unacceptably long waiting times. The country described as the "European champion on medical outcomes" is thus, at the same time, being criticised for its "notoriously poor accessibility situation".[27]

Equal access constitutes an important part of the foundations of Swedish health care, as clearly stated in Section 2 of the Health and Medical Services Act. This provision was later supplemented with the principle of respect for the equal value of all humans and the dignity of the individual human being, together with the principle that those in greatest need of health care must be given priority. These principles do not solve the problems related to prioritising limited health care resources; however, with regard to the need to avoid discrimination, the preparatory works provide important examples of circumstances that do *not*, in themselves, constitute acceptable grounds for prioritisation (e.g. age, weight, lifestyle, or social standing).[28]

In order to tackle accessibility problems, various schemes and reforms have been tried out over the years. Statutory provisions on maximum waiting times were recently adopted, as part of the obligations of public health care providers.[29] Legislation on systems allowing free choice of health care provider in primary care has also been introduced.[30]

For some Swedish patients, the evolution of EU law on cross-border care has provided additional opportunities for improved access to health care.[31] This alternative also has the advantage of being legally enforceable. Even so, most patients still prefer to be treated in their home country, and not everyone has the resources and personal support that may be necessary, in reality, for cross-border health care.

In order to actually make use of the available alternatives and access guarantees, even within Sweden, patients need to be well informed and reasonably resourceful in other respects, too. This means that special attention must be paid to the interests of more vulnerable patient groups, e.g. minors and incapacitated adults, psychiatric patients and immigrants.

---

27 Euro Health Consumer Index 2009 Report, Health Consumer Powerhouse 2009-09-28, p. 9, electronic version available at http://www.healthpowerhouse.com9.

28 Government Bill 1996/97:60 Prioriteringar inom hälso- och sjukvården [Prioritisation in Health Care], pp. 24-25.

29 See Sections 3 g-h of the Health and Medical Services Act, together with the new Care Guarantee Ordinance (2010:349), further described in government Bill 2009/10:67 Stärkt ställning för patienten - vårdgaranti, fast vårdkontakt och förnyad medicinsk bedömning [Improved Status of the Patient – Health Care Guarantee, ?? Contact and Second Opinion], pp. 36 ff. See also L-Å. Johnsson and J. Sahlin, *Hälso- och sjukvårdslagen med kommentarer [Comments on the Health and Services Act]*, (8 ed. Norstedts Juridik, Stockholm, 2010), pp. 117-119 and pp. 164-167.

30 Lagen (2008:962) om valfrihetssystem [Act on Systems for Free Choice], see government Bill 2008/09:74 Vårdval i primärvården [Choice of Care in Primary Care].

31 See, for instance, Edwardsson, *Fri rörlighet för välfärd? Rättsutvecklingen gällande den fria rörligheten för sjukvårdstjänster [Free Movement for Welfare? Legal Development Regarding the Free Movement of Health Care Services]*, (Sieps, Stockholm 2007:5).

There are also patient groups to which the principle of equal access does not fully apply, even formally, e.g. asylum seekers and irregular immigrants.[32] Sweden has been criticised on this point for not meeting its obligations under public international law, with regard to the right of everyone to the highest attainable standard of health.[33] The issue has been subject to renewed investigation and a recent official report now proposes that the principle of equal access to health care services should apply to *all* patients, whether they have a valid residence permit or not.[34]

4.3.2 Health service content and patient influence

Since the late 1970s, there have been considerable developments in legal requirements regarding quality of care and patient participation. The Monitoring of Health Care Staff Act (1980:11) has introduced general rules governing the duties of health care professionals, including, for instance, the obligation to provide patients with expert and conscientious care that is in keeping with science and proven experience, and which is, as far as possible, designed and delivered in consultation with the patient. The patient should be given information on his/her state of health and on the available treatment methods, and must be shown consideration and respect.[35] Similar general requirements were prescribed in the 1982 Health and Medical Services Act, regulating the obligations of health care providers. It was debated whether or not this goal-oriented framework legislation – aimed at also allowing scope for autonomous local and regional decision-making – would offer patients sufficient predictability and legal certainty in their health care.[36] Despite calls for regulation better suited to clarifying the legal status of patients, however, the government argued that duty-based legislation could also be sufficiently focused on the needs of patients.

The general obligations and the characteristics of good health care have been elaborated on and supplemented a number of times since the early 1980s.[37] One such clarification concerned information requirements, which specify, with effect from 1999, that patients must be given *individually-adapted* information on their state of health and the available methods of *examination, care and treatment.*[38] At the same time, new legal duties were introduced, allowing patients to choose between the available treatment methods, under certain circumstances, and to have access to a second opinion in case of particularly serious illness or injury.[39]

32 See Swedish Government Official Report 2011:48 Vård efter behov och på lika villkor – en mänsklig rättighet [Care in Relation to Need and on Equal Terms – a Human Right].

33 Report of the Special Rapporteur on the right of everyone to the enjoyment of the highest attainable standard of physical and mental health, Paul Hunt Addendum Mission to Sweden, United Nations A/HRC/4/28/Add.2, 28 February 2007.

34 Supra note 33.

35 Section 5 of this Act.

36 Government Bill 1981/82:97, pp. 46-49.

37 See L-Å. Johnsson and J. Sahlin, supra note 30, pp. 50-111.

38 Government Bill 1998/99:4 and 2009/10:67, p. 65.

39 Section 3 a of the Health and Medical Services Act. See L-Å. Johnsson and J. Sahlin, supra note 30, pp.145-151.

While the obligations of health care providers continue to be regulated by the 1982 Health and Medical Services Act, the duties of health care staff have been regulated by several consecutive statutes over the years. Today, the relevant rules are laid down in Chapter 6 of the Patient Safety Act (2010:659).

Further improvements have been made to the specific area of information privacy protection, not least by the introduction of the new Patient Data Act (2008:355). While allowing electronic access to medical records across organisational boundaries – under strict conditions that include patient consent – the Act also clarifies internal confidentiality requirements and the need for health care providers to restrict and control their employees' access to medical records. Patients may request that their records be blocked as regards certain types of external or internal health care related access; they also have the right to know who has accessed their medical records. Unfortunately, health care providers seem to be taking a long time to arrange for their electronic systems to comply with the prescribed safeguards.[40]

4.3.3 *Areas still lacking clarified rules*

Although the legal status of Swedish patients has been improved in many areas, by means of clarifying and elaborating on duty-based provisions, a number of unclear areas still remain.

Variations in the services provided by different county councils and municipalities give rise to questions regarding the meaning of equal access and equitable health care, from a national perspective. Problems related to the coordination of services concern not least vulnerable patient groups such as the elderly and those with functional impairments.

With regard to incapacitated adult patients, Sweden still has no legal system of proxy decision-making. The issue has been investigated and a report proposing additional legislation was presented as early on as 2004;[41] however, since the drafts were considered to require further adjustment, no government Bill has been prepared thus far. On the initiative of the Swedish Council on Medical Ethics, a number of public agencies and organisations have recently approached the government requesting that necessary measures be taken without further delay.[42]

The above-mentioned proposed legislation on proxy decision-making also addresses issues of advance directives, whereas no coercive interventions are covered. The need for protective measures in the care of patients suffering from dementia has been investigated by a separate commission of inquiry, resulting in suggestions for

40 See Swedish Data Inspection Board decisions 761-2008, 748-2009, and 1010-2009. Cf. also *I. v. Finland*, 17 July 2008, ECHR no 20511/03, regarding the duty of states to prevent infringements of the right to privacy, instead of merely offering legal remedies after an infringement has already taken place.

41 See Swedish Government Official Report (2004:112) Frågor om förmyndare och ställföreträdare för vuxna [Questions on Guardians and Legal Representatives of Adults].

42 Letter dated 2011-06-14: En sammanhållen reglering avseende ställföreträdare för patienter med bristande beslutsförmåga [A Comprehensive Regulation on Legal Representatives for Adults with Reduced Capacity for Decision-making]. Electronic version available at the web page of the Council, http//:www.smer.se/Uploads/Files/97.pdf, visited 2011-07-06.

special regulation in this field, too.[43] This report, presented in 2006, has not led to any legislation either. As regards the limits of justifiable coercive health care measures concerning incapacitated adults suffering from *other* types of illness or impairment, no investigation has thus far taken place.

Another vulnerable patient group in lack of specific Swedish health care regulation is minors. Parental decision-making is based on the general rules in Chapter 6 of the Parents and Children Code, providing very little guidance regarding, for instance, mature minors or parental disagreements over health care issues. The resulting uncertainties regarding decision-making and protecting the best interests of the child cannot be considered compatible with the UN Convention on the Rights of the Child. Clarifying and supplementing regulation has repeatedly been called for, and this is now one of the issues that the most recently appointed commission of inquiry has explicitly been asked to look into.[44]

4.4 Judicial protection and adequate legal sanctions

It has already been stated that Swedish patients have no enforceable right to health care. In accordance with the Swedish Administrative Procedure Act (1986:223), decisions in health care are exempted from the general provisions on appeal, unless otherwise specified. This means that, as a rule, patients have no possibility of appealing against a doctor's decision not to offer certain treatment, or for that matter, any treatment at all. If the illness is of a particularly serious nature, the doctor may be duty-bound to assist the patient in getting a second opinion, but were he/she to refuse to do so, this decision could not be formally appealed against either. As mentioned above, the Acts on abortion and sterilisation provide for special review by the National Board of Health and Welfare, should the requested intervention be denied; however, patients who are refused other types of health care would normally have no choice but to seek another doctor/health care provider, if the applicable rules regarding referral allow this.

Since patients have such limited legal means of forcing health care providers to fulfil their duties, access to complaints procedures and different legal sanctions becomes all the more important. An efficient system for monitoring health care services and professionals can also constitute a valuable safeguard.

Early improvements were made with regard to paying compensation for health care related injuries, when no-fault patient insurance schemes were introduced in

---

43 Swedish Government Official Report (2006:110) Regler för skydd och rättssäkerhet inom demensvården [Provisions on Protection and the Rule of Law in Care of Patients Suffering from Dementia].

44 Such requests can be found in a number of Swedish Government Official Reports, e.g. 1997:154, 2001:72, 2006:82, and 2007:10. See also E. Rynning, Barns rätt i vården – juridiska aspekter [The Rights of Children in Health Care – Legal Aspects], in (ed.) M. Söberbäck, *Barn och ungas rätt i vården [The Rights of Children and Adolescents in Health Care]*, (Allmänna barnhuset, Stockholm, 2010), pp. 119-152, at p. 149. Electronic version available at http//:www.allmannabarnhuset.se.

the Nordic countries, as early on as the mid-1970s.[45] In Sweden, this insurance was regulated by contract for 20 years or so, until the Patient Injury Act (1996:799) was passed. The Act itself does not cover injuries due to a lack of information or consent; however, in this field, there has been some development by tort law precedents.

In 1980, an important reform of the disciplinary system for health care staff took place. Legally-based disciplinary sanctions had previously been administered by a special Board within the National Board of Health and Welfare, but an independent central agency was now created: the Medical Responsibility Board.[46] Just as under the old system, the decisions of the Responsibility Board could be appealed against, within the administrative court system. A new feature, however, was that patients who had filed a complaint with the Board would be granted leave to appeal. Patients were thus given access to a judicial review, and could put their complaints before a court, if the Responsibility Board did not find sufficient cause to issue a warning or a reprimand. In the preparatory works, it was declared that the independent Responsibility Board would offer improved guarantees of transparency and the rule of law, benefitting patients and health care professionals alike.[47] This legally-regulated system of individual disciplinary sanctions, whereby the patient's standing was that of a party to the procedures, was then abolished after 30 years upon the introduction of the Patient Safety Act in January 2011. Complaints against health care staff are now to be filed with the National Board of Health and Welfare, and cannot result in any formal disciplinary sanctions, only informal criticism.[48] Certain new provisions governing communication were introduced, but neither patients nor professionals have access to appeals against the decisions of the Board, decisions that are now taken by individual civil servants.[49]

The National Board of Health and Welfare is a central agency which, among other things, is responsible for the overall monitoring of Swedish health care providers and their staff. Just like any other citizen, patients also had the option, even previously, to report adverse events or complaints to this supervisory agency, but they had no special standing or rights during the proceedings. The National Board of Health and Welfare has also chosen to focus more on system-related threats to patient safety than on the shortcomings of individual health care professionals. All in all, it is difficult to see this reform as a step forward in the advancement of patients' rights.

---

45 Supra note 9. For a description of the Swedish system, see U. Hellbacher, C. Espersen and H. Johansson, *Patient Injury Compensation for Health-Related Injuries* (Patient Claims Panel, Stockholm, 2007), http://www.pff.se/.

46 See government Bill 1978/79:220 Om samhällets tillsyn över hälso- och sjukvårdspersonalen m.fl. [On Public Monitoring of Health Care Staff].

47 Government Bill [what bill? 1978/79:220], pp. 17 and pp. 21-22.

48 Government Bill 2009/10:210 Patientsäkerhet och tillsyn [Patient Safety and Supervision], pp. 96-101 and Swedish Government Official Report 2008:117 Patientsäkerhet – Vad har gjorts och vad behöver göras? [Patient Safety – What has been done and what needs to be done?], pp. 315 ff.

49 This was considered a problem even when the Act was passed (see government Bill 2009/10:210, pp. 134-137), and the need for some kind of appeal has since been under investigation by the Ministry, but no solution has so far been presented.

In all fairness, however, it should be made clear that the primary aim of the reform was not patient empowerment, but the equally important endeavour to improve patient safety.[50] The system of disciplinary sanctions was only one piece in the jigsaw puzzle, but it was not considered to contribute anything meaningful with respect to patient safety. On the contrary, the risk of individual sanctions was believed to reduce the willingness of health professionals to report adverse events. Whether or not other factors could be more important vis-à-vis being motivated to report such events was not discussed very much in the preparatory works. It was also ignored that the new and expanded criteria for revoking licenses and imposing periods of probation could be a stronger deterrent against reporting adverse events than the risk of a mere warning or reprimand. It thus seems highly questionable that abolishing the system of disciplinary sanctions as such would lead to any significant improvements in patient safety, while losing access to justice, for both patients and health professionals, seems all the more obvious.

5 Implications for the status of Swedish patients

Although the legal status of Swedish patients has been improved in many respects over the past few decades, it is clear that there are also important areas that suffer from a surprising lack of satisfactory regulation. It may, perhaps, be argued that legislation based on the duties of health care providers and professionals can offer the same protection as special patient legislation, if only the contents of the provisions are adequate. Nevertheless, there can be no doubt that comprehensive patient-focused legislation offers considerable advantages with regard to accessibility, overview, and perspective. This was recognised a long time ago, but a number of Swedish governments have ever since neglected to take appropriate action based on this knowledge.

One consequence of unclear and inaccessible legal rules is the increased risk of misunderstandings regarding the contents of the law. Neither patients nor health care professionals can be expected to have sufficient legal training to master the interpretation of combined rules spread out over different statutes. If those most concerned by the regulation do not know their own rights and duties, there will be a substantial risk of the legal requirements not being met.

Regrettably, however, insufficient legal accessibility and a poor overview would not seem to be the only consequences of the fact that the comprehensive patient legislation is repeatedly being postponed. In the other Nordic countries, the process of drafting patient-focused legislation made it clear that certain difficult issues had to be addressed, e.g. decision-making on behalf of incapacitated patients, the status of minors in health care, and medical treatment in emergency situations. The legal solutions chosen by the different countries are not identical, and some of the provisions in the Nordic Patients' Rights Acts are certainly deserving criticisism. Even so, eve-

50 Government Bill 2009/10:210, pp. 71-74 and pp. 97-98.

ry serious attempt at addressing a legal inadequacy must be preferable to ignoring it. In Sweden, the final draft of comprehensive patient-focused legislation has repeatedly been put off, under the excuse that certain issues require additional investigation. Some of these issues have been investigated by separate law commissions; however, as long as no serious attempt is made at actually drafting the comprehensive Patients' Act, other issues will remain unsolved.

It is difficult to avoid noticing that most of the inadequately-regulated areas seem to concern vulnerable patient groups with limited ability to protect their own interests. While freedom of choice and consumerist ideologies may be greatly appreciated by certain patients, these legal developments do not primarily benefit incapacitated adults who lack supportive relatives. It is hardly worthy of a welfare state to focus on the interests of comparatively resourceful patient groups, while at the same time neglecting to protect the fundamental human rights of the most vulnerable ones. Not least in view of important ongoing demographic changes, with a rapidly ageing population and increased immigration, Swedish policymakers would do well to consider more carefully what may be expected of them in order to also safeguard the rights of more vulnerable patients.

Although no Swedish government seems to have put forward any thorough analysis of the overall compatibility of Swedish health law with the requirements of the Biomedicine Convention, it is clear that the lack of a system of proxy decision-making for incapacitated adults in health care constitutes a primary obstacle to Swedish ratification of the Convention.[51] This shortcoming in Swedish law in turn seems closely related to the continuously deferred drafting of comprehensive legislation on the status of patients.

6 Concluding remarks

Contrary to the other Nordic countries, Sweden does not seem to have been able to produce or implement any coherent and effective policy regarding the overall advancement and protection of patients' rights. Although there have been important developments in many areas, it is especially troublesome that the rights of very vulnerable patient groups have remained inadequately protected in Sweden, while our Nordic neighbours have not hesitated to address these difficult issues.

It is, of course, very gratifying that the Swedish government has now, at long last, appointed a commission of inquiry explicitly tasked with actually drafting a comprehensive Act on the legal status of patients. From the terms of reference, however, it is far from clear that the envisaged Act will actually cover all the issues that such a piece of legislation would be expected to address. It can only be hoped that the continuously vague and uninformed Swedish approach to patients' rights will finally be overcome in the report of the commission, which is to be submitted by January 2013.

51 Cf. Article 6.2 of the Biomedicine Convention.

By then, it will perhaps also be possible to make an initial evaluation of the revised complaints system, a system which thus far does not allow independent judicial review.

Another uncertainty concerns which additional steps may be taken in order to introduce a system of decision-making for incapacitated adults in health care. What is absolutely certain, however, is the fact that the problem will not go away, and that Sweden will not be able to ratify the Biomedicine Convention until this has been solved.

Human Rights, Health Care, and Coercion in Norwegian Health Law

By Professor Aslak Syse, University of Oslo[1]

1 Introduction

An important principle of health law and health ethics is that healthcare should be provided with the patient's consent. Respect for autonomy – the obligation to respect the decision-making capacities of autonomous persons – is usually regarded as one of the four main principles of medical ethics.[2] However, this principle may be overridden in cases of emergency. In such situations, health personnel are lawfully obliged to provide any essential healthcare they consider to be of vital importance according to the principle of beneficence. This applies when the patient is incapable of providing consent, and also if the patient objects to treatment. It may thus also be considered as some sort of a "rights provision".

Outside of emergency situations, the provision of healthcare without valid consent requires a stricter basis in law. This follows from the principle of legality relating to, *inter alia*, interference with the right to liberty and private and family life. This principle is not a statutory provision in Norwegian national law, being enshrined, however, in the provisions of the European Convention on Human Rights; see, for example, Articles 5 and 8 of the convention, which are part of Norwegian and Nordic law (see Section 2.2 below).

All the Nordic countries have mental health Acts that provide the authorization to use coercive measures on strict terms within the field of psychiatry, albeit outlined

1 Aslak Syse, MD, cand.jur and dr.juries. Professor of Law and Head of the Department of Public and International Law, University of Oslo. He worked as a physician (1972-88) in Northern Norway and in Zimbabwe. In 1989 he joined the Law Faculty, since 1997 as Professor. His main publications are in welfare law and health law.

2 According to T. L. Beauchamp & J. F. Childress (1979; 2009), *Principles of Biomedical Ethics*, 6th edn, New York: Oxford University Press, the four principles approach to health care are as follows:

a. Beneficence – the obligation to provide benefits and balance benefits against risks.

b. Non-maleficence – the obligation to avoid the causation of harm.

c. Respect for autonomy – the obligation to respect the decision-making capacities of autonomous persons.

d. Justice – obligations of observe fairness in the distribution of benefits and risks.

somewhat differently.[3]

In some of the Nordic countries, there is also an opening to isolate and detain a person with a disease dangerous to society. In this case, as well, the criteria for isolation must be strict, and detention must be used as a last resort, in order to comply with the European Convention on Human Rights. This is demonstrated by the Enhorn case, where the Swedish authorities failed to strike a fair balance between the need to ensure that the HIV virus did not spread and the applicant's right to liberty.[4]

> In 1994, it was discovered that Enhorn, who is a homosexual, was infected with the HIV virus. In response, the county medical officer issued instructions to the applicant constraining his conduct in order to prevent him from spreading the HIV infection. When the authorities were alerted to the fact that the applicant was not complying with these instructions, and had transmitted the virus to a 19-year old man, the County Administrative Court ordered that the applicant be compulsorily isolated for up to three months pursuant to Section 38 of the 1988 Infectious Diseases Act. A psychiatric report on the applicant noted that he "suffered from a paranoid personality disorder and from alcohol abuse. He was considered to be completely void of a sense of being ill and also lacked awareness. The combination of a sexual orientation towards younger men and a possible alcohol related neuro-psychological functional impairment, from the infection-spreading viewpoint, was deemed disadvantageous." As a result of the confinement order, the applicant was in total isolation for approximately one and a half years.
>
> The European Court of Human Rights acknowledged having "only to a very limited extent ruled on cases where a person has been detained in order to prevent the spreading of infectious diseases". Therefore, it established new criteria to assess whether or not a detention was lawful, asserting that a detention is lawful where the spread of the disease is dangerous to public health and safety, and where that detention is used as a last resort. According to the Court, these criteria ensure that the law complies with the principle of proportionality and is free from arbitrariness. In this case, the Court held that HIV does indeed constitute a danger to public health. However, the Court also said that it was not possible to conclude that the repeated confinement orders were employed "as a last resort" because the Swedish government had not provided "any examples of less severe measures which might have been considered for the applicant during the period 16 February 1995 to 12 December 2001, but were apparently found to be insufficient as regards safeguarding the public interest". In addition, the overall duration of the confinement orders showed that "the authorities failed to strike a fair balance between the need to ensure that the HIV virus did not spread and the applicant's right to liberty".

3 A. Syse and T. Nilstun, "Ulike regler – lik lovforståelse? Om tvangsregulering, tvangsbruk og verdikonflikter i nordisk psykiatri" [Coercion in Nordic Psychiatry: Different rules – not that different practices]. *Tidsskrift for Rettsvitenskap* 1997, pp. 837-918.

4 Court judgment, 25 January 2005.

There are three important Acts in Norwegian health law that authorize the use of coercive measures. Two of these have parallels in other Nordic countries: the Act relating to the provision and implementation of mental health care and the Act relating to the control of communicable diseases. A specific piece of Norwegian legislation is the amended Chapter 4A of the Norwegian Patients' Rights Act which allows for the provision of somatic healthcare, including dental services, to persons not competent to consent to, or to decline, such care. Denmark has some provisions which allow treatment by force, but which are more restricted, however, than this Chapter 4A.

The Mental Health Care Act (MHCA) is by far the most important of these three statutes. On a yearly basis, approximately 6,000 patients are civilly committed to mental health institutions. A substantial portion of this Chapter is, thus, devoted to the MHCA, while the last two sections more briefly present the Communicable Diseases Act and Chapter 4A of the Patients' Rights Act.

> In Norway, as in most other European countries, additional statutes for the civil commitment of substance abusers are in place. These regulations are not, however, part of health legislation; neither is the care of persons with general learning difficulties and, in addition, challenging behaviour. These situations are dealt with in compliance with special Chapters of the Social Welfare Act and are thus not covered here.[5]

Coercive intervention in the field of psychiatry today is based on a number of assumptions about the beneficial effects of coercive measures. Despite the lack of an empirical basis which would justify such measures, Norway currently has legislation that allows civil commitment, regardless of whether or not the patient is competent to make somatic treatment decisions. Particular attention will be paid to the new UN Convention on the Rights of Persons with Disabilities and whether or not Nordic regulations in the field of psychiatry comply with this Convention.[6]

---

5 For an actual overview of Norwegian Health Law, see Molven and Ferkis, eds. (2011), *Healthcare, Welfare and Law. Health Legislation as a Mirror of the Norwegian Welfare State*. This Chapter is partly based on a chapter in that book written by this author. However, the text has been revised and updated, and the discussion about the relevance of the *UN Convention on the Rights of Persons with Disabilities* on mental health legislation has been written anew, alongside the case law from ECHR. – The actual provisions in the Social Welfare Act will as from 1 January 2012 be integrated in a mutual Municipal Health and Social Care Act (helse- og omsorgstjenesteloven).

6 In June 2011 a law commission submitted a white paper proposing some changes in the Mental Health Act, see NOU 2011:9 *Økt selvbestemmelse og rettssikkerhet. Balansegangen mellom selvbestemmelsesrett og omsorgsansvar i psykisk helsevern [Increased Self-determination and Justice. Balancing Autonomy and Paternalism in the Mental Health Field]*.

2 The Mental Health Care Act

2.1 Overview

The Mental Health Care Act (MHCA) regulates mental health care in Norway, and contains provisions relating to the establishment and operation of voluntary and compulsory healthcare, both inside and outside hospitals and other health institutions. At any given time, approximately 1,000 persons are being detained in psychiatric institutions, committed on the basis of legal authority under the Act. The number of detained patients has declined considerably over the last few decades due to a general trend of de-institutionalization. As far as possible, mental health care should be administered within the municipality.

The vast majority of admissions are voluntary (approximately 80 %), thus being based on either patient consent or parental consent, in the case of minors. A percentage of admissions are compulsory observations, which may last a maximum of ten days. Most civil commitment decisions are valid for one year, but may be reiterated for an additional year, and for an unlimited number of years.

Patients with mental health problems who are not receiving treatment from specialist psychiatric services – either as in- or out-patients – are outside the scope of the MHCA. This pertains, for instance, to patients treated by their family doctor or patients residing in a nursing home run by the municipality.

A patient must be competent to give his/her valid consent to be admitted voluntarily under the MHCA. However, there is no clear-cut boundary concerning what is registered as a voluntary admission and what is registered as a civil commitment.[7] Next of kin have the right to express their opinions on the appropriateness of voluntary measures being applied to patients who are incompetent to consent and not objecting to the actual treatment. Still, there remains a grey area between civil commitment and voluntary admission, factually as well as legally.

The Act also contains provisions giving parents the right to consent on behalf of children less than 16 years of age.

The most important *terms* used in the Act are defined in Chapter 1 of the MHCA. Special rules are also given relating to certain other Acts, in particular the Patients' Rights Act and the Public Administration Act, both adding to the regulation of the field of psychiatry. The Patients' Rights Act gives all patients the right to obtain necessary treatment, the right to obtain information, involvement in medical decisions, and the right to refuse treatment other than in cases of necessity. A patient is also entitled to view his/her medical records, and there are hardly any exceptions to this rule, even within the scope of psychiatric care. The MHCA overrules the right to refuse treat-

7 This is clearly demonstrated in the Nordic Study on the use of coercion in mental health, see, for instance, G. Høyer, L. Kjellin, M. Engberg, K. Riittakerttu, T. Nilstun, M. Sigurdjonsdottir, and A. Syse, "Paternalism and autonomy: A presentation of a Nordic Study on the use of coercion in the mental health care system". *International Journal of Law and Psychiatry* 2002, Volume 25, pp. 93-108, and T. Nilstun and A. Syse, "The right to accept and the right to refuse". *Acta Psychiatrica Scandinavica* 2000; (suppl. 399), pp. 31-34.

ment in cases of civil commitment, and in such cases, the Public Administration Act also comes into play, containing conditions for the decision-making process.

The following three chapters of the MHCA contain provisions for consenting to mental health care (Chapter 2), for compulsory mental health care (Chapter 3), and for the implementation of mental health care (Chapter 4). This last chapter applies to patients admitted either on a voluntary or an involuntary basis. However, some of the provisions may only be applied to civilly committed patients (see, for instance, the example provided in Section 2.5).

In Chapter 5, the MHCA lays down special rules for the implementation of a criminal sentence involving compulsory mental health care. Such a sentence may only be handed down to a person who was psychotic at the time of the crime, and thus, according to criminal law, not guilty by reason of insanity. In this case, an additional forensic risk assessment is required.

The Chapter 6 of the MHCA contains important provisions relating to control and supervision as exercised by a special review board, the Control Commission. Chapter 7 contains a brief but important provision relating to speedy judicial review in the event that there is any deprivation of liberty (see Section 2.7).

The standard of mental health care has improved considerably over the last ten years. It has become more user-orientated, with out-patient services and municipality-based measures being implemented and refined. Out-patient clinics for child and adolescent psychiatric care have been further developed, and education and research within this field has been stimulated.

By itself, the MHCA provides only limited measures for meeting the qualitative goals of mental health care services. Health policy goals in this field are clearly distinguished from the regulation of patients' statutory rights, and the Act does not provide a claim-right to treatment.

The legal position of patients with mental disorders, who are not receiving treatment under the MHCA, is determined by their rights under the above-mentioned Patients' Rights Act, as well as under the Municipal Health Care Act, and the Specialized Health Services Act.

2.2 *Human rights. A general introduction*

There are a number of international conventions and recommendations with implications for the legal regulation of the mental health field. The European Convention on Human Rights of 1950 contains several important provisions, e.g. Article 3 (Prohibition against torture or inhuman or degrading treatment or punishment), Article 5 (Right to liberty and security of person), Article 6 (Right to a fair trial), and Article 8 (Right to respect for private and family life).

The Court of Human Rights in Strasbourg has dealt with more than 100 "Mental Disability Cases" based on petitions from psychiatric patients concerning breaches of their rights under the above-mentioned articles. The court has ruled in favour of the patient in just a few of these cases; more often than not on the basis of breaches of procedural regulations, not on the grounds of breaches of Articles 3 or 8.[8] So far, no decision has gone against Norway in Strasbourg in such a case.

The United Nations International Covenant on Civil and Political Rights of 1966 also contains relevant provisions in this field, e.g. Article 7 "In particular, no one shall be subjected without his free consent to medical or scientific experimentation"; Article 9 "Anyone who is deprived of his liberty by arrest or detention shall be entitled to take proceedings before a court, in order that that court may decide without delay on the lawfulness of his detention and order his release if the detention is not lawful"; and Article 10 "All persons deprived of their liberty shall be treated with humanity and with respect for the inherent dignity of the human person".

The Norwegian Supreme Court has passed judgment in four cases on the basis of the MHCA. Two judgments passed in 2001, the year the MHCA came into force, dealt with prerequisites for civil commitment. In both cases, the patient wished to be discharged from psychiatric care, claiming that these prerequisites had not been met. The other two Supreme Court judgments dealt with appeals concerning the procedure used when establishing civil commitment, particularly in comparison with the requirements laid down in the European Convention on Human Rights, Article 5. In three of these cases, the patient in question was not discharged. The fourth and successful case (for the patient) is described below, see Section 2.4.

There is no doubt that traditional Nordic Mental Health Legislation complies with the above-mentioned HR instruments.[9] Even if there are discrepancies between the Nordic Mental Health Acts, they are still tailored using the same pattern.[10]

However, there is an ongoing discussion about whether or not this legislation complies with more modern MR instruments, e.g. the Oviedo Convention (The Convention for the Protection of Human Rights and Dignity of the Human Being with regard to the Application of Biology and Medicine, or the Convention on Human Rights and Biomedicine). The Oviedo Convention has a special provision in Article 7 relating to the "Protection of persons who have a mental disorder":

> Subject to protective conditions prescribed by law, including supervisory, control and appeal procedures, a person who has a mental disorder of a serious nature may be subjected, without his or her consent, to an intervention aimed at treating his or her mental disorder only where, without such treatment, serious harm is likely to result to his or her health.

8 P. Bartlett, O. Lewis, and O. Thorold (2007), *Mental Disability and the European Convention on Human Rights.*

9 A. Syse, "Det menneskerettslige vernet mot frihetsberøvelse og tvang i behandlingsøyemed innenfor psykiatrien" [Human Rights as a safeguard for freedom and against coercion in psychiatry]. *Nordic Journal of Human Rights* 2006, Volume 24, pp. 318-342.

10 Syse and Nilstun 1997 (op. cit.).

Furthermore, there is no reason to deal too intensively with the Oviedo Convention as there are new and stricter, binding rules in the new Convention on the Rights of Persons with Disabilities, which will be the next topic.

2.3 *Convention on the Rights of Persons with Disabilities: A shift of paradigm?*

In 2001, the UN initiated a process of drafting a binding convention that would ensure the rights and dignity of persons with disabilities. This process continued without any unnecessary delays, and the preparatory papers were processed promptly from one year to the next. Global organizations representing the disabled were active participants during the state negotiations, in addition to operating to great effect within the different working groups in between general meetings.

The Convention on the Rights of Persons with Disabilities (CRPD) was unanimously adopted on 13 December 2006 at the United Nations Headquarters, and was opened for signature on 30 March 2007. There were 82 signatories to the Convention, 44 signatories to the Optional Protocol (an individual complaint procedure addressed to the relevant committee). This is the highest number of signatories in history to a UN Convention on its opening day. The CRPD is the first comprehensive human rights treaty of the 21st century and the first human rights convention to be open for signature by regional integration organizations. The Convention came into force on 3 May 2008.

> The CRPD has, per 1 February 2011, been ratified by 97 state parties, and there are 60 ratifications of the Optional Protocol.[11] Spain and Austria were the first two European countries to ratify.
>
> Amongst the Nordic countries, Sweden ratified both the Convention and the Protocol on 15 December 2008. Denmark ratified the Convention on 24 July 2009; however, neither country has signed or ratified the Protocol. Iceland and Finland have signed both the Convention and the Protocol, but ratified neither of them. Norway has signed the Convention, but not the Protocol, but has not yet ratified the Convention.

The main reason for Norway not having ratified the Convention is this country's legislation on guardianship, which is currently being modernized to comply with the CRPD. The other topic now being discussed is whether or not the Mental Health Act complies with the CRPD.

From the wording, it is quite clear that the CRDP includes persons with more permanent mental disorders; see Article 1, second paragraph:

> Persons with disabilities include those who have long-term physical, mental, intellectual or sensory impairments which in interaction with various barriers may hinder their full and effective participation in society on an equal basis with others.

11 An updated overview of the ratification processes is available at: www.un.org/disabilities/countries.asp?id=166.

The UN's Special Rapporteur on torture and other cruel, inhuman, or degrading treatment or punishment made the following statement in his 10th Report to the UN Assembly in July 2008:

> The recent entry into force of the Convention on the Rights of Persons with Disabilities and its Optional Protocol provides a timely opportunity to review the anti-torture framework in relation to persons with disabilities. By reframing violence and abuse perpetrated against persons with disabilities as torture or a form of ill-treatment, victims and advocates can be afforded stronger legal protection and redress for violations of human rights.

The Special Rapporteur finds the Convention relevant to protecting psychiatric patients from cruel, inhuman or degrading treatment. In the Report (part III), under the headline *Protecting persons with disabilities from torture*, the wordings are as follows:

> 40. Persons with disabilities are exposed to medical experimentation and intrusive and irreversible medical treatments without their consent (e.g. sterilization, abortion and interventions aiming to correct or alleviate a disability, such as electroshock treatment and mind-altering drugs including neuroleptics).
>
> 41. The Special Rapporteur is concerned that in many cases such practices, when perpetrated against persons with disabilities, remain invisible or are being justified, and are not recognized as torture or other cruel, inhuman or degrading treatment or punishment. The recent entry into force of the Convention on the Rights of Persons with Disabilities and its Optional Protocol provides a timely opportunity to review the anti-torture framework in relation to persons with disabilities.

In addition, the Rapporteur adds that it is against the principles laid down in the Convention as regards accepting involuntary treatment and involuntary confinement on the basis of a disability. All sorts of treatments must be based on valid consent. This is underpinned in the following way:

> 44. The Special Rapporteur notes that in relation to persons with disabilities, the Convention on the Rights of Persons with Disabilities complements other human rights instruments on the prohibition of torture and ill-treatment by providing further authoritative guidance. For instance, article 3 of the Convention proclaims the principle of respect for the individual autonomy of persons with disabilities and the freedom to make their own choices. Further, article 12 recognizes their equal right to enjoy legal capacity in all areas of life, such as deciding where to live and whether to accept medical treatment. In addition, article 25 recognizes that medical care of persons with disabilities must be based on their free and informed consent. Thus, in the case of earlier non-binding standards, such as the 1991 Principles for the Protection of Persons with Mental Illness and for

> the Improvement of Mental Health Care (resolution 46/119, annex), known as the MI Principles, the Special Rapporteur notes that the acceptance of involuntary treatment and involuntary confinement runs counter to the provisions of the Convention on the Rights of Persons with Disabilities.

The Special Rapporteur is also concerned as regards forced treatment:

> 63. Inside institutions, as well as in the context of forced outpatient treatment, psychiatric medication, including neuroleptics and other mind-altering drugs, may be administered to persons with mental disabilities without their free and informed consent or against their will, under coercion, or as a form of punishment. The administration in detention and psychiatric institutions of drugs, including neuroleptics that cause trembling, shivering and contractions and make the subject apathetic and dull his or her intelligence, has been recognized as a form of torture. In *Viana Acosta v. Uruguay*, the Human Rights Committee concluded that the treatment of the complainant, which included psychiatric experiments and forced injection of tranquillizers against his will, constituted inhuman treatment. The Special Rapporteur notes that forced and non-consensual administration of psychiatric drugs, and in particular of neuroleptics, for the treatment of a mental condition needs to be closely scrutinized. Depending on the circumstances of the case, the suffering inflicted and the effects upon the individual's health may constitute a form of torture or ill-treatment.

The Special Rapporteur also calls upon states to ratify the Convention on the Rights of Persons with Disabilities and ensure its full implementation, paying particular attention to the non-discrimination provision, Article 2 (No. 71). States must adopt legislation recognizing the legal capacity of persons with disabilities and must ensure that, where required, they are provided with the support needed to make informed decisions (No. 73). And his conclusion is:

> 76. The Special Rapporteur calls on relevant United Nations and regional human rights mechanisms, including those addressing individual complaints and conducting monitoring of places of detention, to take full account of the new standards contained in the Convention and integrate them in their work.

The UN High Commissioner for Human Rights has given an opinion along the same lines (Dignity and Justice for Detainees week, October 6-12, 2008):

> The Convention on the Rights of Persons with Disabilities (CRPD) states clearly that deprivation of liberty based on the existence of a disability is contrary to international human rights law, is intrinsically discriminatory, and is therefore unlawful. Such unlawfulness also extends to situations where additional grounds – such as the need for care, treatment and the safety of the person or the community – are used to justify deprivation of liberty.

> Under international human rights law, persons with disabilities are entitled to enjoy their rights to liberty and security on an equal basis with others, and can be lawfully deprived of their liberty only for the reasons, and in accordance with the procedures, that are applicable to other persons in the same jurisdiction.

Such well-defined statements make it clear that the CRPD may demand extensive alterations to the Nordic legislation within the field of psychiatry. On the other hand, Sweden ratified the Convention without even discussing this question. Denmark has ratified the CRPD, and one of the five European members on the Committee on the Rights of Persons with Disabilities (twenty elected members in all) is Danish.

It will be mandatory for this Committee, either by means of a general comment or when scrutinizing actual state reports, to clarify whether or not the Nordic – and European – way of regulating the field of psychiatry complies with the Convention.

On the *website* of the CRPD[12], the following statement temporarily underpins the paradigm shift:

> The Convention marks a "paradigm shift" in attitudes and approaches to persons with disabilities. It takes to a new height the movement from viewing persons with disabilities as "objects" of charity, medical treatment and social protection towards viewing persons with disabilities as "subjects" with rights, who are capable of claiming those rights and making decisions for their lives based on their free and informed consent as well as being active members of society.
>
> The Convention is intended as a human rights instrument with an explicit, social development dimension. It adopts a broad categorization of persons with disabilities and reaffirms that all persons with all types of disabilities must enjoy all human rights and fundamental freedoms. It clarifies and qualifies how all categories of rights apply to persons with disabilities and identifies areas where adaptations have to be made for persons with disabilities to effectively exercise their rights and areas where their rights have been violated, and where protection of rights must be reinforced.

It is still not clear whether or not ratifying the CRPD necessitates making significant alterations to Norwegian mental health legislation. However, even if the quotations above are made in a "handicap-friendly" language, they are not official statements with any kind of binding effect on the State parties to the convention, or on general public international law.

Thus, only more official statements by the Committee will make the legal situation clearer. However, such statements by the Committee will not even be binding, in general terms, or on the state in question.

12 www.un.org/disabilities/default.asp?id=150

2.4 Conditions for compulsory mental health care

The most important decision, according to the MHCA, is the decision to carry out civil commitment, which entails depriving the patient of liberty; in principle, for an unlimited period of time if certain prerequisites are met. In such cases, compulsory mental health care may be established, more often than not in a hospital setting, but also in terms of a community treatment order.

The conditions for committing a patient are listed in the MHCA, Section 3-3, first paragraph, and numbered 1-6. They read as follows:

1. Voluntary mental health care has been tried, to no avail, or it is obviously pointless to try this.
2. The patient has been examined by two physicians, one of whom shall be independent of the responsible institution, cf. section 3-1.
3. The patient is suffering from a serious mental disorder and application of compulsory mental health care is necessary to prevent the person concerned from either
    a. having the prospects of his or her health being restored or significantly improved considerably reduced, or it is highly probable that the condition of the person concerned will significantly deteriorate in the very near future, or
    b. constituting an obvious and serious risk to his or her own life and health or those of others on account of his or her mental disorder.
4. The institution is professionally and materially capable of offering the patient satisfactory treatment and care and has been approved in accordance with Section 3-5.
5. The patient has been given the opportunity to state his or her opinion, cf. Section 3-9.
6. Even though the stipulations of the Act have otherwise been met, compulsory mental health care may only be applied when, following overall assessment, this clearly appears to be the best solution for the person concerned, unless he or she constitutes an obvious and serious risk to the life or health of others. When making the assessment, special emphasis shall be placed on how great a strain compulsory intervention will put on the person concerned.

Before a decision about civil commitment can be made, two medical examinations must be carried out; one prior to admission by a physician who is unconnected with the responsible institution, and one after arrival at the institution, cf. Point 2.

Point 1 states that coercion may be used only when "voluntary mental health care has been tried, to no avail, or it is obviously pointless to try this". This is intended to avoid unnecessary coercion. Furthermore, patients must be given the opportunity to state their opinion, cf. Point 5, and the institution concerned must be professionally and materially capable of offering the patient satisfactory treatment and care, cf. Point 4.

The most fundamental requirements are stipulated in Point 3, which states that the patient must be suffering from "a serious mental disorder". However, such a disorder is not a sufficient reason for hospitalization. At least one of the additional requirements under Point 3a (improvement) and/or 3b (dangerous risk) must be met. These two important requirements (serious mental disorder, need for treatment and/or dangerous risk) were interpreted in the above-mentioned Supreme Court judgments. A further important provision in Section 3-3 of the Act is Point 6, which calls for an overall assessment whereby special emphasis shall be placed on how great a strain compulsory intervention would put on the person concerned.

In one of the Supreme Court judgments from 2001, the patient was discharged on the basis of this overall assessment, even though all the other conditions were found to have been met. The patient was an elderly man, obviously actively psychotic, without a realistic view of life outside of the hospital setting, where he had lived for 16 years. However, the Supreme Court found that the patient, following overall assessment, deserved the opportunity to "try a life of freedom", even though he most probably would soon relapse into circumstances necessitating readmission.

A civil commitment decision should be made by a specially-appointed mental health professional, a psychiatrist, or a specialist in psychology, who must have examined the patient personally.

The patient, and their next of kin, can appeal against such a decision to the Control Commission (see Section 2.7).

2.5 *Implementation of in-patient care*

The Chapter 4 of the MHCA contains a number of sections regulating the use of coercive measures during the implementation of mental health care. These are Sections 4-3 on segregation or seclusion, 4-5 on restrictions to contact with the outside world, 4-6 on the inspection of rooms, possessions and body searches, 4-7 on seizures, 4-7a on urine samples, and 4-8 on the use of coercive measures during in-patient care. Furthermore, Section 4-4 on treatment without the patient's consent, contains provisions regulating forced medication and, in the case of a serious eating disorder, the administration of nutrition to a patient without his/her consent (see Section 2.6).

The provisions regulating compulsory interference in mental health care are systematized in roughly the same way: The section starts with an introductory paragraph setting out the patient's rights, followed by one or more paragraphs stating the conditions under which these rights may be restricted. This is followed by provisions stating that a decision is a requirement in the implementation of such limitations, along with rules for appealing against decisions and the complaints/appeals procedure. The section concludes by giving the authority the assignment of issuing further regulations for the purpose of laying down more detailed rules governing the examination and treatment of patients without their consent.

The use of coercion must always remain within the framework of the provisions protecting personal integrity enshrined in the above-mentioned human rights conventions and specified in Section 4-2 of the MHCA. Section 4-1 of the Act contains a provision stating that patients undergoing mental health care, who require prolonged and coordinated services, are entitled to an individual plan.

The discussion below is limited to the provisions of Section 4-4 of the Act, relating to treatment without the patient's consent.

2.6 Treatment without the patient's consent

Right up until the beginning of the 1980s, it was generally the case that patients undergoing compulsory mental health care could be subjected to a range of compulsory care measures when this was considered necessary, either in order to prevent injury or because this would improve the treatment outcome. During this period, a number of invasive forms of treatment were in use, e.g. electroconvulsive therapy and other shock therapies, and brain surgery (lobotomy). None of these interventions was based on sufficient medical evidence and they are currently regarded to be obsolete. Additionally, patients were rarely given adequate information and/or asked to consent. Antipsychotic drugs, with often irreversible side-effects, were administered on a compulsory basis over many years without authorization for this in the legislation. Provisions regulating the use of compulsory medication were not implemented until 1984

Over the last 25 years, a much greater emphasis has been placed upon the benefit of patients' participating in their treatment, cf. Section 3-1 of the Patients' Rights Act, which also applies to mental health care. However, the preparatory work for the MHCA declares that the introduction of effective psychiatric drugs has undoubtedly represented progress, making it possible to treat serious psychotic disorders more effectively and with less harm to patients. A number of judicial decisions by the Supreme Court have also reflected the same positive attitude towards compulsory medication.

Compulsory medical treatment may only be implemented by using registered drugs in commonly-used doses, and only when these are presumed to have a favourable effect clearly outweighing the disadvantages of any side-effects. One problem is that, usually, the physician (and not the patient) is the one who makes this important assessment, and who also makes the decision on this basis.

Under Section 4-4 of the MHCA, a patient undergoing compulsory mental health care may be subjected to "such examination and treatment as is clearly in accordance with professionally recognized psychiatric standards". This means that self-admitted patients, and patients compulsorily admitted solely for observation, may not be subjected to compulsory medical treatment. Furthermore, "no examination or treatment entailing a serious intervention may be carried out unless the patient consents". However, in the following sentence, it is stated that a patient may be treated with medicines, e.g. anti-psychotic drugs, without his/her consent.

In 2007, a separate regulation was introduced into Section 4-4 stating that nutrition may be given without consent when treating a patient with a serious eating disorder, provided this is considered absolutely necessary.

2.7 *Appeals*

The appeal body for most coercive measures is the Control Commission; there are currently more than 50 local commissions in Norway. Each commission consists of four members and is chaired by a lawyer (see the MHCA, Chapter 6). Of the other three members, one must be a physician, and one a member of an organization representing psychiatric patients or their family members, or an appointed spokesman for psychiatric patients. The fourth member should be a layman.

When a patient is committed, he/she, the closest relative, or the patient's guardian, may appeal against the decision to the Control Commission. The refusal of an application to be discharged during the stay may also be brought before the Commission. In such instances, the Commission has the authority to discharge the patient, even against the superintendent's assessment of what is best for that patient. In these circumstances, a meeting of the four members of the Commission is held, at which the patient and the patient's lawyer, on the one hand, and the hospital, on the other, get the opportunity to express their views as to why compulsory care should, or should not, continue. After this exchange of views, the Commission concludes its discussion about the case in a separate room and makes its decision.

If the Commission decides against the patient, he/she may bring the case to court. The court procedures are the same for all administrative compulsory decisions under the MHCA, under the Communicable Diseases Act, and under the Chapter 4A amendment.[13]

These procedures are quite favourable towards persons subjected to administrative coercion. The proceedings are free-of-charge to the person concerned; the person is entitled to free legal aid and representation; the case must be expedited; and

13 The same court procedure is also mandatory for administrative decisions entailing the use of coercion according to the Children Welfare Act, and the Social Welfare Act.

the court should assess all aspects of the case in full, including whether or not it is in the patient's best interest to "try a life of freedom" (see Section 2.4).

3 The Communicable Diseases Act

3.1 Objectives of the Act

The Communicable Diseases Act (CDA) has three main purposes. First, it gives health authorities a legal basis for taking steps to protect the population from communicable diseases by preventing their occurrence, controlling their spread, and preventing them from either being introduced into Norway or propagated from Norway to other countries. The government's recommended vaccination programme for children, which is free-of-charge, is one such measure.

Second, the Act provides health and other authorities with the necessary legal instruments to coordinate their efforts and control communicable diseases. When it is necessary to prevent the occurrence or spread of a communicable disease hazardous to public health, municipalities may decide to prohibit meetings and gatherings, or impose other limitations to social contact wherever people are assembled. The Council may also close public establishments such as day-care centres, schools, swimming pools, or airports, or impose limitations to their activities in order to stop or curtail the spread of disease, as well as order private or public establishments to clean, disinfect, or destroy objects or even entire premises. In the event of a serious outbreak of a hazardous communicable disease, and when the swift implementation of measures can prevent the disease from spreading, the Norwegian Directorate of Health can make decisions which apply to either the whole or part of the country.

Third, the CDA is intended to safeguard the legal rights of individuals who are affected by steps taken under the act. This is of particular interest because the health authorities may decide that a person suspected of being infected with a communicable disease should be hospitalized involuntarily for the purpose of a medical examination and/or short-term isolation (see Section 3.2).

3.2 Coercive measures regarding individual patients

If an infected person objects to isolation, and if other measures that could prevent the occurrence or spread of the disease have been tried without success, the person may be placed in isolation in a hospital for up to three weeks without his/her consent. The term of isolation may be extended for a period of up to six weeks within a time limit of one year from the initial decision. In the event of an extension of the isolation period, it may be decided to implement compulsory drug therapy when this could significantly reduce the term of isolation. Compulsory drug therapy may only be implemented when it can render an infected person non-infectious, and involves limited risk and/or merely minor discomfort.

Generally, persons infected with a hazardous communicable disease are grateful when receiving treatment for their disease and willing to provide the information necessary to prevent further spreading. Therefore, the provisions of the Act for the use of isolation and other coercive actions are seldom used, as there are only a few involuntary hospitalizations each year for persons with hazardous communicable diseases.

There has been no discussion concerning the human rights aspects of this legislation. It conforms to the European Convention on Human Rights, Article 5. This article enables, amongst other things, "the lawful detention of persons for the prevention of the spreading of infectious diseases".

Persons in a position to spread hazardous communicable diseases normally modify their behaviour, and the penal code otherwise prescribes strong remedies if persons intentionally try to spread such diseases. These provisions in the penal code are being discussed these days because the spreading of – or exposing another person to the risk of being infected with – a communicable disease is a criminal act. This applies even in the case of the valid consent of an informed person vis-à-vis the possibility of acquiring HIV, hepatitis, or another communicable disease, e.g. a sex partner or the sharer of a jointly-used needle when injecting drugs.

3.3 *Decisions and appeals*

Administrative decisions regarding coercive treatment under the CDA should be made by an administrative board, the Board for Communicable Diseases, comprising three members – a judge, a doctor, and a layman. In acute cases, the decision may be made by the Chief Medical Superintendent of the municipality. The Board for Communicable Diseases then becomes an appeal board.

The board's decisions may in turn be put before the courts by means of a fast-track procedure when trying administrative coercive decisions in the health and social fields of law (see Section 2.7).

4 The Chapter 4A amendment to the Patients' Rights Act

4.1 *Objectives of the Act*

While the provisions of the Communicable Diseases and Mental Health Care Acts are based on prior provisions and older legislation, Chapter 4A of the Patients' Rights Act represents a new principle in Norwegian health law, coming into force 1 January 2009, enabling the provision of *somatic* healthcare, including dental services, to patients *opposing* such care. The implementation of psychiatric care against the patient's will is subject to the provisions of the Mental Health Care Act.

The measures in Chapter 4A are restricted to persons not competent to make valid decisions, e.g. elderly persons with dementia, persons with serious learning disabilities, and patients who are confused due to mental illness.

The purpose of Chapter 4A is to provide essential care which is necessary to prevent serious deterioration and significant harm to a patient's health. In addition, such regulations also intend to prevent and limit the use of coercion through detailed material and procedural prerequisites.

In 2006, after years of preparatory work, the government submitted a Bill to the Norwegian parliament to amend the Patients' Rights Act. As already mentioned, Chapter 4A came into force in 2009.

During the preparatory work, there was some discussion about whether or not such an amendment would conflict with human rights obligations. The critique was mainly of a procedural nature. In the preparatory papers, the entitlement to make treatment decisions was originally to have been given to health personnel (mainly doctors, dentists, and nurses), with almost no formalities. In the end, all treatment decisions under Chapter 4A are now scrutinized by the Boards of Health Supervision of the counties (see Section 4.3). In addition, the substantive prerequisites are restricted to situations where failure to provide health care would lead to *significant harm* to the patient's health, and where the healthcare is deemed to be *necessary* (see Section 4.2).

If applied correctly, the result is that decisions under Chapter 4A will ensure that patients *opposing* somatic health care will still receive treatment in line with patients who have an intact mental capacity and who would normally appreciate such health care. This is a kind of "mild paternalism", as opposed to "strong paternalism", which may be the case for coercion applied under the MHCA and the CDA.[14]

> Placing a patient with serious dementia in a nursing home without his/her consent may thus be lawful under Chapter 4A, and similarly under the European Convention, as demonstrated in the case of H.M. v. Switzerland (no. 39187/98). The European Court of Human Rights noted that the applicant (H.M., a pensioner) had been given the opportunity to receive care in her own home, but that she and her son had refused to co-operate. She complained, claiming that she had been unlawfully deprived of her liberty, in that Article 5 (1) (e) of the Convention only cites "vagrancy", and not neglect, as grounds for detention. She contended that she did not meet the conditions of vagrancy, as, at the time of her placement, she had a home and was receiving a pension.
>
> The Court concluded that the applicant's placement in the nursing home was a responsible measure taken by the competent authorities in the applicant's own interest, in order to provide her with the necessary medical care and adequate living conditions. It did not, therefore, amount to a deprivation of liberty within the meaning of Article 5 (1). Finding that this Article was not applicable, the Court held, by six votes to one, that there had been no violation of Article 5(1).

14 Syse and Nilstun 1997, op. cit.

If a patient who is not competent to grant valid consent in practice agrees to a proposed healthcare measure, the regulations in Chapter 4A will not apply. A lack of protest is thus taken as tacit or implied consent, making it legal for health personnel to commence treatment. However, if it is clear and evident that an unprotesting patient does not understand what is going on, the medical supervisor may make a treatment decision, presenting this decision to the patient and his/her nearest relative and then entering it into the patient's medical record.

Chapter 4A applies to a protesting patient who is not competent to make healthcare decisions. Then, the provider of the actual health care (a doctor, a dentist, a nurse etc.) must make a special treatment decision according to the procedural rules stated in the chapter.

If a patient who is fully competent to make healthcare decisions objects to medical treatment, such treatment may only be given in cases of emergency, or under extraordinary circumstances.

> In 2010, the Norwegian Supreme Court ruled on an exceptional case where a competent, but stubborn, patient of a municipal nursing home rejected all normal hygienic measures. He was against his bedclothes being washed and changed, and that he should wash, at least now and then. The nurses were not even allowed to change old and ill-smelling bandages on his infected sores, which were medically indicated. As he was mentally competent, the regulation in Chapter 4A was not applicable. [15]
>
> The majority (three judges out of five) ruled that the nursing home could set such conditions for its patients. As there were no alternative forms of care outside the actual nursing home, the judges enabled the use of force, albeit limited to necessary and gentle hygienic measures. The two dissenting judges ruled that, since there was no legislation underpinning such extraordinary care, the nursing home was not permitted to carry out hygienic measures without the patient's consent, due to the principal of legality.

4.2 Use of Chapter 4A

In its year of implementation (2009), the Boards of Health Supervision of the counties, which must obtain a copy of all such treatment decisions, received 1,687 notifications, fewer than 200 of which warranted further investigation. It is estimated that the number of notifications will be approximately the same in 2010.

Healthcare delivered to a protesting patient must be provided in such a way as to assure respect for that patient's physical and mental integrity. Healthcare treatments should, if possible, be minimally invasive, recognize the patient's right to self-determination, and be delivered in accord with the presumed will of the patient.

15 The case is referred to in Norsk Retstidende (Rt.) 2010, p. 612.

Prior to administering care to objecting patients, health professionals must attempt to gain those patients' confidence in order to avoid their protesting, unless such an attempt obviously appears pointless. If patients continue to object to the actual care, or if health personnel know that a patient is likely to maintain his/her objection, an administrative decision may be made to provide the relevant healthcare if, and only if, the following three prerequisites are met:

i) failure to provide health care may lead to *significant harm* to the patient's health,
ii) the care to be provided is deemed *necessary*, and
iii) the measures are *proportional* to the need for health care.

Even when these three conditions are met, diagnostic procedures, treatment, and other care may only be implemented if this clearly appears to be the best solution for the patient following overall assessment.

When assessing whether or not to implement such care, importance must be attached to, *inter alia*, the degree of objection and whether or not the patient may be expected to regain his/her competence to consent in the near future.

The Boards of Health Supervision of the counties, which must obtain a copy of all such treatment decisions, should – as instructed to by the Health Supervision Directorate – look into each and every one of the notifications. If the use of force seems to be unjustifiable, for medical reasons, or hard to justify through ethical reasoning, e.g. seemingly disproportionate, this will call for further investigation.

4.3 *Appeals*

Administrative decisions regarding health care under Section 4A-5 may be appealed against to the Board of Health Supervision in the relevant county, either by the patient or the patient's next of kin. In 2009, seven such complaints were filed, one of which was accepted.

One obvious problem with the appeal system is when the patient has already been found incompetent to make valid decisions, e.g. elderly persons with dementia. Therefore, there are problems associated with the patients making such complaints themselves. Additionally, the next-of-kin may be so relieved sometimes that their mother or father is being taken care of by healthcare providers that they are reluctant to use the complaints procedure. Therefore, the main instrument for avoiding the misuse of these provisions is control and investigation by the Boards of Health Supervision of the counties.

The Board's decision may in turn be brought before the courts using a fast-track procedure for trying administrative coercive decisions (see Section 2.7).

5 Summary

The issue of the use of coercion clearly demonstrates one of the most fundamental ethical and medical dilemmas in health law: Should a patient be allowed to act against what seems to be his/her best interests, or should health personnel be entitled to intercede in a paternalistic manner? In such cases, there is a conflict of values. On the one hand, the patient's right to self-determination and respect for his/her integrity is essential. On the other hand, the principles of beneficence and non-maleficence are of the utmost importance.

The paternalistic approach is often supported by the view that patients with a serious mental disorder, or without the competence to consent, should not be entitled to object to treatment which is assessed to be in their own best interest. However, this position is increasingly being challenged; patients are increasingly becoming entitled to a voice and a choice[16], and there should be more symmetry in the right to accept treatment and the right to refuse it.[17]

At the same time, health legislation is intended not only to promote the best interests of an individual but also to protect the community. In some cases, the two aims are irreconcilable. The dilemma of when to use coercion – and when not to use it – puts a severe strain not only on the patient, but also on the patient's family, and on the health professionals involved.

The regulations governing the use of coercion in health law were agreed upon after weighing the relevant values and principles against one another. The individual health professional may not make an independent decision to diverge from these regulations, except in an acute emergency. However, not all the rules are equally clear and many remain open to, or require, professional assessment in order to be accurately applied. Thus, the use of coercion continues to be a challenging area from a medical, ethical, and legal perspective.

As underscored in the text, there are possibilities that human rights instruments, e.g. the CRDP, may interfere in an unexpected way with states' traditional right to regulate the field of health law, especially the mental health legislation. Up until now, states have to a certain degree had legal possibilities for allowing health personnel to decide to act in a paternalistic way when this is in the "patient's best interest", even when the person in question neither wants nor likes the intervention. Such regulations may in the future be in conflict with binding UN conventions.

16 A. Syse (2007), *Psykisk helsevernloven med kommentarer [The Mental Health Act: a Commentary]*, 2. rev. ed., and A. Syse (2009), *Pasientrettighetsloven med kommentarer [The Patients Rights' Act: a Commentary]*, 3. rev. ed.

17 Nilstun and Syse 2000, op. cit.

References

P. Bartlett, O. Lewis, and O. Thorold (2007), *Mental Disability and the European Convention on Human Rights*, Leiden.

G. Høyer, L. Kjellin, M. Engberg, K. Riittakerttu, T. Nilstun, M. Sigurdjonsdottir, and A. Syse (2002), "Paternalism and autonomy: A presentation of a Nordic Study on the use of coercion in the mental health care system". *International Journal of Law and Psychiatry* 2002, Volume 25, pp. 93-108.

O. Molven and J. Ferkis, eds. (2011), *Healthcare, Welfare and Law. Health Legislation as a Mirror of the Norwegian Welfare State*, Oslo.

T. Nilstun and A. Syse (2000), "The right to accept and the right to refuse". *Acta Psychiatrica Scandinavica* 2000; (suppl. 399), pp. 31-34.

A. Syse. (2007), *Psykisk helsevernloven med kommentarer [The Mental Health Act: a Commentary]*, 2. rev. ed., Oslo.

A. Syse. (2009), *Pasientrettighetsloven med kommentarer [The Patients Rights' Act: a Commentary]*, 3. rev. ed., Oslo.

A. Syse (2006), "Det menneskerettslige vernet mot frihetsberøvelse og tvang i behandlingsøyemed innenfor psykiatrien" [Human Rights as a safeguard for freedom and against coercion in psychiatry]. *Nordic Journal of Human Rights* 2006; Volume 24, pp. 318-342.

A. Syse and T. Nilstun (1997), "Ulike regler – lik lovforståelse? Om tvangsregulering, tvangsbruk og verdikonflikter i nordisk psykiatri" [Coercion in Nordic Psychiatry: Different rules – not that different practices]. *Tidsskrift for Rettsvitenskap* 1997, pp. 837-918.

Detention of Pregnant Women to Protect the Foetus – Nordic Perspectives[1]

By Professor Karl Harald Søvig, University of Bergen[2]

1 Introduction

It is well known that the use of alcohol or other substances during pregnancy may be harmful to the foetus; such risks are mentioned even in the Bible.[3] The most common intoxicating substance used by expectant mothers is alcohol, which can cause FAS (Fetal Alcohol Syndrome). The prevalence of FAS is about 1-2 per 1,000 births,[4] but estimates vary and there is no educated guess regarding the Nordic countries.[5] Children can also contract less severe health problems caused by their mothers' alcohol consumption during pregnancy, and Fetal Alcohol Spectrum Disorders (FASD) has been introduced as a common term for the diversity of negative health consequences which may be caused by alcohol consumption during pregnancy.[6] Substances containing narcotics,[7] both prescription and illegal drugs, can also be harmful to the foetus, but not to the same extent as alcohol. The negative health impact can occur even during the early stages of pregnancy. Thus, public health advice

1 Thanks to Janne Rothmar Herrmann, Anna Leppo, Klaus Mäkelä and Therese Reitan for their provision of useful information and interesting discussions when preparing this paper.

2 Karl Harald Søvig is professor of law, University of Bergen. His research has focused on different forms of coercive measures within the welfare state, as well as rights of children and he is currently working on a project on "Provision of welfare to irregular migrants" funded by the Norwegian Research Council. He has previously served as temporary judge at the district and high court.

3 The Book of Judges, 13:7.

4 P.A. May and J.P. Gossage, 'Estimating the Prevalence of Fetal Alcohol Syndrome: A summary', 25:3 *Alcohol Research and Health* (2001), pp. 159–167.

5 For a discussion on the possible overestimation of prevalence, see K. Mäkelä, 'The cost of Fetal Alcohol Spectrum Disorder', 27:4 *Nordics Studies in Alcohol and Drugs* (2010), pp. 327–333.

6 R.J. Sokol et al., 'Fetal alcohol spectrum disorder', 290:22 *Journal of the American Medical Association* (2003), pp. 2996–2999. FASD, unlike FAS, is not itself a diagnostic term.

7 Research into the subject is usually published with regard to the different substances, and references are not made here.

given in the Nordic countries to pregnant women is abstinence during pregnancy.[8]

Health injuries to children due to the expectant mother's use of intoxicating substances are therefore a significant health problem in most Western countries, although uncertainties exist regarding their prevalence. The Nordic countries are no exception, but a distinctive feature here has been discussions about solving these challenges using coercive measures against the pregnant women. As far as I am aware, Norway is the only country in Europe which has introduced legislation authorizing the deprivation of the liberty of the pregnant women in order to protect the foetus. This contribution will analyze the current Norwegian legislation and the ongoing debate in the other Nordic countries.

There are a variety of terms and concepts in the field. The basic point of legal departure in all Nordic jurisdictions is the principle of 'autonomy' or 'self-determination'.[9] Therefore, the admission to health institutions of addicted patients is, as a general rule, based on informed consent. Under some provisions, admission can be carried out by means of a decision without consent, thereby depriving the concerned person of his/her liberty; a coercive measure. A special feature in Norway and Denmark is admission based on informed consent combined with the possibility of later detention based on the patients' previous consent (the 'Ulysses contract').[10]

In the legal texts, the person concerned is usually described as what can be translated as a 'substance or drug abuser'. Preferred terms due to the lack of stigmatization – and also more in keeping with the systems of medical classification – would be 'substance abuser' or 'drug dependent',[11] but the latter term may cause confusion since it departs from the legal texts. Additionally, a pregnant woman's behaviour may cause harm to the foetus without her being addicted to substances. Thus, I will normally use the terms 'substance abuser' and 'pregnant woman'.

There is an important interplay between substantial, procedural and organizational rules – in addition to the allocation of financial and staff resources – which

8 Denmark: <www.sst.dk/Sundhed%20og%20forebyggelse/Graviditet/Anbefalinger%20til%20gravide.aspx>; Finland: <www.groups.stakes.fi/LAPE/FI/Vauva/index.htm> (the booklet "Meille tulee vauva", also available in Swedish and English); Iceland: <www.lydheilsustod.is/media/afengi/utgefid//1209_Stuttur_utdrattur_-_Afengi-_og_vimuefni_enska.pdf>; Norway: <www.helsedirektoratet.no/gravid/leve_sunt/alkohol/graviditet_og_alkohol_740894>; Sweden: <www.fhi.se/Vart-uppdrag/Barns-och-ungas-halsa/Aktuellt/Alkoholbruk---effekt-pa-foster/>, all visited May 18 2011. For an analysis of the official recommendations on alcohol use during pregnancy in Sweden and Finland, see A. Leppo and D. Hecksher, 'The rise of the total abstinence model', 28:1 *Nordic Studies on Alcohol and Drugs* (2011), pp. 7–27.

9 See H.S. Aasen, 'Dignity and Human Rights in a Modern Welfare State', in H.S. Aasen et al. (eds), *Human Rights, Dignity and Autonomy in Health Care and Social Services* (Intersentia, Antwerp, 2009), pp. 64–67.

10 Named after the hero of Homer's epic poem The Odyssey. Ulysses had himself bound to the mast of his ship to be able to listen to the song of the sirens. On different forms of pre-commitment, see J. Elster, *Ulysses unbound* (Cambridge, Cambridge University Press, 2000). See also T. Tannsjo, *Coercive Care: The Ethics of Choice in Health and Medicine* (New York, Routledge, 1999), pp. 132–134.

11 The *International Statistical Classification of Diseases and Related Health Problems 10th Revision (ICD-10)* by the *World Health Organization* uses 'Mental and behavioural disorders due to psychoactive substance use' as the heading of chapter F, and 'Acute intoxication', 'Harmful use' and 'Dependence syndrome' are amongst the sub categories.

tends to end up in the background of legal analysis. This contribution is no exception, and the focus will be on substantial provisions, although attention will also be paid to procedural rules. In the final part, I will also try to touch on some aspects of the totality of the system, without attempting a comprehensive discussion.

2 Concurring interests

The starting point for the discussion should be the principle of autonomy for the women concerned, which includes the right to make decisions which are not in line with what other members of society, or the authorities, would recommend. However, autonomy is linked with the ability to make decisions based on rational considerations. A special feature of the women concerned is the influence of alcohol or other substances, affecting their ability to make decisions both on their own behalf and on behalf of the foetus. In addition, the interests of the foetus must be considered. In others situations, if a member of society poses a risk to another member,[12] the state may intervene, either to avoid harm in the form of preventative measures, or by criminal sanctions when negative consequences have occurred. In some cases, the state may even be obligated to intervene.[13] Having said this, it is important to emphasize the foetus' unique position as an integrated part of the pregnant woman's body. In this contribution, it is impossible to make an in-depth analysis of the relationship between the foetus and the pregnant woman, but some points should be underlined. In most Western countries, there is tension between protective measures and the abortion issue. Women can, during the initial stage of pregnancy, by having an abortion, prevent further development of the foetus; in later stages, such an intervention may be carried out following a decision by a doctor or a panel. It can be argued that, since society has given women the right to abort, the authorities cannot impose restrictive measures upon her at the same time[14]; however, in my view, this is not a convincing argument. An abortion will terminate further development of the foetus, while substance use during pregnancy may affect the health of the future child and cause lifelong, severe injuries. The foetus is normally protected by society from harm caused by others, and abortion is to be considered the exception rather than the main rule.

The foetus is a *casus sui generis*, and may be seen as a subject in need of relative protection whereby different considerations must be made in different situations. In my view, the possibility of abortion does not rule out intervention during the same period to protect injuries that may occur after birth.

12 The division between intervention to protect the citizens from harming others and themselves is often linked to John Stuart Mill, see J.S. Mill, *On Liberty* (People's edition: London, Longmans, Green Reader, and Dyer, 1872), p. 6.

13 See below with references to ECHR in note 36.

14 See D. Mathieu, *Preventing Prenatal Harm. Should the State Intervene?* (Washington, Georgetown University Press, 2. edn, 1996) suggesting that women have more extensive obligations towards the foetus when the possibility of self determined abortion is no longer open to them.

The two main subjects of this problem are the expectant mother and the foetus, but the interests of the father-to-be will also be assessed. He is a potential agent for the interests of the foetus. In addition, he also has his own interests as a prospective parent. Both these arguments could lead to the conclusion that he should be a part of the process. On the other hand, society has a responsibility to resolve conflicts of interest, like those between the woman and the foetus, and can, in this respect, act in the foetus' interests. The father-to-be still has his own interests as a future parent, but I am reluctant to offer him a legal role in the conflict under discussion here.

The discussions above are all of an ideological nature. In addition, more pragmatic aspects are to be considered, whereby the impact of the argument depends on the effect which would seem to occur in practice. The existence of a coercive measure can deter pregnant women from seeking health care, especially if health personnel are obligated to inform the welfare authorities of substance-abusing pregnant women (like in Norway). Another pragmatic consideration may arise regarding abortion. Facing a potential deprivation of liberty, women may choose to terminate their pregnancies to prevent detention (if this is within the statutory time limit for self-determined and committee-approved abortion). However, this argument is also partly ideological, due to the link with the abortion issue. Which outcome is considered the most undesirable will depend on one's own personal views on abortion.

A complicating factor in this discussion is estimating the health risks to the future child. Uncertainty will normally always surround substance use by pregnant woman, both as regards type and quantity. Medical knowledge of the causality between substance use during pregnancy and health risks is limited. In addition, risks are normally estimated for the pregnancy as *a whole*, while what is needed when considerations are to be made on the deprivation of liberty, is knowledge of the risks associated with continued substance use for *the rest* of the pregnancy.

3 Limitations and obligations under human rights

3.1 Introduction

As stated, there are three actors in this field; the woman, the foetus, and the child. They can all be protected by human rights, with the overall responsibility for balancing competing interests and avoiding violations resting with the state.

Of special interest in this section will be the UN Covenant on Civil and Political Rights (CCPR),[15] the UN Convention on the Rights of the Child (CRC)[16], and the Convention for the Protection of Human Rights and Fundamental Freedoms by the Council of Europe (ECHR).[17] These have all been incorporated into Norwe-

15 General Assembly resolution 2200A (XXI), 16 December 1966.

16 General Assembly resolution 44/25, 20 November 1989.

17 4 November 1950 (CETS No. 5).

gian law through the Human Rights Act (1999), which implements five human rights conventions and gives them supremacy over concurring statutory legislation.[18] Although there are differences in the formal status of these conventions in the Nordic Countries,[19] they all play a significant role within Nordic jurisprudence.

3.2 Protection of liberty

The right to liberty is protected both by ECHR Article 5 and by CCPR Article 9 (and CRC Article 37 if the detainee is a minor). The former will be focused on here due to the development through case law from the European Court of Human Rights (ECtHR). Article 5(1) lays down the general rule that everyone has the right to liberty. The exceptions to this are to be found in Article 5(1) a–f. The relevant exception is Article 5(1) e, which allows the detention of "alcoholics or drug addicts". There have only been a few cases of this type before the ECtHR, but the case law relating to the alternative "persons of unsound mind" is considerable. According to the Court's case law, principles that have evolved with regard to "persons of unsound mind" will also be relevant to the other alternative (and vice versa).[20]

The leading case concerning "alcoholics" was *Litwa* v. *Poland*. One of the main issues here was whether or not the exception for the detention of "alcoholics" was applicable to individuals who were temporarily intoxicated by alcohol but not suffering from a permanent drinking problem.[21] The majority came to the conclusion that the term "alcoholics" also includes persons whose "conduct and behaviour under the influence of alcohol pose a threat to public order or themselves".[22] This approach was followed up in *Hafsteinsdóttir* v. *Iceland*. The crux of the matter was whether or not Icelandic legislation concerning detention in police custody for disturbing the peace while under the influence of alcohol was of sufficient quality to meet the requirement of "lawfulness" in Article 5.[23] The Court stressed the lack of a precise statutory framework or case law regarding the duration of the detention, answering the question in the negative.

The cases show that there are no sharp distinctions between the terms "alcohol-

---

18 Besides CCPR, CRC and ECHR, the UN Covenant of Social, Economic and Cultural Rights (16 December 1966) and the UN Convention on the Elimination of All Forms of Discrimination against Women (18 December 1979) have been incorporated via this Act (Lov om styrking av menneskerettighetenes stilling i norsk rett, "menneskerettsloven"), 21 May 1999 No. 30. It should be added that the supremacy is not limited to the wording of the conventions, but includes the interpretations made by the supervisory bodies.

19 For discussions regarding judicial review in the Nordic Countries, under international influence, see different contributions in: 27:2 *Nordic Journal of Human Rights* (2009), pp. 131-303.

20 *Hutchison Reid* v. *UK*, 20 February 2003, ECHR, no. 50272/99, *Reports of Judgments and Decisions* 2003-IV, para. 51 and *Hafsteinsdóttir* v. *Iceland*, 8 June 2004, ECHR, no. 40905/98, unreported, para. 51.

21 In lack of cases addressing the criterion 'drug addicts', the same approach as in the Litwa judgement must be applied to substances containing narcotics.

22 *Litwa* v. *Poland*, 4 April 2000, ECHR, no. 26629/95, *Reports of Judgments and Decisions* 2000-III, para. 61. For the application of the Litwa principles in recent case law, *see Kharin* v. *Russia*, 3 February 2011, ECHR, no. 37345/03, not yet reported.

23 *Hafsteinsdóttir* v. *Iceland*, supra note 20, paras 53–56.

ics" and "lawful". Besides the traditional demands on national legislation that have been developed by the Court under the notion of "lawfulness", the term also implies substantial demands on national rules. First of all, the Court has held that the deprivation of liberty can only take place after a "fair and proper procedure".[24] Secondly, the Court has set up comprehensive conditions:[25]

> "Moreover an essential element of the 'lawfulness' of the detention within the meaning of Article 5 § 1 (e) is the absence of arbitrariness. The detention of an individual is such a serious measure that it is only justified where other, less stringent measures have been considered and found to be insufficient to safeguard the individual or the public interest, which might require that the person concerned be detained. That means that it does not suffice that the deprivation of liberty is in conformity with national law, it must also be necessary in the circumstances ..."

In this passage, the Court develops two principles: the principle of subsidiarity and the principle of necessity. These are partly overlapping, but together, they provide the Court with a tool for scrutinising national legislation and its application in a rather intense manner.

While the above-mentioned cases all concern detentions of short duration for detoxification, the Court in *Wall* v. *Sweden* was called upon to review the long-term detention of an alcoholic under the Swedish LVM regulation.[26] Since the Swedish authorities had continuously considered less severe measures and strictly scrutinized the necessity for subjecting the applicant to compulsory care, the application was declared inadmissible.

The aforementioned cases all address ordinary procedures regarding the deprivation of liberty. Regarding emergency cases, ECtHR has vested states with a wide margin of appreciation.[27] There is no room in this contribution to elaborate on which situations are to be assessed as 'emergency cases' and which requirements will apply in these cases; however, one point should be emphasized. In jurisdictions with a high frequency of temporary decisions – like Norway – it should not be taken for granted that all of these would be assessed as emergency cases by ECtHR.

In addition to the substantial and procedural requirements regarding the initial decision to detain, cf. Article 5(1), there are also legal demands regarding the review, cf. Article 5(4). These requirements will not be elaborated on in detail here, but due to different regulations in the Nordic countries regarding a person's legal standing after a detention order has been lifted, this issue will be addressed. In the wording of Article 5(4), the remedy of control by the national courts is provided to everyone who 'is' deprived of their liberty. However, in *Herz* v. *Germany*, ECtHR held that

24 See, inter alia, *Winterwerp* v. *Netherlands*, 24 October 1979, ECHR, no. 6301/73, *Series A* no. 33, para. 45 and *Erkalo* v. *Netherlands*, 2 September 1998, ECHR, no. 23807/94, *Reports of Judgments and Decisions* 1998-VI, paras 46–60.

25 *Hafsteinsdóttir* v. *Iceland*, supra note 20, para. 51 with reference to *Litwa* v. *Poland*, supra note 22, para. 78.

26 *Wall* v. *Sweden*, 10 December 2002 (Decision), ECHR, no. 41403/98, unreported.

27 See *X.* v. *UK*, 5 November 1981, ECHR, no. 7215/75, *Series A* no. 46, para. 41.

it was a violation of Article 5(4) when German courts denied a further review of the detention order because the maximum period had expired and the patient had escaped from the hospital.[28]

Until now, the implicit situation has been the classical deprivation of liberty of a person opposed to entering an institution. A special feature of some of the Nordic countries is the 'Ulysses contract'. The question is, then, whether or not a person has been 'deprived of his liberty' under Article 5(1) when that person, at the time of admission, has consented to possible detention. In the Vagabond cases, ECtHR held that the "right to liberty is too important in a 'democratic society' within the meaning of the Convention for a person to lose the benefit of the protection of the Convention for the single reason that he gives himself up to be taken into detention"[29]; thus, persons consenting to detention also enjoy protection under Article 5, notwithstanding that the scope of this protection may vary.

3.3 *The foetus' human rights*

ECHR Article 2 states that "[e]veryone's right to life shall be protected by law", while Article 3 states that "[n]o one shall be subjected to torture or to inhuman or degrading treatment". Under CCPR Article 6, "[e]very human being has the inherent right to life". CRC Article 1 defines a child as "every human being below the age of eighteen years" while in Article 6, the contracting parties recognize that every child has the inherent right to life. In addition, Article 24 (d) makes the appropriate ante- and post-natal health care for mothers an obligation, thus indicating that the foetus, in this respect, is a protected interest. In situations where the foetus can be expulsed due to substance exposure, or where manifest harm can occur, the question arises as to whether or not the foetus is protected under human rights and, if so, whether or not the authorities may be under obligation to intervene in order to protect it. Here too, the focus will be on ECHR.

Most of the cases determined by ECtHR regarding protection of the foetus have been raised in relation to the mother's right (or lack thereof) to have an abortion.[30] These cases give limited guidance on the current issue, which differs from abortion in many aspects, especially since offspring may have to live with the consequences for the rest of their lives. Of special relevance is *Vo* v. *France*, where a foetus was harmed due to alleged professional misconduct, and the question was whether or not the lack of legal protection was in conformity with Article 2. The majority held:[31]

28 *Herz* v. *Germany*, 12 June 2003, ECHR, no. 44672/98, unreported, paras 64–70. See also *Filip* v. *Romania*, 14 December 2006, ECHR, no. 41124/02, unreported, paras 70–78.

29 *De Wilde and others* v. *Belgium*, 18 November 1970, ECHR, no. 2832/66 et al., *Series* A 12, para. 65.

30 See the case law referred to in the recent *A., B. and C.* v. *Ireland*, 16 December 2010 (Grand Chamber), ECHR, no. 25579/05, not yet reported.

31 *Vo* v. *France*, 8 July 2004 (Grand Chamber), ECHR, no. 53924/00, *Report of Judgments and Decisions*, 2004-VIII, para. 84, cf. para. 80. See also *Evans* v. *UK*, 14 April 2007 (Grand Chamber), ECHR, no. 6339/05, not yet reported, regarding destruction of an embryo when the forthcoming father – after conception but prior to insemination – had withdrawn his consent.

"At best, it may be regarded as common ground between States that the embryo/foetus belongs to the human race. The potentiality of that being and its capacity to become a person – enjoying the protection under civil law, moreover in many States, such as France, in the context of inheritance and gifts, and also in the United Kingdom ... require protection in the name of human dignity, without making it a 'person' with the 'right to life' for the purposes of Article 2."

Here, ECtHr introduces a special category and provides the foetus with a form of relative protection. The foetus can, in some situations, be protected by virtue of its human dignity; however, in other situations, like abortion, it is not covered by Article 2. The passage can be interpreted such that the foetus will never enjoy protection as an ordinary human legal entity; rather, simply due to its potential to become a human being. The foetus, then, is more an object of rights than an individual with it owns subjective rights. This approach entails ECtHR not distinguishing between the foetus' possible protection under Article 2 and what the consequences of this protection are, but subscribing to a form of overall assessment. This way of reasoning may be criticized, but in this context it is sufficient to emphasize that the foetus to some extent is protected by ECHR.

3.4 Protection of the prospective father

Questions regarding the prospective father have arisen in many cases under ECHR, with regard to abortion, whereby the potential father has challenged the measure, alleging this was an infringement of his rights. The core of the issue has not been addressed, since ECtHR has held that the abortions were in conformity with the state's human rights obligations.[32] As stated earlier, abortion cases may not be the best road map to use since the current issue concerns the health of both the future child and the foetus. Turning to cases arising after birth, these have mainly been addressed under Article 8 and the term 'family life', or alternatively 'private life'. Under current case law, the father's human rights protection is conditional, and depends on the relationship between him and the pregnant woman.[33]

Given that a potential father has a family life with the pregnant woman,[34] it may be claimed that the woman's substance abuse will interfere with his prospective family life with the offspring. However, if the state is to have a right, or an obligation, to

32 See, inter alia, *Boso* v. *Italy*, 5 September 1999 (Decision), ECHR, no. 50490/99, *Reports of Judgments and Decisions* 2002-VI, with further references to previous case law.

33 See, inter alia, *Lebbink* v. *the Netherlands*, 1 June 2004, ECHR, no. 45582/99, *Reports of Judgments and Decisions* 2004-IV, para. 37 ('family life') and *Mikulic* v. *Croatia*, 2 July 2002, ECHR, no. 53176/99, *Reports of Judgments and Decisions* 2002-I ('private life').

34 *Camp and others* v. *the Netherlands*, 3 October 2000, ECHR, no. 28369/95, *Reports of Judgments and Decisions* 2000-X, concerning inheritance rights when the father dies before the son is born, indicates that the relationship between the father and the foetus is under the ambit of Article 8.

intervene, this should be reasoned on the basis of the health of the foetus and the future child, not under considerations regarding the father.

3.5 *Balancing the implicated parties' human rights: a right to intervene, or an obligation?*

Of the implicated parties, the pregnant women enjoy well-developed protection against the arbitrary deprivation of liberty, while the foetus enjoys the status of a member of the human race. The father's interests are relevant, but his position is secondary. Thus, the question facing national authorities is whether or not they can intervene in the case of pregnant substance abusers without violating the human rights of the persons concerned. If so, a subsequent question concerns whether or not national authorities, in some situations, may be under a human rights obligation to intervene.

Regarding the first question, the starting point for the discussion is the pregnant woman's protection against the deprivation of her liberty under ECHR Article 5, or similar provisions in other human rights instruments. Since Article 5 does not specify the interests that can justify an intervention, detention in order to protect the foetus cannot, as such, be a violation of Article 5, as long as the other requirements are met. When assessing whether or not such an intervention is in conformity with Article 5, the foetus' enjoyment of some sort of protection under ECHR Articles 2 and 3, in line with the reasoning in *Vo* v. *France,* is of relevance[35]. Thus, there is an impact both on the proportionality and the margin of appreciation.

The second question, then, concerns whether or not national authorities may be under a positive obligation to intervene in the case of pregnant women, as in situations where states, according to case law from ECtHR, are under duty to prevent citizens from harming each other.[36] As long as the foetus has limited protection under ECHR Articles 2 and 3, and similar provisions, national authorities will be under no such obligation. In addition, of relevance here is the lack of such provisions in the legal orders of Europe, indicating that there is no common European standard, thus widening states' margin of appreciation.

35 See supra note 31.

36 See, inter alia, *Osman* v. *UK*, 28 October 1998 (Grand Chamber), ECHR, no. 23452/94, *Reports of Judgments and Decisions* 1998-VIII, para. 115 and *Z. and others* v. *UK*, 10 May 2001 (Grand Chamber), ECHR, no. 29392/95, para. 73.

4 The Norwegian legislation

The Norwegian Social Services Act was introduced in 1991.[37] The previous legislation governing the deprivation of liberty of substance abusers was largely continued in Section 6-2, albeit limiting the indications for intervention to risk to the substance abuser's own health and shortening the detention period to three months. Like its predecessor, the 1991 Act also contained a provision authorizing 'Ulysses contracts', cf. Section 6-3.

A separate provision for pregnant women was discussed in the preparatory works, but not proposed.[38] The issue came onto the agenda several times during the following years, but the proposals were turned down until Parliament, in 1995, enacted Section 6-2a. The following is an unofficial English translation of the first and second paragraphs of the provision, which state that:

> "It can be decided that a pregnant substance abuser, without her consent, shall be admitted to an institution appointed by a regional health enterprise, cf. Act no. 61 of 7 July 1999 relating to specialized health care, Section 2-1a second sub-paragraph, and be held there for the rest of her pregnancy if the abuse is such that it is most probable that the child will be born with injuries, and if voluntary measures according to Section 6-1 are insufficient. The County Board shall simultaneously decide whether the institution shall be permitted to take urine samples from the pregnant individual during her detention.
>
> The aim of this detention is to prevent or minimize the likelihood of injury to the child. During detention attention shall be paid to providing the woman with satisfactory help for her substance abuse and enabling her to take care of her child."

The material conditions of the provision will be presented below, but first some background information on the procedure. The process is initiated by the municipal social authorities, and the decision to detain is taken by the County Board. This Board is formally an independent administrative body, but with well-developed procedural guarantees, and functioning like a court. The Board normally consists of a chairman (lawyer), a professional (most often a psychologist), and a lay person. If the case is complex, another professional and lay person can be added, and the chairman can make the decision alone, if the parties consent to it. The decision can upon request be reviewed by the courts, but only while the woman is being detained, which raises discussions regarding ECHR Art. 5(4).[39]

---

37 "Lov om sosiale tjenester", 13 December 1991 No. 81. This Act will by 1 January 2012 be replaced by "Lov om kommunale helse- og omsorgstjenester m.m." ["Act regarding Municipal Health and Care Services"], 6 June 2011 No. 30. The new act has almost the exact same wording as its predecessor, cf. Section 10-3. A selection of Norwegian legislation is translated (unofficially and not always up to date) and available at <www.ub.uio.no/ujur/ulov/>, visited on 11 April 2011.

38 For an analysis of the Norwegian legislation, see K.H. Søvig, *Tvang overfor rusmiddelavhengige [Coercive measures against substance addictives]* (Bergen, Fagbokforlaget, 2007), with an abstract in English. On the discussions about a special provision regarding pregnant substance abusers, see ibid., pp. 55-56.

39 Cf. ECtHR in *Herz* v. *Germany*, supra note 28.

The detention period is the rest of the pregnancy, with a review every three months. Medical personnel have a statutory obligation to inform, ex officio, the social services if it is reasonable to believe that a pregnant woman meets the legal conditions laid down in Section 6-2a, regardless of medical confidentiality.[40]

The legal conditions are based on *five* criteria (besides the woman concerned being pregnant). The *first* criterion relates to both the source of the risk to the foetus and the reduced ability for self-determination. The woman must have been assessed as a 'substance abuser' (Norwegian: *rusmiddelmisbruker*). The 'substance' part of the term includes alcohol, narcotics, and pharmaceuticals containing narcotics, and thus excludes tobacco and social factors not beneficial to the foetus (e.g. the consumption of unhealthy food). The 'abuser' part of the term requires the persistent consumption of substances of a certain quantity. The *second* criterion addresses the negative health consequences for the foetus; thus defining this as an 'injury' (Norwegian: *skade*) to the future child. A proposal about qualifying the injuries as 'significant' was turned down during the legislative process.[41] A regular negative health consequence for newborns who are exposed to substances during pregnancy is abstinence syndrome. This is to be considered an injury despite being temporary, since withdrawal symptoms do not normally occur in newborns. The *third* criterion establishes the link between the perilous behaviour of the woman and the impact on her future child, stating that the negative outcome must be 'likely'.[42] This is partly a question of knowledge of causation; however, it is important to emphasize that it is a challenging task for the decision-maker. The core issue is not whether the foetus will most likely be born with injuries due to substance abuse, but whether the continued use of substances, in cases of non-intervention, will lead to injuries. This is a matter of prognosis, complicated by the fact that the negative health consequences that have already occurred are irrelevant, unless these will deteriorate.

While the aforementioned criteria are specific to the topic, the latter two are based on the common European principles of subsidiarity and proportionality found in most national legislations authorizing the deprivation of liberty, as well as in different human rights instruments. The *fourth* criterion is a concession to the principle of autonomy. Voluntary measures must show themselves to be insufficient (Norwegian: *utilstrekkelige*). This does not mean that all potential measures have to be tried out, but the most common efforts must usually have been made. The *fifth* criterion has its origins in the discretion vested in the decision-maker. The Board has the authority to intervene ('can'), unlike the Swedish legislation where the administrative courts are under a statutory obligation to act if the requirements are met. This criterion requires a classical assessment of proportionality, albeit with some atypical aspects, especially regarding the duration of the detention. Normally, the length of the

40 Cf. inter alia Act relating to Health Personnel of 2 July 1999 No. 64, section 32, second paragraph.

41 See the Parliamentary Committee in Innst. O. (Report to the Parliament Chamber) 68 (1994–95), p. 2.

42 The Norwegian term *overveiende sannsynlig* allows scope for different interpretations that will not be discussed here.

detention is a one-sided argument, but in this case, it is more versatile. An early intervention increases the burden on the woman in the form of a longer time to be deprived of her liberty; but, on the other hand, the probability of preventing harm to the foetus increases.

Due to the judicial nature of the County Board procedure, the decision-making process takes time. A period of eight weeks elapsing between initialization by the social authorities and the decision of the County Board is normal. During this period, the foetus may be exposed to its mother's substance use, and there may be a need to intervene. The legislator has therefore introduced temporary decisions (Section 6-2a, fourth paragraph). For such an intervention to take place, the criteria for an ordinary decision must have been met, supplemented by an urgent need of immediate detention.

5 Ongoing debates in other Nordic countries

5.1 Introduction

Unlike Norway, the other Nordic countries have not introduced any special provisions regarding pregnant substance addicts, despite there being no indications of differences between these countries concerning the public health problems of newborns who are exposed to substances during pregnancy.[43] Regardless of diversity in legal regulations, the public debate has largely featured the same sets of arguments, albeit with a different outcome. In this part, I will give a presentation of the ongoing discussions in the other Nordic countries, focusing on the variety in the legal approaches used. Iceland will not be visited in this section, since the subject does not seem to have been on the public agenda there.

5.2 Sweden

Like Norway, Sweden has an existing regulation governing the detention of substance abusers. Sweden's Care of Drug and Alcohol Abusers Act was enacted in 1988 (Swedish: *Lag om vård av missbrukare i vissa fall: LVM*), continuing the basic principles of former legislation.[44] In contrast to the Norwegian legislation, the Swedish Act has an alternative criterion authorizing intervention if the substance abuser can cause serious harm to a closely-associated person (Swedish: *allvarligt skada [...]*

43 For a discussion of the legal approach in Scandinavia, see E. Nilssen, 'Coercion and justice: a critical analysis of compulsory intervention towards adult substance abusers in Scandinavian social law', 14: *International Journal of Social Welfare* (2005), pp. 134–144.

44 Lag om vård av missbrukare i vissa fall (LVM), No. 1988:870. A selection of Swedish legislation is translated (unofficially and not always up to date) and available at <www.sweden.gov.se/sb/d/3288/>, visited 11 April 2011. See also <www.nyulawglobal.org/globalex/Sweden1.htm>, also visited 11 April 2011.

någon närstående).[45] The maximum detention period is 6 months. In 2009, the administrative courts of first instance made 1,330 decisions (including temporary ones) regarding 807 individuals.[46] The foetus is not considered a "closely associated person".[47] Nevertheless, since one third of admittees are female,[48] pregnant women may be detatined on the basis of the general criteria laid down in the legislation. In recent years, about 15 women per year have been pregnant at some point during their detention.[49]

Sweden has seen regular public discussions as regards including pregnancy as a criterion for detention.[50] The most recent proposal was drafted by the Ministry of Social Affairs.[51] The suggested amendment introduced detention for the rest of the pregnancy and one month beyond.[52] The additional criterion stated that the administrative court should impose detention if a pregnant woman were "exposing her unborn child to a palpable risk of being born with injuries causes by the [substance] abuse" (Swedish: *utsätter sitt ofödda barn för en påtaglig risk att födas med en skada orsakad av missbruket*). During the round of consultation, many authorities and NGOs opposed the idea of a separate criterion for pregnant substance abusers; the government did not follow up on its own proposal to put a Bill before parliament. Among the opponents was the Swedish Parliamentary Ombudsman *[Justitieombudsmannen]*.[53] Her objections were twofold; *firstly*, she argued that the proposal had underestimated the risk of reluctance on the part of pregnant substance abusers to seek medical assistance due to the fear of being detained; *secondly*, she emphasized that a decision to deprive someone of their liberty should not be based on scantly-documented causation between the consumption of substances and the negative impact on the foetus' health.

In a recently-published report, measures for substance abusers (including involuntary care) were evaluated and, among other things, the incorporation of the Care of Drug and Alcohol Abusers Act into the Compulsory Psychiatric Care Act (1991:1128)

45 For an extensive analysis of Swedish legislation on the subject (with a short summary in English), see E. Gustafsson, *Missbrukare i rättsstaten [(Substance)abusers and rule of law]* (Nordstedts juridik, Stockholm, 2001).

46 See, 'Sveriges officiella statistik, Statistik – Socialtjänst, Vuxna personer med missbruksproblem och övriga vuxna – insatser år 2009' ['Official statistics Sweden, Statistics – Social services, Adult persons with an abuser problem and other adults – intervention 2009'], (Stockholm 2010), table 12 (p. 115).

47 Gustafsson, supra note 45, pp. 406–408, with further references.

48 See 'Statistics Sweden', supra note 46, table 13.

49 Information provided by Therese Reitan at the Swedish National Board of Institutional Care. The only public figures are from 2007 and published in the Board's yearbook, see Statens institutionsstyrelse, Årsredovisning 2007, [Swedish National Board of Institutional Care, Yearbook 2007], (Stockholm, 2009), p. 18 (11 pregnant women in 2007).

50 See, inter alia, Ds 1981:6 (Measures against substance abuse during pregnancy), Swedish Government Reports 1987:11 (Protection of the future child. Measures against substance abuse etc. during pregnancy) and Swedish Government Reports 2004:3 (Coercive measures and alteration).

51 Ds 2009:19 (Pregnant women with substance abuse).

52 For a critique of the proposal, see W. Runquist, 'Sverige – om konsten att sila mygg och svälja kameler' [Sweden – On the art of filtering mosquitoes and swallowing camels], 26:3 *Nordisk alkohol- & narkotikatidskrift* (2009), pp. 304–313.

53 See <www.jo.se/Page.aspx?MenuId=106&MainMenuId=106&Language=sv&ObjectClass=DynamX_SFS Decision&Id=3979>, visited 11 April 2011 (only in Swedish).

was proposed.[54] The question of pregnant substance abusers may be back on the agenda again when the report's suggestions regarding a revisit of the regulation are discussed in public and in Parliament; however, this will probably not be the core topic since questions regarding pregnant abusers are not a key issue in the report.[55]

5.3 *Finland*

In Finland, the Care of Abusers Act authorizes the detention of substance abusers either when they pose an immediate and grave risk to their own health ("health risk") or when violence arising from substance abuse jeopardizes the health, security, or mental development of a family member or other person ("violence risk").[56] The maximum detention period is normally 5 days, but detentions of up to 30 days can be ordered by an administrative court in cases where there is a risk of violence. These provisions are hardly ever used,[57] and there are no official statistics on the subject.

In 2008, the Ministry of Social Affairs and Health appointed a working group to ensure the care and treatment of women with substance abuse problems. The group delivered its report in 2009.[58] According to that report, recent estimates indicate that about 6 percent of pregnant Finnish women are excessive users of alcohol and about 600 children with symptoms related to alcohol exposure during the foetal stage are born in Finland every year. These figures are contested,[59] but it seems undisputed that alcohol use during pregnancy is a health problem that is of concern.

One of the designated tasks of the working group was to evaluate the appropriateness of involuntary care and treatment with regard to pregnant women who have substance abuse problems. The working group proposed a provision authorizing care against the woman's will and introduced a 'Ulysses contract'. Additionally, a provision directing physicians to consider the involuntary care of pregnant substance abusers was also suggested.

The working group underlined in its proposal that care and treatment against the person's will cannot and must not replace insufficient substance abuse services, but that this option should be used when all other methods have been exhausted. The

54 See Swedish Government Reports 2011:35 (Improved efforts against [substance] abuse and addiction).

55 Swedish Government Reports 2011:35, pp. 313–314. The report does not introduce pregnancy as a special criterion for detention.

56 Lag om missbrukarvård [Act on substance abuse treatment], 17 January 1986 No. 41. A selection of Finnish legislation in unofficial English translation is available at <www.finlex.fi/en/>, visited 11 April, but the Act which is of current interest is not included.

57 See K. Stenius, 'Synliggør tvånget inom psykiatrin!' ['Reveal coercive measures within psychiatric services!'], 25:5 *Nordisk alkohol- & narkotikatidskrift* (2008), pp. 335–336.

58 Sosiaali- ja terveysministeriön selvityksiä 2009:4, Raskaana olevien päihdeongelmaisten naisten hoidon varmistaminen – työryhmä [The Ministry of Social Affairs and Health, Report of the Working Group to ensure the care and treatment of pregnant women with substance abuse problems], with a summary in English. Available at <www.stm.fi/sv/pressmeddelanden/pressmeddelande/view/1382890>, visited 11 April 2011.

59 See, K. Mäkelä, 'Vård och kontroll av missbrukarmödrar' ['Protection and control of addictive mothers'], 26:3 *Nordisk alkohol- & narkotikatidskrift* (2009), pp. 319–322.

suggested introduction of a special criterion for pregnant substance abusers has been criticized,[60] and it has been argued that such a provision would be a breach of the fundamental rights laid down in the Finnish constitution.[61] Currently, no decision has been taken by the Ministry as to whether to put a Bill before Parliament. Additionally, a working group has been assigned to evaluate the principle of autonomy within the health and social sector. A part of the mandate of this group is to discuss measures against pregnant substance abusers.[62]

5.4 Denmark

Unlike the other mainland Nordic countries, Denmark currently has no separate provision authorizing the deprivation of the liberty of substance abusers without their consent. However, since 1992, the Act governing the detention of drug addicts in treatment has offered the possibility of a 'Ulysses contract'.[63] This provision may only be used in regions where the municipal authorities have introduced such contracts. Both the institution and the person concerned must agree on the terms, and the maximum duration is limited to 6 months. If the institution wants to keep a patient in detention, it must make a decision on the matter and the patient must meet the criteria laid down in the legislation. Such a decision is temporary and must be approved by the municipal authorities. The detention cannot exceed 14 days in each case, and the total period must not exceed 2 months of a total of 6 months. The patient must be a drug (Danish: *stof*) abuser, i.e. a user of narcotics, thus alcoholics are excluded. Although enacted in 1992, such contracts were never offered in practice.[64]

After a public debate, the government proposed, in 2007, amendments that were later adopted by Parliament. The municipal authorities were then under a statutory obligation to offer 'Ulysses contracts' to pregnant drug abusers.[65] However, the amendment only includes pregnant women using "drugs". The use of alcohol is far more widespread among women of a fertile age, and alcohol is considered more toxic to the foetus than narcotics. Against this backdrop, it is not surprising that the leg-

---

60 For a critique of the proposal, see, Mäkelä, supra note 59, pp. 323-325.

61 See A. Leppo, 'Illusionen om enkla lösningar' ['The illusion of simple solutions'], 26:3 *Nordisk alkohol- & narkotikatidskrift* (2009), p. 315, with references to M. Liljeström, 'Sikiön oikeusturva. Sikiön itsenäiset oikeudet vai raskaana olevan naisen oikeusturva sikiön hyvinvoinnin oikeudellisena perustan' ['Legal protection of the foetus. The rights of the foetus or the legal protection of the pregnant woman as the legal ground of the well-being of the foetus'] 56:19 *Suomen Lääkärilehti* (2001), pp. 2171–2175. *See also*, L. Nieminen, 'Raskaana olevien päihteitä käyttävien naisten tahdosta riippumaton hoito perusoikeuksien kannalta - kenen etu ratkaisee?' ['Mandatory treatment of pregnant drug users from the perspective of civil rights - whose interest is decisive?'], 108:4, *Lakimies* (2010), pp. 537–558.

62 See <www.stm.fi/sv/under_arbete/arbetsgrupper/klientens_sjalvbestammanderatt>, visited 11 April 2011.

63 'Lovbekendtgørelse om tilbageholdelse af stofmisbrugere i behandling' ['The Detention of Drug Addicts in Treatment Act'], 14 May 1992 No. 349 with amendments, recently 22 February 2010 No. 170. A selection of Danish legislation in unofficial English translation is available at <www.juraportal.dk/links/010/010/040/?lang=en>, visited 11 April 2011, but the Acts of current interest are not included.

64 D. Hecksher, 'Gravide med rusmiddelproblemer i Danmark' ['Pregnant women with problematic substance use in Denmark'], 26:3 *Nordisk alkohol- & narkotikatidskrift* (2009), p. 299.

65 Act 6 June 2007 No. 542.

islators also made legal facilities for 'Ulysses contracts' for pregnant alcoholics. Such a legal tool was introduced into the Health Act via an amendment in 2007.[66] Unlike the Detention of Drug Addicts in Treatment Act, 'Ulysses contracts', under the Health Act, constitute a set of special provisions only offered to pregnant women and, by contrast, the municipal authorities are under no legal obligation to offer such contracts. The criteria for detention are quite similar to the Detention of Drug Addicts in Treatment Act, and the nuances of legal approach will not be elaborated upon here. Thus, it should be mentioned that the Health Act contains a criterion targeting pregnant women, stating that a decision to impose detention can be made if the pregnant woman poses a present danger of harming the foetus (Danish: *den gravide alkoholmisbruger frembyder nærliggende fare for at skade fosteret*), while the Detention of Drug Addicts in Treatment Act uses a general criterion regarding detention if the drug addict poses a present and imminent danger to himself or others [*stofmisbrugeren frembyder nærliggende og væsentlig fare for sig selv eller andre*]. In the latter case, this provision has to be applied to pregnant women, and the "foetus" must be seen as another person.

According to figures from the National Board of Social Services [*Servicestyrelsen*], from April 2011, five municipalities had offered contracts to pregnant drug abusers. Of these, four had actually concerned two women.[67] Regarding alcohol, the provisions of the Health Act have hitherto never been used.

The right to a court review is guaranteed in both Acts (sections 8 and 141e, respectively) with reference to the Administration of Justice Act, Chapter 43a.[68] Both of the said sections entitle the person concerned to challenge the decision to offer a contract as well as the decision to detain under the contract. In contrast to the Norwegian legislation, which does not offer a court review of 'Ulysses contracts', the Administration of Justice Act additionally enables the continuation of the court review after detention has ceased (Section 469, fourth paragraph). Since 'Ulysses contracts' are seldom used in Denmark, there are no published court decisions on this subject.

Despite the introduction of separate provisions for pregnant women, the public debate has continued. There has been a call for coercive measures which can be made without the prior consent of the women concerned[69]; however, no proposals are currently before Parliament.

66 Sundhedsloven [The Health Act], 24 June 2005 No. 546, as amended by Act 6 June 2007 No. 511.

67 Email from Janne Schacke at "Servicestyrelsen", ' The National Board of Social Services' on April 15 2011. See also a letter from the Social Ministry to the Parliamentary Social Committee dated 17 March 2010 ('Socialudvalget 2009-10, Spørgsmål 287'), but these figures were later revised.

68 Retsplejeloven [The Administration of Justice Act], 11 April 1916 No. 90, as amended by Act 26 October 2010 No. 1237.

69 Hecksher, supra note 64, pp. 300–301.

6 Application of the Norwegian legislation

Since Norway is currently the only Nordic country authorizing the detention of pregnant substance abusers, it is of interest to present the experiences gained from enforcing such a legal tool. The Norwegian Directorate of Health has financed an evaluation of compulsory interventions vis-à-vis substance abusers – including pregnant women – and the figures below are based on a selection of findings from the research report relating to this project (the author was part of the scientific team).[70]

Between 1996 and 2009, 259 ordinary decisions were made under Section 6-2a, along with 427 temporary ones.[71] The figures concern decisions, not women, and information about whether or not the decisions were carried out is not available. During recent years, the frequency has increased. Between 2007 and 2009, the average yearly figure for ordinary decisions was 27, while 48 decisions were temporary.

The said project also included an analysis of the ordinary decisions, with 204 decisions under 6-2a between 1996 and 2008 being collected (of a total of 213 decisions during the same period).[72] Decisions under section 6-2 were also collected (N=572), and these will also be presented here occasionally for reasons of comparison. In 92.5 percent of cases, the County Board concluded that the women in question should be detained. The following figures include decisions on both admittance and release.

The most common substance used by pregnant women subject to decisions regarding detention was narcotics (78 percent). Just 5 percent of the women were using alcohol alone, while 15 percent were combining narcotics and alcohol (the remaining 2 percent were using other forms of substances). In contrast, alcohol was used in 14 percent of cases under Section 6-2 and, if the female population under Section 6-2 is seen in isolation, 25 percent of these use alcohol. Of those using narcotics under Section 6-2a, either exclusively or in combination with alcohol, the use of opiates (usually injections of heroin) was most common (53 percent), followed by cannabis (48 percent), amphetamine (44 percent), and benzodiazepine (41 percent). Given that the use of alcohol is more widespread among pregnant women than different forms of narcotics, and considered more harmful to the foetus, it is surprising that Section 6-2a primarily targets women using narcotics. Of the different narcotic substances, heroin is, as may be period expected, at the top of the list, but it may be a surprise that cannabis is next.

The decisions were also reviewed as regards when the intervention took place, although many of the decisions lack information on this matter. On average, 117 days of the pregnancy remain when temporary decisions are made (N=139). There has been a development in the field regarding this matter, increasing the average from 90 days

70 See I. Lundeberg et al. (eds), *Tvang overfor rusmiddelavhengige [Coercive measures against substance addictives]*, Uni Rokkansenteret, report 2-2010 (Uni Research, Bergen, 2010).

71 Ibid., p. 17.

72 See K.H. Søvig, 'Fylkesnemndsundersøkelsen' ['An investigation on the practice by the County Board'], in Lundeberg et al., supra note 70, pp. 81–109.

during the period 1996-2000 (N=36) to 126 days between 2005 and 2008 (N=62). Since the study dealt with ordinary decisions, this approach leaves a margin of error. Nevertheless, comparison with available studies of admitted women (including those temporarily detained) suggests that there are only minor divergences.[73]

The time taken by the social workers is also of interest. On average, it took 55 days from social services becoming aware of the pregnancy and the corresponding substance abuse to the temporary decision being made (N=107).

As mentioned before, early intervention is preferred in order to enable the decision to have a significant impact on the foetus' health. Birth weight is considered an indicator of the health status of newborn babies. A non-published study, conducted in one of the major institutions for children born of women detained under Section 6-2a, shows a correlation between duration of detention and birth weight.[74] For new-born babies born of mothers detained for more than 140 days, the average birth weight was 3,512 grams (N=31), while it was 3,029 grams when the mother was detained for a period shorter than 140 days (N=79). Although the numbers are low, the results indicate that early interventions have an impact on the health of the newborn child.

One of the counter-arguments against introducing Section 6-2a was the anticipated effect of reluctance on the part of the women in the target group to seek professional counselling from of fear of detention. As stated earlier, Section 6-2a was amended in combination with a legal obligation on medical doctors (and other health personnel) to inform social services if they became aware of pregnant substance abusers. Against this backdrop, it may be seen as unexpected that the women in 41 percent of the cases ending up with an ordinary decision contacted social services themselves (N=108).[75] However, it should be borne in mind that the figures do not give any indications of the vast majority of women, i.e. those not getting into contact with health or social care professionals, despite their addiction during pregnancy.

Another argument presented in opposition to Section 6-2a was the worry that women in the target group would choose abortion in order to avoid detention. There are no official statistics on this subject; however, a study carried out at one of the major institutions admitting patients under Section 6-2a reports 15 abortions out of a total of 135 patients during the period 1996 to 2008.[76]

The normal procedure regarding a decision by the County Board prior to detention is the statutory main rule, with temporary decisions by social authorities ap-

73 V. Grimstad and R. Kristiansen, *Gravide innlagt på Borgestadklinikken etter LOST § 6-2a i perioden 2006-2008 - sammenlignet med funnene fra 1996-2005 [Pregnant women admitted at Borgestadklinikken under Section 6-2a in the period 2006-2008 – compared with the findings from 1996-2005]* (Kompetansesenter rus – region sør, Skien, 2009), pp. 19–20.

74 Carried out by Egil Nordlie (MD). Figures presented here are with his consent.

75 On this matter, the social workers report a lower figure when asked who first contacted them; see E. Nilssen, 'Sosialtjenestens praktisering av tvangslovgivningen' ['The social services use of the legislation authorizing coercives measures'], in Lundeberg et al., supra note 70, p. 57.

76 Grimstad and Kristiansen, supra note 73, p. 20.

proved by the County Board under a simplified procedure being an exception. In practice, the exception is the main rule. A clear indication is found in the annual number of temporary decisions being higher than the ordinary decisions; however, this also becomes evident when observing that only 3 out of 204 ordinary decisions had not been anticipated by a temporary decision (in 2 of these, the women concerned had already been detained on an alternative legal basis).

The competence to initiate a procedure under Section 6-2a is vested in the social authorities. The study (this part includes all ordinary decisions between 1996 and 2008) shows regional differences. Of Norway's 4 major cities, the ratio per 100,000 female inhabitants varies between 0.75 (Trondheim) and 1.97 (Stavanger), thus there is not any indication of corresponding differences regarding the prevalence of pregnant substance abusers in these cities.

Both Sections 6-2 and 6-2a use the term *deprivation of liberty without the consent of the person concerned.* Despite this wording, 28 percent of the women who were subject to decisions under Section 6-2a state, prior to decisions being taken by the County Board, that they agree with the measure being suggested by the social authorities. It can be argued that, in such cases, the Board's decision should be a release case and the women concerned should be offered a 'Ulysses contract' under Section 6-3. This discussion will not be conducted here; however, it should be emphasized that the percentage of consenting women indicates that *some of them* recognize, following a temporary decision, that they needed detention.

7 Discussions: What lessons can be learnt?

This brief presentation of the regulations of the mainland Nordic countries, and the ongoing debates, illustrates that the legal order cannot be identified through studying the legal texts alone, it must be combined with knowledge of the implementation of the legislation. Since Norway is currently the only country that has introduced a separate provision for detaining pregnant substance abusers, I will focus, in the final part of this contribution, on Norwegian experiences that may be transferable to other jurisdictions that are considering introducing such a legal tool.

The core issue is the balancing of competing interests. This discussion is twofold, although the issues are closely related. *Firstly,* this is a legal issue. Is such a provision in conformity with superior legal instruments, e.g. the constitution and fundamental human rights? For Norway's part – and unlike the discussion in Finland – the constitution contains no provision that is of interest. Regarding human rights, the states seem to have the possibility of introducing such legal tools, but are under no obligation to do so. If a state authorizes the deprivation of liberty, actual interference must be in conformity with human rights, primarily ECHR Article. 5. As discussed earlier, the high frequency of temporary decisions in Norway, the time-consuming administrative process, and the lack of legal standing following the end of detention all raise concerns in under Article 5.

Secondly, this is an ethical and moral issue. Notwithstanding legal rules, how should the competing interests be weighed against each other? The answer to this question depends on the preferences of each individual, and on the values of the society they are a part of. In my opinion, the detention of a pregnant substance abuser in order to avoid the loss of life or severe harm to the newborn child is not, as such, an unacceptable intervention in the autonomy of the woman. Intervention in order to protect the foetus may be seen as a strange idea, but it should be emphasized that the main concern is not the foetus as such, but the future child. In other areas, most legal orders accept the foetus as a protected interest, among other things in form of criminal sanctions in the event of depriving the foetus of life (outside of legal abortions) and seeing the foetus as a patient with regard to foetal diagnostics. Against this backdrop, abortion is merely an exception from the general protection of the foetus, and the legal protection of the foetus, as such, is normally ensured.

However, limitation of the woman's liberty in order to protect her foetus can only be accepted if it is likely that any negative health effects on the latter are efficiently prevented. This assessment must partly be conducted in each individual case,[77] but it also brings about discussion on the group level, since the mere existence of such a provision can have implications for women and their foetuses even though the women concerned have not been confronted with an actual intervention in the form of a possible decision to detain.

My reluctance is primarily of a pragmatic nature. Is it possible to design the legislation in such a way that detention has a significant effect on the health of the newborn children of substance abusers? Future discussions will address such a consideration.

A counter-argument to Section 6-2a and the proposed similar provisions has been that both its existence and detention in the individual case can lead to abortions. There is little knowledge of the effect of the mere existence of Section 6-2a, but post-detention abortions have been reported,[78] although these cases have no significant effect on the overall abortion rate. As stated earlier, the evaluation of this effect depends on one's owns viewpoint in the abortion issue. My personal observation is that abortion as well as negative health effects on the future child should be prevented; however, if prioritisation is necessary, abortion is a lesser evil than manifest injuries to the newborn child that may be lifelong. The evident problem with this general approach is implementation in the individual case, whereby it is difficult to foresee the probability of the different outcomes.

77 Such assessments are incorporated into all amended and proposed Nordic legislation, as well as established in case from ECtHR under ECHR Art. 5, cf. supra note 25.

78 Grimstad and Kristiansen, supra note 73, p. 20.

Another side effect of Section 6-2a, both in individual cases and on the group level, is the reluctance of pregnant women to seek medical help for their addiction in order to reduce the risk to the foetus. This argument has garnered much attention in the ongoing debates and thus deserves to be addressed. As with abortion, there is limited knowledge of the effect on the mere existence of the possibility of detention. Turning to individual cases where the pregnant woman has faced a decision to detain her, it is surprising that a significant number (41 percent) of women have called the social authorities on their own initiative.[79] Since the majority have still been introduced to social services by others, and little is known of the important group containing those not ending up with a decision to detain them, one should be careful when drawing conclusions. Nevertheless, the Norwegian experience indicates that this is a grey area, rather than a black or white one, as in some of the ongoing discussions.

Moving on to knowledge of implementation, a striking fact concerning the experiences gained in Norway is the limited number of decisions regarding women using alcohol. The use of alcohol is more widespread among women of a fertile age than narcotics, and alcohol is considered more harmful to the foetus than narcotics. The difficulties of reaching pregnant alcoholics may be a problem peculiar to Norway, and there is no room here for discussions about why this group is underrepresented. However, it should be borne in mind, in countries considering a special provision on the subject, that the main target group may be difficult to address. This also impacts upon the legislative discussions. In many debates, knowledge of the negative health consequences caused by alcohol is often at the forefront, while it should be borne in mind that effectively preventing such injuries may, in practice, be challenging.

In the mainland Nordic countries where a special provision on the subject has not been introduced, there has been an ongoing debate about the issue. This was also the situation in Norway prior to Section 6-2a, but following the amendment, the topic seems to be the subject of public discussion to a lesser extent. One explanation for this may be that there is an impression that the legislator, by means of the provision, has solved the problem, regardless of challenges concerning implementation and hesitations concerning the impact and effectiveness of the legal remedy. Although it is difficult to draw conclusions, it appears that the existence of a special provision has had a cooling effect on the public debate. Such a consequence is, perhaps, unavoidable, and difficult to address using legal remedies, but could be borne in mind by jurisdictions considering introducing special provisions.

The other side of this coin is the allocation of resources. Those against coercive measures have claimed that such a provision may lead to revisiting the distribution of funding. There are no available official figures regarding the distribution of resources (both financial and regarding personnel) prior to and after the introduction of Section 6-2a. Therefore, no conclusions can be drawn on a more systematic

79 See supra note 75 on different estimates.

level. Turning to individual cases, there have been reports about decisions to detain that were made due to insufficient voluntary measures,[80] but these seem more like exceptions than descriptions of the general state of the sector. In individual cases, there are also limitations, since detention may only be imposed if voluntary measures are insufficient. Still, it can be difficult for the deciding body to assess the different measures and why these are not being offered. The knowledge gained in Norway thus shows the necessity of monitoring the allocation of resources if provisions like Section 6-2a are to be enacted. A final point regarding resources that is to be mentioned here is the capacity of the institutions admitting involuntary patients, forming a maximum limit to the number of detainees being held at the same time. In many respects, the number of beds will be the decisive factor regarding the frequency of coercive measures.

If an intervention is to have a significant impact on the development of the foetus, detention must take place during the initial stages of the pregnancy.[81] It is challenging when intervention occurs as early as this is desirable. Women with an ongoing substance abuse must be identified, and a selection must be made on the basis of a prognosis of whether or not harm will come to the newborn child. There is, in this respect, tension between early intervention and the social authorities' need for time to conduct a thorough assessment. Even though the assessment could be done during the course of a working day, it is difficult to design a legal tool that secures early intervention since development of the organs starts shortly after fertilization. Despite a trend towards earlier decisions in Norway,[82] experience there is still that foetuses are exposed to substances for quite a long time before their mothers are detained. Nevertheless, the positive effect of the substance-free time during the rest of the pregnancy, and a delivery without this kind of intoxication, should not be underestimated. In turn, this complex situation should call for the need to make a comprehensive assessment prior to detention, where medical experts are involved in the decision-making process.[83]

Additionally, despite research into the effects on the newborn child of substance use during pregnancy, there is limited knowledge of when the negative effects occur and whether or not an intervention in the form of detention will prevent them. Against this backdrop, it is astonishing that the Norwegian authorities have not introduced systematic evaluation. There is no national register of the health status of the newborn children of formerly-detained women. Even though such a deficiency may not be a human rights violation, from the individual viewpoint, this still gives rise to major concern from the collective viewpoint. The message to jurisdictions

80 See Søvig, supra note 38, pp. 300–301.

81 Indications on the necessity of early intervention may be found in the unpublished study on the birth weight of the newborn children of formerly-detained women, see supra note 74.

82 See supra note 73.

83 In Norway, medical doctors are only to a limited extent involved in the process as expert members on the County Board, see Lundeberg et al., supra note 70, p. 97.

considering introducing provisions like Section 6-2a is to establish systems of evaluation while introducing substantial provisions. The comparison with drug trials could be borne in mind, despite the fact that the golden standard of randomized double-blind testing would be unethical to conduct on pregnant women, and the substantial differences between legal tools and medical drugs. Nevertheless, when enacting a new legal provision, the authorities also have an obligation to investigate whether or not the legal invention will have the intended effect, in addition to any possible side effects. Under current law, this obligation may not be derived from human rights or constitutional provisions; however, in my opinion, it is certainly a moral commitment.

The experience from Norway, after 15 years of having a special provision on the deprivation of the liberty of pregnant substance abusers in order to protect the foetus, may be summarised thus: Section 6-2a has had an impact in individual cases, although it is uncertain to what extent. However, the provision has not been a significant contributor towards solving the public health problem of children exposed to alcohol during pregnancy.

Cultural Accommodation in Health Services and European Human Rights

By Professor Oddný Mjöll Arnardóttir, Reykjvajík University[1]

1 Introduction

Cultural diversity has various consequences in the context of health services. The question of how to deal with these has only recently found its way into legal discourses. Aart Hendricks has pointed out that the problems arising mainly relate to two issues. Firstly, there is a demonstrable link between cultural or ethnic origin and the morbidity and mortality rates for certain diseases. This may call for appropriate attention to the relevance of ethnic origin and cultural heritage for diagnosis and treatment.[2] Secondly, it is clear that cultural diversity may impact on communication during the delivery of health services. On the one hand, the language skills of the patient in question can raise difficulties during diagnosis and when obtaining informed consent. On the other hand, the potential lack of 'cultural sensitivity' on the part of the health service provider may also present difficulties as this can impact on his or her understanding of the patient and the premises behind the patient's communication or decision-making and, consequently, on the diagnosis and treatment offered.[3] The issues arising from cultural diversity in health services are, thus, complex and varied but the question of how to deal with them legally is still relatively underdeveloped. Although Iceland, perhaps along with Finland, is a fairly homogenous society which is not facing cultural diversity on the same scale as Denmark, Norway and Sweden, the issues arising are the same from the legal perspective and need to be taken seriously across the Nordic countries. This article, however, cannot purport to deal with the matter in any definitive manner. Instead, it only has the more modest aim of casting some light on the basic normative foundations of the claim to cultural

1 Oddný Mjöll Arnardóttir, Ph.D, is professor at the School of Law, Reykjavík University, Iceland. Her research is in the field of human rights law, including non-discrimination, disability and health law. She served on the Icelandic National Bioethics Committe 2003-2006 and is a member of the board of the European Association of Health Law.

2 A. Hendriks, 'Ethnic and Cultural Diversity: Challenges and Opportunities for Health Law', 15 *European Journal of Health Law* (2008), p. 285, at pp. 290-291.

3 Ibid., p. 292.

accommodation in health services and of discussing the limits of cultural accommodation from a European human rights perspective, with reference to selected examples from Iceland. Before entering into that discussion, however, some explanation of the term 'cultural accommodation', as applied in the present context, is needed.

2 Cultural accommodation

2.1. *Culture*

The term 'culture' has many meanings, depending on the context. According to Oxford Dictionaries online, one of these meanings refers to "the ideas, customs, and social behaviour of a particular people or society".[4] Similarly the Merriam Webster online dictionary contains the definition that culture can refer to "the customary beliefs, social forms, and material traits of a racial, religious, or social group".[5] As applied in the present context, the term 'culture' focuses on commonalities in values, beliefs and practices among particular social groups. It is emphasised that the relevant groups cannot be any loosely-defined social group such as for example 'teenagers' or 'academics'. Instead, the focus is on relatively clearly-defined social groups that share a common heritage and identity that is characterised by these shared values, beliefs and practices. Such groups have been made relevant in human rights law, most clearly through the concepts of minorities or ethnic and/or religious groups.

The European Court of Human Rights has defined ethnicity and race in the following terms: "Ethnicity and race are related and overlapping concepts. Whereas the notion of race is rooted in the idea of biological classification of human beings into subspecies according to morphological features such as skin colour or facial characteristics, ethnicity has its origin in the idea of societal groups marked by common nationality, tribal affiliation, religious faith, shared language, or cultural and traditional origins and backgrounds."[6] Further, the Court approaches biologically-defined race and socially-defined ethnicity on equal terms legally and has concluded that "[d]iscrimination on account of one's actual or perceived ethnicity is a form of racial discrimination".[7] This coincides with the approach of the UN Convention on the Elimination of All Forms of Racial Discrimination (CERD),[8] under which the concept of racial discrimination reaches discrimination based on race, colour, descent or national or ethnic origin, cf. Article 1. Similarly, in the context of EU Directive 2000/43/EC implementing the principle of equal treatment between

4 <oxforddictionaries.com/view/entry/m_en_gb0196870#m_en_gb0196870>, visited on 4 April 2011.

5 <www.merriam-webster.com/dictionary/culture>, visited on 4 April 2011.

6 *Timishev v Russia*, 13 December 2005, ECHR, no. 55762/00 and 55974/00, *Reports of Judgments and Decisions 2005-XII*, para. 55.

7 Ibid., para. 56.

8 International Convention on the Elimination of All Forms of Racial Discrimination (adopted 21 December 1965, entered into force 4 January 1969) 660 UNTS 212.

persons irrespective of racial or ethnic origin, the ban against discrimination reaches racial and ethnic origin equally (Racial Equality Directive).[9] Conceptually, the difference between 'race' and 'ethnicity' lies in the fact that one is biologically defined and the other is socially defined. In recent years it is possible to discern in human rights discourses an increased emphasis on ethnicity in its social construction. The reason why is best reflected perhaps in the sensitivity towards any implication of racism expressed in the Racial Equality Directive. Although it refers to the commonly-used legal terms of 'racial origin' and 'ethnic origin' alike, the need was felt to qualify the use of the term 'racial origin' by emphasising that the EU rejects theories which attempt to determine the existence of separate human races, cf. recital 6. It seems clear, therefore, that it makes no difference legally which term is used since the legal implications are exactly the same in cases of racial and ethnic discrimination.

The defining line between ethnicity and religion is, however, more complex as the legal norms intended to support the ban against racial or ethnic discrimination do not necessarily also include a ban against religious discrimination, cf. the CERD and the Racial Equality Directive. Instead, the ban against discrimination based on religion or belief may be provided in other instruments. In the context of EU law, for example, there is a separate directive dealing with discrimination based on religion or belief, disability, age and sexual orientation, cf. EU Directive 2000/78/EC establishing a general framework for equal treatment in employment and occupation (Framework Equality Directive).[10] It has been pointed out in the literature, however, that Jews, Sikhs, Copts and Armenians form groups where ethnic origin and religion coincide so closely that these "two dimensions of their collective life are inextricably interwoven".[11] And even in less clear-cut situations, the definition developed by the European Court of Human Rights shows that religious faith is one of the more important factors that contribute to the establishment of ethnicity. Many borderline issues can therefore arise. In conclusion, it can be stated that the concepts of ethnicity, race and religion are all closely connected in human rights law. It is difficult to draw clear-cut dividing lines between them. In the following discussion the term 'culture' should thus be taken to refer to the values, beliefs and social customs common to social groups that are defined with reference to a common racial, ethnic or religious background.

2.2. *Accommodation*

Now that it has been established what is meant by 'culture' in the present context it must also be examined what is meant by the reference to 'accommodation' when the two terms are linked together. The term cultural accommodation can, in fact, refer

9 Directive 2000/43, OJ [2000] L180/22.

10 Directive 2000/78, OJ [2000] L303/16.

11 Banton, 'Discrimination Entails Comparison' in Loenen and Rodrigues (eds), *Non-Discrimination Law: Comparative Perspectives* (Martinus Nijhoff Publishers, the Hague, 1999), p. 107, at p. 116.

to two opposite scenarios. On the one hand, it can refer to instances where a person who belongs to a certain minority culture adapts to some of the values, beliefs or practices which are dominant in the culture he or she finds herself in. On the other hand, it can refer to the opposite situation where dominant cultural practices are modified or changed to accommodate values, beliefs or practices that are associated with minority cultures. The question is which kind of accommodation are we concerned with here and why? This article adopts a human rights approach to the issues discussed. In the Dworkinian conception, human rights essentially function as 'trumps' to protect important individual interests against infringements that might otherwise be justified by the majoritarian or utilitarian arguments that they satisfy the majority of the population or benefit the community as a whole.[12] Human rights, therefore, are much rather concerned with protecting the interests of individuals who find themselves in a minority or marginalised position than with imposing the choices of the majority on that individual. This understanding has, in fact, been repeatedly confirmed by the European Court of Human Rights when it emphasises that "although individual interests must on occasion be subordinated to those of a group, democracy does not simply mean that the views of a majority must always prevail: a balance must be achieved which ensures the fair and proper treatment of minorities and avoids any abuse of a dominant position".[13] The human rights perspective, therefore, focuses our attention on changes in mainstream practices to accommodate the different values, beliefs and social customs of particular minority or marginalised ethnic or religious groups, but not on requiring individuals to assimilate to the majority or mainstream culture. This is the meaning of the term 'cultural accommodation' as applied in the present context.

3 The normative foundations of cultural accommodation in health services

Equality and non-discrimination are fundamental elements of human rights protection.[14] The Universal Declaration of Human Rights (UDHR)[15] exhibits the key position of the principle of equality in human rights law. Article 1 of the UDHR proclaims that all human beings are born free and equal in dignity and rights while Article 2 stipulates that everyone is entitled to all the rights and freedoms set forth in the Declaration without 'distinction' (i.e. discrimination) of any kind. The principle of equality is also reflected in some form or another in all the major international human rights instruments that have been adopted since.

12 R. Dworkin, 'Rights as Trumps' in J. Waldron (ed.), *Theories of Rights* (Oxford University Press, Oxford, 1984), p. 153.

13 *Sørensen and Rasmussen v. Denmark,* 11 January 2006, ECHR, no. 52562/99 and 52620/99, *Reports of Judgments and Decisions 2006-I*, para. 58.

14 See for example H. Lauterpacht, *An International Bill of the Rights of Man* (Columbia University Press, New York, 1945), p. 115: "The claim to equality before the law is in a substantial sense the most fundamental of the rights of man. It occupies the first place in most written constitutions. It is the starting point of all other liberties."

15 Universal Declaration of Human Rights, GA Res. 217 A III (1948).

The issue of equal access and equal quality of health services for all social groups is also a very important theme in health law.[16] Article 2(2) of the International Covenant on Economic, Social and Cultural Rights (ICESCR)[17] requires all the rights protected therein, including the right to health under Article 12, to be guaranteed without discrimination on the basis of race, colour, sex, language, religion, political or other opinion, national or social origin, property, birth or other status. Indeed, the Committee on Economic, Social and Cultural Rights has made it clear that the right to health under Article 12 contains both freedoms and entitlements, including an entitlement to "a system of health protection which provides equality of opportunity for people to enjoy the highest attainable level of health".[18] In its General Comment 14 on the right to health the Committee also repeatedly highlights the importance of non-discrimination and equality of access to health care and health services.[19] Similarly, the European Convention on Human Rights and Biomedicine (Biomedicine Convention),[20] Article 3, provides that states parties "shall take appropriate measures with a view to providing, within their jurisdiction, equitable access to health services of appropriate quality". The Explanatory Report to the Convention clarifies that this requires the absence of unjustified discrimination in access to appropriate health services.[21]

Cultural diversity poses some challenges to the requirement for equal access to appropriate health services. Should health services be designed and implemented in a 'one size fits all' fashion or is it necessary to take diversity into account and offer tailor-made solutions in order to truly provide quality care of an equal standard to all? The right to health under the ICESCR provides an answer to this question. The right to health contains four interrelated and essential elements. These are the *availability* of functioning public health and health care facilities, goods and services, the *accessibility* of these to everyone without discrimination, the *acceptability* of these in light of ethical and cultural considerations and the requirement for *quality* in terms of facilities, goods and services being scientifically and medically appropriate.[22] More precisely, health care facilities, goods and services are not considered *ac-*

16 See e.g. World Health Organization, Commission on Social Determinants of Health Final Report, *Closing the Gap in a Generation: health equity through action on the social determinants of health,* 2008, available at <whqlibdoc.who.int/publications/2008/9789241563703_eng.pdf>, visited on 7 April 2011.

17 International Covenant on Economic, Social and Cultural Rights (adopted 16 December 1966, entered into force 3 January 1976) 993 UNTS 3.

18 Committee on Economic, Social and Cultural Rights, *General Comment no. 14 – The Right to the Highest Attainable Standard of Health,* E/C.12/2000/4, para. 8.

19 Ibid., paras 8, 17-20, 22 and 34-36.

20 Convention for the Protection of Human Rights and Dignity of the Human Being with regard to the Application of Biology and Medicine: Convention on Human Rights and Biomedicine (adopted 4 April 1997, entered into force 1 December 1999) ETS No 164.

21 Convention for the Protection of Human Rights and Dignity of the Human Being with regard to the Application of Biology and Medicine: Convention on Human Rights and Biomedicine (adopted 4 April 1997, entered into force 1 December 1999) ETS No 164, Explanatory Report, available at <conventions.coe.int/Treaty/en/Reports/Html/164.htm>, visited on 15 April 2011, para 25.

22 *General Comment no. 14 – The Right to the Highest Attainable Standard of Health,* supra note 18, para. 12.

ceptable in the sense intended by Article 12 ICESCR unless these are "respectful of medical ethics and culturally appropriate, i.e. respectful of the culture of individuals, minorities, peoples and communities, sensitive to gender and life-cycle requirements, as well as being designed to respect confidentiality and improve the health status of those concerned".[23] Cultural appropriateness has therefore been recognised as constituting one of the fundamental elements of the right to health *per se*. But as pointed out by the Committee on Economic, Social and Cultural Rights, all the normative elements of the right to health are interrelated. The attention given to cultural appropriateness is also closely connected with the emphasis placed on equality and non-discrimination in the context of the right to health. In fact, it can be said to be part and parcel of the requirement for equal treatment and non-discrimination and that the two combine to form the normative basis of the requirement for cultural accommodation in health services.

To understand how cultural appropriateness and non-discrimination come together as the normative pillar supporting the claim to cultural accommodation, it is helpful to look towards the European Convention on Human Rights (ECHR).[24] This is not only because of the relatively advanced state of its jurisprudence, but also because all the Member States to the Convention have incorporated it into domestic legislation[25] with the obvious effect that it is exerting a great influence on their domestic legal systems.

The right to non-discrimination is protected under Article 14 of the ECHR and under Article 1 of Protocol 12 to the Convention. Article 14 ECHR stipulates a general, open model non-discrimination clause. It provides that the rights and freedoms set forth in the Convention shall be secured without discrimination on any ground such as sex, race, colour, language, religion, political or other opinion, national or social origin, association with a national minority, property, birth or other status. On the one hand, it has a very wide range as it is not limited to an exhaustive list of discrimination grounds. On the other hand, Article 14 ECHR has limited scope through being an accessory right applicable only in relation to the enjoyment of the rights and freedoms otherwise protected by the Convention. According to this, Article 14 has no independent existence and the non-discrimination obligation must be linked to the protective scope (the 'ambit') of some other Convention right in order to become effective.[26] Article 1 of Protocol 12 ECHR, however, provides for an independent right to non-discrimination and is not limited to the rights otherwise protected by the Convention. It reaches therefore any kind of discrimination, irrespective of whether or not it relates to the enjoyment of other human rights. Apart from the

23 Ibid.

24 Convention for the Protection of Human Rights and Fundamental Freedoms (adopted 4 November 1950, entered into force 3 September 1953) ETS 5.

25 D.J. Harris, M. O'Boyle, E.P. Bates and C.M. Buckley, *Harris, O'Boyle & Warbrick Law of the European Convention on Human Rights* (Oxford University Press, Oxford, 2nd ed., 2009), p. 23.

26 *Rasmussen* v. *Denmark*, 28 November 1984, ECHR, no. 8777/79, *Series A no. 87*, para. 29.

difference in protective scope, the two provisions incorporate the same conceptual elements.[27]

Prior to 2000, the European Court of Human Rights had always referred to Article 14 ECHR on the ban against discrimination as concerned (only) with safeguarding individuals who are placed in analogous or similar situations against discriminatory differences of treatment.[28] In 2000, however, two interesting conceptual developments took place under the Convention. Firstly, Protocol 12 to the Convention and the explanatory report thereto were adopted. This explanatory report elaborated the principle of equality in a somewhat more detailed manner than had previously been done in case law. It stated the following:

> While the equality principle does not appear explicitly in the text of either Article 14 of the Convention or Article 1 of this Protocol, it should be noted that the non-discrimination and equality principles are closely intertwined. For example, the principle of equality requires that equal situations are treated equally *and unequal situations differently*. Failure to do so will amount to discrimination unless an objective and reasonable justification exists.[29]

The second important development was the judgment of the European Court of Human Rights in the *Thlimmenos* case. The applicant in *Thlimmenos* was a member of the Jehovah's Witnesses and had conscientious objections to military service. For this reason he had served a prison sentence for insubordination, which was defined as a serious criminal offence ('felony') in domestic law. Later he was also denied authorization as a chartered accountant on the grounds that he had been convicted of a serious criminal offence. In this judgment, the Court elaborated a new element of the concept of discrimination under Article 14:

> The Court has so far considered that the right under Article 14 not to be discriminated against in the enjoyment of the rights guaranteed under the Convention is violated when States treat differently persons in analogous situations without providing an objective and reasonable justification [...] However, the Court considers that this is not the only facet of the prohibition of discrimination in Article 14. The right not to be discriminated against in the enjoyment of the rights guaranteed under the Convention is *also violated when States without an objective and reasonable justification fail to treat differently persons whose situations are significantly different.*[30]

27 *Sedjic and Finci* v. *Bosnia and Herzegovina*, 22 December 2009, ECHR, no. 27996/06 and 34836/06, para. 55, <cmiskp.echr.coe.int/tkp197/view.asp?item=1&portal=hbkm&action=html&highlight=P12-1&sessionid=68908807&skin=hudoc-en>, visited on 1 April 2011.

28 *Rasmussen* v. *Denmark*, supra note 26, para. 31.

29 Protocol No. 12 to the Convention for the Protection of Human Rights and Fundamental Freedoms, ETS 177 (adopted 4 November 2000, entered into force 1 April 2005) ETS 177, Explanatory Report, available at <conventions.coe.int/Treaty/en/Reports/Html/177.htm>, visited on 8 April 2011 (emphasis added). Protocol 12 has only been ratified by 18 (mostly Central and Eastern European) Member States to the Council of Europe. Finland is the only Nordic country to have ratified it.

30 *Thlimmenos* v. *Greece*, 6 April 2000, ECHR, no. 34369/97, *Reports of Judgments and Decisions 2000-IV*, para. 44 (emphasis added).

The applicant did not complain of the fact that criminal offenders were excluded from the profession of chartered accountants, but rather that he, as a Jehovah's Witness refusing to serve in the military on religious grounds, belonged to a different class than most other offenders and that the failure to accommodate this difference amounted to discrimination.[31] The Court found there had been a violation of Article 14 taken in conjunction with Article 9 ECHR as the applicant had been found to have been discriminated against when exercising his freedom of religion.[32] This discrimination consisted of failing to treat the applicant differently from other people convicted of a 'felony'. The discrimination was thus the result of failing to fulfil the positive obligation to accommodate the applicant's difference. Since *Thlimmenos,* it has been standard practice by the Court to repeat the conceptual formulation of discrimination provided therein or to state in the context of Article 14 ECHR that "in certain circumstances a failure to attempt to correct inequality through different treatment may, without an objective and reasonable justification, give rise to a breach of that Article ...".[33]

From these developments under the ECHR, it should be clear how the principle of equality, combined with the requirement for 'cultural appropriateness', provides the normative foundations of a claim for accommodation to cultural (ethnic or religious) differences in health services. True equal treatment in the understanding of the ECHR cannot prevail unless significant and relevant differences, which would otherwise lead to or perpetuate exclusion or denial of the full and equal enjoyment of rights, are acted upon with the aim of reducing the disadvantage felt by the person in question.[34] Therefore, if an insensitivity to cultural elements leads to poorer quality health services for those belonging to minority cultural groups, states should endeavour to remedy this through accommodation.

It is not the purpose of the present article to discuss in detail the scope of different human rights norms and their potential reach into public or private health services. Nor is it the purpose to conduct research into whether or not an individual and immediately justiciable right exists to any cultural accommodation in health services under any particular legal norm. For the present purposes it will have to suffice to ascertain that it can be concluded from the developments discussed here that the adaptation of mainstream rules and practices to the needs of minority or marginalised groups, in the context of health services, can certainly be implied by the human rights and non-discrimination perspectives. Regardless of whether an individual and immediately justiciable claim to reasonable accommodation can be raised *de lege lata*

31 Ibid., para. 34.

32 Ibid., paras 42 and 49.

33 E.g. *Sedjic and Finci v. Bosnia and Herzegovina,* 22 December 2009, ECHR, nos. 27996/06 and 34836/06, para. 44, <cmiskp.echr.coe.int/tkp197/view.asp?item=1&portal=hbkm&action=html&highlight=P12-1&sessionid=68908807&skin=hudoc-en>, visited on 1 April 2011.

34 For a more detailed discussion of theoretical develoments relating to the principle of equality in international and European law, see O.M. Arnardóttir, 'Non-discrimination in International and European Law: Towards Substantive Models' 25, *Nordisk Tidsskrift for Menneskerettigheter [Nordic Journal of Human Rights]* (2007), p. 140.

under any particular legal norm, this certainly supports the normative conclusion *de lege ferenda*, that domestic law and practice should endeavour to provide reasonable cultural accommodation in the context of health services.

4 The limits of cultural accommodation in light of the Icelandic experience

To illustrate how some of the issues raised by cultural accommodation in health services might play out in practice and interact with human rights perspectives, I have chosen the publication of a handbook in 2001 called *A Meeting of Cultures: the Effect of Religion, Culture and Heritage on Communication and Treatment in Health Services* by the Directorate of Health and the National University Hospital of Iceland,[35] the revisions that were made in 2008 to *Guidelines in the Event of Death*, originally issued by the Directorate of Health in 1999[36] and *Clinical Guidelines on Palliative Care* issued by the National University Hospital in 2009.[37] In what follows, the guidelines on cultural accommodation provided therein will be described and then assessed in light of the European human rights perspective. The aim is to clarify the limits beyond which cultural accommodation cannot be extended.

4.1. A meeting of cultures

The handbook called *A Meeting of Cultures: the Effect of Religion, Culture and Heritage on Communication and Treatment in Health Services* was published in 2001 by the Directorate of Health and the National University Hospital of Iceland. It focuses attention on the fact that most people find it very important that their religion and cultural heritage are respected and that religion and cultural heritage often have a significant influence on lifestyle choices and personal views regarding treatment and health services. In line with the basic ideology of individualised care, it is asserted that knowledge of the core values adhered to by different social groups is likely to facilitate better communication and more effective treatment and care.[38] The handbook discusses the major world religions and life philosophies; i.e. Judaism, Islam, Buddhism, Hinduism, Taoism, Catholicism, the Eastern Orthodox Churches, Baháism, Mormonism and Jehovah's Witnesses. The general approach is to highlight the beliefs and practices that are different from the ones normally practiced by main-

---

35 Þ. Guðmundsdóttir and V. Ingólfsdóttir, *Menningarheimar mætast: Áhrif trúar, menningar og arfleifðar á samskipti og meðferð innan heilbrigðisþjónustunnar* (Landlæknisembættið og Landspítali háskólasjúkrahús, Reykjavík, 2001), available at <www.landlaeknir.is/Uploads/FileGallery/Utgafa/menningarheim2.pdf >, visited on 8 April 2011.

36 *Leiðbeiningar við andlát: Umönnun látinna og stuðningur við aðstandendur* (2nd ed. revised, Landlæknisembættið, 2008) available at <www.landlaeknir.is/lisalib/getfile.aspx?itemid=3416>, visited on 8 April 2011.

37 Landspítali háskólasjúkrahús, *Klínískar leiðbeiningar Líknarmeðferð: Leiðbeiningar um ákvörðun meðfeðrar og meðrerðarúrræði hjá sjúklingum með lífshættulega og/eða versnandi langvinna sjúkdóma* (1st ed. 2009, updated 2010, Landspítali háskólasjúkrahús, 2010), available at <www.landspitali.is/lisalib/getfile.aspx?itemid=23471>, visited on 8 April 2011.

38 Ibid., pp. 5-6.

stream protestant Icelanders. To give an idea of how, a few examples will be given from each of the religions and life philosophies discussed.

With respect to Judaism, the handbook draws attention, for example, to the basic elements of *kosher* food practices and the fact that Jews are generally opposed to autopsies.[39] As regards abortions, it is explained that they are only accepted in Judaism if the life of the mother is threatened.[40] While most Jews do not oppose treatment and care being provided by persons of the opposite sex it is explained that in some instances, like in the case of pregnant women, some Orthodox Jews may ask for a doctor of the same sex. It is also pointed out that when offering condolences a person of the opposite sex, who is not a part of the family, should not touch the person they are offered to.[41]

Over and above the sometimes similar views and practices related to other major world religions, Islamic beliefs and practices are often singled out for negative discussion in popular culture in Europe. As with other cultural practices, however, the handbook describes these in a neutral manner and gives the general impression that they should be accommodated whenever possible. The issues raised include for example information about the basic elements of *halal* food practices and Islamic hygiene practices.[42] Information is also provided on fasting during Ramadan, including the fact that this includes no medication being administred between sunrise and sunset. As the seriously ill and dying are exempt from the religious obligation to fast, it is recommended that an Imam be involved in order to help negotiate a reasonable solution if this causes significant problems.[43] Further, it is also explained that Muslims are generally opposed to autopsies and that abortions are completely banned in Islam.[44] As regards touching, the handbook explains that Muslims generally do not touch other people, and especially not persons of the opposite sex. It is also explained that if a woman is touched by a man, including a male doctor, she may feel unclean and debased. The handbook also warns that staff should generally avoid bodily contact when offering condolences.[45] Further, the handbook also points out that, as it is considered to be the highest virtue to show prudence and modesty, all Muslims are particularly sensitive towards nudity. Finally, it is explained that Muslims emphasise the separation of the sexes and that this means that interventions and care should be provided by persons of the same sex if at all possible, as this can prevent many problems.[46]

39 Ibid., pp. 8 and 11.

40 Ibid., p. 10.

41 Ibid., p. 11.

42 Ibid., pp. 21 and 23.

43 Ibid., pp. 22 and 25.

44 Ibid., p. 23.

45 Ibid., pp. 23-24.

46 Ibid., p. 24.

As regards Hinduism, the handbook explains that Hindus are generally reluctant to discuss symptoms relating to the reproductive organs, the colon, the bladder and the like, and particularly so when in the presence of others such as family members.[47] Autopsies are considered to show disrespect and are strongly opposed.[48] It is explained that while the emphasis on the separation of the sexes has decreased among Hindus, some might still find it very difficult to be examined and/or treated by individuals of the opposite sex. By the same token, and since Hindus are very sensitive about nudity, it is pointed out that they might find it very difficult to receive help from a person of the opposite sex when bathing.[49]

With respect to Buddhism, it is explained that touching is not as common as is generally the case in Iceland. Many consider the head holy and may consider touching it disrespectful.[50] The handbook also explains that in Buddhism, diseases may be perceived as the result of reprehensible acts in previous lives, which can lead to a certain element of shame being attached to ill health. This may cause a delay in seeking medical treatment compared to other groups. Additionally, since difficulties and suffering are perceived to be a normal part of life and/or a part of repenting past wrongdoings, these patients may complain less than other ones.[51] Finally, as Buddhism emphasises the presence of full consciousness generally and specifically in meeting death, Buddhists may reject pain relief unless it is not sedative.[52]

The handbook also discusses the implications of Taoism for health services. Here, it is the emphasis on the family that raises the most significant issues. In Taoism each family member has a specific status and obligations towards the other family members. The family is the basic social unit and individual interests may have to give way to the interests of the family. The power to make decisions is considered to lie with the eldest member of the family rather than with the individual in question.[53] Touching people is not common practice and healthcare practitioners are warned that touching, and particularly touching the head, might be seen as disrespectful towards the person in question.[54] The handbook further explains that due to the tradition of Eastern medicine, and possibly also the belief that diseases can be the result of past wrongdoings, there may be a delay in seeking (Western) medical attention.[55] As regards communication, the handbook warns that as heritage implies modesty or even an almost submissive attitude towards those who are considered of higher social standing, it is not always possible to assess a person's state by their ap-

47 Ibid., p. 30.

48 Ibid., p. 31.

49 Ibid.

50 Ibid., p. 17.

51 Ibid., p. 15.

52 Ibid., p. 16.

53 Ibid., p. 61.

54 Ibid., p. 62.

55 Ibid., p. 61.

pearance and communication. The handbook also informs that it is a common view that the patient should not be informed immediately of how serious his or her condition is as this may cause increased stress and a worsening of his or her health, whereas patients generally want to be informed when death is near.[56]

As regards Christian denominations and Baháism the main issues discussed in the handbook relate to different views on abortion. The handbook mentions the Catholic opposition to contraceptives and abortion, and points to an emphasis on the provision of the last rites for the dying.[57] Similarly as regards the Eastern Orthodox Church, the main issues relate to opposition to abortion, unless the life of the mother is in danger, as well as opposition to assisted reproduction.[58] When it comes to Baháism and Mormonism, the only significant issue mentioned is a general opposition to abortion unless for special reasons, such as if the life of the mother is in danger.[59] Finally, as regards the Jehovah's Witnesses the main issues mentioned are an opposition to abortion and an opposition to the use of blood or blood products.[60]

4.2. Guidelines in the event of death and clinical guidelines on palliative care

The *Guidelines in the Event of Death*, issued by the Directorate of Health in 1999, were revised in 2008 and now follow many of the recommendations put forward in the handbook *A meeting of Cultures*. Over and above general procedures, applicable across the board, some specific procedures are provided for with regard to Jews, Muslims and those of Asian extraction. In this respect these guidelines often simply repeat the same information that is provided in the handbook, but sometimes in a slightly more direct tone that indicates more clearly what is to be done and what is not to be done. For example, the guidelines provide that that if the body of a Muslim is not prepared for burial by family members, it should be prepared by a person of the same sex as the deceased person, "if at all possible".[61] In the case of those of Asian extraction the guidelines also specifically state that the top of the head of the deceased should not be touched unnecessarily.[62] In all instances it is stipulated that handshakes and hugs are inappropriate when offering condolences[63] and in all instances it is also stipulated that if the slightest language difficulties exist, the assistance of an interpreter shall be sought "if at all possible".[64]

56 Ibid., p. 63.

57 Ibid., pp. 36-37.

58 Ibid., p. 41.

59 Ibid., pp. 47 and 51.

60 Ibid., pp. 55-56.

61 Ibid., p. 13.

62 Ibid., p. 17.

63 Ibid., pp. 14, 18 and 22.

64 Ibid., pp. 16, 20 and 24.

The *Clinical Guidelines on Palliative Care* issued in 2009, are of a somewhat different nature than the other examples discussed here. Instead of the (mostly) discursive style in the handbook *A meeting of Cultures* and in the *Guidelines in the Event of Death,* the *Clinical Guidelines* contain very condensed, specific and direct guidance. They refer to the handbook *A Meeting of Culture,* but also to the *Guidelines on Palliative Care* from the US-based Institute for Clinical Systems Improvement as their main source of inspiration.[65] Cultural issues are discussed in Chapter 5 of the *Clinical Guidelines.* Here, cultural accommodation is generally encouraged and it is also strongly recommended that certified interpreters are used whenever possible since the use of other members of staff or members of the family can lead to inaccuracies, errors or detraction from subjects considered taboo.[66] The *Clinical Guidelines* list the following 'important issues' more specifically:

> Many cultural groups do not wish to know about life threatening diseases.
>
> In cultural groups where patients are not informed about the seriousness of the diagnosis, it is possible that the family wishes that the patient's condition is only discussed with them.
>
> When treatment options are assessed it is necessary to keep in mind that in some cultural groups it is the family that takes decisions regarding treatment and not the patient.
>
> Frank discussions about the progression of a disease and its treatment can be undesirable in situations where this is considered detrimental to the welfare of the patient.
>
> When a conversation takes place through an interpreter, it is important to prepare the interpreter and use a certified interpreter if possible.[67]

Further, the *Clinical Guidelines* recommend that health service providers assess cultural issues from the perspectives of the religion and the concrete background of the patient, the resources available in the patient's community, the views of the patient and his or her family on death and the provision of information and, finally, from the perspective of how decisions are taken within the patient's family and whether the emphasis is on the patient individually or on the family as a decision-making authority.[68] Ethical and legal concerns are discussed in Chapter 9 of the *Guidelines.* Here, it is emphasised that the Act on the Rights of Patients no. 74/1997 must be respected.

65 *Klínískar leiðbeiningar Líknarmeðferð,* supra note 37, p. 2 and 36. For the most current edition of the guidelines of the Insitute for Clinical Systems Improvement, see Institute for Clinical Systems Improvement, *Health Care Guideline: Palliative Care* 3rd. ed., 2009, available at <www.icsi.org/palliative_care/palliative_care_11918.html>, visited on 20 April 2011.

66 Ibid., pp. 36-37.

67 Ibid., p. 36.

68 Ibid.

As regards decision-making more specifically the *Guidelines* remind that informed consent from the patient is needed for treatment decisions, but that, under the Act, specific rules apply if the patient is legally incompetent or otherwise unable to provide informed consent. As regards decision-making by proxy, the *Guidelines* remind that this requires a specific mandate, e.g. as part of a living will.[69]

4.3. *Assessment in light of European human rights*

The publication of the handbook *A Meeting of Cultures* is to be welcomed. It is intended to inform health service staff and it does so effectively through a balanced and neutral overview of the possible needs and expectations of different minority groups in the context of health services. It was carefully researched and its preparation included consultation with people from all the groups discussed.[70] Although the handbook neither positively requires nor bans any specific procedures or approaches, the general tone is one of accommodation, which is well in line with the human rights requirement for equal access to culturally-appropriate health services for all. The handbook has also clearly had an effect on the preparation of subsequent guidelines relating to end-of-life situations and palliative care, and it might have a similar effect on such initiatives in other areas. Such guidelines are of a more direct nature and therefore stipulate more specific do's and don'ts. On a general note, this is to be welcomed as well. The handbook and the *Clinical Guidelines on Palliative Care* both have the express purpose of enabling health service providers to meet the specific needs and expectations of individuals from minority cultural backgrounds.[71] It is also commendable that alongside encouraging cultural accommodation they also warn against overemphasising the relevance of culture since the views of people within each cultural group are not necessarily uniform,[72] and since excessive stereotyping is disrespectful and may lead to discriminatory treatment.[73] However, while cultural accommodation in health services is informed by the human rights requirement for equal access to appropriate health services for all, this can go too far and possibly lead to violations of other human rights. The direct and simplistic formulation of the *Clinical Guidelines on Palliative Care* raises some issues of concern when assessed against other human rights norms.

Article 1 UDHR provides that "[a]ll human beings are born free and equal in dignity and rights. They are endowed with reason and conscience and should act towards one another in a spirit of brotherhood." The references herein to freedom, equality and dignity are in fact indicative of the most fundamental themes of hu-

69 Ibid., p. 43.

70 Þ. Guðmundsdóttir and V. Ingólfsdóttir, supra note 35, p. 67.

71 Ibid., p. 5 and *Klínískar leiðbeiningar Líknarmeðferð*, supra note 37, p. 36.

72 Ibid.

73 Hendriks, supra note 2, pp. 291-292.

man rights law, themes which have a great effect on the interpretation of all human rights norms. The requirements implied by the equality principle have already been discussed in Section 3 *supra*. The interpretative themes of freedom and dignity, how they inform specific rights relevant in the context of health law and interact with equality and cultural accommodation, will be addressed in what follows. For reasons already mentioned, the discussion will primarily focus on the protection provided by the ECHR, but other sources of international and European human rights law will be referred to as and when relevant.

4.3.1. Individual freedom and dignity

Some human rights are defined as rights belonging to groups. Examples include the right of peoples to self-determination under Article 1 of the International Covenant on Civil and Political Rights (ICCPR)[74] and the rights of persons belonging to ethnic, religious or linguistic minorities under Article 27 ICCPR, to enjoy and practice their own culture, religion or language in community with other members of their group. Such group-oriented rights constitute, however, an exception to the main principle that human rights are essentially *individual* rights where the holder of rights is an individual and not a group of individuals such as families, ethnic minorities or 'peoples'. This is clearly expressed in the focus of Article 1 UDHR on the freedom, equality and dignity of individual human beings. Apart from the right to health under Article 12 ICESCR, the most relevant individual rights in the field of health law are the right to life under Article 6 ICCPR and Article 2 ECHR, the prohibition of torture, inhuman or degrading treatment under Article 7 ICCPR and Article 3 ECHR, the right to liberty and security of the person under Article 9 ICCPR and Article 5 ECHR and the right to respect for private and family life under Article 17 ICCPR and Article 8 ECHR.

While the requirement of respect for human dignity is generally not expressed as a right in and of itself in international human rights conventions, its importance as an underlying interpretative theme usually finds expression in either the preambular paragraphs or in general stipulations regarding the purpose of human rights conventions. The ECHR and its preamble, however, never mention human dignity. Even so, the European Court of Human Rights has referred to human dignity as constituting, with freedom, "the very essence" of the ECHR.[75] This reference to freedom and dignity as the very essence of the Convention can be seen not only as confirmation of the importance of human dignity in human rights law *per se*, but also as confirmation of the importance of autonomy in the form of individual freedom to make one's own life choices. In the *Pretty* judgment, concerning assisted suicide, the Euro-

74 International Covenant on Civil and Political Rights (adopted 16 December 1966, entered into force 23 March 1976) 999 UNTS 171.

75 *Christine Goodwin* v. *UK*, 11 July 2002, ECHR, no. 28957/95, *Reports of Judgments and Decisions 2002-VI*, para. 90 and *Pretty* v. *UK*, 29 April 2002, ECHR, no. 2346/02, *Reports of Judgments and Decisions 2002-III*, para. 65.

pean Court of Human Rights accordingly noted that "[a]lthough no previous case has established as such any right to self-determination as being contained in Article 8 of the Convention, the Court considers that the notion of personal autonomy is an important principle underlying the interpretation of its guarantees".[76] This was one of the first express recognitions of the importance of personal autonomy in the case law of the Court. In the subsequent *Evans* judgment, concerning the use of embryos, the Court clearly elevated personal autonomy from the status of an interpretative principle to the status of a right *per se.* In this judgment the Court, sitting as a Grand Chamber, stated that the concept of private life protected under Article 8 ECHR encompasses, *inter alia,* "the right to personal autonomy".[77] However, while emphasised under Article 8 in this manner, personal autonomy like other rights has its limits and can never go so far as to legitimise the violation of the competing rights or personal autonomy of others.[78]

The judgments mentioned above all concern issues closely related to the provision of health services, i.e. the situation of post-operative transsexuals, assisted suicide and the use of embryos. This exhibits how the individual perspective and the emphasis on human dignity and personal autonomy are particularly pronounced in the context of health law. This is also further exhibited in the Biomedicine Convention, Article 1 of which stipulates that the purpose of the Convention is to "protect the dignity and identity of all human beings and guarantee everyone, without discrimination, respect for their integrity and other rights and fundamental freedoms with regard to the application of biology and medicine". Further, its Article 2 emphasises that "[t]he interests and welfare of the human being shall prevail over the sole interest of society or science".

The underlying human rights themes of equality, dignity and freedom provide the deep structures of human rights law, which "open the conceptual space for legal thinking and argumentation, [but] also close it off from essentially different ways of thinking and arguing legally".[79] Thus, they provide the foundations upon which more specific human rights are built, including the right to life and the protection of privacy. With regard to end-of-life decisions made in the health care setting and in concordance with the deep structures of the law these specific rights include the right to take one's own decisions and a right to receive the information necessary for taking them, which have found specific protection under Articles 3 and 8 of the ECHR, in the Biomedicine Convention and in national legislation on the rights of patients.

---

76 *Pretty* v. *UK*, ibid., para. 61.

77 *Evans* v. *UK*, 10 April 2007, ECHR, no. 6339/05, para. 71, <cmiskp.echr.coe.int/tkp197/portal.asp?sessionId=69896487&skin=hudoc-en&action=request>, visited on 19 April 2011.

78 Ibid., para. 90. The case concerned a couple who had stored embryos before the woman underwent the surgical removal of her ovaries. After their divorce, the woman wanted to use the embryos to become a parent in the genetic sense, whereas the man had no wish to have a genetically-related child with her. She had been denied the opportunity to have the embryos implanted into her uterus and this was, with reference to the competing rights of the man, not found to be in violation of her rights under Article 8.

79 K. Tuori, *Critical Legal Positisim* (Ashgate, Aldershot, 2002), p. 193.

4.3.2. Protection of privacy and informed consent

Article 8 is the primary medium of protecting personal autonomy in the context of medical interventions under the ECHR. The European Court of Human Rights has made clear that the protective scope of Article 8 of the ECHR includes the physical and psychological integrity of the person,[80] including a right to personal autonomy,[81] which obviously encompasses all decision-making and interventions in the field of health. It is thus clear that any medical intervention undertaken without the consent of the person in question, or of his or her formally-authorised legal representative, raises serious issues under Article 8.[82] Even minor interferences with a person's physical integrity are considered an interference with the right to respect for private life under Article 8.[83] The Court has also established that as a general rule, the consent relied upon must be "free, express and informed".[84] The *Juhnke* judgment provides an example of how the Court interprets the requirement of free and informed consent. Here, the person in question was held in detention *incommunicado* for several days prior to a gynaecological examination and was, thus, considered to be in a "particularly vulnerable mental state". [85] She resisted the examination, but was persuaded to consent to it by a medical doctor through some unclear references to it being a legal necessity. The Court, of course, concluded that this could not be considered free or informed consent.[86] The Court has also made clear that Article 8 protects the right of a person to decline to consent to life-prolonging treatment.[87] In contrast to the protective scope of Article 8, which reaches even minor interventions, Article 3 protects against torture and inhuman and degrading treatment, which means that the treatment complained of must attain a certain minimum level of severity. This must be assessed in each individual case with reference to "the nature and context of the treatment, the manner and method of its execution, its duration, its physical or mental effects and, in some cases, the sex, age and state of health of the victim".[88] Article 3 would only be implicated in the most extreme cases, e.g. with regard to the forceful administering of food and medication to detainees[89] or the forceful extraction of criminal evidence from detainee's bodies.[90]

---

80 *Pretty* v. *UK*, supra note 75, para. 61.

81 *Evans* v. *UK*, supra note 77, para. 71.

82 *Storck* v. *Germany*, 6. June 2005, ECHR, no. 61603/00, *Reports of Judgments and Decisions 2005-V*, para. 143.

83 Ibid.

84 *Glass* v. *UK*, 9 March 2004, ECHR, no. 61827/00, *Reports of Judgments and Decisions 2004-II*, para. 82.

85 *Juhnke* v. *Turkey*, 13 May 2008, ECHR, no. 52515/99, para. 77, <cmiskp.echr.coe.int/tkp197/portal.asp?sessionId=69642237&skin=hudoc-en&action=request>, visited on 19 April 2011.

86 Ibid.

87 *Pretty* v. *UK*, supra note 75, para. 63.

88 *Kudla* v. *Poland*, 26 October 2000, ECHR, no. 30210/96, *Reports of Judgments and Decisions 2000-XI*, para. 91.

89 *Herczegefalvy* v. *Austria*, 24 September 2992, ECHR, no. 10533/83, *Series A no. 244* and *Nevmerzhitsky* v. *Ukraine*, 5 April 2005, ECHR, no. 5482/00, *Reports of Judgments and Decisions 2005-II*.

90 *Jalloh* v. *Germany*, 11 July 2006, ECHR, no. 54810/00, *Reports of Judgments and Decisions 2006-IX*.

The Biomedicine Convention fills the rough outline provided by the case law under Article 8 ECHR with more specific and detailed provisions on informed consent and the right to information. Its Article 5 stipulates the following:

> Any intervention in the health field may only be carried out after the person concerned has given free and informed consent to it.
>
> This person shall beforehand be given appropriate information as to the purpose and nature of the intervention as well as on its consequences and risks.
>
> The person concerned may freely withdraw consent at any time.

The Biomedicine Convention further stipulates that in emergency situations medically necessary interventions may be carried out for the benefit of the person's health without the consent of the patient or his or her legal representative, cf. Article 8. Article 9 also requires that any previously expressed wishes should be taken into account when the patient is not in a state to express his or her wishes. According to the Explanatory Report to the Convention the main principle of informed consent provided in Article 5 "makes clear patients' autonomy in their relationship with health care professionals and restrains the paternalist approaches which might ignore the wish of the patient".[91] As regards the question of whether 'free and informed' consent must also always be 'express' (verbal or written), the Explanatory Report clarifies that this is not always so. Consent may be implied in the context of routine medical acts, whereas express consent is rather required in cases involving invasive treatments.[92] Similarly, it is explained that consent is only free and informed in the understanding of the Convention "if it is given on the basis of objective information from the responsible health care professional as to the nature and the potential consequences of the planned intervention or of its alternatives, in the absence of any pressure from anyone".[93] As regards information on the state of the health of the patient specifically, the Biomedicine Convention further provides in Article 10(2) that "[e]veryone is entitled to know any information collected about his or her health" and that "the wishes of individuals not to be so informed shall be observed". But as pointed out in the Explanatory Report "[t]his does not, however, obviate the need to seek consent to the intervention proposed to the patient".[94]

Looking, finally, at the domestic legal regulation in Iceland, it can be said that the Icelandic Act on the Rights of Patients no. 74/1997 mirrors the requirements of the ECHR and the Biomedicine Convention. Article 5 provides for the patient's 'right to know' information about his or her health and treatment options and a right to interpretation in the case of language difficulties. Article 6 provides for the 'right not to

---

91 Biomedicine Convention, Explanatory Report, supra note 21, para. 34.

92 Ibid., para. 37.

93 Ibid., para. 35.

94 Ibid., para. 40.

know' any or all of the relevant information. Further, Article 7(3) stipulates that "[n] o treatment may be given without the consent of the patient" and that "[c]onsent shall be in writing whenever possible and indicate the information provided to the patient, and that he/she has understood the information". Article 7(1) also provides that the patient has the right to decide whether or not he or she accepts treatment. Article 7(2) refers to the Act on Legal Competence no. 71/1997 as regards decision-making authority for minors and other legally incompetent patients. In situations where the patient is legally competent, but unable to give his or her consent to highly necessary treatment, Article 9 provides that consent shall be considered implied unless it is known with certainty that the patient would have denied treatment.

4.3.3. *Conclusions on the limits of cultural accommodation in light of the Icelandic experience*

From the above discussion it can be concluded that all the legal norms examined exhibit that the primary focus is on the individual personal autonomy of the patient and not on his or her family. The legal norms on the protection of privacy and informed consent clearly protect against all paternalist approaches and pressures, whether they stem from the health service professionals in question or the patient's family. It is clear that there can be no talk of free and informed consent if information is only provided to the family of the patient and/or if the doctor is too willing to accommodate the family or the eldest member of the family as the actual decision-maker, thus enabling family members either to exert undue pressure on the patient or override his or her will completely. As regards information specifically, the patient clearly also has an individual 'right to know' all of the relevant information concerning his or her health and treatment options. Discussing the relevant issues solely with the patient's family would therefore constitute a violation of the patient's right to know, regardless of his or her cultural background. At the same time, the patient also has a 'right not to know'. It can thus be part and parcel of cultural accommodation to ask about the patient's wishes in this regard in order to enable him or her to exercise that right. It is still the patient who should be asked - not his or her family. And even if the patient exercises this right, his or her consent, or the consent of his or her formally-authorised legal representative, will still be needed. The *Clinical Guidelines on Palliative Care* must be understood in the light of these conclusions. When they state that "it is possible that the family wishes that the patient's condition is only discussed with them" and that "it is necessary to keep in mind that in some cultural groups it is the family that takes decisions regarding treatment and not the patient",[95] they cannot be followed to the letter without violating the human rights of the patient.

---

95 *Klínískar leiðbeiningar Líknarmeðferð*, supra note 37, p. 36.

5 Conclusions

The claim to reasonable accommodation has become a distinct element of the concept of equality and non-discrimination in international human rights law. This implies the adaptation of mainstream rules and practices to the needs of minority or marginalised groups that would otherwise be denied the equal enjoyment of rights. The right to equal access to health care and health services, which is emphasised as a key element of the right to health,[96] cannot be truly enjoyed without appropriate and reasonable cultural accommodation. This is also recognised under Article 12 ICESCR, which requires that health-care facilities, goods and services are 'culturally appropriate'.[97]

Like all other human rights based claims the claim to cultural accommodation, however, has its limits. Firstly, it is clear that it cannot go so far as to destroy or excessively limit other rights.[98] Respect for one person's culture, or autonomy, cannot justify an utter disrespect of, or violations against, the culture or autonomy of others. As always in human rights law, a balance must be struck. In the case of competing individual autonomies or rights, the relative interests and concerns must be weighed up before a decision is reached.[99] The same applies where competing cultures are involved; here, however, the decision-makers must be aware that "although individual interests must on occasion be subordinated to those of a group, democracy does not simply mean that the views of a majority must always prevail: a balance must be achieved which ensures the fair and proper treatment of minorities and avoids any abuse of a dominant position".[100] In any event, the willingness to accommodate culture can never be extended so far as to contravene the basic paradigms that provide the deep structures of human rights law, guide all interpretation and define acceptable ways of thinking and arguing legally. Under European human rights law it is therefore unthinkable that cultural accommodation, commendable as it may be, will ever be able outweigh the respect for the dignity and *individual* personal autonomy of patients that is enshrined in the ECHR and the Biomedicine Convention. Examples from domestic practice indicating otherwise, like Chapter 5 of the Icelandic *Clinical Guidelines on Palliative Care* discussed in this article, should therefore be revised accordingly.

96 *General Comment no. 14 – The Right to the Highest Attainable Standard of Health,* supra note 18, para. 19.

97 Ibid., para. 12.

98 See e.g. Article 17 ECHR.

99 E.g. *Evans* v. *UK,* supra note 77, para. 90.

100 *Sørensen and Rasmussen* v. *Denmark,* supra note 13, para. 58.

Female Genital Mutilation and the Right to Privacy: a Double-edged Sword

By Professor Henriette Sinding Aasen, University of Bergen[1]

1 Introduction and background

As the world becomes more globalized, and as war, hunger and other crises force people to leave their homes, the Nordic and other European societies are becoming increasingly diverse or multicultural. Immigrants tend to bring their culture, traditions and ways of life with them from their countries of origin. Not only have foreign food, music, religions, spices and clothing changed the cultural profile of Norway and other countries, but also traditions that challenge common values in a more fundamental or direct way. Female genital mutilation (FGM) is an example of an old, foreign tradition which has arrived in Norway with immigration, mainly from the African continent and from parts of the Middle East and Asia. In this article, the focus is on coercive or involuntary FGM performed on young girls. Coercive interventions are clearly the most problematic from a human rights perspective, and in light of traditional Western values of individual autonomy and integrity, including the "informed consent" doctrine in European and international health law.

The tradition of FGM is rooted in social structures, practices and gender roles that clearly contradict modern Western views on women's rights and gender equality. FGM is not only associated with gender inequality and inferiority, but also with serious health problems for girls and women, and even death. At the international level (United Nations, World Health Organization), FGM is recognized as a violation of women's right to life, health, integrity and equality. It is viewed as a form of violence against women.[2] In Norway, as well as in the other Nordic countries, the practice is forbidden and criminalized by national law.[3] At the European level, the

1 Henriette Sinding Aasen (dr. juris) is professor at Faculty of law, University of Bergen, Norway. Her main research activities are in the area of health and human rights, with a particular focus on vulnerable groups (children, immigrants, women). She has participated in several national law commissions in the area of health, human rights and biomedical research, and is currently the leader of three interdisciplinary research projects on welfare state law, juridification and the right to health.

2 UN Declaration on the Elimination of Violence against Women (1993).

3 Act of 15 December 1995 No. 74, §1 (Norway).

European Court of Human Rights (ECtHR) has delivered several judgments on FGM, stating that FGM is a violation of fundamental human rights.[4] However, despite legal prohibition and criminalization, very few countries prosecute cases of FGM[5]; from time to time, there is some discussion as to whether or not girls who live in Norway are in danger of being circumcised, either in Norway or when travelling abroad. The media focus on girls from Norway being circumcised abroad[6] has led to heated public debates among politicians, human rights defenders, health personnel, researchers and others about the factual circumstances, as well as what constitutes appropriate and effective preventative measures when protecting girls within Norwegian jurisdiction from falling victim to FGM.[7] In particular, and in addition to the "softer" approaches, the legalisation of systematic and obligatory medical examinations conducted on immigrant girls, and girls with an immigrant background, has been a topic of public debate in Norway since 2000.[8]

This forms the backdrop for the main question posed in this article: Which measures should Norway and other countries take in order to fulfil their human rights obligations and provide the necessary and effective protection against FGM? And which measures should not be implemented, in particular due to human rights concerns? The analysis reflects the increasing need to consider the human rights implications of government policies and regulations in the field of health (and other areas of public interest). It also reflects the interplay and interaction between national and international law, and how human rights provide important legal tools when striking a fair balance between conflicts of interest in the fields of health protection and gender politics. Of particular interest, from a health law perspective, is the analysis of privacy protection, which, in the context of FGM, provides protection in two related but opposing directions: On the one hand, protection against FGM as a clear violation of bodily integrity and privacy, and on the other, protection against privacy interventions in order to prevent FGM, e.g. involuntary health examinations. A compelling question is how to balance these two related, but opposing, needs and interests?

---

4 R. Kool, "The Dutch approach to female genital mutilation in view of the ECHR. The time for change has come", Vol 6, Issue 1, *Utrecht Law Review* (2010), pp. 51-62.

5 Ibid., saying that only France prosecutes reported cases of FGM. In the US (Georgia), a father was sentenced to ten years in prison for FGM on his 2-year-old daughter, *Aftenposten*, 2 November 2006.

6 Example headline in one leading newspaper: "Tusenvis av norske jenter i fare for å bli lemlestet. Norske jenter får klitoris, indre- og ytre kjønnslepper kappet av før de sys igjen" [Thousands of Norwegian girls in danger of mutilation. Norwegian girls have their clitoris and inner and outer labia cut off before being sealed???], *Dagbladet*, 29 August, 2005. In June 2007, national broadcaster NRK reported that 185 Norwegian-Somali girls had been circumcised over the last three years in Hargeisa, Somalia (Lidén and Bentzen, see note 12, p. 16).

7 In Norway, the public debate has ebbed and flowed since 1995, peaking in the summer of 2007 when the government initiated several measures (information campaigns to schools, health personnel, police and others, open health centres in particular areas, the establishment of a national advisory board, new plan of action, etc.) in response to media reports about overseas circumcisions being performed on girls from Norway (H.S. Aasen, *Menneskerettslige aspekter knyttet til kjønnslemlestelse og helseundersøkelser [Human rights aspects of female genital mutilation and health examinations]*, Institutt for offentlig retts skriftserie, Oslo, 2008, No. 5, pp. 2-3, 60-61. This publication is based on a report submitted to the Ministry of Children, Equality and Social Inclusion (May 2008) concerning human rights and the use of medical examinations to prevent FGM.

8 Ibid., p. 2.

2 Female genital mutilation: a brief description and its prevalence in Norway

2.1 Different types of FGM and the consequences for women[9]

FGM comprises all procedures that involve partial or total removal of the external female genitalia, or other injury to the female genital organs for non-medical reasons. The practice is mostly carried out by traditional circumcisers, who often play other key roles within communities, e.g. attending childbirths. Increasingly, however, FGM is being performed by health care providers. Procedures are mostly carried out on young girls, some time between infancy and the age of 15, and occasionally on adult women. In Africa, about three million girls are at risk of FGM annually. Between 100 and 140 million girls and women are living with the consequences of FGM worldwide. In Africa, about 92 million girls aged 10 and over are estimated to have undergone FGM.

Female genital mutilation is classified according to four major types.

- Clitoridectomy: partial or total removal of the clitoris
- Excision: partial or total removal of the clitoris and the labia minora, with or without excision of the labia majora (the labia are "the lips" that surround the vagina).
- Infibulation: narrowing of the vaginal opening by creating a covering seal. The seal is formed by cutting and repositioning the inner, or outer, labia, with or without the removal of the clitoris.
- Other: all other harmful procedures performed on the female genitalia for non-medical purposes, e.g. pricking, piercing, incising, scraping and cauterizing the genital area.

FGM has no health benefits, and harms girls and women in many ways. It involves removing and damaging healthy and normal female genital tissue, and interferes with the natural functions of girls' and women's bodies. Immediate complications can include severe pain, shock, haemorrhaging (bleeding), tetanus or sepsis (bacterial infection), urine retention, open sores in the genital region, and injury to adjacent genital tissue. Long-term consequences can include: recurrent bladder and urinary tract infections, cysts, infertility, an increased risk of childbirth complications and newborn deaths, and the need for surgery later on.

9 World Health Organization, Fact Sheet No. 241 on FGM, February 2010.

2.2 FGM in Norway

Although FGM does not directly affect ethnic Norwegian women and girls, it does affect immigrant women and girls, as well as women and girls with an immigrant background living in Norway (and in other Nordic countries). In some African countries, e.g. Egypt, Sudan, Ethiopia, Eritrea, Somalia, Mali, and Sierra Leone, at least 90 % of women are circumcised.[10] These high numbers indicate that many women from these countries who currently live in Norway have been circumcised. In 2000, around 10,000 circumcised women were living in Norway.[11] In 2008, a study estimated that around 6,047 girls under the age of 20, whose background was in countries practicing FGM (Somalia, Ethiopia, Eritrea, Sudan, Gambia, and Sierra Leone), were living in Norway. Among these were 3,800 girls of the age when circumcision is common in their country of origin.[12] Just how many of these have been circumcised is not known. The study from 2008 concludes with 15 known cases of FGM reported between 2006 and 2007. However, most of these were carried out before 2000.[13] Between 2006 and 2007, six cases were reported to the police.[14] In 2009, 14 child welfare agencies received 41 new case alerts and initiated inquiries in 44 cases. More than one in three alerts were dismissed, with two in three investigated cases being closed without further action.[15] In the same year, a Somali couple were accused and imprisoned over FGM, on two of their daughters, but were later released after the girls had been medically examined at the hospital and it had been established that FGM had not taken place.[16]

Circumcised women not only suffer from the health problems caused by FGM, but also from the stigma associated with this tradition in Norway. These women need the help of the health service, and support groups etc, in handling the physical and psychological pain that many of them experience. Reception centres for asylum seekers are obliged to help circumcised women to obtain medical treatment.[17] However, it is also psychologically painful to lose the dignity associated with circumcision in one's country of origin, something which is replaced, in Norway and other Western countries, by stigma and strong negative attention.

10 A. Talle, "Kulturell og historisk sammenheng" [Cultural and historical context], in Foss (ed.), *Omskjæring. Stopp* (Cappelen Damm, Oslo, 2010), p. 41, with reference to a WHO report from 2008.

11 W. Jonassen and R. Saur, *Arbeid med kjønnslemlestelse i Norge [Work on FGM in Norway]*, Nasjonalt kunnskapssenter om vold og traumatisk stress, Oslo, Rapport 1/2011, p. 32.

12 H. Lidén and T. Bentzen, *Kjønnslemlestelse i Norge [FGM in Norway]*, Institute for Social Research, Oslo, Rapport 2008:8, pp. 65, 74.

13 Ibid., p. 86.

14 Lidén and Bentzen, supra note 12, p. 82.

15 Jonassen and Saur, supra note 11, p. 16.

16 *Verdens Gang*, 30 June 2009.

17 Jonassen and Saur, supra note 11, p. 16.

2.3 *National efforts to combat FGM*

The Norwegian government has undertaken several initiatives in order to live up to its human rights obligations to combat FGM: Legislation which criminalizes any person who wilfully performs an operation on a woman's genitalia which damages them or inflicts permanent change on them. The penalty is dependent on the seriousness of the action, and could be up to eight years' imprisonment if the operation has resulted in death or serious injury to the woman's body or health. Accomplices are liable to the same penalty.[18] Concerning effectiveness, it is also essential that persons who assist in the performance of FGM are liable to punishment, since FGM typically depends on the collaboration of family members or relatives. The Act not only punishes acts performed in Norway, but also acts performed by Norwegians abroad, or by persons who live in Norway, cf. the Criminal Act, Section 12. This means that parents who bring a daughter abroad in order to get her circumcised are liable to be punished upon arriving back in Norway. In the new Criminal Act of 20 May 2005 No.28, the punishment for serious forms of FGM has been increased to a maximum of fifteen years' imprisonment (Section 285, not yet in force), signalling the strong condemnation of FGM in Norway. However, so far, no one has been convicted of FGM in Norway.[19]

The act prohibiting FGM obligates professionals and other relevant persons to avert FGM:

> Professionals and persons employed in child care centres, the child welfare service, the health and social welfare service, schools, day care facilities for schoolchildren, and religious communities who wilfully fail to seek to avert, by formal complaint or in another manner, female genital mutilation ... shall be liable to fines or imprisonment for a term not exceeding one year. The same applies to elders or religious leaders of a religious community. The duty to avert such an act shall apply regardless of any duty of confidentiality (Section 2).

Thus, Norway has taken strong legislative steps to combat FGM, including the strict duty to avert such actions.

In addition to the duty to avert FGM, existing legislation applicable to all health personnel, as well as to public agencies, organizations, and private institutions performing duties on behalf of the state, county, or municipality, are duty bound to report to the child protection service when they have reason to believe that a child is being mistreated by its guardians or exposed to other forms of serious neglect.[20] This means that these groups are obligated to report to the child welfare service if they have reason

18 Act prohibiting female genital mutilation of 15 December 1995 No. 74, section 1. The act was in force from 1 September 2004.

19 From Sweden it is reported of a conviction for FGM in 2006 (see RH 2007:7). In Denmark, the first (and possibly so far the only) court case appeared in 2009 (http://www.svd.se/nyheter/utrikes/forsta-dansk-dom-for-konsstympning_2369063.svd#after-ad, checked at May 6, 2011).

20 Health Personnel Act of 2 July 1999 No. 64, Section 33, and Child Welfare Act of 17 July 1992 No. 100, Section 6-4.

to believe that a specific girl has been exposed to FGM since, according to Norwegian law, this is considered an act of serious mistreatment and neglect.

In addition, due to the observation that legislation alone cannot prevent FGM, the government has also taken several more "soft" approaches in order to combat FGM. The national Plan of Action to combat FGM for 2008-2011 includes several initiatives: the effective implementation of the legislation, including guidelines to professionals regarding their responsibilities,[21] increased competence for health care personnel, teachers, child welfare workers, and other relevant professionals, the distribution of knowledge, the improvement of reporting routines, prevention and campaigns directed at changing attitudes in the affected groups, accessible health care services, augmented efforts concerning holidays as well as augmented international efforts. However, there has recently been criticism that many of the planned initiatives have not yet been implemented.[22] In a recent overview of national efforts, it was pointed out that three organizations are better than the rest when it comes to combating FGM: the health services, the child welfare services, and the reception centres for asylum seekers.[23] However, the authors of this report recommend augmenting the competence of child welfare service staff when it comes to their duty to avert FGM.[24] The asylum reception centres are obligated to inform all newcomers that FGM is prohibited in Norway. In addition, pilot studies and efforts to improve contact and dialogue between the public agencies and the affected groups, are based on the notion that change must come from within the affected groups.[25]

On 13 November 2008, the government decided to offer clinical examinations to all girls and women whose background was in areas where FGM is common. These examinations are to be based on informed consent and offered within a year of arriving in Norway. Girls already living here are offered such examinations in 5th and 10th grade. The government considered obligatory health examinations, but met resistance from researchers[26] and decided not to implement involuntary health examinations of girls from particular groups.[27]

In 2009, two cases sere reported where the immigration authorities had requested Somali parents to have their daughters examined yearly (for 17 years) in order for them to stay in Norway.[28] Thus, it appears that involuntary measures are still being implemented.

---

21 For example, *Veileder om regelverk, roller og ansvar knyttet til kjønnslemlestelse [Guidelines on legislation, roles and responsibilities related to FGM]*, issued by the Ministry of Children, Equality and Social Inclusion and the Ministry of Health and Care Services, Mentor Media as at 06/2008.

22 After 2 years, only 6 of the 41 suggested measures had been implemented, according to *Verdens Gang* 5 October 2010.

23 Jonassen and Saur, supra note 11, p. 16.

24 Ibid., p. 113.

25 Aasen, supra note 7, pp. 60-65.

26 Lidén and Bentzen, supra note 12, and Aasen, supra note 7.

27 Announcement of 13 November 2008, http://www.regjeringen.no/en/dep/bld/pressesenter/pressemeldinger/2008/tilbud-om-underlivsundersokelse.

28 *Verdens Gang* 18 May 2009.

3 Female genital mutilation, human rights and state obligations

3.1 Overview

FGM violates, or represents a threat to, several human rights that are protected by international human rights instruments ratified by all Nordic and European countries: the right to freedom from torture and degrading treatment,[29] the right to life,[30] health,[31] privacy,[32] freedom from discrimination (including gender prejudices and gender stereotypes),[33] and freedom from harmful traditional practices.[34] The human rights provisions mentioned are all enshrined in Norwegian law, and are to be given precedence in the event of conflicting with national law, cf. the Human Rights Act, Sections 3 and 2.[35] They impose duties and responsibilities on states to respect, protect, and fulfil the rights concerned.[36] More specifically, national governments are to protect the rights of women and children and prevent them from being victims of FGM within the relevant state's jurisdiction. State obligations embrace obligations to provide effective protection against harmful practices such as FGM, and the right to physical integrity, privacy, and health, as well as effective protection against discrimination based on ethnicity, nationality, or other status.[37]

Due to limitations of space, this chapter will mainly deal with the duty to provide effective protection against FGM and the duty to protect all citizens from unjustified privacy interventions and discrimination. As we shall see, these obligations might contradict each other, and then the question of how to prioritize and harmonize them arises. This topic is particularly relevant in the light of the debate in Norway concerning coercive health checks on girls from particular risk groups. Norwegian law will be taken as the national point of departure, but the human rights analysis will be of general interest to all countries facing similar challenges.

3.2 FGM and the protection of minority rights

According to the International Covenant on Civil and Political Rights (ICCPR), Article 27, states are under an obligation to protect cultural minorities:

29 European Convention on Human Rights (ECHR), Article 3, International Covenant on Civil and Political Rights (ICCPR), Article 7, Convention on the Rights of the Child (CRC), Article 37a.

30 ECHR, Article 3, ICCPR, Article 6.1.

31 International Covenant on Economic, Social and Cultural Rights (ICESCR), Article 12, Convention on the Elimination of All Forms of Discrimination against Women (CEDAW), Article 12, CRC, Article 24.

32 ECHR, Article 8.

33 ECHR, Article 14, CEDAW, Articles 1 and 2 f, ICESCR, Article 2.2 and Article 3.

34 CRC, Article 24.3.

35 Act of 21 May 1999 No. 30.

36 A. Eide.

37 ECHR, Article 14, ICCPR, Article 26.

> In those States in which ethnic, religious or linguistic minorities exist, persons belonging to such minorities shall not be denied the right, in community with the other members of their group, to enjoy their own culture, to profess and practice their own religion, or to use their own language.

Thus, a relevant and practical question is how far governments must respect and protect the cultural traditions of minority groups that violate the rights of women. The international human rights community has been quite clear on this point, stating that states parties "should eradicate, both through legislation and any other appropriate measure, all cultural or religious practices which jeopardize the freedom and well-being of female children".[38] To my mind, this position is in line with the general attitude in Norway and most Western countries. In addition, most governments of countries where FGM still exists have accepted the same state obligations. Therefore, in the following discussion, the general assumption is that FGM is not a cultural tradition that is to be protected under international law. Rather, from the human rights perspective, this tradition is to be abolished by means of effective and appropriate measures aimed at protecting the rights of women and children.

3.3 The duty to provide effective protection against FGM

This state obligation stems from several human rights provisions, including the Convention on the Rights of the Child (CRC), Article 24.3, and the Convention on the Elimination of All Forms of Discrimination against Women (CEDAW), Article 12, both protecting the right to health. As FGM is most often performed on young girls, Article 24.3 of the CRC is particularly appropriate,[39] declaring that states parties "shall take all effective and appropriate measures with a view to abolishing *traditional practices prejudicial to the health of children*" (italics added). Thus, the state obligation in this regard is to take, within its jurisdiction, all effective and appropriate measures to abolish FGM (which is clearly within the main purpose of the provision). The words "effective" and "appropriate" are both important here as they indicate different and cumulative aspects of state obligations. While "effective" is related to the potentially positive outcome of preventative measures (do they significantly reduce the risk of FGM faced by girls in particular risk groups?), "appropriate" is related to what kind of measures are being used (are they acceptable, for instance with regard to law, ethical or professional standards, and human rights norms, etc.?).

At the regional level, the European Convention on Human Rights (ECHR), Article 8.1, is a key provision that protects the right of every individual to *privacy* ("respect for his private and family life"). At the heart of this provision lies respect for

38 Human Rights Committee, General Recommendation No. 28 (2000). Similar statements from the CEDAW Committee in its General Recommendation No. 14 (1990), No. 19 (1992) and in No. 24 (1999), and from the CRC Committee in its General Comment No. 7 (2005).

39 CRC protects the rights of persons under the age of 18, cf. Article 1.

bodily integrity,[40] which is clearly violated by coercive FGM. With regard to this right, too, the state obligation is to ensure the effective protection of the right to privacy.[41] Thus, the state must take effective measures to prevent girls from being victims of FGM.

The CEDAW Committee has requested states parties to the CEDAW Convention to take appropriate and effective measures against FGM and other forms of violence against women, including the adoption and implementation of effective legislation and the sanctioning of violations. The Committee has developed guidelines regarding what is considered to be additional necessary initiatives, including data collection and statistics, education, information, research, and national health strategies involving health personnel explaining the damaging consequences for women's health. Furthermore, according to the Committee, collaboration with women's organisations and awareness raising by politicians and religious leaders of influence are important. Also, women should be actively involved in the planning, implementation, and monitoring of healthcare services for women. The gender-sensitive training of healthcare workers to detect and manage the health consequences of all kinds of gender-based violence, including FGM, is among the Committee's recommendations to state parties. The Committee has stressed that all health services for women must be voluntary and respect their human rights, including the right to autonomy and informed consent, privacy and confidentiality.[42]

The CRC Committee has made recommendations similar to those of the CEDAW Committee, and has focused in particular on children and adolescents' right to be respected as persons in their own right and to be given appropriate information about FGM and other harmful practices, in addition to appropriate health services. In particular, the needs of adolescents from a minority background must be given special attention.[43]

Other UN instruments express a similar approach to FGM; strong condemnation, a requirement for legislation prohibiting and punishing FGM, and for redressing the wrongs caused by it and other forms of violence, a national strategy including public awareness and the implementation of policies, education, the distribution of information and knowledge, and co-operation with religious institutions and leaders as well as with traditional authorities.[44]

The general impression is that the monitoring human rights bodies at the UN level, as well as other UN instruments, recommend measures like legislation forbidding and sanctioning FGM, as well as "softer" measures like education and training,

40 E. Møse with further references, *Menneskerettigheter* (Cappelen Akademiske Forlag, Oslo, 2002), p. 402.

41 Ibid., P. and J. Aall, *Rettsstat og menneskerettigheter* (Fagbokforlaget, second edition, Bergen, 2004), pp. 177–178.

42 See Aasen, with further references to the CEDAW Committee's General Recommendations Nos 14, 19 and 24, supra note 7, pp. 33-36.

43 Aasen, with references to the CRC Committee's General Comments Nos 7 and 4, supra note 7, pp. 36-40.

44 UN Declaration on the Elimination of All Forms of Violence Against Women (1993); Plan of Action for the Elimination of Harmful Traditional Practices Affecting the Health of Women and Children (1994).

information, data collection and research, awareness raising, and dialogue, etc. in order to combat FGM and other harmful practices over time at the national level. This approach to what constitutes effective and appropriate measures for combating FGM is also relevant when considering what constitutes "necessary" interventions that can be justified under the ECHR, Article 8.2, see the following discussion.

3.4 The duty of abstaining from non-justified interventions in privacy (ECHR, Article 8.2)

As we have seen, the right to privacy requires effective protection against involuntary FGM. However, the right to privacy not only protects girls from being the victims of FGM, it also protects the same – and other – girls from other privacy interventions, e.g. involuntary health checks in order to prevent FGM. As mentioned above, in Norway, as well as in other countries, there has been public discussion about using obligatory (meaning involuntary) health checks as a strategy for preventing FGM, both at the individual level (the protection of particular girls at risk) and as a general measure against FGM. Thus, the right to privacy provides protection in two opposing directions, which means possible tension or conflict in situations where girls considered to be at risk of FGM, e.g. due to the fact that they belong to particular "risk groups", do not want to undergo such health checks. Such rejection could take place when the girl (or her parents if she is very young) has decided not to continue the practice, although she/they belong to an FGM risk group (e.g. being of Somali origin and from areas that still practice FGM). Another scenario is that rejection takes place because of a wish to hide the fact that FGM has actually taken place, e.g. after a visit to the country of origin, thereby also preventing legal prosecution for a criminal offence. A third possibility is that the girl or her parents think that an "official check" on the most private part of the girl's body conflicts with their values and norms and thus they will not allow it.

Then the question arises as to whether conducting involuntary examinations on the genitalia of girls from certain ethnic groups[45] is an appropriate measure in preventing FGM.

It follows from the CRC, Article 24.3, that measures aimed at abolishing traditional practices prejudicial to the health of children must be both "effective" and "appropriate". Thus, although a measure is considered very effective, it cannot be implemented if it is not also appropriate. Also, CEDAW requires that measures against discriminatory customs and practices must be appropriate, cf. Article 2 f. Clearly, in order for national measures to be appropriate, they must comply with common human rights standards, including the right to privacy. The CEDAW Committee has pointed out that all measures aimed at combating FGM and other harmful traditions

45 The option of examining the genitalia of all girls at a certain age has been ruled out as inappropriate, since only a very small percentage of girls are affected by FGM.

need to respect the human rights of women, including autonomy and privacy.[46] With regard to ECHR, Article 8, the tension between preventative purposes and privacy protection must be resolved in line with paragraph 2 of the article:

> There shall be no interference by a public authority with the exercise of this right [privacy] except such as is in accordance with the law and is necessary in a democratic society ... for the prevention of disorder or crime, for the protection of health or morals, or for the protection of the rights and freedoms of others.

This means that only when the intervention, e.g. a coercive health check on a particular girl's genitalia, is allowed under national law and "necessary" for the purposes mentioned will it be justified. Both these requirements must be met. In Norway, we have no legislation allowing such involuntary health checks. Thus, the discussion has been about whether or not Norwegian law should be amended in order to allow such involuntary examinations for the purpose of preventing FGM. However, even if Norway were to amend its national legislation (which has not happened yet), in my view, this law could, and most likely would if the European Human Rights Court is presented with a case, be considered a violation of ECHR, Article 8.2. The reason for this is that a strong privacy intervention like examining the genitalia of specific girls (even amounting to discrimination, see 3.6 below) cannot be considered "necessary", given the precise circumstances in Norway; see the following discussion.

3.5 What is "necessary" according to ECHR, Article 8.2? Striking a fair balance between conflicting interests

An analysis of what is "necessary" requires a broad assessment of several factors. The overall theme is whether or not the involuntary intervention represents a fair balance between considerations of individual privacy and the need to avert FGM.[47] The legal guidelines given by other human rights bodies, like the CEDAW and CRC Committees, regarding what constitutes "appropriate" measures when combating FGM and other harmful practices, should be taken into consideration. As we have seen, these committees recommend legislation prohibiting such practices, as well as education, information, and other "soft" approaches aimed at eradicating these practices over time. In particular, the CEDAW Committee's statement that the rights of autonomy and privacy must be respected,[48] is also important when considering what is "necessary" under ECHR, Article 8.2. Practice from the European Court of Human Rights (ECtHR) shows that it is not sufficient for the intervention to have a good purpose (e.g. preventing FGM), it must also be "necessary in a democratic

46 Aasen, with reference to General Recommendation No. 24 para. 31 e, supra note 7, p. 35.

47 Møse, supra note 40, p. 405, with reference to practice from the European Court of Human Rights (ECtHR) on "fair balance".

48 See 3.4 above (note 45).

society", which entails the need for a more substantial justification. In human rights theory, with reference to practice from the ECtHR, it is said that "necessary" corresponds with *a pressing social need*,[49] which lies somewhere between "indispensable" and "useful"/"desirable".[50] In addition, the intervention must be "proportionate to the legitimate aim pursued".[51] The intervention will be considered a violation of ECHR, Article 8.1, if it is not suitable for meeting its objective (e.g. preventing FGM), if the objective is not important enough, or it could be achieved using other less intrusive measures. The final evaluation must depend on the degree of sensitiveness/intrusiveness, on the one hand, and the urgency of the social interest, on the other.[52]

Concerning the use of involuntary health checks when preventing FGM, it must be assessed whether or not this is a necessary and proportionate measure in Norway. Such involuntary health checks could be organized using two categories: 1) involuntary examinations of the genitalia of girls belonging to a particular "risk group", and 2) involuntary examinations of the genitalia of all girls (also ethnic Norwegians) of certain ages. While the first alternative could be accused of discrimination, this is not the case for the latter. However, both alternatives must be considered intrusive as they are not based on informed consent, which is the main rule regulating all health care, including all kinds of health examinations, under Norwegian health care law.[53] In what follows, I will only focus on the first alternative, as this is the suggestion that has been given the most serious attention by the Norwegian authorities.[54]

One of the problems that occur with regard to health checks on girls belonging to certain target groups is the identification and delimitation of these groups ("risk groups"). In Norway, FGM is most common among immigrant women from Somalia,[55] since in that country, around 98 % of women have been circumcised.[56] In Somalia, it is common to circumcise girls aged between 6 and 10. Based, in particular, on age and how long they have been in Norway, researchers have roughly estimated that around two fifths of the Somali girls living in Norway are at risk of FGM.[57] However, it is stressed that this is a very rough estimate, as cultural, social, and political factors, including individual attitudes, level of education, access to health care and information, interaction with different people etc., play an important role. Many immigrants change their attitudes and priorities when they move to

49 Aall, with reference to *Handyside*, supra note 41 p. 127.

50 J. Aall, with reference to ECtHR practice, supra note 41, p. 127.

51 Ibid., with reference to *Olsson*.

52 Ibid., pp. 127-129.

53 Patient Rights Act of 2 July 1999 No. 63, Section 4-1.

54 Aasen, supra note 7, pp. 72-85.

55 In 2008, around 4,516 women who have either immigrated to Norway from Somalia themselves, or have Somali parents, were living in Norway (Aasen, with further reference to Lidén et al. (preliminary report), supra note 7, p. 12).

56 Ibid., p. 12.

57 Ibid.

a new country and are exposed to new values, opinions, and information. Thus, it is not easy to determine exactly who is at risk of FGM, and who is not, without the risk of generalization and even stigmatization. Immigrants themselves, including those opposing FGM, have expressed concern for the possible stigmatizing effect of involuntary health checks on immigrant girls from particular ethnic groups.[58]

Another factor to consider is the possible negative effects on young girls exposed to involuntary health checks, also including the possibility of discovering that the girl has actually been circumcised, resulting in parents or relatives possibly being sent to jail for that criminal offence (which has not happened in Norway, as yet, but which could be the outcome of systematic health checks). Although it is important to have effective legislation against FGM, it is also necessary to consider the degree of effort the state should put into pursuing potential criminals in particular groups, and whether or not these efforts are in the best interests of children from these groups who have been affected, children who, among other negative effects, risk losing their provider for several years in a foreign country, cf. CRC, Article 3.1. Although preventing FGM and protecting potential victims from this human rights violation is an important aim, it is also necessary to consider the potential and predictable effects of various preventative measures.

The risk of undermining immigrants' trust in the health authorities is also an important concern with regard to which measures should be chosen in order to combat FGM. Many immigrants arrive in Norway with little trust in official authorities, and thus many are sensitive to coercive measures directed towards them as individuals, in particular as members of a specific group. Such measures could be an efficient barrier to the development of a trustful relationship with Norwegian health care personnel, something which is essential for advancing good health in new citizens, including the prevention of FGM within particular groups.

There is no scientific documentation showing positive effects from involuntary health checks aimed at preventing FGM. The reason for the lack of academic studies is most likely the legal and ethical problems associated with involuntary measures directed at particular ethnic groups.

As stated earlier, the prevalence of FGM in Norway is unknown. However, existing research indicates that the actual number has fallen.[59] It seems that the increased level of attention and information regarding the legal prohibition and threat of punishment, the strengthened competence of health care personnel and other professionals, the increased awareness among affected groups, and the more systematic routines for filing reports to the child welfare service by health care centres for children, by schools, and by hospitals, as well as closely monitoring asylum-seekers, have all had an effect.[60] It is clear that the Plan of Action of 2008 has strengthened the

58 Ibid., p. 79.

59 This is also the trend internationally, in Somalia (Lidén and Bentzen, supra note 12, pp. 32, 35-36) too.

60 Lidén and Bentzen, supra note 12, p. 86.

control aspect in order to make the measures more effective, i.e. involving health personnel, the child welfare service, and the police more actively. Therefore, although the measures still ought to be increased and improved, it seems that the Norwegian strategy is working, and that a radical measure like involuntary health checks on girls from particular groups cannot be considered necessary under ECHR, Article 8.2.

3.6 The duty of non-discrimination

The last point to mention is the duty of non-discrimination, which is an independent human rights obligation on all the ratifying states, stemming from ECHR, Article 14, as well as all the UN human rights instruments. Under ECHR, Article 14, enjoyment of the rights and freedoms set forth in the Convention, including the right to privacy, "shall be secured without discrimination on any ground such as sex, race, colour, ... national or social origin, ... or other status". Clearly, involuntary privacy interventions directed at particular ethnic groups, or girls considered to be at risk of FGM, will be viewed as extremely problematic in the light of the non-discrimination principle.[61] Although dissimilar treatment may be justified on objective and reasonable grounds, especially if the interventions are proportional with regard to the expected benefits, it could be acceptable. However, the same considerations mentioned in 3.5 above will also be relevant here and, accordingly, the non-discrimination principle will also be a legal barrier to involuntary health checks on girls from particular ethnic groups, or from other defined groups.

4 In conclusion

FGM is a serious human rights violation which all states that have ratified ECHR, CRC and CEDAW are obligated to provide effective protection against, including via legislation. In Norway, FGM is forbidden by law, and it is the duty of the relevant professionals and others to seek to avert it, using formal complaint and reporting procedures. Both these legislative measures are essential and form the basis of all the other measures aimed at preventing and combating FGM in Norway. In addition, information, education, and dialogue, aimed at spreading knowledge, developing competence, and raising awareness, are important as regards bringing practical effect to the legislation. However, the existing measures need to be constantly monitored in order to improve them, e.g. with regard to more effective collaboration between different actors, the identification of "best practices", improved dialogue and co-operation with professionals from minority backgrounds and affected groups, and the more efficient sharing of knowledge, etc.[62] In the context of existing national efforts to provide effective protection against FGM, which seems to have the intended ef-

61 Aall, supra note 41, p. 62.

62 Jonassen and Saur, supra note 11, pp. 112-113.

fect, involuntary health examinations seem to be too intrusive. ECHR, Article 8.2 requires privacy interventions to be necessary and proportional, implying a fair balance between the interests in conflict, in order to be justified. In light of the uncertainty surrounding the actual problem and when defining which girls are at risk, the fact that this practice seems to be declining in the affected groups both in Norway and abroad, the increased attention and control provided by health care workers, teachers, and child welfare workers, and the information campaigns aimed at newcomers, it is hard to defend involuntary health checks, with their potentially negative effects (stigma, discrimination, loss of trust) as appropriate and justified.

Infant Male Circumcision – Finnish Supreme Court Ruling on a Multicultural Legal Problem

By Professor Raimo Lahti, University of Helsinki[1]

1 Introduction

The acceptability and practical aspects of religiously-based, non-medical infant male circumcision have given rise to brisk debate in Finland, from time to time, over the past two decades. Depending on perspective, this debate has, on the one hand, emphasised the right of the infant male, unable to give his consent, to physical integrity and, on the other, the protection of religious freedom and minority culture, as well as the protection of family life as enjoyed by certain communities. Similar debates have been conducted in many other countries.[2] In the international arena, the main focus has been on the circumcision of girls and women for non-medical reasons. While this is unanimously rejected in all Western legal cultures, views vary as to the appropriate preventative means.[3]

This article is an examination of Finland's legal and ethical debate on this topic, extending back to the 1990s, and centres on the Finnish Supreme Court ruling in precedent *KKO 2008:93*. Some comparative observations will be made on the situation in the other Nordic countries.

---

1 Raimo Lahti, LL.D., M.Soc.Sc. Professor of Criminal Law since 1979 and responsible teacher in Medical Law and Biolaw 1997-2011, University of Helsinki, Faculty of Law. Permanent Expert for the National Board of Health 1970-91, and for the National Authority of Medicolegal Affairs 1992-2008. Member of the National Advisory Board in Health Care Ethics 1998-2002. Member of the Steering Group of the Nordic Network for Research in Biomedical Law 2006-2011.

2 On the international debate, see, for instance, Smith, *Male Circumcision and the Rights of the Child*; Fox & Thomson, *Law, Ethics, and Medicine*; Putzke, *Die strafrechtliche Relevanz der Beschneidung von Knaben [The criminal-law relevance of the circumcision of boys]*.

3 For an overall review, see, for instance, Denniston et al. (eds.), *Circumcision and Human Rights*. On the circumcision of women, in particular, see, for instance, Oba, *Female Circumcision as Female Genital Mutilation*; Gozdecka, *Religions and Legal Boundaries of Democracy in Europe*, pp. 166–168.

2 Reactions to infant male circumcision in the 1990s

The original impetus to the attention paid to the topic was the circular dispatched by the Ministry of Social Affairs and Health to municipalities in 1992 recommending that male infant circumcisions be performed within the public health system. Whilst the small Jewish and Tatar (muslim) communities in Finland, among whom the practice is common, had little need for public health services in the performance of circumcisions, this situation changed with the increasing influx of immigrants from Islamic countries.

In a complaint to the Parliamentary Ombudsman dated 12 August 1997, Professor and Chief Physician Esko Länsimies criticised the conducting of infant male circumcisions at university hospitals and asked the Ombudsman to review the matter. Resolving the complaint on 30 November 1999, Deputy Ombudsman Riitta-Leena Paunio initially assessed the issue in a general legal perspective and then arrived at the following conclusions, deemed well justified by this author: in respect of the Status and Rights of Patients Act, and legislation concerning the duty of municipalities to organise health care and medical treatment, public health care units were under no obligation to carry out non-medical circumcisions on infant males. While Paunio did not consider such procedures to be clearly unlawful, bearing in mind that there were no express legal provisions or regulations governing these, and bearing in mind that the Ministry of Social Affairs and Health had recommended, in the early 1990s, a positive stance on the conducting of these procedures within the municipal health care system, she held the circumcision of infant males, who were incapable of giving their consent, in the absence of any medical indication, to be highly questionable from a legal point of view. According to Paunio, public health care units should refrain from conducting the said procedure until such time that the child in question is of an age when he is capable of giving his informed consent.[4]

In the statement issued by the National Advisory Board on Health Care Ethics (ETENE) on 15 June 1999[5], before resolution of the complaint by Deputy Ombudsman Riitta-Leena Paunio, the majority of the advisory board members held non-medical infant male circumcision to be an ethically-acceptable procedure which could be carried out within public health care on members of the Jewish and Islamic faiths; the rationale being to avoid intolerance and the disparagement of religious traditions. Moreover, a policy of accepting such circumcisions was deemed capable of protecting the children concerned from the traumatising physical and psychological experiences of pain when the procedure was performed by experienced health care professionals.

As a member of the Advisory Board who was in the minority, this author criticised the majority statement for not attaching sufficient weight to the child's interests: an intervention in the field of health on a person who does not have the

4 See the Annual Report of the Parliamentary Ombudsman (1999), pp. 273–275.

5 See publication of ETENE 5/2002, pp. 40–43.

capacity to consent is acceptable – except in certain situations for which express provisions have been laid down – only when the procedure entails direct health-related, or other, benefits for the person concerned. In support of this reasoning, this author made particular reference to Article 6 of the Council of Europe's Convention on Human Rights and Biomedicine[6], which Finland had signed immediately but had not, at that time, ratified yet. Furthermore, this author also made reference to what has been stated in the preparatory documents of the Basic Rights Reform Act (969/1995) regarding the relationships between the various basic rights and their relative balancing. Freedom of religion or freedom of conscience cannot justify actions which infringe upon human dignity or other basic rights, or which are contrary to the foundations of legal order. All in all, this author held that the acceptability of infant male circumcision, conducted without medical indications, was highly questionable in respect of the Finnish legal order.[7]

3 Investigations by the authorities in 2004

The approach to non-medical infant male circumcision took a new turn when the Ministry of Social Affairs and Health, together with the Association of Finnish Local and Regional Authorities, reaffirmed, in its circular of 3 March 2003, the recommendation issued by the same Ministry during the early 1990s, despite this compliance with the circular being tantamount to a wholesale dismissal of the views of a supervisor of legality, i.e. Deputy Ombudsman Riitta-Leena Paunio. It was also around this time that State Prosecutor Päivi Hirvelä was considering charges in a case which involved a physician and Muslim fathers who were suspected of assault for having boys circumcised on religious grounds without any medical reason and without their own consent in unsafe health conditions.[8]

Owing to conflicting opinions as to the legality of the circular, and the acceptability of infant male circumcision in general, the Ministry of Social Affairs and Health felt a compelling need to set up a working group to investigate the matter. The members of this group, appointed on 11 April 2003 and headed by Archiatre Risto Pelkonen, were selected to represent a wide range of expertise. Kristina Stenman was appointed rapporteur in order to assist the working group in its investigation of international and Finnish infant male circumcision practices.

According to the memorandum produced by the working group, the non-medical circumcision of boys was to be allowed subject to certain conditions. The working group based this view on the good of the child, which concept was nonetheless examined in a wider perspective than just the health-related benefit "in emphasising

---

6 Opened for signature on 4 April 1997 in Oviedo (Spain), subsequently the Biomedicine Convention.

7 Regarding this author's views, besides the publication of ETENE, see also supra note 5, pp. 43–43, also Lahti, *Ärztliche Eingriffe und das Selbstbestimmungsrecht des Invidiuums [Medical interventions and the individual's right to self-determination]*, p. 522.

8 State Prosecutor Hirvelä issued a decision, on 30 June 2004, that there would be diversionary non-prosecution in the case.

socially adequate grounds arising from religious and cultural traditions". As in Sweden[9], provisions setting out the conditions for circumcision should be laid down in a special Act, as the procedure represents an intervention in the physical integrity of male infants. Circumcisions could only be performed by licensed physicians, or duly authorised ones, and only with the consent of the male infant's guardians. The working group went on to propose that male infant circumcision should be carried out within the public health system in the same manner as medically-indicated procedures.[10] According to rapporteur Kristina Stenman, male infants should be provided the performance of circumcisions in safe conditions and on equal grounds throughout the nation. A special Act, in line with the Swedish model, might, in her opinion, bring clarity to the situation.[11]

These official investigations did not result, however, in a government Bill for a special Act.

4 Main substance of precedent ruling *KKO 2008:93*

In its ruling *KKO 2008:93*, Finland's Supreme Court held that the conduct of a mother who – as her child's sole guardian – had her Muslim son of 4½ circumcised for religious reasons was not to be deemed illegal, and that her conduct was thus not punishable as an assault (either through complicity or instigation). At the legal core of the ruling was the question of whether or not the intervention in a person's physical integrity, which circumcision entails (the irrevocable removal of the foreskin), constituted the elements of the offence of assault and, if the answer was in the affirmative, whether or not the religious, cultural, and social reasons behind the procedure might be deemed, once other potential conditions had been met, grounds for exemption from criminal liability (para. 6 of the reasoning). A charge was brought against the boy's guardian who arranged for the circumcision, while the person who actually performed the procedure remained unidentified, although, according to the Supreme Court's evaluation of the evidence, that person was a physician (para. 1 of the reasoning).

In this case, the judgement issued by Turku Court of Appeal on 14 March 2007 was the same in terms of outcome as the unanimous ruling returned by the Supreme Court on 17 August 2008, despite the fairly considerable difference in the reasoning of the two decisions, whereas the court of first instance, i.e. Tampere District Court, had held that the constituent elements of the offence of assault had been proven and that no justification had been put forward or had come to light. Nonetheless, Tampere District Court held the illegal conduct of the accused to be manifestly excusable

9 See *Lag* (2001:499) *om omskärelse av pojkar [Circumcision of Boys Act]*.

10 See Ministry of Social Affairs and Health Working Group memorandum 2003:39 (subsequently ministerial memorandum), passim.

11 See Ministry of Social Affairs and Health stencil 2004:3, passim.

owing to a mistake as to the unlawfulness of the act (Criminal Code, Chapter 4:2), thus dismissing the charge.

As regards the legal issues relating to infant male circumcision, the ruling initially addressed the question of whether or not non-medical infant male circumcision, as commissioned by the child's guardian in circumstances where the child, due to his age, is unable to make a decision on the procedure, constitutes punishable instigation or other participation in assault, as was charged. In the Supreme Court's view, the constituent elements of the offence of assault were proven: the point of departure, therefore, was that this conduct prima facie constituted the actus reus of the offence of assault, or petty assault at least (para. 6 of the reasoning).

When the Supreme Court, nonetheless, resolved to dismiss the charge, one had to pose the second question regarding the grounds on which such intervention in physical integrity is non-punishable, either through a restrictive interpretation of the constituent elements of assault or by holding such intervention to be a justified (acceptable) or an excusable (understandable) measure. As a result of the legislative amendments enacted in 2003 (515/2003), the grounds for exemption from liability laid down in Chapter 4 of the Criminal Code now differentiate, to a greater degree of clarity and consistency, between justification and excuse. According to the reasoning of the Supreme Court's ruling, the case involved an evaluation of whether a justification ground which removes illegality was at hand (paras 19 and 29), although the position was not formulated in a clear way. The question of justification was evaluated in the ruling by balancing divergent basic and human rights without reference, in this context, to the concept of 'social adequacy', developed in criminal law theory – unlike the Supreme Court of Sweden, in its ruling of 29 September 1997, in an equivalent case[12].

In this author's opinion, the Supreme Court, in its precedent ruling KKO 2008:93, adopted a novel justification that is not governed by the Criminal Code's grounds for exemption, i.e. a justification not written into law; the alternative would have been a restrictive interpretation of the constituent elements of assault.[13] Being for the benefit of the accused, the outcome is not contrary to the principle of legality in criminal law. With regard to the values underlying the principle of legality (predictability and equality), it is nonetheless desirable for such grounds for exemption, benefitting the accused, also to be provided in law.[14]

12 See *Nytt juridiskt arkiv [Judicial records]* 1997, 636-645 (NJA 1997:107). A critical review of the case and its outcome has been published by Ravn, *Omskærelse i strafferetten [Circumcision in criminal law]*. On the previous legal situation in Sweden, see Rynning, *Samtycke till medicinsk vård och behandling [Consent to medical care and treatment]*, pp. 296–298.

13 Thus also Frände, *Yleinen rikosoikeus [General criminal law]*, p. 57 note 124. Cf. Tolvanen, Comment on *KKO 2008:93*, p. 143, according to whom the circumcision of the boy should have been examined as an issue of the interpretation of the constituent elements of assault.

14 See also Melander, *Kriminalisointiteoria [A Theory of Criminalization]*, p. 501.

5 On the balancing of basic and human rights in ruling *KKO 2008:93*

According to the Supreme Court, the central legal issue in this case was whether or not the religious, cultural, and social reasons behind circumcision could be considered to constitute grounds justifying conduct constituting the elements of assault. As relevant background information (para. 7 of the reasoning), the ruling states that non-medically indicated infant male circumcision is a global phenomenon and a common practice within several communities for reasons connected with religion, culture, or tradition. It is estimated that roughly 200 boys are circumcised for non-medical reasons each year in Finland. According to the Supreme Court, nowhere in the world is infant male circumcision, based on religious or cultural tradition, banned outright, although a special Act governing the procedure had been enacted in Sweden.

Among Muslims, infant male circumcision is deemed to be based on religious tradition and is a deeply-rooted practice within the said communities. According to the Supreme Court, the information put forward in the case demonstrates that circumcision is also an integral component of the identity of the community's male members; the circumcision performed on Muslim boys between the ages of four and thirteen serves to attach them to their religious and social community. (para. 8 of the reasoning.) It is this author's observation that, in this respect, the Supreme Court's reasoning relies more or less directly on the ministerial memorandum[15].

The reasoning proper of the Supreme Court consists of balancing divergent basic and human rights; the outcome of this balancing being a decision on whether or not compelling reasons exist to adopt an unwritten justification. Balancing of this kind has been fairly uncommon in Finnish court decisions, although the incorporation of such considerations into the decision-making process is on the rise. In criminal law, the prohibition of analogy and the prohibition of vague statutes set the boundaries for balancing to the detriment of the accused. However, as stated above, as grounds for exemption from criminal liability not written into law, the Court may have relied on the concept of 'social adequacy'. The Supreme Court of Sweden defined this concept as a conflict between the protected interest, under the criminal provision concerned, and an opposing interest, appearing in unwritten grounds for exemption: circumcision conducted for religious reasons met the requirements of social adequacy in light of the fact that the parents had given their consent and the fact that the children, aged between 18 months and 7 years, had not been caused excessive pain (although the circumcisions had been performed without analgesia and four out of the six had suffered infections as a result of the procedure).[16]

The reasoning of the Supreme Court in ruling *KKO 2008:93* is considerably more detailed and weighed with a greater degree of differentiation than in the equivalent

15 Ministerial memorandum, supra note 10, p. 34.

16 NJA 1997, supra note 12, pp. 642–644.

Swedish decision. The argumentation used in the decision, focusing on basic and human rights, strives comprehensively to identify all the relevant rights, to prioritise these rights, and to balance them against each other, the apparent aim being to pay optimum heed to divergent rights.

Ahead of a more detailed analysis of that consideration, this author wishes to draw the reader's attention to a shortcoming of the Supreme Court's decision: it fails to mention the Biomedicine Convention. Admittedly the Convention had not been ratified before the committal of the offences charged; however, as an instrument signed by Finland in 1997 and which came into international effect in 1999, the Convention constituted an important permitted[17] source of law. As regards this Biomedicine Convention, it has also been argued that, in the case law of the European Court of Human Rights, when the Court applies the European Convention on Human Rights, the Biomedicine Convention will constitute the 'European standard' and influence application of the European Convention on Human Rights additionally in respect of states which have not ratified the Biomedicine Convention.[18] Finland ratified the Biomedicine Convention and its two Protocols in 2009 to pass into law on 1 March 2010 (23/2010).[19] These instruments have thus become binding sources of law with an interpretative effect, in particular upon the future application of Finnish legislation in the sector.

In this author's opinion, the reasoning of the Supreme Court, when addressing the relevant basic rights and human rights norms (paras 10–18), is appropriate, with the exception of ignoring the Biomedicine Convention. The relevant provisions of the Finnish Constitution, along with its legislative drafts[20] and the relevant Articles of the European Convention on Human Rights and the related case law of the European Court of Human Rights, are reviewed in a laudable manner, as are the relevant Articles of the UN Convention on the Rights of the Child. Among basic and human rights, the protection of family life is raised alongside the right to physical integrity and freedom of religion.

The evaluation portion of the reasoning (paras 19–27) presents the core issue of balancing divergent basic and human rights as the question of whether or not a male child's right to physical integrity prevents his guardians from deciding to circumcise him on his behalf, as someone who is unable to give consent, when the grounds for the procedure are not medical but involve the family's religious traditions. The acceptability of the procedure is thus linked to both the protection of family life and freedom of religion. In the reasoning, the protection of a child's right to physical integrity is also found to be strong relative to the rights of the guardian, the protection

17 The term 'permitted' refers to the fact that such a Convention (not yet ratified) does not belong to the binding legal sources to be observed in the first place.

18 See Roscam Abbing, *The Convention on Human Rights and Biomedicine*, p. 380; Nys, *The Biomedicine Convention as an Object and a Stimulus for Comparative Research*, p. 277.

19 Of the ratification instruments, see, in particular, government Bill 216/2008.

20 See, in particular, government Bill 309/1993, p. 56 (para. 17 of the Supreme Court's reasoning).

of family life, and religious freedom (para. 21). An emphasis such as this, relying on the legislative drafts of the basic rights reform, is important when prioritising these basic and human rights.

In determining and balancing the relative weight of the said basic and human rights, the argumentation of the Supreme Court can be boiled down to the following: "Intervention in a male child's physical integrity, taking the form of a medically appropriate circumcision conducted on religious grounds may be deemed a defensible measure with regard to the child's overall interests and also, when assessed as a whole, as an intervention of such minor significance that there is no cause to consider the conduct of the child's guardians, in having their child circumcised in this manner, as constituting such an act, in infringement of the interests and rights of the child, that would be punishable in terms of the offence of assault" (para. 26). In other words, an infant male circumcision with his guardians' consent is thus justified if it is both defensible with regard to the child's overall interests and represents only a relatively minor intervention in the child's physical integrity, irrespective of the child's own will (para. 24 of the reasoning).

The requirement regarding the overall interests of the child, according to the Supreme Court, was to be read as a procedure having the purpose of promoting the child's well-being and development while at the same time not running contrary to the interests of that child even in an objective assessment (para. 23). Here, the Court, earlier in its reasoning (para. 8), relies mainly on the view of keeping with the wording of the ministerial memorandum[21], viz. that circumcision performed for religious reasons has a positive impact on the boy himself, on the development of his identity, and on his bonding with his religious and social community (para. 26).

In the decision, infant male circumcision is judged to be a fairly harmless procedure when carried out with the appropriate medical care, in hygienic conditions, and when using the analgesia warranted by the procedure. It is stated that the procedure may give rise to some discomfort but not to any health-related, or otherwise permanent, injuries. Even though the procedure is irreversible, no qualities are associated with it that will stigmatise either the child or the adult into whom the child will develop (para. 25).

The degree of intervention in physical integrity is judged to differ materially in the circumcision of boys and girls. Circumcision of the latter, according to the Supreme Court, constitutes conduct that is primarily to be categorised as aggravated assault – genital mutilation – which under no circumstances can be justified using religious or social reasons (para. 27).

21 Ministerial Memorandum, supra note 10.

6 Critique of the balancing argumentation in ruling *KKO 2008:93*

Criticism may be levelled at the balancing argumentation recounted above on the basis of the Biomedicine Convention and international debate. Primarily, with regard to the argument of 'overall interests of the child' in circumcision.

Under Article 6(1) of the Biomedicine Convention, an intervention may only be carried out on a person who does not have the capacity to consent when the intervention benefits him/her directly.[22] Article 26(1) provides an exhaustive list of the grounds for restricting the rights secured under the Convention ("in the interest of public safety, for the prevention of crime, for the protection of public health or for the protection of the rights and freedoms of others"). It would appear that the kinds of religious, cultural, or social reasons mentioned in the Supreme Court's reasoning, in reliance upon which infant male circumcision would be justified in the sense intended in that Article, cannot be derived from the grounds listed above. This non-fulfilment of the requirement for direct benefit under the Biomedicine Convention was a key argument in this author's minority opinion of 15 June 1999 to the National Advisory Board on Health Care Ethics, as well as in Deputy Ombudsman Riitta-Leena Paunio's complaint resolution of 30 November 1999, and State Prosecutor Päivi Hirvelä's decision regarding diversionary non-prosecution of 30 June 2004.[23]

Regardless of whether or not Article 6 of the Biomedicine Convention is used when assessing 'the interests of the child', criticism has been directed, in the international debate, against the definition of the entire concept. British researchers Marie Fox and Michael Thomson have called for a re-formulation of the concept of the "best interests" of the child, used in common law countries in connection with infant male circumcision. In assessing the permissibility of the procedure, from the viewpoint of a male child's best interests, it is not enough to pay attention to the degree of intervention in physical integrity or other direct impacts; instead, a much wider interpretation has to be given to the concept of 'interests'. Factors to be taken into account in this assessment include issues such as the effects of the procedure on a maturing child's right to choose and on his subsequent sex life.[24]

One may also ask if the factors described in the Supreme Court's ruling, in respect of the child's overall interests, refer to the community interests of family life as defined by the relevant religious community and the guardians, rather than to the individual interests of the maturing child, e.g. in the sense referred to by Fox and Thomson. A key aspect of the Supreme Court's reasoning in this respect is that circumcision is deemed to foster the development of the boy's identity and his bonding with his religious and social community. In his critical commentary, Matti Tolvanen

22 On Article 6 of the Biomedicine Convention and its effects in ratifying States, see Stultïens et al., 'Minors and Informed Consent'.

23 For details, see supra Chap. 2.

24 Fox and Thomson, *Reconsidering 'Best Interests'*, p. 26.

brings up the danger of circumcision constituting a bond between a boy and his religious community that is so tight as to render impossible any future breaking with that bond when it is time for the child to form his independent world view.[25]

The question has also been posed in the international debate regarding whether or not there is any cause to differentiate so radically between male and female circumcision on the basis of intervention in physical integrity, as is currently the case, and as also done in the Supreme Court's reasoning. Dutch researcher Jacqueline Smith, for example, contests this double standard that is commonplace in the West and finds discrimination against circumcised (Jewish and Muslim) boys inasmuch as they are not afforded the same protection against the pointless causing of pain as are girls and those boys who do not belong to the religious communities practicing ritual circumcision.[26] In its reasoning (para. 27), the Supreme Court rejected this allegation of discrimination.

7 Male circumcision and Supreme Court ruling *KKO 2008:93* as examples of multicultural legal issues

The circumcision of boys and related case *KKO 2008:93* illustrate the issues faced by multicultural criminal law and by the entire legal regime. What kind of flexibility can there be in the application of the conditions of legal liability and the grounds for exemption from liability, and to what degree can practices diverging from the dominant legal order be accepted, or at the very least tolerated, as a defence on the grounds of religious or (sub)cultural tradition, in the spirit of cultural diversity?[27] With its regard to multiculturalism, the argumentation in ruling *KKO 2008:93* is to a laudable extent based on a balancing of basic and human rights, even if the details of the argumentation leave room for criticism.

Being a part of the religious traditions of the Jewish community, male infant circumcision is anything but a new phenomenon in Finland. As it becomes more prevalent as a result of the immigration of people of the Muslim faith, and when public health services have to adopt a position on a procedure of this kind, performed for non-medical reasons, increasing attention is being paid to the issue.

Within the same timeframe, the sector of medicine and health care has grown increasingly legalistic: that which is not clearly condoned by society on the basis of existing legislation or customary norms (by established legal practice) requires justification through new legislation. In Finland, this development is influenced by the growing emphasis on human rights and basic rights, which started in the 1990s. For example, when personal integrity is protected by basic rights and human rights

25 Tolvanen, comment on *KKO 2008:93*, p. 144.

26 Smith, *Male Circumcision and the Rights of the Child*, conclusion.

27 On multiculturalism in modern (criminal) law, see, for instance, Foblets and Renteln, *Multicultural Jurisprudence*, and, on divergent Finnish views, Tolvanen, Comment on *KKO 2008:93*, p. 144, and Nuotio, *Kulttuurien kohtaaminen rikosoikeudessa [Multiculturalism in criminal law]*, p. 144.

norms, as well as criminal law norms, any derogation from that must be backed by solid reasons based on the legal system.

The portions of ruling *KKO 2008:93* that are susceptible to criticism demonstrate the difficulty of drafting thoroughly compelling and readily-applicable legal rules by means of weighing up basic and human rights. In order to safeguard the diversity of the phenomenon in question, and its full regulation, legislation would be in order – the special Act in keeping with the Swedish model and proposed in the ministerial memorandum.[28] In drafting this special Act, the degree of national margin of appreciation potentially permitted under Article 6 of the Biomedicine Convention should be determined.

The status of physicians and other health care professionals, as well as the role of public health care in the performance of circumcisions, should also come into consideration in the drafting of the special Act. Since case *KKO 2008:93* was a criminal one, the status of the physician who performed the procedure could not come under distinct examination in terms of, for instance, how the acceptability of the procedure should be assessed in the light of the disciplinary liability and professional supervision to which the physician is subject. Owing to these liabilities, a double standard is imposed on health care professionals, with the preclusion of criminal liability not necessarily ruling out incompatibility with professional obligations. In assessing these, compliance with professional codes of ethics[29] must also be taken into account, and in these a negative, or at the very least cautious, position has been adopted vis-à-vis male infant circumcision.[30]

References

Denniston, George C. et al. (eds.), *Circumcision and Human Rights*. Springer, Dordrecht 2009.

Foblets, Marie-Claire & Renteln, Alison Dundes, *Multicultural Jurisprudence. Comparative Perspectives on the Cultural Defense*. Hart Publishing, Oxford and Portland, Oregon 2009.

Fox, Marie & Thomson, Michael, Law, Ethics, and Medicine. A covenant with the status quo? Male circumcision and the new BMA guidance to doctors. *Journal of Medical Ethics* 31, 2005, 463-469.

– – –Reconsidering 'Best Interests': Male Circumcision and the Rights of the Child. In: Denniston *et al.* (eds.), *Circumcision and Human Rights*. Springer, Dordrecht 2009, pp. 15–31.

28 As to the Swedish Act and the ministerial memorandum, see supra notes 9 and 10. See also Tolvanen, Comment on *KKO 2008:93*, pp. 143–144, and the Opinion of the Finnish League for Human Rights on non-medical infant male circumcision, 18 December 2008.

29 See section 15 of the Health Care Professionals Act (559/1994) and Article 4 of the Biomedicine Convention.

30 See ministerial memorandum, supra note 10, p. 25; Äärimaa, Editorial; Opinion of the *Svenska Läkaresällskapet* [Swedish Medical Association] on the non-medical circumcision of boys, 25 February 2010.

Frände, Dan, *Yleinen rikosoikeus [General criminal law]*. Edita, Helsinki 2005.

Gozdecka, Dorota A., *Religions and Legal Boundaries of Democracy in Europe: European Commitment to Democratic Principles*. Doctoral thesis. University of Helsinki 2009. (http://ethesishelsinki.fi)

Lahti, Raimo, Ärztliche Eingriffe und das Selbstbestimmungsrecht des Individuums [Medical interventions and the individual's right to self-determination]. In: *Festschrift für Heike Jung [Publication in honour of Heike Jung]*. Nomos, Baden-Baden 2007, pp. 511–528.

Melander, Sakari, *Kriminalisointiteoria - rangaistavaksi säätämisen oikeudelliset rajoitukset. [A Theory of Criminalization – Legal Constraints to Criminal Legislation.]* Suomalainen Lakimiesyhdistys, Helsinki 2008.

Nuotio, Kimmo, Kulttuurien kohtaaminen rikosoikeudessa [Multiculturalism in criminal law]. *Oikeus* 39, 2010, pp. 138-145.

Nys, Herman, The Biomedicine Convention as on Object and a Stimulus for Comparative Research. *European Journal of Health Law* 15, 2008, pp. 273-280.

Oba, Abdulmumini A., Female Circumcision as Female Genital Mutilation: Human Rights or Cultural Imperialism? *Global Jurist* 8, Iss. 3 (Frontiers), Article 8, 2008. (http://www.bepress.com/gj/vol8/iss3/art8)

Putzke, H., Die strafrechtliche Relevanz der Bescheidung von Knaben. [The criminal-law relevance of the circumcision of boys]. In: *Festschrift für Rolf Dietrich Herzberg [Publication in honour of Rolf Dietrich Herzberg]*. Mohr Siebeck, Tübingen 2008.

Ravn, Lene, Omskærelse i strafferetten [Circumcision in criminal law]. In: *Kriminalistisk årsbok [Yearbook in criminal sciences]. 1998*. Københavns Universitet [University of Copenhagen] 1999.

Roscam Abbing, Henriette, The Convention on Human Rights and Biomedicine. *European Journal of Health Law* 5, 1998, pp. 377-387.

Rynning, Elisabeth, *Samtycke till medicinsk vård och behandling [Consent to medical care and treatment]*;. Iustus Förlag, Uppsala 1994.

Smith, Jacqueline, Male Circumcision and the Rights of the Child. In: Bulterman, M. et al. (eds.), *To Baehr in Our Minds: Essays in Human Rights from the Heart of the Netherlands*. Netherlands Institute of Human Rights, Utrecht 1998. (http://www.nocirc. org/legal/smith.php)

Stultiëns, Loes et al., Minors and Informed Consent: A Comparative Approach. *European Journal of Health Law* 14, 2007, pp. 21-46.

Tolvanen, Matti, Kommentti, [Comment on] *KKO 2008:93*. In: *KKO:n ratkaisut kommentein [Supreme Court decisions with comments]*, II, 2008. Talentum, Helsinki 2009.

Äärimaa, Markku, Pääkirjoitus [Editorial]. *Suomen Lääkärilehti [Journal of the Finnish Medical Association]* 14/2003, p. 1631.

Mutual Recognition within the EU of the Concepts of Sickness and Incapacity for Work in a Rehabilitative Situation

By Professor Lotta Vahlne Westerhäll, University of Gothenburg[1]

1 Point of departure

It is difficult to describe the legal situation of European migrant workers who are in need of medical/vocational rehabilitation. For the sick or disabled migrant worker, living in one country and having his/her workplace in another, medical/vocational rehabilitation often raises complicated issues which have to be resolved by an equally complex framework of legal rules. Rehabilitation consists of measures that enable individuals to regain their capacity for work, which implies the precondition for rehabilitation that an individual has been declared incapable of working. Previous EC Regulation 1408/71 and, from May 2010, EC Regulation 883/04 aim to co-ordinate and safeguard the social security rights of migrant workers. No special rules covering rehabilitation exist in the regulation. Instead, it is sickness and health care benefits in general that are applicable. Under national social insurance schemes, the preconditions for receiving benefits (cash or in kind), e.g. what is to be considered sickness or invalidity generating incapacity for work, are set within national legal frameworks. The legal interpretation of the concepts of sickness and incapacity for work may differ from one member state to another, sometimes resulting in big losses for the individual.

What can make up for these shortcomings? One may argue that these basic conditions for social security within the EU should be interpreted in the same way across all the member states. Accordingly, the concepts ought to be *harmonised* in conformity with, for example, the concept of worker, which has been given a specific legal content in the EU through its application by the ECJ.

---

1 Lotta Vahlne Westerhäll is Professor in Public Law and Social Law at the School of Business, Economics and Law, University of Gothenburg, since 1996. Former Vice Chancellor of the School of Business, Economics and Law. Doctor of Law from Lund University. Research interests in social insurance law, social welfare law, medical law and administrative procedural law.

Another approach, on the national level, is to work for *mutual recognition* of doctor's certificates. This would facilitate a mutual recognition of each member state's legal definition of the concepts of sickness and incapacity for work. In itself, this is not inconsistent with the basic principle that social security is a national concern. Consequently, the delicate question of a constitutional balance between the EU and the member states would not be touched upon.[2] This paper will present my hypothesis that the content of international medical-scientific documents on diagnoses and functional ability can serve such a purpose.

A circumstance advocating such an interpretation is the fact that Article 5 of Regulation 883/2004 contains a general principle of the *equalisation* of facts and legal relations; that could be an instrument for improving the legal certainty of migrant workers. This principle clearly signals to administrations and courts in the member states that they should regard all facts and events as relevant to an insurance case, even when these facts and events relate to another member state.

I will give a short description of the rules in Regulation 883/2004 and in its implementing Regulation 987/2009 concerning the legal right to sickness benefits and documents proving the right to such benefits, that means the occurrence of sickness and the inability to work, before I start on my investigation.

In the preamble to Regulation 883/2004, it is said that it is necessary to respect the special characteristics of national social security legislation and to draw up only one system of coordination. It is also necessary, within the framework of such coordination, to guarantee equality of treatment under the different national legislations for those concerned. This general principle of equal treatment is of particular importance to workers who do not reside in the member state where they are employed. The coordination rules must guarantee that a person moving within the Community retains any rights and advantages acquired.

Article 4 of Regulation 883/2004 says that persons to whom the regulation applies shall enjoy the same benefits and be subject to the same obligations under the legislation of any member state as nationals thereof. The above-mentioned Article 5 of Regulation 883/2004 includes the important settlement of equalisation dealing with equal treatment regarding benefits, income, facts or events, also saying that, where the receipt of social security benefits and other income has certain legal effects, the relevant provisions of that legislation shall also apply to the receipt of equivalent benefits acquired under the legislation of another member state. The article also says that where legal effects are attributed to the occurrence of certain facts or events, that a member state shall take into account similar facts or events occurring in any other member state as if they had taken place within its own territory.

2 As examples, see *22/86 Guiseppe Rindone v. Allgemeine Ortskrankenkasse Bad Urach-Münsingen* (ECR/1987/1339) and *45/90 Alberto Paletta and others v. Brennet AG* (ECR/1992/I-3423). Compare B. Schulte – H.F. Zacher, *Wechselwirkungen zwischen dem Europäischen Sozialrecht und dem Sozialrecht der Bundesrepublik Deutschland [Interaction between European Social Law and German Social Law]* (Duncker & Humblot, Berlin, 1991), pp. 98-102.

The key article concerning sickness cash benefits stipulates that an insured person residing or staying in a member state other than the competent member state shall be entitled to cash benefits provided by the competent institution in accordance with the legislation it applies (Art. 21). By agreement between the competent institution and the institution of the place of residence or stay, such benefits may, however, be provided by the institution of the place of residence or stay at the expense of the competent institution in accordance with the legislation of the competent member state. The preamble of implementing Regulation 987/2009 points out that closer and more effective cooperation between social security institutions is a key factor in allowing those covered by Regulation 883/2004 to access their rights as quickly as possible, under optimum conditions. One example of this is that documents issued by the institution of a member state and showing the position of a person for the purposes of the application of Regulations 883/2004 and 987/2009, and supporting evidence on the basis of which the documents have been issued, shall be accepted by the institutions of the other member states as long as they have not been withdrawn or declared to be invalid by the member state in which they were issued (Regulation 987/2009 Art. 5).

Where there is doubt about the validity of a document, or the accuracy of the facts on which the particulars contained therein are based, the institution of the member state that receives the document shall ask the issuing institution for the necessary clarification and, where appropriate, the withdrawal of that document. The issuing institution shall reconsider the grounds for issuing the document and, if necessary, withdraw it. Where there is doubt about the information provided by those concerned, the validity of a document or supporting evidence or the accuracy of the facts on which the particulars contained therein are based, the institution of the place of stay or residence shall, insofar as this is possible, at the request of the competent institution, proceed to the necessary verification of this information or document. Where no agreement is reached between the institutions concerned, the matter may be brought before the Administrative Commission by the competent authorities no earlier than one month following the date on which the institution that received the document submitted its request. The Administrative Commission shall endeavour to reconcile the standpoints within six months of the date on which the matter was brought before it.

Regulation 987/2009 stipulates that, if the legislation of the competent member state requires the insured person to present a certificate in order to be entitled to cash benefits relating to incapacity for work, pursuant to Article 21 of Regulation 883/2004, the insured person has to ask the doctor in the member state of residence who determined his state of health to certify his incapacity for work and its probable duration. The insured person has to send the certificate to the competent institution within the time limit laid down in the legislation of the competent member state. Whenever doctors providing treatment in the member state of residence do not issue certificates of incapacity for work, and whenever such certificates are required under the legislation of the competent member state, the person concerned has to apply directly to the institution in the place of residence. That institution immediately has to arrange for a medical assessment of the person's incapacity for work. The certificate has to be forwarded to the competent institution forthwith.

At the request of the competent institution, the institution in the place of residence has to carry out any necessary administrative checks or medical examinations on the person concerned in accordance with the legislation applied by the latter institution. The report of the examining doctor concerning, in particular, the probable duration of the incapacity for work, has to be forwarded without delay by the institution in the place of residence to the competent institution.

The competent institution reserves the right to have the insured person examined by a doctor of its own choosing. For the purposes of the application of Article 21 of Regulation 883/2004, the particulars on the certificate of incapacity for work for an insured person drawn up in another member state, on the basis of the medical findings of the examining doctor or institution, will have the same legal value as a certificate drawn up in the competent member state.

The above said can suit as a basis for the "EU possibilities" of equalisation and mutual recognition and, in the extension, harmonisation within the legal fields of sickness and inability to work.

2 An illustrative example

I will now use Sweden and Norway as a cross-border example in order to illustrate the problems facing an insured person and the social security administration during rehabilitation. The legal problems are basically attributable to differences between social security systems within the EU.

The example is a case taken from the Swedish Administrative Court of Appeal, presented in the article 'Legal Aspects of Cross-Border Rehabilitation to Work' by Associate Professor Thomas Erhag.[3] The case illustrates the problems facing migrant workers who are moving after a period of long-term sickness and rehabilitation.

Jan A, a plumber with Norwegian citizenship, was born in 1948. He had been living and working in both Sweden and Norway when he sustained work-related injuries in 1988, 1991, and 1993. Subsequently, he suffered from problems with his arms, back, and neck. He had limited movement in his arms and hands and suffered from severe neck and shoulder pain, which was later diagnosed as frozen shoulder. After periods on sick leave and undergoing rehabilitative measures in Sweden (including medical treatment and a change of profession), Jan A moved back to Norway in November 1997, where he worked as a plumber for 10½ months. In 1998, his problems again stopped him from working and he was given Norwegian sick pay for one year.

3 *European Journal of Social Security* (EJSS) Vol. 7 No. 2 (2005), pp. 139-166.

After that, Jan A applied for Norwegian invalidity benefit. He could have received full invalidity benefit in Norway on the grounds that he had no capacity for work, based on medical opinion; however, the Norwegian administration rejected his application, referring to a special qualification rule in Norwegian legislation that requires at least one year's income from employment. This qualification rule is applicable to both rehabilitation and invalidity cases. Jan A was lacking 1½ months.

His application for invalidity benefit was also rejected by the Swedish Social Insurance Agency, as well as by the County Administrative Court and the Administrative Court of Appeal. They noted that, in the opinion of the Social Insurance Agency's medical adviser, Jan A's capacity for work was not limited. This left Jan A in a peculiar situation as he could have received full invalidity benefit in Norway on the grounds that he had no capacity for work, based on medical opinion, if we set the qualification rule aside. On the other hand, the same medical opinion could not be used to obtain invalidity benefit in Sweden. Without a working record, and living in a country that would not award him benefits of any kind (Norway), and with no help from his previous country of employment (Sweden), Jan A had to turn to social security. The retraining of a person in Norway to a new job on the basis of his work capacity in Sweden was not an option. Thus, the basic principles of free movement and equal treatment are not sufficient in many cross-border situations.

3 Incapacity for work due to sickness under the WHO classification

The constitution of the WHO requires the creation of an international health classification system to enable governments, care-givers, and consumers to use a shared interpretation in a meaningful manner. It is the WHO's classification register for sickness (functional status) and incapacity for work (functional ability) that are of interest in this context.

There is a Classification Implementation Database containing information on the implementation of the classifications in the different member states. A number of member states belong to the WHO Family of International Classifications (WHO-FIC). The purpose of the WHO-FIC is to implement classifications of health and medical care regulations in different countries.

The following classificatory documents have been approved by the executive body of the WHO for international use: International Classification of Diseases (ICD), International Classification of Functioning, Disability and Health (ICF), and International Classifications of Health Interventions (ICHI). I will discuss the first two of these. In October 2001, the full printed version of the ICF was available in the six official languages of the WHO (English, French, Spanish, Russian, Chinese, and Arabic). Translation of the ICF into other national languages is complete, in most cases, and the classification has been published in book and digital form in several countries. Of the Nordic countries, only Iceland has not yet translated the ICF.

I start with the ICF and the meaning of incapacity for work. The ICF describes the functional status and the (negative) effect on it. The classification says that it may be categorized as constituting a *"medical model"* and a *"social model"*. The medical model sees an effect on functional status as a problem with the individual, caused by sickness. The social model regards functional impairment as a socially-created problem and as a question of the integration of the individual into society. The ICF is based on a combination of these different models. Thus, a *"biopsychosocial"* approach has been used to capture the different perspectives on the functioning of the individual. With the ICF, efforts are made to achieve a synthesis of perspectives in order to offer a coherent view of functional status and health based on a biological, an individual, and a social perspective.

The medical incapacity for work is thus something that is determined on the basis of a holistic perspective of the individual, something that was originally also emphasized when determining the *legal* content of the concept of incapacity for work. I will come back to this legal content.

Now I will turn to the concept of sickness under the WHO international classifications. "Health conditions", e.g. *sickness,* disorders, injuries etc., are classified in accordance with ICD-10, which is short for the International Classification of Diseases, Tenth Revision. ICD-10 provides diagnoses of sicknesses, whereas the ICF provides information on the functional status. Sweden's National Board of Health and Welfare emphasizes the importance of using these two documents together.[4]

It is important to note the overlap between the ICF and ICD-10. Both are based on the body systems. Two people with the same illness may have different levels of functional status while two people with the same level of functional status may not necessarily have the same illness (health condition). It is pointed out that use of the ICF "must not ignore customary medical diagnostics".

Which medical diagnoses does ICD-10 contain? Are they based on the biological/biomedical sickness concept or are they based on the socio-medical sickness concept, both concepts often used in social insurance contexts? The question is easy to answer. The classification takes up all biomedical sicknesses, both of a somatic and a mental nature, as well as a number of diagnoses of symptoms, of which several might be classified as socio-medical states of ill health. Traditional definitions of sicknesses that focus on observable changes on the organ level are clearly insufficient in ICD-10.

The medical concept of sickness is thus very broad and inclusive in a bio-psycho-social perspective.

4 Socialstyrelsen (2003) 'Klassifikation av funktionstillstånd, funktionshinder och hälsa' – kortversion, Inledning, s. 10. [National Board of Health and Welfare, 'Classification of Functioning, Disability and Health' – short version, Preamble, p. 10].

4 Incapacity for work due to sickness in a legal perspective

I have chosen Sweden and Norway as legislative examples. I start by summarizing reviews of Swedish and Norwegian law, done by myself earlier[5], with regard to the content that has been given to the concepts of sickness and incapacity for work in the field of social insurance. I have studied the legislation of the last two decades, and in some cases further back, as well as its preparatory material, e.g. binding material, but also non-binding material used for guidance. Here, I have paid attention to whether or not there have been references to the WHO classification register for the purposes of figuring out whether or not the content of the national concepts has been interpreted on the basis of the content given to the concepts by the WHO.

Let us first consider the *concept of sickness* in the Swedish regulation. From the Swedish preparatory material, it is clear that the general rule is that the content of the concept of sickness in sickness insurance legislation has to correspond with the medical content.[6] It has been shown, in practice, that the strictly objective "biological" concept of sickness was abandoned in the 1990s in favour of a "socio-medical" one. The question concerns just how much the legal "clarification" (in Swedish *renodling*) during the latter half of the 1990s has affected the content of the legal concept. From the analysis I have carried out, the addition to the legal text that was regarded as representing this "clarification", i.e. that "labour market, social, economic and similar circumstances" should be disregarded, did not greatly influence the sickness concept as it had become established in legal application.[7] References to the ICF and ICD-10 in the preparatory materials show that there was perceived to be an agreement between the medical concept of sickness and the legal concept of sickness. The

5 *Books:* Ed. *Arbets(o)förmåga i ett mångdisciplinärt perspektiv [Inability to work from a multidisciplinary perspective]* (Santérus Förlag, Stockholm 2008); *Läkarintyget i sjukförsäkringsprocessen – styrning, legitimitet och bevisning [Doctor's Certificate in the Social Insurance Process – Control, Legitimacy and Proof]* (together with S. Thorpenberg – M. Jonasson, Santérus Förlag, Stockholm 2009); *Rehabiliteringsvetenskap. Rehabilitering till arbetslivet i ett flerdisciplinärt perspektiv [Rehabilitation Sciences. Rehabilitation to the Labour Market from a Multidisciplinary Perspective]* (together with A. Bergroth – J. Ekholm, 2nd ed., Studentlitteratur, Lund 2009).
Articles: 'Begreppet arbets(o)förmåga inom sjukförsäkringsrättslig lagstiftning och rättstillämpning' ['The Concept of (In)Ability to Work in Social Insurance Legislation and Application'], in *Arbets(o)förmåga i ett mångdisciplinärt perspektiv [Inability to work from a multidisciplinary perspective*], (ed. L. Vahlne Westerhäll, Santérus Förlag, Stockholm 2008); 'Den försäkrades rättsliga ställning i rehabiliteringsprocessen' ['The Individual`s Legal Position in the Rehabilitation Process'], in *Rehabilitering – en etisk utmaning för vården [Rehabilitation – an ethical challenge for the health care sector*] ed. G. Silfverberg, (Ersta Sköndal, Stockholm, 2008); 'Det socialförsäkringsrättsliga arbets(o)förmågebegreppet' ['The Concept of (In)Capacity for Work in the Social Insurance Regulation], in *Arbetslinjens återkomst?[The Return of the Work-line?]* (Försäkringskassan, Socialförsäkringsrapport [National Social Insurance Board, Social Insurance Report] 2009:3, p. 73); 'Är innehållet i begreppen sjukdom och arbets(o)förmåga en fråga för Regeringsrätten?' ['Is the Content of the Concept of Sickness and (In)Capacity for Work a Question for the Swedish Administrative Supreme Court?'], in *Regeringsrätten 100 år [The Swedish Administrative Supreme Court 100 years]*, (Iustus Förlag. Uppsala, 2009, p. 549); 'Komparativ- och migrationsrättsliga perspektiv på sjukdom och arbetsoförmåga för rätt till kontantförmån. Det svensk-norska exemplet' ['Legal Comparative and Migration Perspectives on Sickness and Inability to work for Cash benefits. The Swedish-Norwegian Example'], in *Tidsskrift for Rettsvitenskap [Journal of Legal Science]* (Oslo 2001, forthcoming).

6 SOU 1944:15 'Lag om allmän sjukförsäkring' (Swedish Government Official Report 1944:15 'General Sickness Insurance Act'), p. 162.

7 SOU 1995:149, p. 215; Prop. 1995/96:209 'Försäkringsskydd vid sjukdom, m.m.' ['Government Bill 1995/96:209 'Insurance protection when ill']; L. Westerhäll, 'Rättsliga aspekter på arbetsoförmåga p g a sjukdom' ['Legal aspects of incapacity for work due to sickness'], in *Socialmedicinsk tidskrift [Journal of Social Medicine]* (1997), p. 255.

restriction that has been imposed, in the non-binding document "Insurance Medical Decision Support" (in Swedish *Försäkringsmedicinskt beslutsstöd*), by the National Social Insurance Board and the National Board of Health and Welfare, entails that only objectively-verifiable states of ill health are to provide entitlement to sickness benefit. As this restriction is to be found only in non-binding quasi-legal material, it means, in my opinion, that it cannot be accorded any great significance, if the aim is to ascertain what current Swedish law is with regard to the concept of sickness. An interpretation, based on traditional legal sources, of the concept of sickness in Swedish social insurance law is that it corresponds entirely to the medical one and that the medical concept is the one which, consistent with "scientific knowledge and proven experience", exists in the said international documents.

In Norway, too, there has been a desire to remove the influence of social circumstances from the concept of sickness and this ambition has been apparent in both the established legal sources and in quasi-legal material, even if the pronouncements made have been far from unambiguous. This ambiguity would seem to have implications with regard to how, in practice references to the international documents are to be understood. The preparatory materials for the Norwegian legislation contain numerous references to the WHO classification register. However, the preparatory materials also speak of "the sliding scale" on which a number of conditions with psychosocial components, all assessed as states of ill health in ICD-10, are to be assessed in a legal context. [8]

In Norwegian circulars (not binding documents), it is maintained that certain medical states of ill health should not be given an equivalent in social insurance law.[9] These medical states are not very numerous, so it may well be asked whether or not such savings are involved that would make it worth keeping them outside the system. They are on the "sliding scale", as the Norwegian preparatory material puts it. However, to grant the right to benefits at all, these medical states have to, of course, as in all other cases, give rise to an incapacity for work. Only then will it be of interest to decide, in a legal context, whether or not they are sicknesses. Legal implementation in Norway would undoubtedly be simpler, if the references made to the international documents were to cover all medical sicknesses without any restrictions. A doctor who has assessed, in issuing a certificate for entitlement to sickness benefit, a patient as sick with a diagnosis included in an international document, should not risk having this rejected by a social insurance officer simply because the diagnosis falls outside of what is considered sickness in the social insurance regulation. From the *de lege ferenda* point of view, the Norwegian concept of sickness ought to be given a similar content to the Swedish one, as I have interpreted the latter.

8 NOU 1977:14, NOU 1990:20 and NOU 1990:23 [Norwegian Government Official Report].

9 See *Arbeids-og velferdsdirektoratets rundskriv [Circular of Labour and Welfare Directorate]* concerning the interpretation of *Folketrygdloven* § 8-4 [*Social Security Act* § 8-4].

It is mainly in Sweden that the legal *concept of incapacity for work* has been discussed. The concept has been related to the individual as he/she is insured in an "as is condition" [*försäkrad i befintligt skick*]. From references to the ICF, it is clear that the medical content of the concept of incapacity for work is closely connected to the individual and his/her functional capacity based on the context in which he/she currently is. This gives the legal incapacity for work concept a material content that is in agreement with the medical content. At the same time, this view is rejected in a contradictory manner by the use, in the social insurance policy rhetoric, of the concept of incapacity for work as if this were an empty legal-technical concept.

In Norway, the material content of the incapacity-for-work concept in sickness insurance law has been neither defined nor analysed to any appreciable extent; it has instead been seen as a consequence of the sickness. However, the *work* to which the incapacity is to relate has been put on a more formal footing than has been the case in Sweden. In Sweden, it is the original work of the insured person that has been considered, until it becomes clear that he/she cannot return to that. In practice, this focus on the original work has previously been able to continue for a very long time, sometimes several years. With amendments to Swedish law in 2008, it can no longer continue for more than 90 days; in some cases, up to 180 days from the start of the sickness. Thereafter, the main rule is that the incapacity for work is related to the entire regular labour market in general. This is a definite tightening-up in comparison with the previous state of affairs.

In Norway, there is a rule that special incapacity for work (incapacity to practice one's profession) must be confirmed during the first two or three months of a period of sickness; after which, it is to be replaced by a concept of general incapacity for work that is more extensive.[10] At the same time, it is argued that this rule is not to be observed literally and that there must be an assessment of what is reasonable in each individual case.

Even if the rules differ somewhat in form between Swedish and Norwegian legislation, the result ought to be roughly similar in practical application. The Swedish 90- and 180-day rules may correspond to Norway's rule about reasonableness.

5 Conclusions

As has become apparent, the Swedish and Norwegian concepts of sickness and incapacity for work do not differ greatly. The differences that actually do exist are not a problem when insured migrants are not involved. It is up to the state itself to decide on the content of these concepts. However, the problem takes on a different guise in a situation involving a migrant. In such cases, the differences may give rise to consequences such as those suffered by Jan A in the example given above, which cannot be considered particularly integration-friendly. However, what is now actually required

10 NOU 1990:20, p. 192.

is mutual acknowledgment of each other's concepts of sickness and incapacity for work. This does not, in itself, require the concepts to be applied with a uniform content, but that there is recognition of the other state's way of assessing its content. However, such mutual recognition becomes much easier when the concepts are similar in the legislations concerned. In the case of Swedish and Norwegian law, it should be apparent that the prospects of mutual recognition are very good. It is to be hoped that Swedish and Norwegian social insurance administrations and courts will see the scope for mutual recognition which the regulation in EU law allows.

And to go further, now that both Swedish and Norwegian preparatory materials refer to the WHO classification register vis-à-vis the two concepts, there are good prospects of being able to argue *de lege ferenda* for greater precision in the concepts in line with the WHO definitions, something which would mean a lot to the individual in a situation involving migration. An effort to bring this about would require Sweden and Norway to begin applying uniform concepts of sickness and incapacity for work, which would be wholly consistent with the opportunities for flexible application afforded by Regulation 883/2004 Art. 5. Some countries must begin to argue for what would ultimately represent a harmonization of such vital concepts, in an integration context, as those of sickness and incapacity for work. Sweden and Norway should be able to lead the way in taking such action.

References

Official materials

Preparatory work

Swedish Government Official Report 1944:15
Swedish Government Official Report 1995:149
Norwegian Government Official Report 1977:14
Norwegian Government Official Report 1990:20
Norwegian Government Official Report 1990:23
Government Bill 1995/96:209

Administrative circulars

Socialstyrelsen (2003) 'Klassifikation av funktionstillstånd, funktionshinder och hälsa' – kortversion, Inledning [The National Board of Health and Welfare, 'Classification of Functioning, Disability and Health' – short version, Preamble].

Arbeids-og velferdsdirektoratets rundskriv [Circular of Labour and Welfare Directorate] concerning the interpretation of Folketrygdloven § 8-4 [Social Security Act § 8-4].

Case law

22/86 Guiseppe Rindone v. Allgemeine Ortskrankenkasse Bad Urach-Münsingen (ECR/1987/1339).

45/90 Alberto Paletta and others v. Brennet AG (ECR/1992/I-3423).

Literature

Books

B. Schulte – H.F. Zacher (1991), *Wechselwirkungen zwischen dem Europäischen Sozialrecht und dem Sozialrecht der Bundesrepublik Deutschland [Interaction between European Social Law and German Social Law]* (Duncker & Humblot, Berlin).

L. Vahlne Westerhäll, Ed. (2008), *Arbets(o)förmåga i ett mångdisciplinärt perspektiv [Inability to work from a multidisciplinary perspective]* (Santérus Förlag, Stockholm).

L. Vahlne Westerhäll – S. Thorpenberg – M. Jonasson (2009), *Läkarintyget i sjukförsäkringsprocessen – styrning, legitimitet och bevisning [Doctor´s Certificate in the Social Insurance Process – Control, Legitimacy and Proof]* (Santérus Förlag, Stockholm).

L. Vahlne Westerhäll – A. Bergroth – J. Ekholm (2009), *Rehabiliteringsvetenskap. Rehabilitering till arbetslivet i ett flerdisciplinärt perspektiv [Rehabilitation Sciences. Rehabilitation to the Labour Market from a Multidisciplinary Perspective]* (2nd ed., Studentlitteratur, Lund).

Articles and book chapters

T. Erhag, 'Legal Aspects of Cross-Border Rehabilitation to Work', in *European Journal of Social Security* (EJSS) Vol. 7 No. 2 (2005).

L. Vahlne Westerhäll, 'Begreppet arbets(o)förmåga inom sjukförsäkringsrättslig lagstiftning och rättstillämpning' ['The Concept of (In)Ability to Work in Social Insurance Legislation and Application'], in *Arbets(o)förmåga i ett mångdisciplinärt perspektiv [Inability to work from a multidisciplinary perspective]*, (ed. L. Vahlne Westerhäll, Santérus Förlag, Stockholm 2008).

L. Vahlne Westerhäll, 'Den försäkrades rättsliga ställning i rehabiliteringsprocessen' ['The Individual's Legal Position in the Rehabilitation Process'], in *Rehabilitering – en etisk utmaning för vården [Rehabilitation – an ethical challenge for the health care sector]* ed. G Silfverberg, (Ersta Sköndal, Stockholm, 2008).

L. Vahlne Westerhäll, 'Det socialförsäkringsrättsliga arbets(o)förmågebegreppet' ['The Concept of (In)Capacity for Work in the Social Insurance Regulation'], in *Arbetslinjens återkomst? [The Return of the Work-line?]*, Försäkringskassan, Socialförsäkringsrapport 2009:3, s. 73 [National Social Insurance Board, Social Insurance Report 2009:3, p. 73].

L. Vahlne Westerhäll, 'Är innehållet i begreppen sjukdom och arbets(o)förmåga en fråga för Regeringsrätten?' ['Is the Content of the Concept of Sickness and (In)Capacity for Work a Question for the Swedish Administrative Supreme Court?'], in *Regeringsrätten 100 år [The Swedish Administrative Supreme Court 100 years]*, (Iustus Förlag, Uppsala, 2009).

L. Vahlne Westerhäll, 'Komparativ- och migrationsrättsliga perspektiv på sjukdom och arbetsoförmåga för rätt till kontankförmån. Det svensk-norska exemplet' ['Legal Comparative and Migration Perspectives on Sickness and Inability to work for Cash benefits. The Swedish-Norwegian Example'], *Tidsskrift for Rettsvitenskap [Journal of Legal Science]* (Oslo, 2001, forthcoming).

Westerhäll, L. (1997), 'Rättsliga aspekter på arbetsoförmåga p g a sjukdom' ['Legal aspects of incapacity for work due to sickness'], *Socialmedicinsk tidskrift [Journal of Social Medicine]* (1997).

Part 3

Biomedical Science

Human Dignity as a Legal Argument in the Era of Modern Biomedicine

By Laura Walin, University of Helsinki[1]

1 Introduction

Human dignity, as an attribute of every born human being, was mentioned for the first time in the Universal Declaration of Human Rights in 1948. Today, over 60 years later, humankind is still far from implementing the principle in practice, but at least overall consensus exists as to what the sentence 'All human beings are born free and equal in dignity and rights'[2] means, and what kind of actions translate the essence of the Declaration into reality. These include, among others, equality and non-discrimination, a ban on degrading and/or inhumane treatment, the right to a private life, and freedom of conscience and religion, as also codified in the European Convention on Human Rights.

Developments in modern biomedical sciences have complicated our understanding of human dignity, and it has been rightfully asked how the concept should be understood in an era when it is possible to produce human embryos outside of a woman's body, when human tissue and organs can successfully be transferred from one individual to another in order to cure serious illnesses, and when even single genes can be isolated and patented. To make matters even more complex, there is major commercial interest, in the wealthy Western world, in the abovementioned human material. Thus, nowadays, the protection of human dignity has to take the potential for commercialization into account, if it is agreed that this protection needs to be extended to embryos, tissues, and genes.

1 Laura Walin holds a PhD (evolutionary genetics) and LL.D. (medical law), both from the University of Helsinki. In the field of law, her research has centred on the regulation of human embryonic stem cell research within Europe, where such wider themes as limits of scientific freedom, human dignity as a legal concept and principles of biolaw have emerged. She has also published scientific papers on viral biochemistry and evolutionary genetics. Apart from working as an academic researcher, Ms. Walin has been employed as a scientific secretary by the Academy of Finland and as a science journalist. She currently works at the European Chemicals Agency.

2 Universal Declaration of Human Rights, Article 1.

Research into the concept of human dignity emerged in the field of philosophy, and today it is often developed in bioethics. While ethical and philosophical considerations of the concept bring welcome novel viewpoints to the discussion, it is essential to note that when human dignity is used as an argument in international conventions, as well as national legislation, our understanding of the contents and the effect of the *legal* concept of human dignity is warranted.

This article analyses human dignity as a legal concept. Its starting point is freedom of science, and the use of the human dignity argument to restrict it. Critical scrutiny of the criminalization of certain types of research into human embryos, based on human dignity in Finland, is presented and, finally, taking stock from this and other examples of modern biotechnology, the idea of developing a collective understanding of human dignity in a given society is examined.[3]

2 Freedom of science – and justified restrictions

2.1 Scientific research as a basis of our welfare

Since the Age of Enlightenment, researched knowledge has been considered one of the cornerstones of wealth and wellbeing in Western societies.[4] It has been felt that increased human comprehension of the surrounding world will benefit the whole of humankind.[5] Scientific research is expected to result in solving problems such as curing various severe diseases, developing efficient production systems, and the optimum use of natural resources. One of the central prerequisites for producing this scientifically-justified information has been the freedom of science, as it guarantees that the scientifically most interesting and relevant problems will find a place in the research programmes of scientists, i.e. that research questions arise from the scientific community itself without any outside influence.[6]

In Finland, freedom of science is one of the basic rights. The Finnish Constitution (731/1999) states that "[t]he freedom of science, the arts, and higher education is guaranteed"[7]. The preparatory works elaborate on the meaning of this provision thus: Freedom of science is needed to guarantee the framework of cultural development in a society. Furthermore, it is also seen to be intimately connected with the freedom of speech, being one expression of this key human right. Freedom of science includes the researcher's right to choose his/her object of study and the rele-

3 The ideas behind this article began to emerge during the course of the author's LLD research into regulating research into human embryos and these were partly published in Finnish as part of the author's LLD thesis in January 2010.

4 J.E. McLellan III, *Science and technology in world history*. John Hopkins University Press 2006, pp. 249–273 and J. Gribbin, *Science. A history 1543–2001*. Penguin Books 2002.

5 Codified in Article 15 of the International Covenant on Economic, Social and Cultural Rights: "1. The States Parties to the present Covenant recognize the right of everyone: [...] (b) To enjoy the benefits of scientific progress and its applications."

6 P.G. Werskey, The perennial dilemma of science policy. *Nature* 233:529–532 (1971) and Science and society. *Nature* 184:127–129 (1959).

7 Section 16.3.

vant research methods. The focus and themes of research should originate primarily from within the scientific community itself, and via critique practiced by it. [8] Freedom of science is further protected by the Universities Act (558/2009), establishing the principle of autonomy for the universities of Finland.[9]

In Finland, there are, however, only a few basic freedoms and liberties which are absolute and it can be relatively safely stated that the freedom of science is certainly not one of the core rights. On the contrary, the freedom of science is one of those rights that can be limited in order to respect other, more central human rights and basic freedoms such as the right to life, a ban on torture and cruel, inhuman, or degrading treatment, or the right to privacy.[10] The Constitutional Law Committee of the Parliament of Finland, the authority that scrutinizes whether or not a proposed law is in line with the Constitution, has defined the following prerequisites for restrictions to basic freedoms and liberties: 1) Restrictions must be enacted through parliamentary law. This authority cannot be delegated to a lower level of statutes. 2) Restrictions must be precise and delimited. The relevant content of the restriction must become evident in the law. 3) The restriction must be acceptable and required by a cogent societal need. 4) The core area of the basic freedom in question must remain intact. Restrictions must be essential for the objective, and no other, less-interfering means of implementing that objective are to be found. 5) The restriction should be proportional and hence as limited as possible when weighing the societal interest and limited basic rights against each other. 6) Guarantees of the due process of law must be ensured when limiting basic and fundamental rights, and 7) the restrictions must be consistent with the international human rights obligations of Finland.[11]

It is not often that scientific research is subjected to specific restrictions in Finland. However, two examples are clear: Restrictions on studying genetically-modified organisms, both in the laboratory and in the field[12], and the form of human embryonic research banned in the Criminal Code[13]. I will next analyse these and other reasons behind the restrictions, and their validity.

2.2 Restricting the freedom of science – from precautionary principle to the protection of human dignity

The ideal of the freedom of science has been maintained by Western societies from the Enlightenment right through to the early 20th century. The two World Wars,

8 Government Bill 309/1993.

9 Section 3.1: "The universities are autonomous, which guarantees the freedom of science, the arts and higher education."

10 As expressed, in for instance, Articles 6, 7, and 17 of the United Nations International Convention on Civil and Political Rights, or Articles 2, 3, and 8 of the Convention for the Protection of Human Rights and Fundamental Freedoms by the Council of Europe, respectively.

11 Report 25/1995 of the Committee for Constitutional Law.

12 Chapters 4 and 5 of the Gene Technology Act (377/1995).

13 Chapter 22, Section 4 of the Criminal Code (39/1889).

however, forced humankind to re-evaluate the situation; since those days, the freedom of science has been restricted by means of varying justifications. First, it can be noted that between the World Wars, national security became an accepted justification for restricting freedom of science. When basic research into nuclear physics and related technology gained strategic importance in warfare, the publication of research results was restricted by several countries. In the present day, it could be seen that the prevention of bioterrorism might lead to similar restrictions.[14] WWII also had a profound effect on the regulation of scientific research on human beings, i.e. clinical trials. The basic principles for regulating medical research on human beings were established at the Nuremberg trial in 1947[15], with the protection of the health of research subjects and the guarantee concerning voluntary participation in experiments being established as guidelines.

With the emergence of environmental law in the 1960s, the precautionary principle and risk management have become typical justifications for restricting scientific research.[16] The idea is that the freedom of science is restricted because it is thought that new experiments will cause novel risks whose unpredictability warrants societal control. For example, research into genetically-modified organisms in laboratories, their release onto the market, and their cultivation in natural surroundings are all strictly controlled, because is it felt that there is not yet enough knowledge about the effects of these novel organisms on human health and the environment.

When research is conducted on human embryos, it is not so easy to apply the abovementioned, fairly-established criteria for restricting the freedom of science. Research takes place under very controlled conditions in a laboratory environment, so it is difficult to see any risk to the environment. The protection of human health can be approved as a principle for restricting research if clinical trials are conducted on patients, i.e. when cell products derived from human embryos are tested as medicines.[17] Then, the research protocol needs to comply with the principles laid down for clinical trials. However, as most countries do not see human embryos as human beings with a full moral status[18], the protection of human embryos as human beings, along the lines of the Nuremberg principles, cannot serve as the basis for restricting research on them. The principle that has been revived to

14 M.J. Selgelid A tale of two studies. Ethics, bioterrorism, and the censorship of science. *Hastings Center Report* May-June 2007:35–43.

15 R. Macklin, Universality of Nuremberg code, pp. 240–257 in G.J. Annas and M.A. Grodin, *The Nazi doctors and the Nuremberg code. Human rights in human experimentation*. Oxford University Press 1992.

16 Z.K. Forsman, Community regulation of genetically-modified organisms: A difficult relationship between law and science. *European Law Journal* 10:580–594 (2004).

17 Patient safety is the main argument against starting clinical trials on stem cell products, voiced even by researchers who, in principle, approve of research on human embryos per se. See A.P. Chidgey, D. Layton, A. Trounson & R.L. Boyd, Tolerance strategies for stem-cell-based therapies. *Nature* 453:330–337 (2008), B. Siegel, Reflections on the cloning case. *Cloning and stem cells* 9:40–46 (2007) and I. Wilmut, How safe is cloning? *Cloning* 3:39–40 (2001).

18 R.M. Isasi & B.M. Knoppers, Mind the gap: policy approaches to embryonic stem cell and cloning research in 50 countries. *European Journal of Health Law* 13:9–26 (2006), pp. 12–16.

justify restrictions on the application of modern biotechnology is the protection of human dignity.[19]

3 Human dignity argumentation in the era of biolaw

3.1 Traditional lines of thought: Utilitarianism and human rights view

The ethical issues related to biotechnology can be approached from two fairly opposing, but traditional, viewpoints: either from a utilitarian or from a human rights perspective. As an example, the collection of tissue samples from a whole population for a biobank can be examined. The utilitarian argument would be that, as the benefits of collecting and researching these tissues greatly override the minor harm caused to individuals – e.g. harm related to the physical inconvenience of giving the sample and harm related to the loss of privacy due to making personal genetic information available to researchers – the collection of samples should be allowed. The human rights position would centre on the freedom of action of any individual – did the people have the opportunity to provide their free and informed consent when they were asked to donate their tissue to the biobank.

Provisions restricting the patenting of human genes can be analysed in a similar manner. From a human rights perspective, gene patenting is not a problem if the research subjects have given their informed consent regarding the procedure and the use of their genetic material. The utilitarian would consider the benefits of the incentives produced by the patent system against the harm of the act. The same goes for human embryonic and stem cell research: The utilitarian would emphasise the expected benefits for human beings that have already been born, and would use this argument to justify the research. From the traditional human rights perspective, there would not be any problem either as the human embryo, as a pre-natal form of human life, would not be seen as subject to human rights. The problems start when one tries to define the harm done in these cases, as human dignity then comes into the argument.

3.2 Human dignity has two sides

In the early 2000s, David Beyleveld and Roger Brownsword put forward the idea that human dignity can attain two totally opposite meanings in the era of biotechnology.[20] In the traditional sense, the concept is manifested in such documents as the Universal Declaration on Human Rights, the International Covenant on Civil and Political Rights, the International Covenant on Economic, Social and Cultural

19 For the application of the human dignity principle, in restricting research on born human beings, see A. Barbosa da Silva, Human dignity, the value of knowledge and the limits of scientific freedom, pp. 145-160, in H. Sinding Aasen, R. Halvorsen and A. Barbosa da Silva (eds.), *Human rights autonomy in health care and social services: Nordic perspectives*. Intersentia 2009.

20 D. Beyleveld & R. Brownsword, *Human dignity in bioethics and biolaw*. Oxford University Press 2001, pp. 9–47.

Rights, and the European Convention on Human Rights. It links with the rise of human rights thinking after World War II and derives from Immanuel Kant's idea that no man shall be treated solely as a means, but as the end. The traditional approach emphasises individual autonomy and the right to self-determination. It is also fairly uncontroversial that the legal documents attach human dignity to born human beings, which is understandable considering that assisted reproduction techniques were not available at the time of their writing. The traditional view of human dignity still has a lot of significance, especially in the field of criminal law, and more widely, considering that, although the idea is accepted, not even Western societies are there yet as regards full implementation.

In the Nordic countries, the principle of human dignity, in the traditional sense, has long been recognised in legislation. In all countries, human dignity underpins legislation relating to healthcare and patients' rights.[21] The concepts of human dignity, autonomy, and integrity are interwoven in the Nordic health law tradition, and informed consent is the central vehicle for guaranteeing that these principles are respected as far as possible. The starting point of the traditional thinking is the born human being with full mental capacity. The tricky questions on respecting human dignity central around the groups that are concerned to have limited capacity to decide for themselves such as minors and individuals with cognitive impairment, or situations where coercive treatment is concerned medically necessary.[22]

Since the 1990s, the concept of human dignity has taken on completely the opposite interpretation; it can actually be used nowadays to restrict the choices of born human beings. The object of protection has shifted away from protecting the individual towards protecting something more collective, and simultaneously more abstract. A classical example of this view of human dignity is the case of a person short in stature who was forbidden by court order to earn his keep by acting as an object in midget throwing competitions, since the act itself was considered to be contrary to human dignity.[23] In the area on medical law such well known procedures as euthanasia and abortion, and in within biolaw research on human embryos and patenting human genes have been said to be against human dignity. It is typical that human dignity serves as an argument for both sides of the discussion. For example, it can be claimed that respect for human dignity requires the protection of human life and, hence, euthanasia should be banned, or that the right to a dignified death is something required by human dignity and euthanasia should be allowed.

21 Finland: Patients' Rights Act (785:1992) Section 3; Sweden: Health Act (763:1982) Section 2; Denmark: originally Section 1 of the Patients' Rights Act (482:1998), currently dignity is mentioned in the guidelines regarding information and consent (168:1998); Norway: Patients' Rights Act (63:1999) Section 1; Iceland: Patients' Rights Act (47:1997), Section 1.

22 H. Sinding Aasen, R. Halvorsen and A. Barbosa da Silva (eds.), *Human rights, dignity and autonomy in health care and social services: Nordic perspectives.* Intersentia 2009, pp. 71-144 and 161-203.

23 Conseil d'Etat 27 October 1995, search for case no 143578 at http://www.conseil-etat.fr/cde/fr/base-de-jurisprudence/, visited 23 March 2011.

The approach to this novel interpretation in the Nordic countries is still to be established, and the outcome clearly voiced in legislation. This has, however, been touched upon when the legislation concerning human embryonic research was revised in the 2000s.[24] While it is clear in Sweden's Ethical Approval of Research on Humans Act that this Act, including its underlying principle of respect for human dignity, also encompasses research on biological material of human origin, it was not spelt out in much detail in the preparatory works what this would mean in practice.[25] The emphasis seems to be on informed consent, which would imply that the traditional human rights view has guided the legislator.[26] In the Bill concerning human embryonic research (148:2003/4), the human dignity principle is explained in more detail. Emphasis is put on avoiding the instrumentalisation of human life and on the discussion about when human life begins. The Swedish legislator argues that the implantation of an embryo into the womb is as important a prerequisite for human life as gestation, concluding therefore that embryos not yet implanted are different in terms of human dignity than those already implanted.

Human dignity is mentioned as the fundamental principle of Finland's Medical Research Act (488:1998, Section 3), but it has not been spelt out what the principle would mean, for example, for research on human embryos or human genes.[27] In Norway, too, human dignity is mentioned in the very first Section of the Use of Biotechnology in Human Medicine Act (100:2003). In contrast, Iceland's Artificial Fertilisation and Use of Human Gametes and Embryos for Stem Cell Research Act (55:1996, as amended by Act 27:2008) does not specifically mention human dignity; however, it is evident from Sections 12-13 of this Act that ethical evaluation is a prerequisite for any research on human embryos. It can be fairly safely assumed that scrutinizing the preserving of human dignity is part of such evaluation. In Denmark's Artificial Fertilisation Act (932:2006), human dignity is not mentioned either.

24 The purpose of this article is not to provide a complete comparison of the legal understanding of human dignity in the Nordic countries. Therefore, the paragraphs outlining the Nordic state-of-play should be considered only as an overview of some pieces of legislation where human dignity has been mentioned/elaborated on, either in the legal texts or in the preparatory works. The examples relate mostly to human embryonic research.

25 E. Rynning, Legal aspects of human-animal chimeras and hybrids: Country report Sweden, pp. 689-705, in J. Taupitz & M. Weschka (eds.), *CHIMBRIDS – Chimeras and hybrids in comparative European and international research*. Springer 2009, p. 692.

26 See Sections 1 and 7 of Act 2003:460. In the preparatory works (Bill 2002/03:50, Section 7.1), it is clear that the basis for the human dignity argument is the Biomedicine Convention. While it is noted that there are different interpretations of when human life begins, there is no further elaboration to explain what the Swedish view would be. See also Sections 5.5. and 8.4 of Bill 2003/04:32, which iterates informed consent as the major underlying mechanism for protecting human dignity.

27 The Section on human dignity was, in fact, only added by the Committee on Social and Welfare Issues in their reading, and was thus never discussed in detail during the legislative process. This has been criticized by the author and by Salla Lötjönen in their respective dissertations.

3.3 *Against human dignity or just a threat to it?*

Human dignity is a multifaceted, multilayered concept that has been developed within the disciplines of philosophy, theology and law.[28] Therefore, it is essential that the party using the human dignity argument is prepared to clearly express where the threat to human dignity lies in the action that is being restricted. Otherwise, human dignity will be reduced merely to a mantra that can be recited without further explanation against any novel technology related to (using) human beings. This "dignitarian alliance" may gain unduly strong support in society as it is fairly difficult to argue against respecting human dignity.[29] It is feared that the human dignity argument will only be used to silence societal discussion of novel applications of biotechnology, and thus its use equals oppression. Whenever a novel technology arises, the "dignitarian alliance" immediately claims that it is against human dignity and tries to end discussion about the matter. It has been argued that the human dignity argument is specifically inappropriate in the context of criminalising acts of modern biotechnology.[30]

Since the roots of the dignitarian alliance lie in the traditional understanding of human dignity, i.e. human dignity in terms of granting rights to human beings; in the case of biobanks, its argumentation would presumably be fairly close to that of a human rights position.[31]

The situation is trickier in the case of human embryonic research. The dignitarian alliance simply states that research on human embryos needs to be banned because it violates human dignity. Without further specification, this argument does not hold, as the status of the human embryo is perceived very differently by different societies, and not all of them share the view that the research use of human embryos would be against human dignity. Therefore, it would be fruitful to try to specify which actions are directly against human dignity, and which actions are such that they potentially endanger human dignity.[32]

Take, for example, the criminalisation of certain forms of research on human embryos in Finland.[33] Is it really perceived to be against human dignity in Finland's

28 For an overview, see, for instance, A. Barbosa da Silva, Autonomy, dignity and integrity in health care ethics – a moral philosophical perspective, pp. 13-52, in H. Sinding Aasen, R. Halvorsen and A. Barbosa da Silva (eds.), *Human rights, dignity and autonomy in health care and social services: Nordic perspectives*, Intersentia 2009; M. Häyry, Another look at dignity. *Cambridge Quarterly of Healthcare Ethics* 13:7–14 (2004) and E. Shuster, Human cloning: Category, dignity, and the role of bioethics. *Bioethics* 17:517–525 (2003).

29 R. Brownsword, Bioethics today, bioethics tomorrow: Stem cell research and the "dignitarian alliance". *Notre Dame Journal of Law, Ethics and Public Policy* 17:15–51 (2003).

30 T. Caulfield & T. Bubela, Why a Criminal Ban?: Analyzing the Arguments Against Somatic Cell Nuclear Transfer in the Canadian Parliamentary Debate. *American Journal of Bioethics* 7:51–61 (2007); Caulfield & Chapman 2005; T. Caulfield, L. Knowles & E.M. Meslin, Law and policy in the era of reproductive genetics. *Journal of Medical Ethics* 30:414–417 (2004); Brownsword 2003 and R. Shapiro 2003. Legislative research bans on human cloning. *Cambridge Quarterly of Healthcare Ethics* 12:393–400.

31 D. Resnik, DNA patents and human dignity. *The Journal of Law, Medicine & Ethics* 29:152–165 (2001).

32 Ibid., p. 153.

33 Bill 156/2008, pp. 21–22.

fairly liberal society? It seems to me that these forms of research, were they to be allowed, could endanger the inviolability of human dignity; however, they are not a direct infringement of it in societies where human embryo do not have the full moral status of a human being. Research into, for instance, cloning can also be scientifically justified, so it does not match the definition of a biomedical trial which is given as an example of a banned act on the basis of human dignity violations in the government proposal regarding the constitution. However, it seems completely plausible that if, for instance, cloning were to be allowed, this practice could, over time, change our perceptions on the early developmental stages of human life, thus allowing cloning can be seen as a potential threat to human dignity.

In a similar manner, the act of patenting human genes per se would not be against human dignity[34]. Instead, the patenting of human genes is once again something that potentially endangers human dignity, as our perceptions of the human body may change if parts of it were to become commodities.[35] The threat is even bigger in the case of patenting entire embryos, as these are, in a sense, entire human beings, albeit very primitive ones. This thinking coincides well with the decision by the European Patent Office when ruling that innovations which require the destruction of human embryos are not patentable.[36]

3.4 Human dignity in the 2010s: New ideas, old findings

Since the groundbreaking analysis of the dichotomy of human dignity by Beyleveld and Brownsword in the early 2000s, the development of human dignity as a legal concept has been less evident. One recent opening is the proposal to consider a human being as more than an autonomous individual, on the other hand, and to see the concept in wider terms over time.[37] The idea that a human being should be considered not only as an individual, but also as a part of his/her society is, in my opinion, related to Beyleveld and Brownsword's thought that human dignity should be always defined for a certain society.[38] Dupré develops the idea further by including the psychological inner self in the concept, since he wants to develop the concept of human dignity away from listing only fears and threats towards such positive elements as individual hopes and aspirations.

As a collective concept, Dupré restructures the public settings of the human being, adding the working environment to the well known public and private environments. He claims that all three areas need to be considered whenever respect for

34 Universal Declaration on the Human Genome and Human Rights 11 November 1997, Articles 1-4 are entitled "Human dignity and human genome".

35 Resnik 2003.

36 EPO Enlarged Board of Appeal, Decision in the matter G02/06, 25 November 2008.

37 C. Dupré, Unlocking human dignity: Towards a theory for the 21st century. *European Human Rights Law Review* 2:190–205 (2009).

38 Beyleveld & Brownsword 2001, p. 65.

human dignity is an issue for the legislator. Otherwise one will fail to understand the entire human being, something which in itself is a violation against human dignity. When considering human dignity in time, Dupré notices that time is perceived differently when we talk about individuals, human being as a species, and, for instance, about planets. He sees it as important that we try to reconcile all these views when interpreting human rights. To him, it is also crucial that the concept of human dignity include the potential for change over time: no human being is locked into his/her unsatisfactory situation forever, but he/she can always strive for change.

Professor Christopher Rudden, from the University of Oxford, has analysed human dignity from a more traditional human rights viewpoint. He concludes, like many others, that the concept is bound in time and cannot be transferred 1:1 from one legal culture to another.[39] He claims that both Catholic and left-wing cultures have been favourable breeding grounds for human dignity argumentation and have led to the use of arguments first in legislation and then in the courts.

Based on his analysis of human rights, documents, and global case law, he concludes that the minimum content of human dignity can be crystallized into three elements: i) every human being is a subject of human dignity due merely the fact that they are human beings, ii) all others must respect this dignity, and therefore some acts are required and some are banned, and iii) the state is for individuals and not the other way around. Also, Rudden comes to the conclusion that, while these three conditions per se are almost universally recognized, differences in opinion start as soon as one tries to define more precisely the content of each claim.[40] He is surprised by how easily national courts, despite this, borrow human rights argumentation from other legal cultures. In the end, this proves to Rudden that human dignity is an element which courts can use when needing to balance non-commensurate rights against each other. It is also a means whereby national courts transfer international human rights conventions into the national judicial process.

4 Towards community-based understanding of human dignity

It seems that human dignity is used, or can be used, in three different ways in legal instruments when restricting biomedical research. The first, and a very typical use of the argument, is to present it as a general principle underpinning the entire legislation. In my view, this is the route taken in the Biomedicine Convention[41] and the

39 C. McCrudden, Human dignity and judicial interpretation of human rights. *European Journal of International Law* 19:655–724 (2008).

40 Ibid., pp. 679–680.

41 Convention for the Protection of Human Rights and Dignity of the Human Being with Regard to the Application of Biology and Medicine: Convention on Human Rights and Biomedicine. ETS 164, 4 April 1997, Article 1: "Parties to this Convention shall protect the dignity and identity of all human beings."

Finnish Medical Research Act[42]. In practice, this means that all the remaining provisions of the legislation should be interpreted in a way that ensures maximum respect for human dignity.

In my opinion, this way of using the human dignity argument is acceptable as the concept is not used to establish new rights for individuals, nor is it used to restrict the rights of individuals. Therefore, it does not matter that the concept is vague and is not defined further. This vagueness, however, causes the problems stemming from this declarative use of the concept. As an example, one can take Article 18(2) of the Biomedicine Convention which states that, if a country allows research on human embryos, it will have to ensure the proper protection of them. What does this mean, in practice, in the light of respecting human dignity? The interpretation remains open, as highlighted in, for instance, the respective legislations of Germany and Sweden: in the former, research on human embryos is forbidden while in the latter, it is even permissible to create human embryos purely for research purposes.[43]

The second way to use human dignity as an argument in the legal texts is to ban something because it is against human dignity, or because it violates human dignity. This approach has been taken in the Finnish Criminal Act, where three specific types of experiments have been banned because they are against human dignity.[44] The argumentation does not go any deeper into the reasons why these specifics acts – and nothing else – are against human dignity, which renders the justification unduly vague. In practice, the provision means that certain experiments cannot be done by a researcher even if he/she considers them scientifically relevant. Taking into account the fact that there are relatively heavy sanctions, up to two years' imprisonment, for breaching the provision, the justifications should be transparent and understandable to the addressees.

The third possibility to use the human dignity argument in the legislative texts is an expanded version of the above: certain acts are banned because they are against human dignity, but the *travaux préparatoires* would explicitly spell out how the legislator came to that conclusion. It is important that it is transparently outlined exactly who is behind the judgement that certain acts are against human dignity – is it only the opinion of a single civil servant, or of the working group behind the legislative proposal, or is it considered to be the opinion of the majority of the people. In a democratic society, one should aim for the last option.

In order to find out the opinion of the majority in society, a broad public debate on difficult ethical issues should be conducted before legislative work starts. This public debate can then be filtered into the legislative proposal via, for instance, the

42 Section 3: "Medical research shall respect the inviolability of human dignity."

43 S. Halliday, A comparative approach to the regulation of human embryonic stem cell research in Europe, *Medical Law Review* 12:40–69 (2004).

44 These are studies that violate the physical immunity of human beings, foetuses or embryos and which aim to 1) clone human beings 2) create a human being by combining [two or more] embryos or 3) create a human being by combining human gametes and animal genes.

respective working group.[45] It might be worthwhile, for example, to conduct a poll among a representative sample of people to find out why a certain act is seen as being against human dignity. This would add transparency in a situation where an individual's (researcher's) rights are restricted. The ban would become acceptable since it would represent the collective will of a given population. Human dignity would become a means of communicative regulation, a vehicle for expressing community values in legislation. In a representative democracy, it is, of course, Parliament that represents the whole nation in a legislative process; however, in my opinion, in the ethically tricky questions, a broader public debate would be needed to support Parliament in its work. I think also that the national ethical committees could take a key role in initiating and organizing such a discussion.

In conclusion, it seems that, as a universal argument, human dignity only works if it is left undefined.[46] Therefore, it works well as a declarative principle in, for instance, international conventions where the parties are often individual states. Whenever human dignity is invoked in order to restrict individual rights, or to impose new obligations on individuals, a level of conceptual non-ambiguity is required such that the use of the concept has to be limited to a defined geographical area over a given period of time. It is important to emphasise the last point: human dignity is a concept whose content varies not just in space, but also in time. One has to be aware of this when using the concept in national legislation, since the interpretation of a legal provision may change over time in society due to the evolving understanding of the human dignity concept.[47]

45 A filtering body may be needed because it is more likely that extreme opinions in the public debate are louder than the moderate ones, often representing the majority. J. Dombrink & D. Hillyard, *Sin no more. From abortion to stem cells, understanding crime, law, and morality in America.* New York University Press 2007, pp. 225–256.

46 C. Perelman, *The realm of rhetoric*, 1982, p. 31.

47 A recent example from Finland is the case of the compulsory treatment of addicted pregnant women. For decades, the understanding was that foetal rights could not override women's rights, even if the situation where foetal life was in danger due to the superior status of a born human being over a foetus. In 2010, human dignity arguments are now being used to argue more strongly on behalf on unborn life.

European Integration – a Case Example from European Biomedical Research Law

By Dr. Sigmund Simonsen, Norwegian University of Science and Technology [1]

1 Introduction – the challenge of European integration

European integration is a vision in many fields. In European law, it translates into the aim of regulatory harmony, meaning that people in one European country will be subject to basically the same legal standards as those in another. This is especially practical and important if people in different countries interact across borders, as many do, increasingly also in health care and biomedical research. Regulatory initiatives from both the European Union (EU) and the Council of Europe (CoE) are aimed at regulatory harmony. But since those agencies have different bases, aims, and methods of expression, their initiatives may conflict and thus be regarded as counterproductive to regulatory harmony and European integration.

In this article, I will approach this topic by discussing the challenges facing European integration in European biomedical research law. More specifically, with reference to the challenges faced in my own recent research project on acceptable risk in biomedical research, I will clarify whether or not European integration and regulatory harmony are legally feasible. I will also discuss whether regulatory harmony is a mandatory consideration and an aim in the interpretation of legal instruments in this field. At the end, I offer three concrete examples of the implications of European integration, its challenges, and its possibilities.[2]

---

1 Dr. Sigmund Simonsen is a lawyer in private practice (www.AdvokatSimonsen.no). He is also associate professor in biomedical research law at the Norwegian University of Science and Technology (NTNU). Simonsen is a member of the Norwegian National Committee for Medical and Health Research Ethics (NEM).

2 S. Simonsen, *Acceptable risk in biomedical research*. Doctoral thesis. Trondheim, NTNU 2010. A revised book version is being published by Springer. This publication is partly based on that work, and contains findings and unmarked excerpts from it.

2 The regulation of biomedical research in the Nordic countries in brief

Biomedical research has traditionally been regulated by means of professional guidelines, e.g. the Declaration of Helsinki adopted by the World Medical Association in 1964, which is based on the so-called Nuremberg code as expressed in the judgement from the Nuremberg Doctors Trial of 1947.[3]

Denmark was among the first countries in Europe to adopt a general legal framework for biomedical research; its first Act dates back to 1992. Finland and Iceland adopted similar acts in 1999, while Sweden adopted an Act in 2003. Norway adopted its Biomedical Research Act in 2008. The Norwegian legislation was heavily influenced by international legal and professional regulations, primarily the so-called Oviedo Convention adopted by the CoE in 1997.[4] All countries have also implemented, however, the Clinical Trial Directive of 2001 from the European Union, concerning clinical trials with pharmaceutical products.[5] Additionally, all countries have adopted legal regulations concerning biobanks, biotechnology, and the handling of personal data, which are all relevant in a biomedical research context.[6]

Thus, regulation in most countries appears rather complex since several instruments are partly overlapping, and since some are based on partly overlapping international instruments. There are some publications which are aimed at clarifying the legal framework, but few address the challenge posed by European integration.[7]

Biomedical research law may be seen as founded on three core principles: 1) a requirement for proportionality between risks and potential benefits, 2) a requirement for the informed consent of the research participant, and 3) a requirement for an independent ethical review of the research project. The first principle was the topic of my research project.

---

3 The Nuremberg Military Tribunal's decision in the case of the *United States v. Karl Brandt et al.* of 19th of August 1947. Control Council Law No. 10 was adopted by the allied forces.

4 Convention for the Protection of Human Rights and Dignity of the Human Being with regard to the Application of Biology and Medicine: Convention on Human Rights and Biomedicine of 1997.

5 Directive 2001/20/EC of the European Parliament and Council, of 4 April 2001, on the approximation of the laws, regulations, and administrative provisions of the member states relating to the implementation of good clinical practice in the conducting of clinical trials of medicinal products for human use.

6 Nordic Committees on Bioethics. Legislation on Biotechnology in the Nordic Countries – An overview. *TemaNord* 2006:506.

7 U. Hybel, *Forsøgspersoner [Research Persons]* Copenhagen: Jurist- og Økonomforbundets Forlag, 1998; S. Lötjönen, Medical research in clinical emergency settings in Europe, *J. Med. Ethics* 2002; 28(3): 183-187; S. Lötjönen, Medical research on patients with dementia – the role of advance directives in European legal instruments, *Eur. Jour. Health Law* 2006 (13): 235-261; S. Simonsen 2010 op. cit.; S. Simonsen, *Helseforskningsloven [Health Research Act]. Norsk Lovkommentar [Norwegian Law Commentary]*. Oslo: Gyldendal Rettsdata, 2010.

3 A presentation of some concrete challenges: Are regulatory harmony and European integration feasible?

The level of acceptable risk in biomedical research is a key issue when determining whether or not a human experiment is justifiable. In my research project, I investigated what level of risk and burden it is acceptable to expose human subjects to in European biomedical research.

The answer is basically that risk and burden are acceptable *if* they are outweighed by (proportionate to) the potential benefits accruing to the participant or others.

That follows from the requirement (principle) of proportionality, which is an old and fundamental legal norm in biomedical research law.

The requirement for proportionality is a legal standard in Europe, as well as in the US.

However, the requirement for proportionality is vague and difficult to apply in practice. The content of the norm has largely been unexplored in legal literature, and the rich bioethical literature is inconclusive. The content of the requirement was thus unclear. The aim of my research project was therefore to clarify the more precise content of the requirement for proportionality.

In a legal analysis of this nature, the natural starting point was the wording of the norm in the relevant legal instruments.[8] However, the challenge, as indicated above in Section 2, lay in the fact that the requirement for proportionality is expressed using different words in *several* legal instruments adopted by different agencies at different levels (international and national).

In convention (ECHR/CoE) law[9], Article 6 (1) of the Additional Protocol[10] to the Oviedo Convention[11], contains the following formulation of the requirement for proportionality:[12]

> Research shall not involve risks and burdens to the human being disproportionate to its potential benefits.

Article 3 (2) (a) of the Clinical Trials Directive contains the corresponding provision in Community (EU) law[13], which states:[14]

8 See the Statues of the International Court of Justice, annexed to the UN Charter of 1945, and the Vienna Convention on the Law of Treaties of 1969.

9 "Convention law" refers to the legal framework under the auspices of the Council of Europe (CoE).

10 Additional Protocol to the Convention on Human Rights and Biomedicine, concerning Biomedical Research, of 2005.

11 Convention for the Protection of Human Rights and Dignity of the Human Being with regard to the Application of Biology and Medicine: Convention on Human Rights and Biomedicine of 1997.

12 The provision is a restatement of Article 16 (ii) of the Oviedo Convention (with the addition of the word "burden").

13 "Community law" refers to the legal framework under the auspices of the European Union (EU).

14 Directive 2001/20/EC of the European Parliament and Council, of 4 April 2001, on the approximation of the laws, regulations and administrative provisions of the member states relating to the implementation of good clinical practice in the conducting of clinical trials of medicinal products for human use.

> A clinical trial may be undertaken only if, in particular: (a) the foreseeable risks and inconveniences have been weighed against the anticipated benefit for the individual trial subject and other present and future patients. A clinical trial may be initiated only if the Ethics Committee and/or the competent authority comes to the conclusion that the anticipated therapeutic and public health benefits justify the risks and may be continued only if compliance with this requirement is permanently monitored.

The scope of application of these instruments is partly overlapping. The Clinical Trial Directive applies to interventional clinical trials on human beings using pharmaceutical products, while the Oviedo Convention and its Additional Protocol apply to any interventional human experiments, including clinical trials using pharmaceutical products.

Anyway, member states are obliged, as already mentioned, to make those principles effective and implement them into national law. In Norway, the principles of convention law are incorporated into § 22 of the Health Research Act, 2008, while the principles of community law are incorporated into secondary legislation concerning clinical trials of 2009, § 2-1. Since Norway has used its margin of appreciation, the implementations are not exact translations. This means that, in Norway, we have four authoritative expressions of one norm, or is it four slightly different norms? The situation is probably similar in the other Nordic countries.

To add further complexity to the regulatory situation, the principle of proportionality is supplemented and specified by a number of partly overlapping provisions in all the aforementioned instruments.

This regulatory reality obvious poses some real and difficult challenges, both in practice and with regard to the vision of European integration and regulatory harmony.

In the field of biomedical research law, judges, research ethics committees, biomedical researchers, research subjects, and legal scholars etc. may thus ask questions such as: Which wording is correct or should take priority? What about the additional specifying provisions? What exactly is the normative content? What level of risks and burdens is it legally permissible to expose a human being to in biomedical research?

These are legal questions that must be dealt with in an integrated European reality. Research Ethics Committees (RECs) need to know in order to know whether or not they can approve a research project. Judges need to know, for example, when faced with a tort suit concerning negligence and hazardous, i.e. excessively risky, research. Biomedical researchers and other practitioners need to know what levels of risk it is legally acceptable to expose human participants to. It is, for example, difficult to conduct a multinational clinical trial involving children, if children in one country can apparently be exposed to a certain degree of risk for the sake of helping others while the level of acceptable risk to children is lower in another.

European integration and regulatory harmony are thus clearly necessary and feasible, from a practical point of view as well as from an overarching regulatory point of view.

4 Are regulatory harmony and European integration possible and mandatory?

In this section, the relationship between the Oviedo Convention, and its Additional Protocol, and the Clinical Trials Directive is further addressed.

Different wordings and legal systems may support the notion that the provisions have a different normative content, and that harmonisation is legally impossible. Moreover, while convention law's aim is regulatory harmony, by ensuring minimum standards of protection, community law's aim is an integral market and regulatory harmony. The instruments are distinct, and it can be argued that they should therefore be analysed and kept distinct. However, such a position is neither feasible nor legally sustainable.

It is not feasible because member states are obligated to implement and observe both instruments. Not all European states are member states vis-à-vis both instruments. However, most European states are, arguably through their commitment to the European Convention on Human Rights of 1952 and through international customary law (which the principle of proportionality is probably a part of), obligated at some level by a similar standard.

In practice, that entails that biomedical researchers, RECs, judges, and the government are obligated to observe both instruments. They cannot neglect one of them. A state cannot simply say that the Clinical Trial Directive applies to clinical trials using pharmaceutical products while the Oviedo Convention and its Additional Protocol apply to other interventional studies. The reason for this is that the Oviedo Convention and its Additional Protocol also apply to clinical trials using pharmaceutical products.

Thus, in circumstances where the instrument addresses the same issue, e.g. the level of acceptable risks and burdens during clinical trials, an ambiguous legal command is intolerable, in practice as well as in legal theory.

That European regulatory harmony is an overarching aim of both community law and convention law is clear. In this regard, the Clinical Trials Directive states:

> Clinical trials are a complex operation, generally lasting one or more years, usually involving numerous participants and several trial sites, often in different Member States. Member States' current practices diverge considerably on the rules on commencement and conduct of the clinical trials and the requirements for carrying them out vary widely. This therefore results in delays and complications detrimental to effective conduct of such trials in the Community.

> It is therefore necessary to simplify and harmonise the administrative provisions governing such trials by establishing a clear, transparent procedure and creating conditions conducive to effective coordination of such clinical trials in the Community by the authorities concerned.

Although, this statement is not directed at the relationship between community law and convention law, it is clear that regulatory harmony is desirable in any form to promote legitimate biomedical research. This suggests that regulatory harmony should be possible and a legitimate aim in the interpretation of legal instruments.

Moreover, the European Court of Human Rights, in its case law, has established a "presumption of Convention appliance", which entails having to presume that community law is in harmony with (and not in breach of) convention law, since "respect for fundamental rights has become 'a condition of the legality of Community acts'".[15] Moreover, the provisions concerning the assessment of proportionality in both instruments have a mutual origin in international law and ethics, e.g. international human rights law from 1945, the Nuremberg Code of 1947, and the Declaration of Helsinki of 1964.[16] These instruments are, by and large, subject to corresponding principles of legal interpretation.

A likely reason why the question about harmony has not been raised in the instruments is that the bodies of both the CoE and the EU are cautious about unduly interfering with each other's domains. Silence cannot be taken as a sign of hostile competition or of a "turf fight" between the EU and the CoE; rather, this is about caution and mutual respect.[17] The two institutions have also cooperated in this field, signifying the underlying aim of regulatory harmony.[18]

Since the Clinical Trials Directive is limited to interventional clinical trials using pharmaceutical products, it may be argued that it should be seen as a *lex specialis* (that is more specific) to the Additional Protocol, and hence given preference.

This may be a plausible position when it comes to the more technical provisions that regulate the testing, production, and manufacturing of pharmaceutical products. As mentioned, the EU is specifically aiming at uniting national markets into one single market for pharmaceuticals, thus promoting commercial interests in this field.[19] Both the European Parliament and the EU Council have stressed, in their res-

15 Judgement by the ECtHR in *Bosphorus Hava Yallari Turizm ve Ticaret Anonim Sirketi v. Ireland* of 30 June 2009 (Grand Chamber, with dissenting opinion), paragraph 159.

16 The first expression of modern human rights law is to be found in the UN Charter, which is specified in the Universal Declaration of Human Rights of 1948 and the covenants of 1966; The Nuremberg Code is an integral part of the premises of the Nuremberg Military Tribunal's decision in the case of the *United States v. Karl Brandt et al.* of 19th of August 1947; the Declaration of Helsinki is a widely-recognised set of professional guidelines adopted by the World Medical Association. The legal instruments discussed in this article may be seen as a juridification of those guidelines. For more details, analysis, and further references, see Simonsen 2010, op. cit., parts II and III.

17 Personal communication with the CDBI of the Council of Europe, April 2007.

18 P. Zilgalvis, Placebo use in Council of Europe biomedical research instruments. *Sci Eng Ethics* 2004; 10(1): 15-22, p. 16.

19 I. McLeod, *Legal method*. Basingstoke: Palgrave, 2005, p. 329.

olutions of 16 and 23 April 1996, that: "Completion of the single market in pharmaceuticals is essential in order to protect the health of patients, to ensure rapid access to the market and to encourage innovation in therapies".[20] The Clinical Trials Directive was an important means towards that end, and was thus prepared under the auspices of the European Commission, the Directorate General Enterprise and Industry, and the Pharmaceuticals Unit.

However, the requirement for proportionality has little to do with the aim of a single market beyond facilitating a single standard of acceptable risks and burdens for the research participants. The primary purpose of the requirement for proportionality is to safeguard the safety and dignity of the research participants, their basic human rights.[21] The promotion of commercial interests is, thus, at best, a subsidiary goal. In such a perspective, the Additional Protocol appears to be more specific and thus a *lex specialis.*

Additionally, the problem of overlap between convention law and community law is not new or limited to the regulation of biomedical research. The need to harmonise also exists in the more general field of human rights.[22] Ensuring the protection of human rights is not only the aim of the Council of Europe, it is also the aim of the European Union. Article 6 (2) of the EU Treaty states:

> The Union shall respect fundamental rights, as guaranteed by the European Convention for the Protection of Human Rights and Fundamental Freedoms signed in Rome on 4 November 1950 and as they result from the constitutional traditions common to the Member States, as general principles of Community law.[23]

The European Convention on Human Rights, which all EU member states have ratified, is also one of the bases of the European Charter of Fundamental Rights and the draft constitution of the European Union.[24] Moreover, the European Court of Human Rights regards the EU as a creature of the EU member states, while the EU member states remain "fundamentally responsible for the Community's actions – and for those of the Union".[25]

In effect, the ECtHR regards the EU member states and the EU to have the primary responsibility for securing human rights; the European Court of Human Rights will only step in where those entities (including the European Court of Justice) fail.[26]

20 See http://europa.eu/legislation_summaries/other/l21227_en.htm (accessed 26-03-11).

21 See Simonsen 2010, op. cit., Part V.

22 See J. Steiner, L. Woods & C. Twigg-Flesner, *EU Law.* 9th ed. Oxford University Press, 2006, pp. 120-124.

23 Consolidated Version of the Treaty of the European Union 2006.

24 McLeod 2005, op. cit. p. 87.

25 J. Steiner, L. Woods & C. Twigg-Flesner, op. cit. 2006, p. 123.

26 See J. Steiner, L. Woods & C. Twigg-Flesne, op. cit. 2006, p. 124 with further references.

Apparently, that implies that the ECtHR has the final word in human rights issues, in which that Court specialises. Clearly, the Oviedo Convention and the Additional Protocol are human rights instruments. The Explanatory Report to the Oviedo Convention states:

> The term 'Human Rights' refers to the principles laid down in the Convention for the Protection of Human Rights and Fundamental Freedoms of 4 November 1950, which guarantee protection of such rights. The two Conventions share not only the same underlying approach but also many ethical principles and legal concepts. Indeed, this Convention elaborates some of the principles enshrined in the European Convention for the Protection of Human Rights. The concept of the human being has been used because of its general character. The concept of human dignity, which is also highlighted, constitutes the essential value to be upheld. It is at the basis of most of the values emphasised in the Convention.[27]

This means that the Oviedo Convention and its Additional Protocol may be seen as part of the body of international human rights law which concerns the protection of the individual's fundamental freedoms and basic human rights. The Oviedo Convention and its Additional Protocol must then also be seen as law-making treaties. Indeed, current legal regulation concerning biomedical research on human beings may be seen, when it comes to the rules concerning the protection of individual research subjects' freedoms and rights, e.g. the requirement for proportionality, as *a special branch of international human rights law*.[28] Consequently, the values, interests, and general principles of international human rights law are relevant to the interpretation of the requirement for proportionality in European law.

Furthermore, the provisions entailed in the Oviedo Convention and its Additional Protocol are *minimum standards*, which means that they are intended to ensure that the individual has "a common, minimum level" of protection throughout Europe.[29] This is expressed in the Additional Protocol, Article 34, thus:

> None of the provisions of this Protocol shall be interpreted as limiting or otherwise affecting the possibility for a Party to grant research participants a wider measure of protection than is stipulated in this Protocol.

The same can probably be said in relation to the Clinical Trials Directive.

In other words, it is difficult, if not legally impermissible, to argue, in community law, that an EU directive and commercial considerations trump human rights.

That the requirement for proportionality must be interpreted in the light of, and in conformity with, European human rights law may also be seen as implied in the overarching principle of human primacy recognised in both convention law and

27 Explanatory Report to the Oviedo Convention, paragraph 9.

28 Simonsen 2010, op. cit. Part III.

29 Zilgalvis 2004, op. cit. p. 17.

community law, stating that the "interests and welfare of the human being shall prevail over the sole interest of society or science".[30] The principle of human primacy is thus a powerful means of interpretation, in both convention law and community law, which may be employed to promote harmony and to ensure respect for the minimum standards enshrined in the instruments which aim to protect the individual research participant's interests, welfare (including health), and human dignity.

This underscores the necessity and duty of undertaking a harmonising legal analysis of the Oviedo Convention, and its Additional Protocol, and the Clinical Trials Directive in this field, where both instruments must be interpreted in line with international and European human rights law.

Harmonising does not, however, necessarily mean equality in all respects. The Additional Protocol and the Clinical Trials Directive are distinct instruments which only partly overlap. It is the conflicts of law that the overlap may result in which represents legal challenges that must and can be overcome.

In areas where there is no conflicting overlap. The instruments may supplement each other. The Additional Protocol is obviously a relevant source of law in community law, and vice versa. In an integrated Europe, the instruments are independent, but also interdependent. The instruments may thus be seen as mutually reinforcing, rather than conflicting.

At any rate, member states, lawyers, biomedical researchers, RECs, and others must observe both instruments, as they are operational in the same context.

A harmonising interpretation implies a dynamic and, and to a certain degree, pragmatic interpretation. Such a method is consistent with the interpretational principles adopted and applied by the European Court of Justice, and by the European Court of Human Rights.

It may thus be concluded that regulatory harmony and European integration are legally possible. In light of the practice of the ECtHR and the European Court of Justice; seeking regulatory harmony in this field is a mandatory requirement in this domain of law.

5 Three examples of the challenges facing European integration

The implication of the findings above is that European lawyers must seek harmonising, interpretational results. I will illustrate this implication, and its challenges, using three examples from my research project.[31]

30 See the Additional Protocol Article 3, and similar, in GCP Directive Article 2 (1) (Commission Directive 2005/28/EC of 8 April 2005, laying down principles and detailed guidelines for good clinical practice as regards investigational medicinal products for human use, as well as the requirements for authorising the manufacture or import of such products); see also paragraph 6 of the Declaration of Helsinki. See Simonsen 2010, op. cit. section 12.2.5.

31 See Simonsen 2010, op. cit., part VII for more details, analysis, and further reference.

i) *Basic literal challenges*

One example is the challenges in relation to the differences in wording vis-à-vis the principle of proportionality itself.

The Additional Protocol uses the wording "not disproportionate" while the Clinical Trial Directive uses "justify"; similarly with "burdens", which resembles "inconveniences" in the Directive, as "potential benefit" clearly resembles "anticipated benefit" in the Directive.

A semantic analysis of the wording can be taken to suggest a different normative content. However, legal instruments are not merely subject to statically literal interpretation. On the contrary, my legal analysis showed that the linguistic nuances are too small to make any difference in practice, especially in light of the aim of regulatory harmony. It was thus safe to conclude that, even though the wording of Article 6 (1) of the Additional Protocol and Article 3 (2) (a) differs slightly, the core normative content is the same. The normative content is, for all practical purposes, *a traditional requirement of proportionality* between means and ends in the field of biomedical research.[32]

ii) Non-therapeutic research on children

A more difficult interpretational challenge concerns non-therapeutic research on children and adult persons not able to consent. Non-therapeutic research is research undertaken solely for the sake of other people than the participants themselves, e.g. future patients, entailing that the participants themselves cannot reasonably expect any real and direct health benefits.

In such situations, Article 17 (2) of the Oviedo Convention and Article 15 (2) of the Additional Protocol identify two additional conditions: 1) The potential benefits should consist of a "significant improvement" (i.e. significant potential benefits) and be related to the participants' condition (i.e. a certain closeness to the beneficiaries), and 2) the risks and burdens facing the participant should "only [be] minimal" (no matter how great the potential benefits are to others).

This implies that non-therapeutic research can only be carried out on those who are unable to consent if another person who is unable to consent may benefit, and only if the risks and burdens involved can be characterised as minimal.[33] According to the Explanatory Report to the Additional Protocol, an extra injection or X-ray may only involve minimal risk, suggesting that more than one extra injection or

32 It may be noted that the requirement/principle of proportionality is familiar in other domains of law, e.g. administrative law, general human rights law, general community law, and the laws of war, see Simonsen 2010, op. cit. Part IV, for more details.

33 Article 17 of the Additional Protocol defines minimal risk and burdens thus: "1. For the purposes of this Protocol it is deemed that the research bears a minimal risk if, having regard to the nature and scale of the intervention, it is to be expected that it will result, at the most, in a very slight and temporary negative impact on the health of the person concerned. 2. It is deemed that it bears a minimal burden if it is to be expected that the discomfort will be, at the most, temporary and very slight for the person concerned. In assessing the burden for an individual, a person enjoying the special confidence of the person concerned shall assess the burden where appropriate."

x-ray may involve more than minimal risk. One exposure to magnetic resonance imaging (MRI) *with* a contrast medium is regarded to involve more than minimal risk. A research intervention like this would thus be illegal and unacceptable on children, unless the child him- or herself can expect real health benefits. This is the case no matter how great the benefits might be to society, science, and future minor patients. The minimal risk standard, which is also applicable in US federal law, is a relatively strict, and thus controversial, standard.

Article 4 of the Clinical Trial Directive, which concerns research on children, is vaguer than the Additional Protocol. This vagueness might be interpreted as suggesting that community law is more flexible and liberal when it comes to the level of risk to children that is acceptable. However, the Directive also indicates that a more rigorous and strict approach is needed in assessing acceptable risks and burdens, when Article 4 (g) of the Directive states that clinical trials must

> have been designed to minimise pain, discomfort, fear and any other foreseeable risk in relation to the disease and developmental stage; both the risk threshold and the degree of distress have to be specially defined and constantly monitored.

Closer analysis, including a harmonising interpretation, suggests that the Clinical Trial Directive should be interpreted in the light of the standards adopted by convention law and in the US, leading to a standard of minimal risk. This must surely be the case in Norway, where both the Clinical Trial Directive and the Oviedo Convention legally obligate the government, and considering that children, as a matter of principle, should be entitled to better protection.

iii) Non-therapeutic research on adults unable to consent

The situation is even more challenging when it comes to research on adults who are unable to consent. In convention law, the same standards apply as for children, which make sense since, basically, the same considerations apply.

In community law, however, different standards obviously apply since Article 5 (i) of the Clinical Trial Directive states that: "There are grounds for expecting that administering the medicinal product to be tested will produce a benefit to the patient outweighing the risks or produce no risk at all". A literal interpretation would clearly imply that no additional risk is acceptable at all in non-therapeutic research on adults who are unable to consent.

This means that, if the potential benefits for future patients with dementia are great, it will not even be acceptable for participants with dementia to be exposed to minimal risks, since minimal risks are greater than "no risk at all". Such an interpretation problematic since a medical intervention, regardless of how innocent it is, always involves risk. Even a regular injection or the taking of a placebo drug (e.g. a sugar pill) involves risks, albeit very small ones (i.e. minimal risks).

Taken literally, the Clinical Trial Directive thus implies that non-therapeutic clinical trials involving adults who are unable to consent are simply illegal. A harmonising interpretation would suggest that "no risk at all" should be taken to mean "no more than minimal risk".

However, if adults who are unable to consent are to be afforded improved protection, one might just as well argue that convention law should be interpreted in line with the stricter standard in community law, see the aforementioned Article 34 of the Additional Protocol.

In my thesis, I argue that an interpretational result like this is probably unintended, not very reasonable, and thus probably legally unsustainable. In Norway, for example, non-therapeutic interventional research on adults who are unable to consent is accepted by research committees and regularly carried out, despite the fact that Norway is obligated to implement the Clinical Trial Directive. My interpretation is, nevertheless, controversial and uncertain. Speaking frankly, I am not sure whether or not I would advise my clients to put their heads on the chopping block for it. This illustrates an unacceptable regulatory situation, which calls for immediate revision.

6 Final reflections on European integration and regulatory harmony

In summary, European integration is easier said than done, as the legal framework has not been harmonised.

Nevertheless, legal insecurity and conflicts of law must be overcome, strongly suggesting harmonising interpretation. This implies a certain degree of latitude when it comes to conflicting wordings, as other sources of law must also be considered, including the overarching aim of regulatory harmony in European law. European integration, in biomedical research law for instance, is feasible in practice, legally possible, and even legally required.

The Human Body and Norwegian Property Law – Ancient and Modern

By Professor Marit Halvorsen, University of Oslo[1]

1 The problem

The legal regulation of human biological material is, at first thought, a very modern problem. It has become increasingly urgent following the development of transplantation surgery, the entire biomedical revolution related to the discovery and mapping of the human genome, and the commercialization of biobanks. It may seem a little odd to approach this problem through a legal historical analysis, and a Roman law analysis at that. However, as so often happens when you are working with new problems, they contain elements of well-known and often-asked questions: What kinds of interests dominate the field and whose are they? Who can make use of the things in question, and for what purpose? Who will or ought to harvest the economic gain? Who owns the things, and can they be described as property at all?[2]

The term 'legal regulation of human biological material' leads to a number of discussions. These all center around the same main questions: Who can harvest such material, and who can use it, and for what purpose. The topic is a meeting place for medicine, ethics, privacy issues, and data technology. Regulation serves various interests: best medical practice in diagnosis, treatment and research; the sufficient protection of personal integrity and self determination; making things easier for the pharmaceutical industry. But discussions are often clouded by the simple fact that we may not be in total agreement about the core issue: what, in actual fact, *are* the 'things' we are talking about? How should they be described in legal terms?

---

1 Marit Halvorsen is professor at the Department of Public and International Law, University of Oslo. She holds a LL.M degree from Yale Law School and a Dr. juris degree from the University of Oslo. She has published mainly within the fields of welfare law, health care law, and legal history. She has participated in law commissions, research ethics committees and consulting bodies within the field of medical ethics.

2 This article is based on research done for my book *Norsk biobankrett. Rettslig regulering av humant biologisk materiale [Norwegian Biobank Law. The legal regulation of human biological material]* (Fagbokforlaget, Oslo 2006), and for the article Romersk rett, norsk tingsrettsteori og eiendomsrett til humant biologisk materiale, [Roman Law, Norwegian property law and human biological material as personal property], *Tidsskrift for Rettsvitenskap* 4-5/2008 (Universitetsforlaget, Oslo 2008), pp. 580-598.

The main purpose of finding the legal terms for any subject is to be able to match the legal discussion with reality in the best possible way. A legal description of any subject or issue ought to be recognized as fitting, not only by lawyers but also by the public. If the legal language is intuitively perceived as suitable, it will benefit the legal system in general. If we can regulate the harvesting and use of human biological material, using concepts and terms that sound 'right', the regulation may earn greater acceptance. This search for good language makes it tempting to go back a bit and look for where in the legal system similar facts are discussed, and search for inspiration. Human biological materials are physical things, albeit of a specific nature; however, they are, nonetheless, tangible, limited things. So maybe property law can offer some fruitful insights?

2 The current Norwegian position

In Norway, the discussion about human biological material and property rights came up in connection with the passing of the *Biobanks Act (lov om biobanker 21. Februar 2003 nr 12)* and the *Medical and Health Research Act (lov om medisinsk og helsefaglig forskning 20/ 6 2008 nr 44)*. Both Acts reflect international thinking and the regulation of, among other issues, human biological material, as seen, for example, in the *Convention* on *Human Rights and Biomedicine*,[3] and various EU directives (e.g. the so-called Blood Directive and the Human Tissue Directive[4]). To make a long story short, the preparatory works discuss property rights – among them ownership – in a fairly superficial way, and with no regard to traditional Norwegian property law. The legal sources drawn upon are, in other words, limited and not really helpful.[5] The conclusions are cloudy.

The argument largely goes like this: people can perhaps be described as owners of the biological material that originated from them, but it is not ethically suitable to use property law terms in connection with humans and, as you cannot own another human being, neither can you own human biological material. The originator of the material may not sell it, and may only give it away on condition that she can determine its usage and reclaim it at any point. But when the material is processed, the processor, not the originator, owns it. Well, maybe not owns it, but can use it for commercial purposes – perhaps.

It should be noted that these cloudy conclusions only apply to some biological material; some kinds of material are exempted and some are not discussed at all. It is

3 *Convention for the Protection of Human Rights and Dignity of the Human Being with regard to the Application of Biology and Medicine: Convention on Human Rights and Biomedicine (1997 ETS 164) and additional protocols.*

4 *Directive 2002/98/EC of the European Parliament and Council of 27 January 2003, setting standards of quality and safety in the collection, testing, processing, storage and distribution of human blood and blood components* and *Directive 2004/23/EC of the European Parliament and Council of 31 March 2004 on setting standards of quality and safety in the donation, procurement, testing, processing, preservation, storage, and distribution of human tissues and cells.*

5 For a fuller account, see my book *Norsk biobankrett. Rettslig regulering av humant biologisk material [Norwegian Biobank Law. The legal regulation of human biological material]*, Chapter 13 (in particular 13.3).

quite confusing. One thing is clear, though: the preparatory works demonstrate that the committee members, as well as the legislator, find it unseemly to use language connected to property law when speaking about the human body and its parts. At a stretch, they agree to use the concept of 'possession'; if you possess such material (i.e. if it originates from you, or somehow came into your possession through donation, sale, or whatever), you can make use of it in ways described in the law. Thus, the discussion lacks the boldness necessary to clarify the issues.

As for most things, movables or immovables, the discussion on property rights and, in particular, ownership of human biological material is intimately tied up with the question of economic value. This truth is shown in the fact that the ownership discussion is raised when things that have traditionally had no economic value become valuable because of new technology, or for other reasons, as well as in the fact that things lose their economic value for the same reasons. A lot of examples, also from the realm of human biological material, demonstrate this. As long as hairpieces have been fashionable, false hair has been bought and sold. The women of ancient Rome spent great sums of money on imported false hair; in fact, imports were big enough to merit customs duty.[6] The invention of synthetic hair has not destroyed the market for human hair, instead providing cheaper substitutes. Teeth used to be valuable; today, however, modern materials are more suited to the production of dentures. Human breast milk became economically valuable with increasing knowledge of its biological value and the development of refrigerating and freezing technology. Norwegian women can deliver milk to certain hospitals and get paid by the litre. These hospitals sell it to maternity units and to other worthy customers. Umbilical cord blood is a good example of something recently considered to be just waste, but which today has great economic value.

Economic value is also one of the underlying factors explaining why international legislative activity concerning human biological material, in various forms – from solid organs to DNA – has been accelerating over recent decades. Unfortunately, not all legislative or regulatory initiatives have produced good legal regimes. At least in Norway, an issue like 'self determination' has been debated and regulated *in absurdum*. The property law discussion, however, has barely been touched upon.

Generally speaking, two different models are used in legislation and regulation: The transplantation model and the blood transfusion model.[7]

The transplantation model complies with the ethics of organ donation – altruism, close relationship between donor and recipient (provided the donation takes place *inter vivos*), great care of the donor, a noble (life-saving) purpose for the donation – whereas the blood transfusion model concentrates on control of the product, as-

6 Jêrome Carcopino, *Daily life in ancient Rome*, (Penguin, London 1991), p. 187.

7 George J. Annas explains and elaborates on these models in "Waste and Longing", in *American Bioethics. Crossing Human Rights and Health Law Boundaries*, (Oxford University Press, Oxford; New York 2005).

sumes little or no risk regarding the donor, requires no relationship between donor and recipient, and frequently paves the way for commercial activities. The blood transfusion model has few problems recognizing the person who gave the blood as its owner. The transplantation model is less in need of property terms. Some of the confusion in the Norwegian (and other) legislators' legal analysis may stem from choosing the wrong model for the material to be regulated.

3 The traditional Norwegian property law position

Neither the legal debate nor the preparatory works for the relevant legislation have conducted any research into general Norwegian property law theory. One reason for this may be that the latest textbooks and general monographs[8] in property law mention neither the body nor human biological material at all. All the classical texts from the first half of the twentieth century, on the other hand, dedicate whole paragraphs to the human body and its parts.

The two major monographs from 1912 and 1919 (Herman Scheel and Nikolaus Gjelsvik[9]), a large study from 1974 (Mons Sandnes Nygard[10]), and the most recent summary (Kåre Lilleholt[11]) all find reason to write more or less extensively on the body and property rights.

In a paragraph called "On things in general", Scheel writes: "The human body is a thing, be it dead or alive. This is not contrary to the living human also being a legal person, in other words, much more than a thing. While the living human may never be subject to property rights, the parts separated from the human body are in all respects similar to other things. On the contrary, things brought into intimate contact with the human body to make up for natural human deficiencies, for example spectacles, wigs, dentures, artificial eyes or limbs, have thereby become subject to special legislation, by being exempt from execution and seeing that a contract of sale or other transference may be seen as contrary to good and honourable practice."[12]

Gjelsvik does not share the opinion that the human body is a thing, but agrees that parts separated from the body are things. He writes: "Legal subjects can never be reckoned as things. ... Accordingly, the living human body is not a thing. There can be no kind of property right. Or as the Romans said: No man can own his limbs (D. 9-2 fr. 13 pr.). The legal protection enjoyed by our bodies is no part of property law. When any part of the human body is separated from it, the separate part is a

8 Thor Falkanger, *Tingsrett [Property Law]*, (Universitetsforlaget, Oslo 2000); Thor Falkanger/Aage Thor Falkanger, *Tingsrett [Property Law]*, (Universitetsforlaget, Oslo 2007); Sjur Brækhus og Axel Hærem, *Norsk tingsrett [Norwegian Property Law]*, (Universitetsforlaget, Oslo 1964).

9 Herman Scheel, *Forelæsninger over norsk Tingsret [Lectures on Norwegian Property Law]*, (Brøgger, Kristiania 1912) and Nikolaus Gjelsvik, *Norsk tingsret [Norwegian Property Law]*, (Kristiania 1919).

10 Mons Sandnes Nygard, *Ting og rettar, [Properties and Rights]* (stensilert, Oslo 1970).

11 Kåre Lilleholt, 'Alminnelig formuerett' [Property Law] in *Knophs oversikt over Norges rett*, 12th ed., (Universitetsforlaget, Oslo 2004).

12 Scheel, op. cit. pp. 30-31.

thing, and the person from whose body it came, owns it. The inanimate body is also no one's property (compare the Criminal Code §§ 143 and 341). Skeletons, specimens and mummies are on the other hand things that can be owned."[13] Gjelsvik also points out that his concept of property is the same as Torp's (a Danish jurist) and Heinrich Dernburg's (a German pandectist).

Property law is often considered a very national legal subject, intimately connected with local topography, living conditions, old usage, and other factors that typically differ between countries. Although Norwegian property law has retained certain distinctly national legal constructions since mediaeval times, the international (read German) influence on property law theory is easy to trace. Gjelsvik referred to Dernburg, whose treatment of property law drew heavily on Roman law references.

In his book *System des Römischen Rechts, der Pandekten*[14], Dernburg discusses the different aspects of the concept of 'thing', establishing, through references to Roman law, the basis for opinions later voiced by Torp and Gjelsvik. He treats the human body under the headline *Die res extra commercium* (*körperliche Gegenständen, welche dem Verkehr entzogen sind*; i.e. things exempted from the commercial sphere). Things are exempted from the commercial sphere either because positive rules say so or *auf natürlichen Gründen*; the latter is the case for the human being, he says. Therefore, a human being is not a thing that can be bought or sold. But as soon as something is no longer a part of the body, it can become subject to ownership and can then be treated like any other thing. A corpse also assumes the status of a thing. ("*[W]as ferner nicht mer einen Teil des Lebenden menschlichen Organismus* bildet, ist unmittelbar des Eigentums fähig. Das jemandem abgeschnittende Haar wird ein Eigentum. Folgerecht ist auch der Leichnam Sache."[15])

Nygaard holds forth that, according to Norwegian law, a human being cannot be treated as property, whether dead or alive. There are strict rules governing what can and cannot be done with dead bodies, and it is clear that nobody 'owns' them in any legal sense of the term. He goes on to discuss the new (at that time) Organ Transplantation Act, saying: "Parts separated from the human body can be reckoned as regular things, for example hair plaits for the production of wigs. Blood donation based on consent is practical today; if the transfusion is not direct, the blood is, in the meantime, a regular commodity like medication."[16] In other words: Biological materials separated from the body, enter the realm of things (and property law).

And, finally, Lilleholt: "Humans, on the other hand, dead or alive, are never considered as things. The legal rules concerning things do not apply to the human body. As said before ... separate rules apply for donation of organs for transplantation etc.

13 Gjelsvik, op. cit. pp. 14-15.

14 Berlin 1911 (with Paul Sokolowski).

15 Dernburg, op. cit. p. 118.

16 Dernburg, op. cit. pp. 21-22.

... and from legal usage follows that property law applies to bones and skeletons traded for the purpose of research and education."[17]

We can now discern an opinion in Norwegian property law: A human being is a legal person, and therefore not a thing. This is expressed by Gjelsvik, Nygård, and Lilleholt. Neither is a dead body a thing; however, if it is treated and changed into a mummy or a skeleton, its status will change from not-thing to thing. And parts removed from the living (or dead) body will change their status from legal persons (subjects) to objects, or things. Things are generally owned by someone, and that someone, unless prohibited from doing so, may avail him- or herself of the ownership by means of gift, bequest, sale, destruction, or whatever method he/she prefers. This, then, is a possible point of departure regarding human biological material: as long as it is an integral part of a living person, it complies with the legal status of that person. However, when it is removed (NB in a way conforming to legal requirements!), the person owns it and can dispose of it in any way he/she chooses that is in accordance with the law. Norwegian law, for example, prohibits the commercial exploitation of human biological material *per se*. This provision relates directly to Art. 21 of the *Convention on Human Rights and Biomedicine*.

Some kinds of human biological material are not treated in accordance with the law, even if they are not exempted. Breast milk has already been mentioned; it is treated as a fairly regular commodity. Nobody has argued that there is anything illegal or unethical in this practice. Clearly, the women who produce and deliver the milk are entitled to payment; the milk is theirs to sell.

According to Norwegian law, 'ownership' is not defined positively, but negatively; i.e. 'ownership' is never total or unlimited, but surrounded by rules and regulations pertaining to the owner's freedom to possess, enjoy and dispose of his/her property. Perhaps the very fact that we find it necessary to list the various limitations on ownership suggests that we have a notion of the original or perfect ownership as total and unlimited. However, as any lawyer can tell you, ownership in this manner does not exist. Even classical Roman Law, which recognized a more 'total' form of ownership than we do, maintained that ownership did not confer unlimited rights. Neighbours enjoyed protections against certain activities on a property, and heirs could prevent a testator from disposing of his/her entire fortune without making them beneficiaries.[18] However, the notion of limitations on ownership nevertheless implies a hypothetical and unlimited ownership.

As opposed to negatively-defined ownership, 'right of possession' is defined positively: this is the right to perform specified actions on or with specified things. The owner usually has possession of the thing he/she owns, but he/she is free to confer his/her rights, including possession itself, on anyone of his/her choosing, law permitting. The owner can decide that others have possession in concert with him-/her-

17 Lilleholt, op. cit. p. 167.

18 R.W. Lee, *The Elements of Roman Law*, 4th ed. (Sweet & Maxwell, London 1987), pp. 160-163 and pp. 217–218.

self, instead of him/her, or superseding his/her own rights. This kind of 'secondary right of possession' does not follow from the 'primary right of possession' that lies at the core of ownership, but from an act of transfer from the owner to the possessor. Thus, when someone is the possessor of a thing, but does not own it, we expect the existence of an owner; an owner who transferred his/her right of possession; an owner whose ownership rights are negatively defined, and who can act out his/her ownership in the areas not covered by the rights of the possessor. Alternatively, the right of possession did not originate from an act of transfer, but because the thing was not owned by anyone. However, in that case, the main rule is that the finder becomes the owner. Thus, being in the legal position of the 'possessor' of a thing, without the existence of a legal owner, is a very unusual status.

Nevertheless, this seems to be the legal construction favoured by the Norwegian legislator when faced with the seemingly new problem of categorizing the status of human biological material: Nobody can own it since nobody can own another human being. Not even the person from whom the material originated, can own it. He is just a possessor. The material can be owned only after being processed, then being owned by the processor. And he/she is free to use it and exploit it just as any other owner is with any other thing.

It does not escape the legislator that this solution sits uncomfortably with the rest of the legal system. All the more so since the 'originator' who donates material for biobanks can recall the gift as long as it is not irrevocably joined with other material (or used up). This is a privilege not even conferred on most regular owners, indeed indicating strong ownership.

That biobank material consists, in reality, of 'things' – in spite of the reluctance to call it that – is emphasized by the fact that, in other legal situations than sale and purchase, it is quite natural to treat the material like other movables. If stolen, it can be recovered. If destroyed, tort law may be applied and, since a biobank can be insured, insurance is an issue. The owner of a biobank can probably give it away as a gift or bequest as long as the receiver complies with the law and the gift is not in conflict with the contract made with the donors. The biobank can constitute the balance of a corporate account, or a bankruptcy estate, or an estate of inheritance. The more you look at it, the stranger and more strained it becomes trying to keep human biological material outside the scope of property law. There must be ways to overcome the ethical itch felt by the legislators. And there are; however, the careful references to Roman law made by the old property lawyers has been forgotten.

4 Returning to the Romans: a viable way?

Let us resume the position. In the vernacular, we speak of our bodies as if we owned them: "It is my body", "move your leg", "can I take a blood sample from you?" and so on. But does the vernacular reflect something more than our awareness of our own being, as separate from other beings? I *am* my body, but do I *own* it? Perhaps one must make a distinction between the body *in integrum*, as Scheel, Gjelsvik and Nygard (and the old Roman lawyers) did. I cannot sell my hair as long as it is still on my head; however, when I cut it off, I can sell it if I want to. If I lose a finger because someone cuts it off me in a fight, I can claim it back if the person wants to keep it as a trophy.[19] If a researcher asks me for 10 ml of my blood, I should be allowed to give it to him. A lactating woman can sell her milk.

It is not easy to find any compelling arguments against characterizing individuals as owners of the biological material that comes from their bodies. In fact, ownership fits very well with what the few relevant legal sources say and with what is intuitively right: of course I own my body and what stems from it!

The National Committee for Research Ethics in Medicine (NEM) suggested, as early as 1996, that human biological material can perhaps best be classified as *res extra commercium*, i.e. things outside the commercial sphere. *Res extra conmmercium* includes things that are not subject to private ownership, and as such impossible to exploit for commercial purposes. *Res extra conmmercium* includes the things classified as *res divini iuris*, i.e. temples, holy gravesites, holy monuments etc, as well as the *res humana iuris* which, according to law, are things held communally. These are the *res omnium communes*, i.e. the soil, air, and water etc, and the *res publicae*, i.e ports, arenas, marketplaces, theatres.[20] Justinian maintains the doctrine when speaking of things *in nostro patrimonio – extra nostrum patrimonium*. [21] Now we can return to Heinrich Dernburg, and his description of *res extra commercium* as classified as such either for natural reasons or by positive law. As we have seen, Dernburg maintains that the human body (NB the bodies of free men as opposed to slaves) is *res extra commercium* for natural reasons, whereas that which is separated from the body is not necessarily exempted from the commercial sphere.

NEM does not follow Dernburg's distinction of the *res extra commercium* in those that are so classified for natural reasons and those that are so classified because of positive law. But we can further apply his reasoning in our search for the most suitable legal description of human biological material.

The Latin word *res* is often translated as 'thing', but it was also used by the Romans to describe a case, e.g. 'a case in court'.[22] They categorized *res* using several parameters. There were the *res corporales* and the *res incorporales*; tangible or intangible things: *Corporales hae sunt, quae tangi possunt, velut fundus, homo, vestis, aurum, argen-*

19 A similar example is described by Jean-Pierre Baude, *L'affaire de la main volée*. Une histoire juridique du corps, (Des traveaux Seul, Paris 1993): A carpenter loses his hand using a chainsaw; his colleague (who could have put the hand in a plastic bag and taken the carpenter and the hand to hospital to have it sown back on) throws the hand in an oven to get rid of his competitor. With this example, Baud shows how French law, by insisting that the body is a thing that cannot be owned, actually leads to the hand becoming a thing only when it is cut off, and that, at the moment when it is cut off, it has no legal owner and as such is an object to be appropriated by anyone who picks it up. Thus, the man who threw it into the oven can justly claim it as his own, and cannot be punished for his deed. This solution is, of course, horrendous and Baud's point was to show the unsoundness of French doctrine.

20 Gaius, *Institutiones* II, 1–11; Justinian, *Instituiones* II, I, De rerum divisione.

21 Justinian, *Institutiones* II, I, introduction to *De rerum divisione.*

22 Compare the English legal terms 'chose in possession' and 'chose in action'.

tum et denique alias res innumerabiles (tangible things are those that can be touched, for example the land, a man, clothes, gold, sliver and innumerable other things).[23]

Another category was the *res in commercio* and the *res extra commercium*; things subject to commercial activities and things exempted from the commercial sphere. The point of *res extra commercium* is that these things can neither be bought nor sold. Thus, nobody, or everybody, owns them; nobody can buy them or sell them. In Roman law, the definition of *res* in the sense of case was tied up with the commercial value. *Res extra commercium* was therefore 'thing' but not 'case', as such things could have no price.

The quotation from *Gaius* (supra) tells us that *homo*, man, was categorized as *res corporales*. Slaves were, according to law, both "thing" and "case", and were bought and sold according to the ancient proceedings of *res mancipi*. Free citizens who were *sui iuris* were also 'things', but not 'cases'; they were, for natural reasons, *res extra commercium*.[24]

The *res extra commercium* laid down in law comprised, among other things, the natural resources that everyone could freely enjoy. This, then, must be our analogy: human biological material is a natural resource and, as such, protected from economic exploitation, but to be used for the common good. However, for the Romans, body parts separated from the body were *res* in both senses of the concept. Just like they are, in fact, today as well: many kinds of human biological material have commercial value and are, at least to some extent, treated like personal property.

One should ask oneself whether or not legal regulations prohibiting the commercialization of human cells and tissues indeed have the same rationale as Roman law's classification of some things as *res extra commercium*. It is a beautiful idea to regard human biological material as a natural resource to be enjoyed freely, like wind, water and air, for the common good. But somehow, the notion does not quite fit. Firstly, there is an inherent difference between human biological material and wind, water and air (or churches, theaters, marketplaces, roads, docks, beaches etc.) Through DNA analysis, every bit of human biological material can (at least in theory) be traced back to an individual. The *res extra commercium* of the Romans had no such connection with human beings. And secondly, it is a fact that many kinds of human biological material are not subject to any prohibition from commercial exploitation, even in states with very strict biomedical legislation. Even under Norwegian law, which attempts to exempt human cells and tissues of all kinds from the commercial sector, it is neither correct nor expedient, in my opinion, to drag human biological material away from property law, even though the regular body of law pertaining to movable objects cannot be applied to its full extent.

---

23 Gaius, *Institutiones* II, 12–14; almost identical to Justinian *Institutiones* II 2, 2.

24 According to arcane Roman law, *pater familias* could sell his family, but this part of the *patria potestas* disappeared during the Late Republic.

I maintain that there are good reasons to take the departure point that each individual is the owner of the biological materials that stem from his/her body. The vernacular suggests that popular opinion agrees; not in itself a decisive argument for a legal rule, but at least of some importance when considering the legal options. In my opinion, no specific ethical caveats preclude the use of the concept. There are, of course, legal constrictions to the owner's right to commercialize the material, but this is the case for many things that are subject to ownership. The fact that one cannot own other people is no viable argument for not being considered the owner of oneself or, indeed, for owning biological material legally obtained from another. And, as demonstrated, I see a tradition in Norwegian property law (picked up from German law and, indeed, from the Romans) that supports this view.

When Scheel, in 1912, wrote that the human body is a thing, he repeated sound Roman law; *homo* is *res corporales.* When Gjelsvik seven years later wrote that subjects of law can never be counted as things (objects), that too was in line with the Romans: man is thing, but not case; *homo* is *res extra commercium.*

Nygard picked up the Roman thread in 1974 and led us into modern times. All in all, the bits and pieces quoted from Norwegian property theory are sufficient to form a coherent doctrine, which, in addition, sits well with Roman law and is thus internationally understandable. Why not tag onto the old learned property lawyers? Perhaps they might show us a sensible way of navigating the troubled waters of modern biomedical legal issues.

Biobank Regulation in Finland and the Nordic Countries

By Dr. Salla Silvola, University of Helsinki[1]

1 The biobank as a concept

The term biobank, or *biopankki*, in Finnish, is not used in everyday life in Finland. Neither does the concept of the biobank appear in the existing legislation in Finland.[2] The word itself refers to the storing of biological material. As it does not directly refer to any research activities, the average layman could easily mistake its purpose; guesses can range from collections of rare plants to human organ banks. However, the word is commonly used amongst Nordic biomedical researchers, and has been in use in the ethico-legal debate since the mid-1990s, although there is no single universal definition for it even in this forum.[3] Biobanks may be established not only for research, but also, for example, for patient safety, quality assurance, transplantation, assisted procreation, or for manufacturing medicinal products. Many biobanks have been set up for a combination of purposes.[4]

For present purposes, I will refer to a biobank as a collection of human biological samples combined with health and lifestyle information on the provider of the sample.[5] The information may or may not be linked to an identifiable person (personal data), and the information may or may not contain genetic information.

---

1 Dr. Salla Silvola (formerly Salla Lötjönen) works as Senior Advisor in Legislative Affairs in the Ministry of Justice, Finland. She is also a Docent in Medical and Bio Law and teaches part-time at the Faculty of Law at the University of Helsinki. She is a former member of the board of the Nordic Committee on Bioethics (2002-2007) and a former member of the board of directors of the European Association of Health Law (2008-2009).

2 Whereas the terms tissue bank and cell bank appear in Finland's Act on the Medical Use of Human Organs and Tissues (§§ 1, 1a).

3 See, for instance, L. Nielsen et al., *Health Science Information Banks: Biobanks* (Danish Central Scientific-Ethical Committee, Danish Council of Ethics, Danish Medical Research Council, Copenhagen, 1996) and G. Hermerén, Protecting Human Integrity, in M. Sorsa & J. Eyrfjörö (eds.), *Human Biobanks* (Nordic Committee on Bioethics, Copenhagen, 1997).

4 See, for instance, E. Rynning, Legal Challenges and Strategies in the Regulation of Research Biobanking, in J.H. Solbakk et al. (eds), *The Ethics of Research Biobanking* (Springer, New York, 2009) pp. 280-281.

5 A rather similar definition was used by a group of experts working for the European Commission. They considered biobank collections to mean "the biological samples themselves, plus the related databases, allowing a certain level of accessibility, availability and exchange for scientific studies". European Commission, *25 Recommendations on the ethical, legal and social implications of genetic testing* by Eryl McNally, Anne Cambon-Thomsen, Celia Brazell, Jean-Jacques Cassiman, Alastair Kent, Klaus Lindpaintner, Paula Lobato de Faria, Detlef Niese, Henriette Roscam Abbing, Jan Helge Solbakk, Hélène Tack, Erik Tambuyzer, Thomas R. Weihrauch, Erik Wendel (Brussels 2004).

The collection and use of biological samples is regulated in several legal instruments in Finland, depending on the purpose for which the sample has been collected.[6] The research community has repeatedly criticised the scattered legislation in this area. In an attempt to clarify the situation, a Bill was put before Parliament specifically aimed at regulating biobanks on 30 December 2010.[7] However, due to the Parliamentary elections in April 2011, the particular Parliament that the Bill was put before was unable to finalise the processing of this Bill before it was dissolved. Hence the Bill lapsed. The new government has decided to continue with this legislative project, but whether or not the principles of the lapsed Bill will be followed, is not yet confirmed.

Regarding the use of the concept of the biobank in the legal arena, it is interesting to note the different approaches taken in the Nordic countries. According to the legislations of Iceland, Norway, and Sweden, biobank regulation does not apply to the temporary keeping of samples. However, there are duties that fall on the owner of the biobank after a certain period of time without regard to the action (or non-action) of the biobank owner.[8] According to the (now defunct) Finnish Biobank Bill, a collection of samples would not qualify as a biobank until it had fulfilled the rather extensive requirements needed for national registration. If a collection of samples does not seek the status of a biobank, it could remain outside the proposed legislation independent of the time period that the samples are retained.

2 Structure and nature of regulation

More interesting Nordic variation can be found in the different approaches taken in the structures regulating biobanks.

The Icelandic Biobanks Act is the oldest in the Nordic countries, adopted in 2000.[9] It covers all collections of biological samples irrespective of whether these have been collected in connection with health care or research.

Sweden's biobank legislation currently contains specific provisions only as regards biobanks connected with health care (I will subsequently refer to these as diagnostic biobanks).[10] Research on humans is covered by the Act on Ethical Re-

6 The samples collected for diagnostic use are governed by the Act on the Status and Rights of Patients, no. 785 from 1992, samples collected for research use are governed by the Medical Research Act, no. 488 from 1999, and samples collected from the deceased, as well as the secondary use of biological samples, are governed by the Act on the Medical Use of Human Organs and Tissues, no. 101 from 2001.

7 Bill on the Biobank Act and the Act amending the Act on the Medical Use of Human Organs and Tissues and the Act on the Status and Rights of Patients, no. 325 from 2010.

8 This period of time varies. In Iceland, keeping temporarily means storage up to 5 years. In Norway and Sweden, the time period for keeping temporarily has not been stated on a legal level. In practice, however, it has been set at a maximum of 2-4 months.

9 No. 110 from 2000.

10 Biobanks in Health Care Act, no. 297 from 2002.

view of Research on Humans (the Ethics Review Act)[11] and the Medicines Act[12]. However, as neither of these Acts contains any specific provisions on biobanks used in research, a committee report has been published which proposes to expand the scope of the current Biobanks in Health Care Act to include biological samples collected and used for research.[13]

In Norway, the regulation of biobanks also began with biobanks connected with medical care.[14] However, in 2009, the new Medical and Health Research Act[15] came into force, which not only contains provisions on medical research on humans in general, but also provisions on biobanks collected and used for research purposes.

Denmark has the most centralised health legislation of all the Nordic countries; here, the main principles of nearly all health-related regulation have been gathered under one Health Act.[16] In addition, the Act on Research Ethics Committees and Biomedical Research Projects (the Committee Act)[17] applies. Danish provisions regarding the collection of biological samples are concise and very liberal vis-à-vis the needs of biomedical research.

The current Finnish regulation of biobanks is, as previously said, spread across different laws, depending on the original purpose of the sample for which it was collected. The provisions regarding the secondary use of biological samples are, however, enshrined in the Act on the Medical Use of Human Organs and Tissues (the Tissue Act).[18] These provisions are almost as concise and liberal as in the Danish regulation. However, if the Biobank Bill is passed unchanged by the next Parliament, the Finnish regulation will not be the strictest, but the most extensive and detailed amongst the Nordic countries.

3 Preconditions for setting up a biobank

Based on the currently existing Nordic legislation, only the Danish and Finnish biobanks need no separate approval, besides ethical approval, in order for each research project to proceed.[19] At the other extreme, only the Icelandic biobanks require actual licensing. The Icelandic licence is provided by the Ministry of Welfare

11 No. 460 from 2003.

12 No. 859 from 1992.

13 *En ny biobankslag*, Betänkande av Biobanksutredningen, Statens Offentliga Utredningar [*A new Biobanks Act*, Report by the Biobank Inquiry, Swedish Official Reports] SOU 2010:81, Stockholm 2010.

14 Health Care Biobanks Act, no. 12 from 2003.

15 No. 44 from 2008.

16 No. 95 from 2008, latest consolidated version no. 913 from 2010.

17 No. 402 from 2003.

18 Act no. 101 from 2001.

19 However, if the cells or tissue that are processed in the biobank are transferred to another human, the provisions of the EC Directive on setting standards of quality and safety for the donation, procurement, testing, processing, preservation, storage and distribution of human tissues and cells (2004/23/EC, Tissue Directive) will apply. All 'tissue establishments' falling under the scope of the application of the Tissue Directive require a tissue licence.

following recommendations from both the Medical Director of Health and the National Bioethics Committee.[20]

In Sweden and Norway, no licence or previous ethical evaluation is required from biobanks connected with health care.[21] In Norway, founding a research biobank requires the approval of a regional research ethics committee.[22] According to the Swedish committee report, ethical approval would also be required before samples could be collected for a research biobank in Sweden.[23] In addition, the supervisory authority should be notified of both types of biobanks. In Norway, this is done by a regional ethics committee after approval has been granted,[24] whereas in Sweden, the duty to notify the National Board of Health and Welfare would rest with the biobank.[25]

If the next Parliament decides to follow the principles of the lapsed Biobank Bill, the Finnish biobanks would also have to undergo extensive evaluation. According to the Bill, the biobank would first have to ask the National Research Ethics Committee for a statement on the fulfilment of the standards set out in the Biobank Act, and in other legislation (e.g. the Personal Data Act), in addition to the ethical acceptability of the biobank in general.[26] Once the biobank has started up its activities, it would inform the National Supervisory Authority for Welfare and Health about commencing operations.[27] The Authority will then add the biobank to the national register of biobanks. If the operations of the biobank do not meet the requirements laid down by law, the Authority will be entitled to withhold registration or take the biobank off the register until the standards have been met.[28]

4 Provisions on consent

4.1 Competent adults

One of the most controversial issues with regard to biobanking is the form of consent required from sample providers. With regard to clinical medical research, which involves physical touching of the research participants, this question is a non-issue. All Nordic countries are in agreement regarding the need for written informed con-

20 Biobanks Act, Art. 4.

21 However, if the tissue is intended for use in human applications, the provisions of the Tissue Directive 2004/23/EC will apply and a license will be required. The Tissue Directive has been implemented in Sweden by means of the Quality and Safety Standards in the Processing of Human Tissue and Cells Act (2008:286).

22 Medical and Health Research Act, § 25.

23 Proposal for Biobanks Act, Chap. 2, § 4.

24 Medical and Health Research Act, § 44.

25 Proposal for Biobanks Act, Chap. 2, § 6.

26 Biobank Bill, § 6.

27 Biobank Bill, § 9.

28 Biobank Bill, §§ 33, 34.

sent.[29] Collecting samples for a diagnostic biobank is also relatively unproblematic. Most of the Nordic countries rely on presumed consent with regard to retaining samples in health care related biobanks.[30] Giving consent to treatment is regarded to include giving consent to the retrieval, storage, and processing of samples in diagnostic biobanks. The two exceptions are Finland and Sweden, where documented informed consent is required, if samples are stored for longer than temporary diagnostic use requires.[31]

Research on biological samples is somewhat more complicated. If samples are collected directly from sample providers, the same rules as for clinical medical research will apply, i.e. written informed consent is required. However, if samples have been derived previously, either from a diagnostic biobank or from a research biobank, the participant will not be in the physical presence of the research team at any time. Will the biobank or researcher need to go back to the participant every time his/her sample is needed; can consent be given to an unlimited number of future research projects; or can consent either be presumed or given by someone representing the sample provider's interests?

Solutions to this question vary between the Nordic countries. If the research sample is taken from a diagnostic biobank, the situation can always be described as a situation of secondary use, i.e. a change in the original purpose for which the sample had originally been derived. Therefore, the sample provider's consent should not be presumed, if he/she was unaware that samples from diagnostic biobanks could be used for research purposes. Nevertheless, presumed consent is the current standard in Denmark for the secondary use of diagnostic samples.[32] The patient can, however, take action to register his/her objection to the secondary use of his/her sample in anything other than what is directly related to his/her treatment. The person in charge of retaining the samples is obligated to consult the register and honour the patient's objection, if samples are requested to be used for another purpose than the treatment of the patient.[33] The patient can also ask for his sample to be destroyed or given back to him/her in order to ensure that it is not misused.[34]

In all the other Nordic countries, the departure point for the secondary use of diagnostic samples lies in explicit informed consent rather than presumed consent. However, there is a variety of possibilities for exceptions from the main rule. Mainly, the possibility of using diagnostic samples for secondary research purpose involves permission from a supervisory authority or the approval of a research ethics committee.

29 Committee Act, § 16 (Denmark), Patients' Rights Act (no. 74/1997), Art. 10 (Iceland), Medical Research Act, § 6 (Finland), Medical and Health Research Act, § 13 (Norway) and Ethics Review Act, § 17 (Sweden).

30 Health Act, § 29 (Denmark), Biobanks Act, Art. 7 (Iceland), Health Care Biobanks Act, § 11 (Norway).

31 Tissue Act, § 7 (Finland), Biobanks in Health Care Act, Chap. 3, §§ 1, 7 (Sweden).

32 Health Act, § 32.

33 Health Act, § 29, para. 4.

34 Health Act, §§ 33, 34.

The Icelandic provisions are the strictest here, as the approval of three actors is required before samples can be used for secondary use in research without consent: i.e. the Board of the biobank, the Data Protection Authority, and the National Bioethics Committee. They all have to agree that exigent interests are at stake, and that the potential benefit outweighs the potential inconvenience, either to the donor of a biological sample or to other parties.[35]

In Sweden and Norway, the regional ethics committees have been empowered to safeguard the interests of the sample providers. In Sweden, the general rule is that explicit consent for the new purpose is required, but a regional ethics committee can determine which criteria can be used for obtaining consent. Depending on the circumstances, an ethics committee can even decide that no additional information or consent is required (for instance, when the purpose and method of the study are very close to the purpose that the samples were originally collected for), or that the sample providers must be informed about the new purpose and are given the possibility to opt out (for instance, in studies that involve a considerable number of sample providers and the study could not be carried out without this exception).[36]

Also in Norway, the regional research ethics committees can grant an exemption from the requirement for express informed consent for the secondary use of diagnostic samples. The criteria to be used during evaluation include considerable societal interest and due consideration being paid to the welfare and integrity of the sample providers.[37]

Currently in Finland, the National Supervisory Authority for Welfare and Health may grant permission to use samples from a collection of diagnostic samples, if informed consent is not possible to obtain because of the large number of samples, the age of the samples, or other similar reason, or because the person has died. The provisions for secondary use differ with the original use of the samples. If the samples were originally provided for use in research, the Authority can grant permission only if the sample provider has died.[38]

According to the Finnish Biobank Bill, researchers would primarily use samples from a biobank that has been entered into the national biobank register. Samples could be taken into the biobank in two ways. Firstly, new samples could be collected directly into the biobank, or in connection with a specific research project. In this case, informed consent would be required. However, the consent could be given in broad terms, which would allow future research on the sample without

35 Biobanks Act, Art. 9, para. 5.

36 Biobanks in Health Care Act, Chap. 3, § 5, para. 3, Ethics Review Act, § 15, Bill on the Ethics Review Act, no. 50 from 2002/03, and Swedish Research Council, Scientific Council for Medicine, *Biobanker: nya forskningsetiska riktlinjer för nyttjande av biobanker för forskningsändamål* [*Biobanks: new guidelines in research ethics for the use of biobanks in research*], May 2003.

37 Medical and Health Research Act, § 28.

38 Tissue Act, § 20, paras 1, 2.

renewing it for each new research use.[39] The second method of including samples in a biobank is by transferring 'old samples' from current diagnostic collections. As this operation would in the best (or worst) case scenario involve thousands or even hundreds of thousands samples, it has been considered impossible to require explicit consent from all sample providers. Hence, the presumed consent model has been selected, coupled with an extensive information campaign about the possibility of opting out.[40] This option would come very close to the Danish solution, although a more stringent regime would be complied with regard to the 'new samples' collected after the new Act had come into force.

As establishing a biobank would be voluntary in Finland, according to the Bill, researchers would continue to be allowed to also use samples from existing collections of biological samples. First of all, there would be a five-year transition period, during which the National Supervisory Authority for Welfare and Health would be able to grant permissions to use diagnostic biological samples without informed consent, according to the current criteria, provided that suitable samples are not available from existing biobanks.[41] The five-year transition provision would apply to diagnostic samples only. After the transition period, the conditions governing secondary use would become stricter. In order to use diagnostic samples without the informed consent of the sample provider, the approval of both an ethics committee and the National Supervisory Authority for Welfare and Health would be required. Six conditions have been written into the Bill regarding evaluation by the Authority: 1) the research must be medically or socially significant, 2) the research must be approved by an ethics committee, 3) the required samples must not be available from any existing biobanks, 4) adequate premises, equipment and staff must be available for the research, 5) there must be a designated physician in charge of the project, and 6) the privacy of the sample providers must not be endangered.[42]

4.2 Children

With regard to children, the general starting point is the same in most of the Nordic countries: i.e. in order to collect and retain a biological sample from a minor to a diagnostic biobank, the provisions corresponding to patient care will apply. In Sweden, no specific age limits have been introduced into legislation as regards the age when a child is capable of giving his/her independent consent to treatment. Reference is only made to the child being of a sufficient age, development, and under-

39 The information provided to the sample provider would contain nature of biobank research, possible harms, the purpose of taking and retaining the sample, information on the owner of the sample and the biobank that retains it, voluntariness of consent, and the possibility of restricting it or withdrawing it without any negative consequences (§ 11, para. 3).

40 Biobank Bill, § 13.

41 Biobank Bill, proposal for amending the Tissue Act, transitory provisions.

42 Biobank Bill, proposal for amending the Tissue Act, §§ 20, 21 a.

standing.[43] In Finland, the Act on the Status and Rights of Patients applies to the collection of tissue; however, if the tissue is retained, the provisions of the Tissue Act will apply. However, for children, essentially the same standard is used in both Acts, i.e. the child's consent is valid, if he/she has sufficient understanding to give it.[44]

In Denmark, children over 15 may give their independent consent to treatment under the Health Act. However, the child's parents (or guardians) will be included in decision-making. If health care staff are of the opinion that the child lacks the necessary understanding to decide about his/her treatment, even if he/she has reached the age of 15, decision-making will be referred to those with parental responsibility.[45]

In Iceland and Norway, the age of 16 is considered as the starting point for independent decision-making. However, the views of the child are to be given increasing importance from the age of 12 and up, after which time the child is always to be consulted.[46]

When the sample from the child is required for research, the starting point is, as with adults, that the standard provisions governing participation in clinical medical research will apply. This regularly means that the views of those with parental responsibility will have more relevance. For example, Finland and Sweden require parental involvement in order to gain valid consent for all minors under 15,[47] and the consent of those with parental responsibility is required, without any age limits, for tissue retrieval in Denmark and Norway.[48] According to the Finnish Biobank Bill, if the sample is collected for a biobank, the child's consent will be sought in addition to that of his/her legal guardian.[49]

When a sample previously-collected from a child is required for research, the rules for representation change again. For example, according to the Finnish Tissue Act, the self-determination of the minor is not given any weight, but decision-making is transferred in its entirety to the legal representative of the child.[50] Similar provisions are proposed for the amended Swedish Biobanks Act: if those with parental responsibility object to the minor's sample being included in a biobank, that sample may only be used directly for the benefit of the child.[51]

43 Biobanks in Health Care Act, Chap. 3, § 2.

44 Tissue Act, § 7.

45 Health Act, § 17.

46 Patients' Rights Act, Arts. 25 and 26 (Iceland), Rights of Patients Act (no. 63 from 1999), Chap. 4, § 4 (Norway).

47 Medical Research Act, § 8 (Finland), Ethics Review Act, § 18 (Sweden).

48 Committee Act, § 17 (Denmark), Medical and Health Research Act, § 17, para. 3 (Norway).

49 § 11.

50 § 20.

51 Proposal for Biobanks Act, Chap. 3, § 5.

4.3 Adults who lack the capacity to make decisions

Similar principles are applied to the collection of samples from adults who lack the capacity to make decisions concerning their treatment: provisions regarding consent to treatment apply mostly also to the collecting of the samples. In Denmark, Finland, Iceland, and Norway, those close to the patient are given the power to make decisions on behalf of the adult who lacks the capacity to decide to various degrees: in Norway, those closest to the patient are to be interviewed in order to discover what the patient him- or herself would have decided,[52] while in Denmark, Finland, and Iceland, the actual decision-making power is given either to those who are close to the patient or to the patient's legal representative, provided one has been appointed to the patient.[53]

Sweden is the only country amongst the Nordic countries still lacking overall legislation with regard to dealing with adults who lack the capacity to decide for themselves. Hence, the current Biobanks in Health Care Act does not contain provisions on this matter either. The Biobank Committee, however, proposes a new provision which would enable the health care provider to collect and store samples from adults like these without their express consent. Such samples would not be available for research purposes, but would only be used in direct treatment.[54] If a sample was collected and retained for research purposes, the provisions of the Ethics Review Act would apply. According to the Ethics Review Act, if the research participant did not have the capacity to consent to the procedure, the participation would take place with consent of his or her closest relatives.[55]

4.4 Deceased

In Finland, Norway, and Sweden, the collection and retaining of samples for research from deceased people, is regulated in the same Act that governs organ transplantation.[56] In these countries, the collection of biological samples is prohibited if it is known that the deceased would have objected to it.[57]

In Denmark, the informed consent of the closest relatives is required in order to conduct research on the deceased.[58] In Norway and Sweden, those close to the deceased have an opportunity to object, although specific consent is not necessary.[59]

52 Rights of Patients Rights Act, Chap. 4, § 6.

53 Health Act, § 18 (Denmark), Tissue Act, § 7 (Finland), Patients' Rights Act, Art. 6, para. 3 (Iceland).

54 Proposal for Biobanks Act, Chap. 3, § 6.

55 Ethics Review Act, § 22.

56 In Denmark, the Committee Act is applied unless the provisions governing transplantation (Health Act, §§ 52-56) take specific priority (Committee Act, § 18). To my knowledge, transplantations are not performed, and thus not regulated, in Iceland.

57 Tissue Act, § 12, para. 2 (Finland), Medical and Health Research Act, § 21 and Transplantation, Hospital Autopsies and the Donation of Body Act (No. 6 from 1973), § 2 (Norway), Transplantation Act (No. 831 from 1995), § 3 (Sweden).

58 Committee Act, § 18.

59 Transplantation, Hospital Autopsies and the Donation of Body Act, § 2 (Norway), Transplantation Act, § 4.

Only in Finland have the relatives of the deceased been left entirely without a say in the matter.[60] This is well in line with the recent change to the other provisions of the Tissue Act, whereby the earlier possibility of objecting to organ transplantation on the part of those close to the deceased was lifted.[61] If the deceased is a child, or an adult who was never able to form his/her own opinion on organ or tissue retrieval, objections on the part of his/her representative will, however, prevent the procedure.[62]

If the samples from the deceased have been collected while he/she was alive, and are requested to be used for a secondary purpose after death, the situation would seem somewhat more complicated. Not all countries have specific provisions with regard to this. In Finland, for research purposes, the diagnostic samples of the deceased may be used with the permission of the National Supervisory Authority for Welfare and Health.[63] The Biobank Bill proposes that the possibility of using these samples would continue. If the samples have been transferred to a biobank, only ethics committee approval would be required, while non-biobank samples would also require the permission of the National Supervisory Authority for Welfare and Health. In neither case could samples be used if there was reason to believe that the deceased would have objected to it.[64]

In Norway, it is presumable that approval by a regional research ethics committee would also suffice for changing the purpose of samples from a deceased person without involving relatives. However, the Swedish Biobank Committee proposes that the provisions of the Transplantation Act would also continue to apply to secondary use of the samples of the deceased.[65] That would mean that not only are the wishes of the deceased relevant, but also that those close to the patient would need to be contacted.

5 Withdrawal of consent

As in all regulation of medical research, the right to object or to withdraw one's consent seems to be the most stringently protected right in biobank research. Denmark and Norway have both set up specific electronic registers where people can opt out of their samples being used for research. If the Biobank Bill is passed in its current form by the new parliament, this kind of register will also be introduced in Finland.

60 Tissue Act, § 12.

61 In effect, the relatives are still able to exert an influence on decision-making, as they will be asked about the wishes of the deceased. If they state that the wish of the deceased was for his/her organs (and tissue) to be left intact, then health care professionals will not be able to conduct an intervention.

62 Tissue Act, § 9.

63 Tissue Act, § 20.

64 Biobank Bill, proposal to amend the Tissue Act, §§ 20, 21 a.

65 Proposal for Biobanks Act, Chap. 3, § 7.

However, although a lot of effort has been put into enabling people to state their wishes on the use of their samples, Denmark, Iceland, and Norway all have provisions in place whereby even a specific objection or wish to withdraw can be overridden. Interestingly, in Denmark and Iceland, a patient's request for sample destruction can be overridden as regards to a *diagnostic* biobank,[66] while in Norway, the regional research ethics committees may allow the continued use of the sample in a *research* biobank, if strong societal or research interests favour it. In Denmark, the withdrawal of consent is not accepted at all regarding samples collected for clinical research;[67] in Iceland and Finland, however, the right to withdraw one's consent as regards research is inviolable. In Iceland and Norway, however, specific provisions prevent material that has been produced from a sample in a study, or in the results of studies already carried out, from being destroyed.[68]

6 Informing the public

It would seem that any country using the presumed consent model and emphasising the right to object would be under obligation to make this right known to those involved. Curiously, no specific obligation to inform the public can be found in the Danish Health Act.

However, although the Norwegian system cannot be categorised as a system based purely on presumed consent in this regard, Norway has introduced an obligation to inform the public by requesting that those who give samples to diagnostic biobanks are to be informed of the possibility that their samples may be used for research and of their right to opt out.[69] This is related to the possibility that a regional research ethics committee might grant an exception from the main rule if considerable public benefit is at stake. In addition, sample providers who have given their broad consent to biobank research, are entitled to periodic information about the research project.[70]

In Sweden, the duty to inform the public may be placed by an ethics committee, if it decides to grant an exception from explicit consent for secondary use.[71]

If Finland implements the ideas in the current Biobank Bill, the duty incumbent on both the supervisory authorities and the biobanks themselves to inform the public about the existence of biobanks, their operations, and the rights of those provid-

66 In Denmark, requests for sample destruction or retrieval can be overridden by the health care provider who is in charge of the sample if considerable private or public interest calls for it to be kept. See Health Act, §§ 33, 34.

67 This is the position taken by the National Committee for Biomedical Research Ethics. See *Den Centrale Videnskabsetiske Komités Årsberetning [Annual Report of the National Committee for Biomedical Research Ethics]* 2003, p. 37.

68 Biobanks Act, Art. 7, para. 2 (Iceland), Medical and Health Research Act, § 16 (Norway).

69 Medical and Health Research Act, § 28.

70 Medical and Health Research Act, § 14.

71 Bill on the Ethics Review Act, no. 50 from 2002/03, p. 128, and Swedish Research Council, Scientific Council for Medicine, *Biobanker: nya forskningsetiska riktlinjer för nyttjande av biobanker för forskningsändamål [Biobanks: new guidelines in research ethics for the use of biobanks in research]*, May 2003, p. 6.

ing samples to prevent their already existing samples from being transferred to a biobank, will be extensive. With regard to the possibility of preventing the transfer of old samples to a biobank, information would primarily be sent to all sample providers individually. If this is not possible at reasonable effort, due to the large number of samples, the age of the samples, or other similar reason, information would have to be provided via the official journal, the public information network (Internet) and, where applicable, via one or more newspapers.[72]

7 Financial aspects and benefit sharing

Traditionally, researchers have held onto their sample collections like treasure, and have only granted access to other researchers in exchange for something of benefit to them. This may have been the case even when samples were collected using public funds, and as a team effort. Private enterprises continue to apply this method of operation, as many of them see exclusivity as a means of gaining a competitive edge.

The public sector cannot, however, operate in line with the same ideology. It is in the public interest to provide good research opportunities to researchers working in both the private and public sectors. The results of public and private research may materialise in different ways and on a different timescale, but neither should be overlooked. Providing researchers in the public field with access to biological samples may yield better results in publications and in the sharing of information generally, but the well-being of private biotechnology enterprises means employment, tax returns, healthy competition, and, in the best case scenario, better products for diagnostics and health care. Hence, biological samples, even if they have been collected using public funds, should not be reserved exclusively for a specific public research institute – or a private one either.

As the Danes have the least restricted access to biological samples, it could be said that Denmark has taken the biggest leap of faith in supporting its biotechnology research. In order to protect participants, and perhaps private enterprises as well, the Health Act contains a specific provision regarding the requirement for private enterprises to enter into a contract with the sample providers, for example, with regard to the purpose of the sample collection, the length of time the sample will be retained, and the possibility of terminating the contract.[73]

The Norwegian and Swedish legislation includes specific conditions for others than the owner of the biobank accessing and using biobank samples. If access is denied, there is a possibility of obtaining a second opinion in both countries.[74] The Norwegian legislation recognises, for example, the biobank owner having a research

72 Biobank Bill, § 13.

73 Health Act, § 35.

74 Health Care Biobanks Act, § 15, Medical and Health Research Act, § 31 (Norway), Biobanks in Health Care Act, Chap. 4.

priority. In addition, the quality of the research plan of the party asking for access, and its relevance to the purpose of the specific biobank, are criteria that will be taken into account when evaluating a request for access.[75]

The Finnish Biobank Bill specifically recognises open access as the starting point of the Bill. This is clearly shown even in the opening provisions of the proposed Act. Section 1 of the proposed Act states that the purpose of the Act will be to support research on human samples and further openness in the use of biological samples, and to protect privacy and self-determination in the handling of biological samples. The Bill would create several registers, including a national register of biobanks, which would be accessible to researchers, citizens, and supervisory authorities, and which would contain information on the existing biobanks, their owners, and those in charge of these biobanks, in addition to general information about the quantity and usability of the samples being stored.[76] The biobank would only be able to restrict access to the samples in compliance with the conditions set forth in the Act, which do include the research priority for the study that the samples were collected for, but the priority does not extend to any subsequence studies by the biobank owner. In return, the Bill proposes that the party requesting access to the samples should be duty bound to publish the research results accruing from the samples.[77] If access to the samples were not to be granted, a complaint regarding the decision by the biobank owner could be lodged with the National Supervisory Authority for Welfare and Health.[78]

8 Conclusion

Historically, it is easy to imagine that the collection of biological samples began as a necessity and as a side effect of therapeutic activity. It is also easy to picture how very quickly the activity became combined with scientific ambitions. For decades, if not centuries, Nordic researchers have utilised these collections without much public interest. Together with the development of data processing and genetics, and an increased awareness of the protection of personal data, states also began regulating the various sources of the data. Apart from patient records, confidential information can be derived from the biological samples being collected from us, especially when the sample provider is still identifiable.

The extent to which the handling of these collections is regulated is primarily dependent on international agreements, which have been shamelessly ignored here.[79]

75 Medical and Health Research Act, § 31.

76 Biobank Bill, § 30.

77 Biobank Bill, § 27.

78 Biobank Bill, § 42, para. 3.

79 On the international documents in this area, see, for instance, S. Lötjönen, Biopankit [Biobanks] in L. Lehtonen (ed.), *Bio-oikeus lääketieteessä [Biolaw in medicine]* (Edita Publishing Oy, Helsinki, 2006), pp. 156-159 and E. Rynning, Legal Challenges and Strategies in the Regulation of Research Biobanking, in J.H. Solbakk et al. (eds), *The Ethics of Research Biobanking* (Springer, New York, 2009) pp. 280-281.

Within the remaining sphere of national discretion, the extent to which biobanks are regulated nationally depends on the trust placed on the research community to keep our secrets safe.

At present, it seems that, out of the Nordic countries, this trust is thriving in Denmark, where the regulation of biobanks is minimalistic, and where researchers are given ample opportunity to utilise their samples. The strictest Nordic country, in this sense, is Iceland, where exceptions from explicit consent have to be approved by three authorities. In Sweden and Norway, the regional research ethics committees may grant the exceptions, whereas in Finland this has been left with a government agency.

The Icelandic biobanks were feverishly discussed at the beginning of this century, when access to Iceland's health sector database was given to one private research enterprise.[80] People were also concerned about the appropriateness of the presumed consent of the data subjects in this regard. Curiously enough, presumed consent is not the standard for access to biological samples in Iceland, as we have learnt from the above.

Based on the comparisons made above, it would seem that the Icelandic example has led us in two different directions. Firstly, despite the controversy attached to presumed consent, it is alive and well in the Nordic context. Denmark applies it to diagnostic biobanks, while Finland has concrete plans to use it in order to organise all the existing samples into a handful of large biobanks mostly located adjacent to university hospitals. Traces of presumed consent can also be found in Norway and Sweden, where regional research ethics committees are empowered by law to allow large-scale exceptions from the requirement for explicit informed consent – in much the same way as the current situation in Finland (even though permissions are granted by a government agency).

However, although presumed consent has started to grow in the Nordic countries, the other example brought to us by Iceland has not. The notion of granting exclusive access to important national databases seems to be one that has been expressly rejected by the rest of the Nordic countries. On the contrary, denying access to samples must be justified on the basis of criteria laid down in law, and the decision can be appealed. The Finnish Biobank Bill seems to continue to develop this idea as well.

Depending on the nature and level of experience of the researchers in our own countries, it may be relatively easy to trust those in our own region who share our values and whose samples are probably part of the Nordic biological mass lying in freezers, or whose data is part of the digitalised universe in the same way as ours. However, bioscientific research does not recognise state or regional boundaries. This article has focused on comparing the regulations of the Nordic countries with regard

80 See, for instance, O.M. Arnardóttir et al., The Icelandic Health Sector Database, 6 *European Journal of Health Law* (1999) pp. 307-362.

to biobanks. As can be seen, even in this small geographical area with its close historical, cultural, and scientific co-operation, there are significant differences in the approaches adopted concerning biobank research. Efficient collaboration in biobank research requires some level of harmonisation in the standards being applied. Some endeavours have already been undertaken by various international bodies, e.g. UNESCO, OECD, the Council of Europe, and even, to some extent, the European Union;[81] however, none of these has been efficient enough to result in common standards, even in the Nordic region.

81 For a more detailed account of the content of the documents provided by these bodies, see the references listed in footnote 79.

Genetic Privacy: Autonomy or Solidarity?

By Assistant Professor Line Bune Juhl, University of Aalborg[1]

1 Challenges of gene technology – a patients' rights perspective

Genetic privacy challenges the way we traditionally think of and protect patients' rights. Gene technology – and its inherent possibilities for genetic diagnosis and treatment – is an example of a new technology that challenges the rules and regulations of the health care sector.

These challenges are related to the fact that genetic diagnosis involves the entire family, whereas health law typically protects patients through individual rights. Therefore, where genetic diagnosis is concerned, conflicts can arise between the different individual rights of the different family members. The question of how to resolve such conflicts is on the agenda, both internationally and regionally, of the Nordic countries; however, there are various legal approaches to the issue. In Denmark, the field of genetic privacy is almost entirely regulated through general Acts with no specific focus on genetic diagnosis. A different solution can be found in Norway, where the Biotechnology Act contains provisions that address some of the issues connected to genetic diagnosis specifically.[2]

This chapter identifies the relevant conflicts between various individual patients' rights which can arise in relation to genetic diagnosis. Once the potential conflicts have been uncovered, it is discussed how to resolve them by weighing and balancing each individual right against the other. Furthermore, it is described how a duty of solidarity towards blood-related family members might sometimes tip the scales when weighing and balancing conflicting rights. Finally, the Danish legal situation is explored, with the problems related to regulation through general rules – as is the case in Denmark – being pinpointed.[3]

---

1 Line Bune Juhl is an assistant professor at the Department of Law at the University of Aalborg, where she teaches constitutional law, human rights law, and health law. Her research has a rights based perspective and focuses on human rights in general and patient's and children's rights in specific.

2 The Norwegian Biotechnology Act: LOV 2003-12-05 nr. 100, Lov om humanmedisinsk bruk av bioteknologi m.m. (bioteknologiloven).

3 The chapter is largely based on the author's Ph.D dissertation concerning the handling of genetic information: L.B. Juhl: *Interesseafvejninger i sundhedsretten – med særligt fokus på håndtering af genetiske oplysninger om slægtninge*. This dissertation has not yet been published.

2 Autonomy or solidarity?

Since World War II, patients have been protected through individual rights, e.g. the right to confidentiality, the right to know, and the right not to know. To some extent, however, genetic information is shared by an entire family. Therefore, an exclusive focus on the individual does not always seem appropriate. On the contrary, when dealing with genetic diagnostics, it becomes apparent that it is not possible to regard the individual as completely separated from his/her surrounding family, society, and relations with other individuals. More appropriately, "[i]n genetics, the 'true patient' may be a family with a shared genetic heritage".[4]

Thus, it might be more in line with reality to speak of the entire family as "the true patient". The trouble is, however, that current regulations - in Denmark, in the other Nordic countries, and internationally - regard patients as individuals and protect them through individual rights. Information that is the result of genetic diagnostics is potentially relevant to the health of every blood-related member of the same family. Thus, it could be argued that every member has the right to access such knowledge. This individual right, however, could risk coming into conflict with the individual right of confidentiality enjoyed by other members of the same family. This problem is not addressed in current regulations and, as a result, the genetic counsellor who has to apply the law is provided with barely a hint of what to do when different individual rights are in conflict.

Because of the family's shared genetic heritage, the concept of solidarity comes into play when dealing with genetic diagnostics. The question is whether or not a duty of solidarity exists – and, if it does, to what extent this might tip the scales when weighing and balancing different individual rights against each other. Before even beginning to answer the question of how to carry out this weighing and balancing, as well as what emphasis to put on the interests and duties of solidarity, it will be necessary to understand what types of conflicts can arise in relation to genetic diagnostics. These are best illustrated using an example. This example is rather extensive, but then again, so is reality in such cases.

3 George and his family

The example begins with a man named George. George's brother, John, died of colon cancer when he was 45 years old. George's sister, Charlotte, is still alive, but has recently been diagnosed with colon cancer. Fortunately, Charlotte's disease has been discovered at a much earlier stage than John's was. Therefore, she stands a much better chance of being cured, because there is an available treatment for colon cancer, and the sooner you are diagnosed, the better will be your chances of being cured.

4 Consultants' report by WHO Professors D.C. Wertz, J.C. Fletcher, K. Berg: "Review of Ethical Issues in Medical Genetics", WHO, 2003, p. 50 with reference to K. Berg, 1989. Preface in: D.C. Wertz and J.C. Fletcher (eds.), *Ethics and Human Genetics: A Cross-Cultural Perspective.*

George has never been that close to his brother and sister, and he does not know that Charlotte has been diagnosed with colon cancer. He only knows that she is sick, and that she has some sort of cancer. He is, however, a bit worried that he himself might get cancer because their father also died of the disease. George is a man of action. He makes an appointment with his doctor and courageously asks the doctor to level with him and tell him when he can expect to fall ill with cancer. It is not an easy task to answer George's question. What the doctor *can* do, however, is refer George to genetic counselling at one of the major hospitals in the country.

3.1 The first visit to the genetic counsellor – and the first conflict

The genetic counsellor tells George that colon cancer *can* be hereditary but that this is not necessarily the case in his family. Just because one member of the family has been diagnosed with the disease, it does not automatically follow that the rest of the family is genetically predisposed to it. George is then asked to tell the counsellor about all the cases of cancer in the family that he is aware of. On the basis of this information, the counsellor makes a family tree into which all members of the family are entered, along with all known information about their diseases.

The counsellor now has the rather extensive task of verifying George's information. People like George can rarely recite the correct medical history of the entire family. Sometimes, misunderstandings or misinformation can occur. And sometimes, they just do not have all the facts; like George, who only knows that his sister is suffering from some sort of cancer. The counsellor has to gather information from the medical records of George's family members in order to make sure that the information in the family tree is adequate and correct. The counsellor approaches Charlotte and tells her that she would like to have a copy of her medical records in order to be able to give George a risk assessment that is as precise as possible. However, Charlotte does not want to consent to this because she does not want to know whether a hereditary mutation exists within the family. The reason for this is that Charlotte has a daughter – Jennifer – who recently died of colon cancer. Charlotte feels that she would be responsible for her daughter's death if she had passed on a genetic mutation to her, and she cannot bear the thought of that.

In this situation, consideration can be given to whether or not Charlotte's medical records should be made available without her consent. The quality of the counselling that George receives depends on whether or not this information is available. Whether or not consent is necessary can also be of relevance to how soon George can be offered preventive examinations, because it can often be rather time-consuming to obtain such consent from all the relevant family members; especially from those who are in doubt, like Charlotte. Given that the chances of being cured increase when the disease is diagnosed early on, the amount of time spent on the family tree is important. You could argue that George has a right to know genetic information of relevance to his own health, as well as a right to be treated if he has an inherited predisposition. These rights, however, come into conflict with Charlotte's right to confidentiality, and her right not to know whether the disease is hereditary.

However, let us just assume that Charlotte decides to consent after all. When the family tree has been drawn up and verified, the counsellor assesses whether or not there are indications of hereditary disease. In George's case, there are indications of hereditary colon cancer. George is thus encouraged to undergo preventive examinations at regular intervals. These preventive examinations consist of a rectal arthroscopy aimed at discovering cancer at the earliest possible opportunity in order to increase his chances of being cured.

3.2 *The second conflict arises: a family member wants a genetic test*

George has a daughter named Michelle who is also encouraged to follow the preventive programme of regular examinations. She finds the examinations quite unpleasant. They hurt and are, quite frankly, embarrassing. Therefore, Michelle would like to know for certain whether or not she has an inherited predisposition for colon cancer. If she does not, the examinations will then not be necessary. If Michelle is to be tested, this will require that the geneticists have something to compare Michelle's DNA with. The mutation causing this disease is often specific to the individual family, and the geneticists have to know the exact mutation in order to be able to examine Michelle's DNA.

Consequently, it will be necessary to obtain a blood sample from a member of the family who is already ill and thus certain to have inherited the mutation. For that reason, Michelle approaches Charlotte, but this time Charlotte is even more resistant and hesitant. A genetic test will enhance her sense of guilt, which is already hard to bear on top of having to bear the loss of a daughter. If Charlotte decides not to give a blood sample, Michelle cannot be tested.

Consideration can be given to whether or not it should be possible to force Charlotte to cooperate. Michelle has a right to know and a right to be treated which cannot be respected if Charlotte refuses to cooperate. However, Charlotte still has a right to confidentiality and a right not to know which will be violated if she is forced to cooperate. Most people would probably reject the idea of forcing Charlotte to give blood. But what if a sample of Charlotte's blood was already being stored in a biobank somewhere? In that case, Charlotte can be forced to cooperate without violating her bodily integrity.

Let us imagine that Charlotte is persuaded to cooperate voluntarily. That could, for instance, be the case if Charlotte's daughter Jennifer had a child before she died. This child might also benefit from the information that Michelle is seeking in order to avoid preventive examinations. So Charlotte gives blood, a mutation is found, and Michelle can now be tested. Both George and Michelle are tested, and it turns out that neither of them has inherited the mutation. Consequently, they no longer have to follow the preventive programme.

3.3 The third conflict: should other family members be informed?

The story does not end here. The family has yet another member. The deceased brother, John, had a son named Michael. The genetic counsellor encourages Charlotte to tell Michael that there is a risk that he could have inherited the mutation. But Charlotte flat out denies this! She has never been close to any of her brothers and she finds Michael to be every bit as eccentric and mean as his father. Before they broke off all contact, he acted inexcusably towards her and she does not feel that she owes him anything. Hence, she refuses to be the bearer of information that is already hard for hear to deal with. She also feels that Michael must himself be responsible for considering the risk of a hereditary disease, since he is aware that both his father and grandfather died of cancer.

In this situation, the genetic counsellor is facing two conflicts. Firstly, she has to consider whether or not she is allowed to breach doctor-patient confidentiality and inform Michael herself. You could argue that the results of the test are relevant to Michael's health and thus included in his right to know. This right, then, is in conflict with Charlotte's right to confidentiality.

Secondly, the genetic counsellor has to consider, whether or not it is in Michael's best interest to be informed at all. Besides the right to know, Michael also has a right not to know. In this situation, it is impossible to respect one right without violating the other. The right not to know has been formulated with a focus on situations where patients are capable of deciding for themselves whether they want to know or not. But in this case, it will be impossible to ask Michael without disclosing at least some of the very information he might wish not to know about.

When it comes to hereditary colon cancer the decision of whether or not to inform Michael may not be so hard since it is a serious hereditary disease that can be prevented and treated with good results; most people would probably agree that it is best to be informed. But what if we change the example and think of a serious disease that *cannot* be prevented or treated? Should Michael still be informed in that case?

4 Ways of resolving the conflicts

The example concerning George and his family illustrates that genetic testing can lead to conflicts between the individual rights of different family members, and even to conflicts between the same individual's opposing rights.

Once the potential conflicts have been identified, it is relevant to consider who is supposed to solve these conflicts and how. The solution to any such conflict must be found by weighing and balancing the various rights on either side.

The weighing and balancing necessary to resolve potential conflicts can be achieved by legislators by means of specifying a fixed solution written directly into the law. When it comes to regulation that concerns patients' rights, a fixed solution of some sort is generally offered through consent. If the genetic counsellor obtains valid consent from the party whose right may be violated, violation will no longer pose a problem. With Charlotte's consent, her medical history and the information extracted from her biological samples can be shared with any member of her family – provided, of course, that the consent given meets the requirements stipulated in the law.

The legislators can also leave the solution of potential conflicts to the genetic counsellors. They will have to resolve the conflicts themselves if this is specifically indicated in the law or if the law says nothing about the subject. Either way, the counsellor will have to practice the art of weighing and balancing. If Charlotte refuses to consent, this might become relevant.

The point of this chapter is not to offer a solution to all the potential conflicts, but to point out that such conflicts may often occur, and to illustrate how difficult weighing and balancing is, and how much, or rather how little, guidance is offered in the relevant Danish and international legal instruments. Therefore, this chapter will merely concentrate on the conflicts that might occur *prior to or in relation to* the actual genetic test.

In the example of George and his family, this would be the conflicts between Charlotte on the one hand and George and his daughter Michelle on the other. Conflicts that might occur after the test has been conducted, such as the conflict between Charlotte and her rude nephew Michael, can be just as difficult to resolve, but they will not be mentioned in detail here.

5 Resolution of conflicts in relation to diagnosing/testing

The following section will give a brief overview of how the conflicts in question are regulated in Danish law. The focus will be solely on the Danish Health Act even though the stipulations in the Danish Act on Processing of Personal Data are of relevance at times, too.[5] The intention of this chapter is to illustrate the level of guidance; the Act on Processing of Personal Data does not offer more guidance than the Health Act. The solutions found in these Acts are, in fact, very similar.

Characteristic of both the Health Act and the Act on Processing of Personal Data is that they are general Acts regulating a very large legal field. With the exception of a few rules about the use of genetic information by employers and insurance companies, there are no specific rules concerning genetic testing in Denmark. Some guidelines can be found in various international instruments, especially from the Council of Europe; however, all in all, specific legal instruments concerning this topic are sparse. Therefore, Danish genetic counsellors are primarily left with the general regulations found in the Health Act and the Act on Processing of Personal Data.

5 The Danish Health Act: Act no. 913 from 13/07/2010 with subsequent changes. The Danish Act on Processing of Personal Data: Act no. 429 from 31/05/2000.

In § 40 of the Danish Health Act, it is stipulated as a main rule that doctor-patient confidentiality must be respected. Confidentiality is a central part of health law everywhere and its main purpose is to ensure that patients trust the system, which will benefit both the individual patient and society as a whole.

It is, however, quite obvious that, in some situations, it must be possible to share information regarding a patient's health. For instance, this is the case when two or more doctors are involved in treating the same patient. Therefore, the Danish Health Act allows the processing of health-related personal data in some cases. For the purpose of treatment, processing can take place in three different situations, pursuant to §§ 41 and 42 a:

1. If consent is given.
2. If there is a presumption that the patient would consent if asked.
3. If there is what is called a value gap.

Consent is probably well known to most people. The presumption of consent is used in situations where it would be unnecessarily formalistic to require expressed consent. For instance, when several doctors are involved in the ongoing treatment of a patient, it is only natural that these doctors exchange relevant information about the patient without having to obtain the consent of that patient for each and every exchange.

The value gap rule offers the possibility to process information in spite of confidentiality when other opposing interests are found to be of a higher value. This is an example of the law specifically requiring the genetic counsellor to weigh and balance opposing rights.

Originally, this rule regarding value gaps was intended for unconscious patients; however, in 2006, the law was changed slightly and, according to the preparatory works, the expressed intention is that, to some extent, the presence of a value gap can justify a breach of confidentiality in relation to genetic testing.[6]

Most of the time, the processing of health-related data will occur on the basis of either consent or the presumption of such consent when it comes to genetic diagnostics, too. There is no question that this is the main stipulation in the law. In these cases the legislators have indicated a fixed solution by prescribing that e.g. Charlotte's right of confidentiality must be respected unless Charlotte herself allows something else.

The challenge for the genetic counsellor lies in identifying when the so-called gap of values is present and justifies processing without consent. The genetic counsellor must perform the task of weighing and balancing opposing rights and inter-

6 Section 4.2.4. of the general remarks and the specific remarks for § 1, no. 8 in the proposal for the change in the Health Act: forslag nr. L 50 af 25. oktober 2006 til lov om ændring af sundhedsloven og lov om klage- og erstatningsadgang inden for sundhedsvæsenet (1 måneds behandlingsfrist, IT-anvendelse i sundhedsvæsenet, elektroniske helbredsoplysninger, adgang til Medicinprofilen m.v.).

ests in these situations. As an example George's and Michelle's right to know and their right to be treated could be mentioned. Consideration for these rights must be weighed and balanced against consideration for Charlotte's right to confidentiality.[7]

The Danish Health Act contains two provisions that allow the processing of health-related data without consent for the purposes of treatment because of a gap of values. They both state that processing must be necessary because of justified considerations of an essential nature. Little is said, however, about which considerations should be deemed justified and when they will be of an essential nature. The question is how far shared genetic interests and the idea of genetic solidarity can justify restricting the rights of individual family members.

In these situations, the principle of proportionality can be of some help to the genetic counsellor.

6 The art of weighing and balancing

The art of weighing and balancing is well known in the legal field. In public law, it is common for legislators to provide the administrative authorities with scope for discretion. From a rights-based perspective, this entails both risks and benefits.

The possibility of leaving at least part of the weighing and balancing to the administration, instead of always offering a fixed solution in the law, provides legislators with a flexible legal tool. It makes it possible for the administrators to take the specifics of each individual case into account and to apply their own professional expertise to the process. This flexibility can be used to provide strong protection of patients' rights.

Along with the flexibility, however, comes a lack of foreseeability which can potentially threaten the very same patients' rights. To minimize that threat, while at the same time maintaining the benefits, it is often desirable to provide individual administrators with some sort of guidance as to which elements carry particular weight in the relevant legal field.

The genetic counsellors, however, are left with very little guidance in this regard because the existing regulation has a general objective, and does not address the specific issues that can arise in relation to genetic counselling and testing.

Apart from guidance based on the relevant legal instruments, it is also widely recognized that when weighing and balancing opposing rights and interests, the principle of proportionality plays an important part. The wording of the Danish regulation indicates that this is also supposed to be the case when a genetic counsellor has to decide whether or not to breach or uphold confidentiality.

7 If data is, in fact, processed without consent because of a gap of values, then a duty might exist to inform the person whose data is being processed. For an in-depth analysis, see L.B. Juhl: *Interesseafvejninger i sundhedsretten – med særligt fokus på håndtering af genetiske oplysninger om slægtninge*, pp. 93 ff. This dissertation has not yet been published; however, it is outside of the scope of this chapter to address the issue in detail.

The principle of proportionality has evolved over time, and can be found today in various forms in different legal fields. A common way of describing the principle of proportionality is to divide the principle into three independent, but still connected, sub-principles:

1. The principle of suitability
2. The principle of necessity
3. The principle of proportionality *stricto sensu*

Thus, according to the principle of suitability, a genetic counsellor faced with conflicting rights must initially consider whether or not the violation of a specific patient right is even fit to achieve the purpose that the counsellor is trying to serve. In our case, there must be consideration of whether or not the violation of Charlotte's right to confidentiality is fit to achieve the diagnosing of George and Michelle. In this regard, four questions that are typically necessary to consider can be derived from the relevant legal instruments:[8]

1. Is the disease genetic?
2. Is the disease hereditary?
3. Will the available method of testing render reliable results?
4. Is the information that the counsellor wishes to process relevant to the purpose?

In our case, all the questions can be answered affirmatively. This leads me to conclude that the breach of confidentiality is, in fact, fit to achieve the desired purpose. This is not, however, enough to meet all the criteria of the principle of proportionality.

Furthermore, according to the principle of necessity, the counsellor must consider whether or not there are any less intrusive ways of achieving the desired purpose. Typically, it will be relevant to consider whether or not less information will suffice. In our case, the counsellor has to know what kind of cancer Charlotte is suffering from in order to produce an accurate family tree. The counselor also needs the blood sample in order to test Michelle. Thus, no other and less intrusive way is available.

Lastly, according to the principle of proportionality *strictu sensu*, the counsellor must consider which of the opposing rights or interests is compelling enough to outweigh the other; herein lies the real challenge. It will always be necessary, when weighing and balancing, to evaluate the specific case and determine the nature of the rights or interests of each side. Once the relevant rights and interests have been identified, the process of determining which right or interest is the most compelling can begin. Here, on the one hand, we have Charlotte's right to confidentiality. This is an

8 In particular, the Health Act and its preparatory works. The elements found here are supported, for instance, by Council of Europe Recommendation No. R (97) 5 of the Committee of Ministers to member states on the Protection of Medical Data and the Explanatory Memorandum to the Recommendation.

essential patient right and as such it requires weighty arguments in order to justify a breach. On the other hand, we have George's or Michelle's right to know and their right to be treated. These are also basic patients' rights.

Such a conflict with basic patients' rights, on either side, is difficult to solve at first glance. None of these rights can be said to be automatically more compelling than the other.[9] To reach a solution, it will be necessary to take a closer look at the specifics of the case at hand and then come up with arguments that take these details into account. It is, of course, impossible to generate an exhaustive list of specifics that will be relevant to consider in every case, since each case has its own individual characteristics. Some elements that will be relevant to any case, however, can be extracted from the available legal instruments.[10] These elements are:

1. *The nature of the disease.*
   How serious is the disease, for instance, and what are the implications to the health of the patient? The more serious/the greater the implications – the more justified it will be to breach patient confidentiality.
2. *The magnitude of the risk of actually falling ill if you have a genetic predisposition.*
   The greater the risk – the more justified it will be to breach patient confidentiality.
3. *Available points of action once you have been diagnosed.*
   Is it possible to prevent or treat the disease, for instance? Is it important to know about the disease when making reproductive decisions? The more you will be able to actually *do* – the more justified it will be to breach patient confidentiality.
4. *The time factor.*
   The more the patient's prognosis depends on a quick diagnosis and treatment – the more justified it will be to breach patient confidentiality, instead of spending time obtaining consent.

9 If, on the one hand, we still had a basic patient right such as confidentiality, but on the other, something that was not a patient right but merely a general interest/consideration, this would place a much more difficult burden of proof on such an interest or consideration and the arguments supporting it in order to outweigh a fundamental patient right. As an example, it is stated in the preparatory works for a change in the Danish Health Act that it can sometimes be justified to breach patient confidentiality in order to avoid *unnecessary concern* for the patient himself; see the specific remarks for § 1, no. 8 in the proposal for the change: forslag nr. L 50 af 25. oktober 2006 til lov om ændring af sundhedsloven og lov om klage- og erstatningsadgang inden for sundhedsvæsenet (1 måneds behandlingsfrist, IT-anvendelse i sundhedsvæsenet, elektroniske helbredsoplysninger, adgang til Medicinprofilen m.v.). It is not a patient right to avoid unnecessary concern and it would seem that the legislators have not been bearing in mind the difference between a legal right and what is merely an interest. For further analysis, see L.B. Juhl: *Interesseafvejninger i sundhedsretten – med særligt fokus på håndtering af genetiske oplysninger om slægtninge*, pp. 76 f. This dissertation has not yet been published; however, it is outside the scope of this chapter to address the issue in detail.

10 The Health Act and the Act on Processing of Personal Data and their preparatory works are, of course, essential. International instruments of particular relevance include: Council of Europe Recommendation No. R (92) 3 of the Committee of Ministers to member states: Genetic testing and screening for health care purposes and the Explanatory Memorandum to the Recommendation. Council of Europe Recommendation No. R (97) 5 of the Committee of Ministers to member states on the Protection of Medical Data and the Explanatory Memorandum to the Recommendation. Council of Europe Additional Protocol to the Convention on Human Rights and Biomedicine, concerning Genetic Testing for Health Purposes and the Explanatory Report to the Additional Protocol. The issue is further addressed in L.B. Juhl: *Interesseafvejninger i sundhedsretten – med særligt fokus på håndtering af genetiske oplysninger om slægtninge*, pp. 79 f. This dissertation has not yet been published; however, it is outside of the scope of this chapter to address the issue in detail.

5. *The risk of spreading information outside the group of people bound by confidentiality.*
   The smaller the risk of spreading information to people without a duty of confidentiality – the more justified it will be to breach patient confidentiality.

7 Solidarity – a relevant weight on the scales?

The final result of weighing and balancing will be influenced by whether or not the legislators support a duty of *solidarity*. The interesting question is whether or not such a duty even exists and, if so, whether or not it will sometimes be able to tip the scales.

This question can be answered in two very different ways depending on your point of view. You may either be convinced that genetic information is the shared property of all members of the family or you may be convinced that autonomy should be protected at any cost.[11] You could also argue that solidarity is more of a moral obligation and that this area is best regulated by social and cultural norms rather than legal ones.[12]

As previously mentioned, it has been specifically pointed out, in the preparatory works for a change in the Danish Health Act, that it will sometimes be possible to process medical data without consent when dealing with genetic testing.

This indicates that, at least to some extent, a duty of solidarity can influence the final result of weighing and balancing. Thus, it appears that the Danish legislators are somewhere in between these two opposing points of view. However, neither the law nor its preparatory works are clear about this in any way, and the international guidelines pull in different directions.[13] This lack of clarity forces genetic counsellors to act with great caution within their boundaries of discretion. The possibility of pro-

11 Article 29 Data Protection Working Party: Working Document WP 91, 12178/03/EN, on Genetic Data, adopted on 17 March 2004, Human Genetics Commission: *Inside Information - Balancing interests in the use of personal genetic data*, 2002, Chapter 2, Michael Parker, Anneke M. Lucassen: "Genetic information: a joint account?", *BMJ*, 2004, 329:165-167.

12 Robin Pierce: *Comparative Approaches to Unconsented Disclosure of Genetic Test Results to Relatives: A Social Norms Approach*.

13 Relevant international instruments include: Principles 5, 6, 9, and 11 of Council of Europe Recommendation No. R (92) 3 of the Committee of Ministers to member states: Genetic testing and screening for health care purposes; Principles 3 and 7 of Council of Europe Recommendation No. R (97) 5 of the Committee of Ministers to member states on the Protection of Medical Data, and paragraphs 146 and 152 of the Explanatory Memorandum to the Recommendation Arts 5 and 10 of the Council of Europe Convention for the protection of Human Rights and dignity of the human being with regard to the application of biology and medicine: Convention on Human Rights and Biomedicine and paragraph 88 of the Explanatory Report to the Convention; Arts 9, 14, 15, and 18 of the Council of Europe Additional Protocol to the Convention on Human Rights and Biomedicine, concerning Genetic Testing for Health Purposes, and paragraphs 86 and 138-140 of the Explanatory Report to the Additional Protocol; Arts 5 (b) and 9 of the UNESCO Universal Declaration on the Human Genome and Human Rights and Art. 8 (a) of the UNESCO International Declaration on Human Genetic Data; Sections 9 and 11 in "Proposed International Guidelines on Ethical Issues in Medical Genetics and Genetic Services", WHO, 1997 and sections 8.2.2 and 19 in Report of Consultants to WHO Professors D.C. Wertz, J.C. Fletcher, K. Berg: "Review of Ethical Issues in Medical Genetics", WHO, 2003. For an in-depth analysis, see L.B. Juhl: *Interesseafvejninger i sundhedsretten – med særligt fokus på håndtering af genetiske oplysninger om slægtninge*, pp. 133 ff. and 159 ff. This dissertation has not yet been published; however, it is outside the scope of this chapter to address the issue in detail.

cessing medical data without consent can only be certain to include regular information and not biological samples. On the one hand, George might be able to obtain a diagnosis based on an accurate family tree, including information about Charlotte's disease. Michelle, on the other hand, will probably not be able to be tested without Charlotte's consent, even if a sample of Charlotte's blood were already in storage.

I therefore strongly urge the legislators to bring some clarity to this matter, because the situation at present is unsatisfactory, for both genetic counsellors and patients.[14] Counsellors must, of course, be able to weigh and balance conflicting rights while drawing on their professional experience. Written guidelines would, however, help strengthen patients' rights; most particularly, there should be clarification of how much weight to attribute to the idea of genetic solidarity.

14 In Norway, the solution to potential conflicts is much clearer. In paragraphs 5-9 of Norway's Biotechnology Act, it is stipulated that information relevant to the patient's family members cannot be disclosed against the patient's expressed wish. Only in situations where the patient is unable to consent can information in some cases be disclosed. Thus, legislators have determined that, in Norway, a duty of solidarity cannot outweigh respect for the patient's autonomy. Interestingly, in the previous Biotechnology Act, it was actually possible, under certain conditions, to disclose information against the patient's wishes. This possibility was introduced in a revision of the Act in 2000. In 2004, however, the Act was changed again, and the possibility of disclosing information against the patient's wish was removed. In the preparatory works, it is expressly stated that, in these situations, the right to confidentiality and the right not to know are the most important, see section 5.12.5 of Ot.prp. nr. 64 (2002-2003).

Death Before Life: The Legal Status of Cadaveric Foetuses

By Associate Professor Janne Rothmar Herrmann, University of Copenhagen[1]

1 Introduction

The issue of how to dispose of aborted foetuses is a sensitive ethical and legal issue which relates directly to the legal status of the foetus. An illustrative example of this issue's practical legal relevance is the Danish Council of Ethics' recommendation[2] of March 3, 2011, in reply to the Municipality of Odense regarding the establishment of a separate anonymous lawn for aborted foetuses at the town's principal cemetery in order to provide parents with a free and optional alternative to the current procedure. The aim of this article is to analyse death before life in Danish law and to offer some general reflections on the legal status of cadaveric foetuses.

2 Person or thing?

The human foetus has always been an entity which has proved difficult to place within the legal landscape, as it is located in the border territory between the legal concepts of personhood and property. In the traditional legal way of thinking, this distinction between persons and property is essential: as Immanuel Kant pointed out, 'a person cannot be property and so cannot be a thing which can be owned, for it is impossible to be a person and a thing, the proprietor and the property'.[3] Accordingly, how an entity is categorised in terms of these basic concepts is pivotal for the scope of legal protection afforded to it. Persons are individuals who possess integrity and basic liberty rights, and thus cannot be owned by other individuals. Property, on the other hand, is an object that a person can possess, both in a physical and a legal sense. Rights and duties concerning property relate to the person who owns the

1 Janne Rothmar Herrmann is Associate Professor at the Faculty of Law, University of Copenhagen. She was awarded the PhD-degree in 2008 on the basis of a dissertation on the legal status on foetuses and embryos, on which this article is based.

2 Available at http://etiskraad.dk/Aktuelt/Hoeringssvar-og-udtalelser/2011/03-03-2011-kremering-af-flere-fostre-i-samme-kiste.aspx. Accessed March 9, 2011.

3 I. Kant, *Lectures on Ethics* (Methuen and Co., London, 1930), p. 65.

thing or regulate the relationship between different persons with regard to possession of the thing. The distinction between person and property stems from ancient Roman law, e.g. the *corpus juris civilis* distinguished between the law of persons and the law of property.[4] Not all human beings were categorised as persons, e.g. wives and slaves were considered property. The human foetus was afforded a special status in between an anticipated person and a *res futura* (future thing). The foetus did not have a legal status in general, except in relation to rights pertaining to property and inheritance, where the law applied the principle *nasciturus pro iam nate habetur* (he who is about to be born should be considered already born). The rights were, however, dependant upon the foetus being born alive as a foetus which did not result in the birth of a child was considered a "thing" which had never existed.[5] The human body and bodily parts have also traditionally been seen as property, regardless of whether alive or dead. Since components of the human body, such as genes, tissues and cells, can now be isolated and used therapeutically as products, the issue of whether bodily components can be categorised as objects is an item on the modern legal agenda in relation, for example, to the patentability of stem cells and stem cell lines.[6]

2.1 The traditional legal classification of foetuses

All scientific disciplines group objects under scholarly study and analysis into various categories. In biology, we refer to the classification of species, while in medical science, illnesses are grouped under superordinate labels such as cancer or motor neuron disease. In legal terminology, we categorise the subjects of legal regulation on the basis of assumptions regarding their typical properties (e.g. patients, consumers, single parents, etc.), thus essentialising them as such. It is, however, within the theoretical framework for legal personhood that the initial and perhaps most important legal classification occurs, as it is in this area of law that the subjects of the law are identified or created as persons in the legal sense. This identification has wide implications for the subject's legal status, most notably regarding his/her ability to be a holder of rights.

Notwithstanding modern day controversies surrounding cells and tissues of embryonic origin, most Western theories on legal personhood maintain the traditional distinction between person and property developed by Roman law and, as a result, are unable to offer an adequate and comprehensive theoretical framework for the legal status of embryos and foetuses.

---

4 See in more depth L. Björne, *Deutsche Rechtssysteme im 18. und 19. Jahrhundert* (Verlag Rolf Gremer, Edelsbach, 1984), p. 176 and L. Björne, *Nordische Rechtssysteme* (Verlag Rolf Gremer, Edelbach, 1987), pp. 95-100.

5 See *Roe* v. *Wade*, 410 US 113, 1973, para. VI, 1.

6 J. Rothmar Herrmann & M. Rowlandson, The Role of Ethics and Morality in EU Law, 5(6) *Journal of International Biotechnology Law* (2008), pp. 241-251.

According to the traditional view, the concept of legal personhood is closely linked to the autonomous individual. The idea of one legal person being inside the womb of another legal person is hard to grasp in this mindset and, according to this logic, either the pregnant woman or the foetus must necessarily be classified as something accessory (or a vessel) in order for the other to be classified as a person.[7] Consequently, birth is seen as the all important demarcation line separating those who are able to be holders of rights from those who are not, implying that there are no legal grounds for distinguishing between the legal status of a recently-fertilised egg and that of a viable foetus. This rather binary rationale not only accommodates the legal questions facing modern society, it also implies that entities such as fertilised eggs, embryos, and foetuses cannot be classified legally.[8]

To illustrate the ensuing legal uncertainty surrounding the foetus and the embryo, I would like to highlight a few cases:

In a case reviewed by the Danish Supreme Court in 2006[9], a couple of young men had been racing their cars in a busy street in Copenhagen, hitting several pedestrians. A young woman was injured severely and, as a result, lost her foetus of 26 weeks gestational age. The young man was only prosecuted for and convicted of injuring the *woman's body*, illustrating the fact that the foetus was not considered to be something separate, but rather something that should be dealt with via the woman's rights and her legal protection. This was also the case in a European Court of Human Rights (ECtHR) judgment in *Vo v. France*,[10] where the applicant had to abort her foetus of 6 months gestational age on medical grounds due to an error by a doctor.

However, in a case heard by the Danish Abortion Appeals Board[11], a 13-year-old girl who was 24 weeks pregnant was refused an induced abortion on the grounds that the foetus was thought to be viable in the sense that it would survive if born prematurely. In this case, the foetus was not something identical to the woman, as in the two other cases; it was something separate that limited the scope of the girl's right to reproductive autonomy and bodily integrity. Along these lines, the former European Commission on Human Rights, in its first ever case on abortion, stated that "the claim to respect for private life is automatically reduced to the extent that the individual himself brings his private life into contact with public life or into close connection with other protected interests ... pregnancy cannot be said to pertain uniquely to the sphere of private life. Whenever a woman is pregnant her private life becomes closely

7 See also M. Davies & N. Naffine, *Are Persons Property?* (Ashgate, Aldershot, 2001), pp. 84-86.

8 See in more depth in my PhD dissertation *Retsbeskyttelsen af foster og befrugtede æg* (Jurist- og Økonomforbundets Forlag, Copenhagen, 2008), Chapters 2-3.

9 UfR2006.1089H (10 January 2006) in *Ugeskrift for Retsvæsen* 2006, p. 1089.

10 *Vo* v. *France*, application no. 53924/00, 8 July 2004.

11 Case no. 0-608-02-38/1. A summary of the case is available in Danish in the Abortion Appeals Board's annual report, 2006 (www.sst.dk).

connected with the developing foetus."[12] As such, the legal uncertainty regarding the status of the foetus permeates international human rights law as well.

The purpose of this article is to challenge this view by demonstrating that embryos and foetuses are, in fact, located in a number of different legal categories with distinct and multifaceted ensuing legal implications. I have chosen the legal status of the dead foetus as an illustrative case in order to analyse:

3 Death before life

Modern legal discourse is very much affected by developments in the biosciences and medicine.

Issues to be dealt with by law now include questions such as what to do when surplus embryos are no longer useful in the treatment of couples undergoing fertility treatment in clinics - can we 'pour them down the drain' or do the embryos have another status that requires them to be handled and disposed of with respect and dignity?

The cadaveric foetus represents a particular challenge in terms of how we handle it legally, as the status of both the dead body and the foetus gives rise to discussion. When looking at the legal status of the dead foetus, the question arises as to whether we should regard the tissue as something identical to the woman or as something individual and with a status of its own.

First of all, I want to briefly point out the interests at stake. In Denmark, both the deceased person and the cadaveric body are protected by the Criminal Code and the Data Protection Act. Consequently, there are issues relating to both the *privacy of the deceased* (e.g. under § 264d of the Danish Criminal Code, it may be unlawful to publish photographs or information about a suicide on account of the privacy, not only of the family, but also of the deceased) and the dead person's *bodily integrity* (e.g. the Danish Criminal Code requires that the cadaveric body be treated respectfully; in a case from the High Court of Eastern Denmark[13], the defendant was convicted for cutting off the finger of a corpse, illustrating that the dead person has a degree of bodily integrity which is protected legally).[14] The issue of *women's privacy* is also at stake. In a case before the European Court of Human Rights[15] a woman in a Swiss institution for asylum seekers had miscarried. The foetus of 27 weeks gestational age was not considered a dead child under Swiss law. The local authorities had arranged burial without the woman's knowledge and participation. They had also transported the miscarried foetus in a van instead of the proper hearse. Both acts violated the

12 *Brüggemann & Scheuten* v. *Germany*, application no. 6959/75, Report adopted by the Commission on 12 July 1977, paras 55-56 and 59.

13 UfR 2002.1382/1Ø (19 March 2002) in *Ugeskrift for Retsvæsen* 2002, p. 1382.

14 See further J. Rothmar Herrmann, 'Use of the Dead Body in Healthcare and Medical Training: Mapping and Balancing the Legal Rights and Values', 18:3 *European Journal of Health Law* (2011), pp. 271–299.

15 *Hadri-Vionnet* v. *Switzerland*, application no. 55525/00 (Cour – Cinquième Section), 14 February 2008.

woman's right to respect for her private life and her family life under Article 8 of the ECHR.

Under Danish law, the cadaveric foetus is categorised legally as a *dead child* if born after 22 weeks gestational age and without showing any signs of life, regardless of the circumstances, i.e. the tissue expelled during the course of a late-induced abortion is also considered a dead child.[16] The limit was changed in 2004[17] from 28 weeks, with respect to progress in the treatment of prematurely-born children. The primary reason for changing the limit was, however, to respect parents' wishes to have their grief over the loss of a child acknowledged legally. The 22 week limit has various legal implications because it triggers the applicability of the rules and regulations concerning children, child birth, and the deceased: the cadaveric foetal body is protected by criminal law, registration of the birth with the authorities is mandatory, and the body must be buried or cremated. The legal category in question also has implications for the parents, who are entitled to receive public welfare benefits such as financial aid towards the cost of burial and maternity benefits. Furthermore, paternity can be recognised legally. Consequently, the pedestrian who was hit by a car in a busy Copenhagen street, in the case mentioned above, would be treated as a mother in all other respects and her foetus as a dead child, although the foetus was not considered a separate entity in the criminal case.

A foetus that is stillborn, miscarried, or aborted using an induced procedure prior to the 22 week limit is considered an *aborted foetus*. The cadaveric foetal body is not required to be treated respectfully according to criminal law, a doctor is not required to make out a death certificate, and burial/cremation is not required by law. Instead, the aborted foetus must be disposed of as *clinical risk waste*,[18] not because the tissue is considered to pose a risk to anyone's health or to those handling the waste, but because it is required to be incinerated beyond recognition due to ethical concerns for the possible discomfort others might feel if any remaining parts, such as an arm or a foot were to be recognisable. Parents wishing to bury their aborted foetus can do so, but unless special preferences are requested, the cadaveric foetus is legally regarded as clinical risk waste and disposed of with other clinical waste products. The fact that the cadaveric foetus can be placed in various legal categories may also be illustrated using the British case *R. v. Gibson*.[19] In this case, a freeze-dried human embryo of 3 to 4 months gestational age had been displayed as an earring in a gallery. If a cadaveric foetus of this age had the same legal status as a dead person, using the foetus in this way would clearly be a violation of the protection of the dead body. However, in this case, the gallery's display was considered to be an *obscene publication*.

16 The Health Act (lovbekendtgørelse nr. 95, 7 February 2008), § 189 (1).

17 See the act lov nr. 133, 2 February 2004 om ændring af lov om ligsyn, obduktion og transplantation m.v. og børneloven (Ændring af grænsen mellem abort og dødfødsel og forenkling af reglerne om registrering af faderskab til dødfødte børn).

18 Ministerial order no. 1634, 13 December 2006, para. 13.2 and instruction no. 60178, 1 August 1998, para. 3.2.

19 R. v. *Gibson* [1990] 91 Cr. App. R. 341.

When further examining the question of how the aborted foetus is categorised, i.e. whether it is considered identical to the woman or a separate entity with a status of its own, it is interesting to note that Danish law seems to distinguish between tissue of cadaveric foetal origin and other bodily cells and tissues obtained by a medical intervention on the woman. The woman cannot register restrictions concerning the foetal tissue in the Central Registry on the Usage of Tissue, which, as a general rule, allows patients to restrict the use of their stored tissue to purposes of treatment, implying that the tissue is not identical to the woman. On the other hand, due to the fact that the tissue does not contain information relating to an *identified* or *identifiable* individual, tissue from foetuses categorised as abortions, rather than dead children, falls outside the scope of the Data Protection Act. As a result, hospitals can freely process, store, and disclose the tissue. In this respect, the tissue is neither considered to be something identical to the woman nor something separate that relates to an identifiable person. As a result, the processing of this tissue operates in a legal void, [20] as the regulation governing clinical risk waste only applies from the moment the hospital wants to *dispose* of the tissue due to it no longer serving a purpose in relation to medical treatment or research.

Cells and tissues from aborted foetuses can be used in many contexts; for research purposes, for diagnostic or therapeutic purposes, or for commercial purposes. While the processing of foetal tissue is unregulated on the whole, the specific usage of foetal tissue and foetuses for *research* and *commercial* purposes is subject to regulation that requires the woman's informed consent. In the latter case, it would be possible to categorise the aborted foetus as property if it has been subjected to scientific processes in order to use it commercially and, consequently, it would be possible to patent stem cell lines derived from foetal (as opposed to embryonic) cells under Danish law. As for the use of foetal tissue for research purposes, Denmark's Act on Biomedical Research Ethics Committees, which regulates biomedical research on humans and human materials, is based on the general principle that research on humans requires the informed consent of the research subject. Occasionally, the Act accepts consent from the closest relative, e.g. in the case of research on cadaveric foetuses. In rare cases, the requirement to obtain an informed consent – either from the intended research subject, by proxy, or from the closest relative – can be derogated from with the permission of the regional Committee for Biomedical Research Ethics. This only applies, however, to cases where the intended research subject is of age, i.e. at least 18 years old. In a case from 2004[21], the Central Committee for Biomedical Research Ethics relied on this very section of the Act when allowing a research project on foetal tissue to go ahead without obtaining the informed consent

20 In both Norway and Sweden, specific provisions have been made that offer safeguards in relation to the processing of foetal tissue, see the Norwegian Transplantation Act (Transplantasjonsloven, LOV-1973-02-09-6, as amended by law no. 31 of June 8, 2001), Chapter II A, and the Swedish Biobank Act (Biobankslagen, Lag (2002:297) om biobanker i hälso- och sjukvården m.m. of May 23, 2002), Chapter 3, § 3.

21 Case no. 2004-7041-12, The Committee's Annual Report, 2004 (www.im.dk/cvk).

of the women, thereby implying that the foetal tissues were identical to the women in question – unlike the provisions of the Health Act regulating the Central Registry on the Usage of Tissue where foetal tissue is exempted from the woman's autonomy in this respect. Whether or not the latter provision is compatible with the fundamental rights to autonomy and privacy, recently applied by the ECtHR, as mentioned above in a case regarding the disposal of foetal tissue, is highly dubious. The Danish government would have to demonstrate the *necessity* of such a restriction to the women's right to control their personal information, an argument which seems highly improbable.

4 Concluding remarks

As illustrated, the cadaveric foetus is located in a number of legal categories, each with its own distinct set of legal implications for the dead foetus, the parents, the healthcare professionals, and the authorities etc. The fact that sometimes the cadaveric foetus has the legal status of tissue and sometimes that of a dead child offers a new perspective on the legal status of the foetus: when examining how the (cadaveric) foetus is handled legally, it seems that it is a dynamic entity that takes many shapes: sometimes, it is a *dead child*, sometimes it is *tissue that is identical to the woman*, sometimes it is *tissue that is separate* from the woman, without having an identifiable status of its own, and sometimes it is *waste*.

Thus, the law does indeed operate with a number of different categories. This illustration is probably easily accepted by most people in relation to dead foetuses. However, the pattern of categorising foetuses legally on the basis of a number of governing parameters extends to foetuses in vivo as well, as I have demonstrated elsewhere[22] and, as a result, the traditional theory that views the period between conception and birth as a uniform one does not seem to adequately describe the legal position of the foetus and the embryo. As a result, in hard cases such as Vo v. France, there is a tendency to rely on the traditional and inadequate conceptual framework, instead of viewing the foetus as a *casus sui generis* with a dynamic and flexible legal status.

22 See my PhD dissertation.

www.ingramcontent.com/pod-product-compliance
Lightning Source LLC
LaVergne TN
LVHW020651300926
849161LV00004B/900